Globe Law and Business

Patent Subject Matter Eligibility

A Global Guide

Consulting Editors
Paul W Browning, Christopher C Johns and **Sara A Leiman**

Consulting editors
Paul W Browning, Christopher C Johns and Sara A Leiman

Managing director
Sian O'Neill

Patent Subject Matter Eligibility: A Global Guide
is published by

Globe Law and Business Ltd
3 Mylor Close
Horsell
Woking
Surrey GU21 4DD
United Kingdom
Tel: +44 20 3745 4770
www.globelawandbusiness.com

Patent Subject Matter Eligibility: A Global Guide

ISBN 9781787424463
EPUB ISBN 9781787424470
Adobe PDF ISBN 9781787424487

Table of contents

Introduction

Paul W Browning
Christopher C Johns
Sara A Leiman
Finnegan LLP

Every year patentees file more patent applications in a wider range of countries. Since the Patent Cooperation Treaty came into force in 1978, nearly four million PCT applications have been filed to enable patentees to obtain international protection for their inventions – and more than half of these PCT applications were filed in the last ten years.[1] A broad patent portfolio has increasing importance to large and small companies in a variety of fields. Because of its potential reach, each international patent increases the strength of a company's patent portfolio for corporate valuation and potential assertion.[2]

Yet, prosecuting patents in different countries can be challenging. Each country has its own laws for pursuing patent applications and achieving enforceable patents. And while treaties and other agreements (like the Paris Convention and the PCT) lay a foundation for many countries' patent systems, local patent law varies widely on the issue of patent eligibility.

For example, while all regions or countries addressed in this publication forbid the patenting of abstract ideas and scientific principles, individual jurisdictions may take different approaches in determining whether a patent claim is improperly directed to an abstract idea or scientific principle and thus not eligible for patent protection. There is widespread recognition that all claimed inventions rely to some extent on abstract ideas and/or scientific principles. These are the fundamental 'building blocks' of all inventions and thus most jurisdictions recognise that the prohibition against patenting abstract ideas and scientific principles cannot be applied too strictly. However, individual regions or countries differ on how they address the often extremely challenging question of whether a claimed invention recites abstract ideas or scientific principles (and thus is not eligible for patenting) or reflects inventive insight in incorporating abstract ideas and/or scientific principles into a patent-eligible invention.

Moreover, some countries, such as the United States, allow for the patenting

1 WIPO IP Statistics Data Center, www3.wipo.int/ipstats/pmhindex.htm?tab=pct (data gathered July 2020).
2 www.oecd.org/site/stipatents/3-3-Useche.pdf – each international application may add €1.42million to each US company; 2012 paper.

of a wide range of subject matter, including business methods, methods of medical treatment and genetically modified life forms. Other countries are much more restrictive. For example, India does not allow the patenting of business methods, any methods of medical treatment (including 'Swiss-type' use or composition-for-use claims), or other specific subject matter including methods of agriculture or horticulture and topography of integrated circuits.

Though not comprehensive, the following chart illustrates the range of approaches that different jurisdictions take in considering the patent eligibility of various subject matter. The specific jurisdiction chapters should be consulted for further clarification and examples of what subject matter is eligible for patenting in each individual country or region.

The individual jurisdiction chapters in this publication provide detailed information about how local patent offices and courts police claims for conformity with that jurisdiction's rules on patent eligibility. These chapters demonstrate the diverse approach to this topic, which informs what subject matter is eligible for patenting in each country or region. With this information in hand, practitioners can have a firmer grasp on where patentable subject matter may be protected and what types of claims to pursue in each jurisdiction.

Exemplary subject matter (see individual chapters for more details)					
Jurisdiction	**Business method**	**Naturally occurring compositions**	**Genetic material**	**Method of treatment**	**Diagnostic method**
Australia	Yes, if there is ingenuity in how the method is carried out on a computer	Yes, if isolated (unless a polynucleotide)	No, but prohibition is narrowly applied	Yes	Yes
Canada	Yes, if implemented using unconventional physical means or if manifests an unconventional discernible physical effect or change	Yes, in principle, if isolated	Yes, if isolated or modified	Yes, as Swiss-type use claims, Canadian-type use claims, or composition-for-use claims, and provided that claim features do not require the professional skill of a medical practitioner	Yes, in light of recent changes to patent office guidelines
China[3]	No, unless involving technical means to solve technical problems	No, unless isolated and practically applied (exception does not apply to a plant or animal)	No, unless isolated or modified and practically applied	No, unless as Swiss-type use claims	No, unless as Swiss-type use claims or as 'virtual device' (eg, a computer-assisted method)

3 China tends to view these types of subject matter unfavourably, although exceptions exist.

Exemplary subject matter (see individual chapters for more details)					
Jurisdiction	**Business method**	**Naturally occurring compositions**	**Genetic material**	**Method of treatment**	**Diagnostic method**
EPO	No	Yes, if isolated and there is a demonstrated technical effect	Yes, if isolated or modified and there is a demonstrated technical effect	Yes, as composition-for-use claims	Maybe, depending on how claimed
India	No, unless involving technical means to solve technical problems	No	Yes, if modified	No	No, but appropriate claim changes may help on case-to-case basis
Israel	No, unless computerised in such a way to be different from a manual activity	Yes, if isolated (unless a plant or animal)	Yes, if isolated or modified	Yes, as composition-for-use claims	Yes
Japan	No, unless implemented as a technical idea utilising a law of nature	Yes, if isolated	Yes, if isolated or modified	Yes, as Swiss-type use claims or composition-for-use claims	Maybe, depending on how claimed

Exemplary subject matter (see individual chapters for more details)					
Jurisdiction	**Business method**	**Naturally occurring compositions**	**Genetic material**	**Method of treatment**	**Diagnostic method**
South Korea	Yes, if the invention is implemented in a specific manner on a computer	Yes, if isolated and practically applied	Yes, if practically applied	Yes, as composition-for-use claims	Yes, as composition-for-use claims
Taiwan	Yes, if practically applied	Yes, if isolated and practically applied (unless a plant or animal)	Yes, if isolated or modified and practically applied	Yes, as Swiss-type use claims	Maybe, depending on how claimed
United States	Yes, although claim requires improvement to technology	No	Yes, if not naturally occurring	Yes, although claim may require some specificity	No, unless using an unconventional technique

Australia

Steve Gledhill
Madeleine Kelly
FB Rice

1. Introduction

Australia has traditionally been viewed as a patentee-friendly jurisdiction, though the legal landscape continues to evolve as the effects of a revised Patents Act start to play out at the Patent Office (IP Australia) and the Australian Federal Court, together with frequent, rigorous analysis by the courts of the stalwarts of patent law – patentability, novelty and inventive step. In the biotechnology and pharmaceutical fields, much attention has been given to the emerging impact of the revised Patents Act (which entered into force in April 2013) and its new, raised standards for patent specifications to meet in providing a sufficient disclosure of the invention across the entire scope of the claims. Otherwise, various quirky Australian provisions such as those relating to the 'promise' of the invention or the obtaining of a patent by false suggestion or misrepresentation continue to trap the unaware.

Within the evolving legal landscape, the fundamental question of patentability remains an important topic for consideration. The Australian Patents Act 1990 retains a distinct, overarching provision for patentability, which is that a patentable invention must be a 'manner of manufacture' as that term is used in the old UK Statute of Monopolies 1623.[1] This requirement has been interpreted by the Australian courts over many decades, resulting in a suite of case law that elaborates on this archaic statutory provision.

In the fields of computer-implemented inventions and business methods, the mere recitation of computer implementation in the claims used to be sufficient to comply with the manner of manufacture requirements. However, following the Australian Full Court Federal rulings in *Research Affiliates LLC v Commissioner of Patents* [2014] FCAFC 150 (*Research Affiliates*) and *Commissioner of Patents v RPL Central Pty Ltd* [2015] FCAFC 177 (*RPL*), the threshold for patent eligibility has been significantly raised, particularly for computer-implemented business methods. And although computer-implemented business methods where the invention lies in the computerisation are still considered patentable subject matter, there has been much uncertainty and flux in the approach taken by IP Australia in assessing the patent eligibility of such inventions.

1 Patents Act 1990, Section 18(1)(a).

In the biotechnology and pharmaceutical arenas, the question of patentability is somewhat clearer. Since the Australian High Court ruling in *D'Arcy v Myriad Genetics Inc* [2015] HCA 35 (*Myriad*) that 'isolated' nucleic acids are unpatentable by virtue of the substance of the claim (the genetic sequence information) being a naturally occurring phenomenon despite the form of the claim (with its 'isolated' limitation) attempting to suggest otherwise, IP Australia has settled into a reasonably predictable practice in reading *Myriad* narrowly. Thankfully, the impact of the Australian *Myriad* decision on the biotechnology industry has not been significantly detrimental. In addition, the Australian courts have confirmed that diagnostic methods remain patentable, including those carried out on the human body. These developments serve to reinforce the distinction between Australia's patent-friendly stance in the biotechnology and pharmaceutical fields and the decidedly more challenging environment in the United States.

2. Electrical and computer arts

2.1 Case law summary – key factors in assessing inventions for patentable subject matter

Over recent years, the Full Court of the Federal Court of Australia has endorsed a two-step test for assessing patent eligibility of computer implemented inventions as depicted in Figure 1.

In particular, it has been recognised that even if the subject matter of a claim is a computerised scheme, the invention may nonetheless reside in the computerisation or implementation of that scheme and be patent eligible.

In *Research Affiliates*,[2] the claims of the application under consideration were directed towards a computer-implemented method for generating an index for use in securities trading which involved a computer being used to receive data associated with assets and apply a weighting to each of the assets to generate the index.

The Full Court noted that the substance of the invention as described in the specification was directed towards the index itself, and although the inventors created an algorithm to gather, process and manipulate the data to cause the computer to generate the index, such algorithms were not 'foreign' to the normal use of computers; there was no technical contribution to the invention or artificial effect of the invention by reason of the intervention of the inventors.

The Full Court held that mere recitation of computer implementation in the claims was not sufficient to render a business method patentable and accordingly, the invention was not a manner of manufacture.

2 *Research Affiliates LLC v Commissioner of Patents* [2014] FCAFC 150.

Figure 1. Patent eligibility of computer-implemented inventions

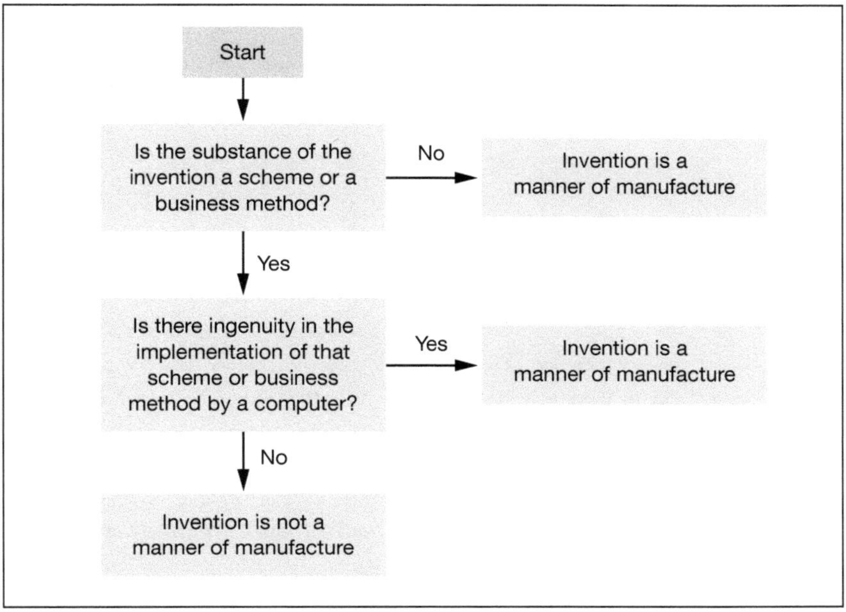

Nonetheless, the Full Court did recognise that a computer-implemented business method or scheme can be patentable if there is some ingenuity in the way in which the method or scheme is carried out in the computer. Taking note of key decisions from other jurisdictions, including the judgment by the Court of Appeal of England and Wales in *Aerotel Ltd v Telco Holdings Ltd; Macrossan's Application* [2006] EWCA Civ 1371 (*Aerotel*), and the judgment by the United States Supreme Court in *Alice Corp v CLS Bank International*, 573 US 208 (2014), the Full Court set out some key factors for consideration in assessing an invention for patentable subject matter holistically, including:

- whether the contribution to the claimed invention is technical in nature;
- whether the invention solves a 'technical' problem within the computer or outside the computer, or whether it results in an improvement in the functioning of the computer, irrespective of the data being processed;
- whether the claimed method merely requires generic computer implementation;
- whether the computer is merely the intermediary, configured to carry out the method using a computer-readable medium containing program code for performing the method, but adding nothing to the substance of the idea; and
- whether the ingenuity is in the physical phenomenon in which the

effect may be observed and which has the requisite economic utility or artificial effect, rather than in the scheme.

In RPL,[3] the invention under consideration by the Full Court involved gathering evidence relevant to an assessment of an individual's competency relative to a recognised qualification standard.

The Full Court sought to identify the substance of the invention to determine where the inventiveness or ingenuity of the inventors resides, and accordingly, whether the claimed invention involved a manner of manufacture. At [96] the Full Court notes:

A claimed invention must be examined to ascertain whether it is in substance a scheme or plan or whether it can broadly be described as an improvement in computer technology. The basis for the analysis starts with the fact that a business method, or mere scheme, is not, per se, patentable. The fact that it is a scheme or business method does not exclude it from properly being the subject of letters patent, but it must be more than that. There must be more than an abstract idea; it must involve the creation of an artificial state of affairs where the computer is integral to the invention, rather than a mere tool in which the invention is performed. Where the claimed invention is to a computerised business method, the invention must lie in that computerisation. It is not a patentable invention simply to "put" a business method "into" a computer to implement the business method using the computer for its well-known and understood functions.

In doing so, the Full Court found the claimed steps of retrieving the criteria from the server, presenting the questions to a user and receiving responses to the questions to be commonplace computer functions that merely reflect the normal use of a computer. The substance of the invention was therefore deemed to be the idea or scheme and not the actual implementation of the idea by the computer. Accordingly, the Full Court held that invention was not a manner of manufacture.

More recently, in *Commissioner of Patents v Rokt Pte Ltd* [2020] FCAFC 86 (*Rokt*), the Full Court again applied the two-step test to consider whether a computer implemented method for linking a computer user to an advertising message by way of an intermediate engagement offer to drive higher engagement with an advertising message was a manner of manufacture. Ultimately, the Full Court held that the substance of the invention was a 'marketing scheme', which relied on computing hardware and software only for their "well-known and understood functions", as "a vehicle for implementing the scheme", and that the claimed invention was patent ineligible.

---

3 *Commissioner of Patents v RPL Central Pty Ltd* [2015] FCAFC 177.

2.2 The role of prior art and expert evidence

Akin to the approach taken by the United Kingdom Intellectual Property Office (UKIPO) following the *Aerotel* decision, IP Australia had adopted the 'contribution test' for assessing inventions for patentable subject matter; that is, identifying the substance of the invention as being the actual contribution to the prior art. The application of the 'contribution test' thereby necessitates a direct comparison of the claimed invention with the prior art, arguably conflating the distinct requirements of novelty and inventive step with manner of manufacture. The appropriateness of this enquiry was considered in two recent decisions: *Encompass Corporation Pty Ltd v InfoTrack Pty Ltd* [2019] FCAFC 161 (*Encompass*) and *Rokt.*

In *Encompass*, the Full Court considered whether the primary judge erred in finding that a computer-implemented invention which merely involved a concatenation of three known methods did not provide an improvement in the computer and was therefore patent ineligible.

Although the Full Court chose not to emphatically reject this approach as illegitimate, it suggested that in inquiring whether the claimed method results in an improvement in the computer, the primary judge was not seeking to import any particular test into his consideration; he was instead searching for patentable subject matter by reference to a "touchstone of such subject matter".[4] However, the Full Court did endorse the view that manner of manufacture is a conceptually distinct element of patentability, referencing a similar caution set out in *CCOM Pty Ltd v Jiejing Pty Ltd* (1994) 51 FCR 260[5] and reiterated in *Research Affiliates*.[6]

In *Rokt*, the Full Court reversed the primary judge's decision, which had found that although the invention solved a business problem, that being how to attract the attention of a user and have that user choose to interact with an advertiser, it also solved the technical problem of how to use computer technology to address the business problem. Notable was a heavy reliance placed by the primary judge on expert evidence submitted by the two parties, particularly in determining what constituted prior art at the priority date of the application.

The Full Court decided that the primary judge was mistaken in relying on expert evidence for a manner of manufacture determination and clarified that the role of expert evidence in such circumstances is limited to familiarising the court with the state of the art at the priority date, assisting the court in construing the meaning of words that are terms in the art, and explaining technical concepts relevant to understanding the invention. It emphasised that

---

4 *Encompass Corporation Pty Ltd v InfoTrack Pty Ltd* [2019] FCAFC 161, at [109], [110] and [113].
5 *CCOM Pty Ltd v Jiejing Pty Ltd* (1994) 51 FCR 260 at [291].
6 *Research Affiliates LLC v Commissioner of Patents* [2014] FCAFC 150 at [111].

it is fundamentally a matter for the court to determine and characterise the invention.

The Full Court further clarified that the role of the common general knowledge in the manner of manufacture assessment is limited to allowing for an informed construction of the specification so the substance of the invention can be identified.

2.3 Mechanisms of a particular construction

In *Aristocrat Technologies Australia Pty Limited v Commissioner of Patents* [2020] FCA 778 (*Aristocrat*), the claims under consideration were directed towards an electronic gaming machine (EGM), which includes a combination of physical parts and computer software to produce a particular outcome in the form of gameplay.

The Court found the substance of the invention to be "a mechanism of a particular construction, the operation of which involves a combination of physical parts and software to produce a particular outcome in the form of an EGM that functions in a particular way". The Court determined that this combination of features work together to provide a particular outcome, distinguish the claims from being a scheme and therefore bring the claims into the realm of patentable subject matter. It was therefore unnecessary to consider the second step of the test (whether there was ingenuity).

This decision contrasts with earlier Patent Office decisions for similar subject matter, such as *Aristocrat Technologies Australia Pty Limited* [2017] APO 1, where the substance of the invention was instead considered to reside in the game play.

The *Aristocrat* decision was appealed to the Full Court of the Federal Court of Australia, and a decision is expected to be handed down imminently.

2.4 IP Australia practice

Following the *Encompass* and *Rokt* decisions, the Australian Patent Examiners' Manual was updated and no longer directs Examiners to apply the 'contribution test' when assessing inventions for a manner of manufacture. Instead, and as shown recently in *Jagwood Pty Ltd* [2020] APO 38, IP Australia is assessing inventions for a manner of manufacture by focusing on the key factors set out in *Research Affiliates*, with a greater weighting being placed on whether the invention is technical in nature.

Computer-implemented inventions that merely rely on generic computing hardware, and that do not provide a technical improvement, tend to be objected to by IP Australia as not being patent eligible.

However, if the computer-implemented invention improves computing technology, or uses non-standard computing hardware in a new and useful way, it may be possible to have IP Australia recognise the patent eligibility of such inventions. To maximise chances of success, it is advisable to include, in the description of a patent specification, technical details of the mechanisms that achieve the specific implementation and emphasise the technical advantages over generic implementations. The invention should also be characterised to a sufficient degree in the claims to distinguish it from generic computer implementations.

On other hand, where it can be demonstrated that the invention solves a technical problem in a technical way, it is likely that the invention will be considered patent eligible by IP Australia. To assist in demonstrating the technicality of the claimed invention, it is helpful to include in the description specific examples of technical difficulties that were overcome in implementing the technology, along with any particular technical effects or advantages provided by specific features of the invention.

And, as has been demonstrated recently in *Aristocrat*, computer-implemented inventions that include software claim features that work in tandem with specialised hardware to provide a new and useful result, such as a mechanism of a particular construction, may be considered patentable subject matter.

3. Biotechnology

3.1 *Myriad*

In October 2015, the Australian High Court handed down its eagerly anticipated decision in *Myriad*.[7] The patent profession awaited the decision with some trepidation as commentators pondered the potential outcome of the decision on issues such as access to genomic material, the growing diagnostics industry and the momentum building behind personalised medicine. Ultimately, whilst the Court's decision that a claim to an "isolated nucleic acid coding for a mutant or polymorphic BRCA1 polypeptide" was unpatentable, IP Australia was quick to issue a practice guideline indicating that the decision would be read narrowly, consistent with the reasoning in the decision. In particular, IP Australia indicated that it would interpret the decision as having specific applicability to nucleic acids, rather than broader applicability to such subject matter as isolated proteins, antibodies, stem cells and diagnostic methods.

IP Australia's quick indication that it would apply *Myriad* narrowly provided welcome relief to patent practitioners. The decision itself appeared to permit a potentially broader application, which could have had a more significant impact on the biotechnology industry in Australia. This potential resulted from the reasoning in *Myriad* that the question of patentability should focus on the substance of the claim, rather than its form:

7 *D'Arcy v Myriad Genetics Inc* [2015] HCA 35 (*Myriad*).

Despite the formulation of the claimed invention as a class of product, its substance is information embodied in arrangements of nucleotides. The information is not 'made' by human action. It is discerned.[8]

Further, the High Court took into account the scope of the claim and its potential economic consequences:

Claims 1 to 3 include the products of applying any process, known or unknown, to the cells of a human being ... The size of the class of the products as defined is large. ... There is a real risk that the chilling effect of the claims, on the use of any isolation process in relation to the BRCA1 gene, would lead to the creation of an exorbitant and unwarranted de facto monopoly on all methods of isolating nucleic acids containing the sequences coding for the BRCA1 protein.[9]

Perhaps this is a result of Australia's 'manner of manufacture' provision representing an overarching requirement for patentability as a whole, which lends itself to the possibility of such discrete considerations as support for claim breadth, and economic ramifications thereof, coalescing into one.

Further, amongst the multiple reasons expressed by seven Justices of the High Court, the decision invoked the memory of principles established in the United States Supreme Court, indicating that:

For a claimed invention to qualify as a manner of manufacture it must be something more than a mere discovery. [...] The question then is whether the subject matter of the claim is sufficiently artificial, or in other words different from nature, to be regarded as patentable.[10]

However, divergence from the US *Myriad* decision[11] was also apparent, on the point of cDNA. Consistent with the reasoning that the consideration of patentability should focus on the substance of the claim rather than its precise form, the majority in the High Court stated that:

It was common ground that if claims 1–3 did not contain patentable subject matter, then those claims would not be saved where they extend to forms of nucleic acid that have been synthesised in the laboratory (cDNA).[12]

Potential ramifications on the Australian diagnostics industry lay in statements of the High Court judgment such as:

[...] the requirement, essential to the concept of a "manner of manufacture", that the subject matter of a claim have about it a quality of inventiveness which distinguishes it from a mere discovery or observation of a law of nature;[13] and

[...] the discovery of a naturally occurring correlation between the presence of the specified mutations and polymorphisms in an isolated fragment comprising the BRCA1 gene and an increased likelihood of actual or potential malignancy in the

---

8 *Ibid* at [6].
9 *Ibid* at [8].
10 *Ibid* at [126]–[127].
11 *Association for Molecular Pathology v Myriad Genetics, Inc*, 569 US 576 (2013).
12 *D'Arcy v Myriad Genetics Inc* [2015] HCA 35 at [283].
13 *Ibid* at [131].

cell from which the fragment is derived is not what was contemplated by a "manner of new manufactures" in the Statute of Monopolies.[14]

The decision therefore brought to mind immediate questions on the fate of patent applications concerning natural products (for example, regulatory RNA, polyclonal antibodies, naturally occurring proteins or small molecules, vaccine antigens, stem cells) and diagnostic methods, particularly if the claims were broad and vulnerable to the accusation of having a 'chilling effect' on the progress of research (arguably an inevitable vulnerability given the effect of a patent as a monopoly right, and tempered by exemptions from infringement such as "experimental use"[15] and acts performed for the purpose of obtaining regulatory approval of pharmaceuticals[16]).

3.2 IP Australia practice

In December 2015, shortly after *Myriad* was handed down, IP Australia issued its guidelines on how it would apply *Myriad* and these guidelines have been incorporated into the Examiner's Manual of Practice and Procedure.[17] Many patent practitioners were relieved to read that IP Australia's position was that Myriad should be interpreted as having specific relevance to claims to isolated nucleic acid sequences, the Guidelines stating that:

The Court made clear that it was not concerned with 'gene patenting' generally and did not make any finding with respect to the remaining claims of the patent directed to probes, vectors, methods of production and methods of diagnosis.

The decision does not set out a general rule that isolated natural products or their derivatives are excluded from patentability. The majority did not engage in a debate about 'products of nature' versus 'artificially created products', but found that, in a case where the substance of the claimed invention was genetic information that was not 'made', the claiming of the alleged invention as an isolated product did not confer patent eligibility.[18]

IP Australia has been consistent with these guidelines in applying *Myriad* narrowly, as has the Federal Court. For example, the following subject matter has been held to be patentable.

(a) Interfering RNA[19]

A claim to a double stranded iRNA composition wherein the antisense strand is complementary to a target nucleic acid sequence was held to be patentable. IP Australia reasoned that the claimed, double stranded structure of the iRNA was essential to its function and that "[a]s a consequence, the informational,

---

14 *Ibid* at [165].
15 Patents Act 1990, Section 119C.
16 Patents Act 1990, Section 119A.
17 http://manuals.ipaustralia.gov.au/patents/Patent_Examiners_Manual.htm.
18 *Ibid* at 2.9.2.6.
19 *Arrowhead Research Corporation* [2016] APO 70.

structural and chemical content of the dsRNA molecules may all be considered essential elements of the invention as claimed, and as a result the substance of the invention encompasses each of these elements, not merely the genetic information conveyed by the molecule."[20]

(b) Codon-optimised sequences[21]

IP Australia found that a codon-optimised sequence had been 'made' and had an effect which differed from the naturally occurring sequence.[22]

(c) Antisense oligonucleotides[23]

A claim to an antisense oligonucleotide comprising at least one locked nucleic acid (LNA) was found by IP Australia to be patentable, including because it comprised non-coding exon sequence information, a chemical modification, and was used to induce exon skipping in a therapeutic application.[24]

(d) Methods of identifying cattle having useful traits using genetic information[25]

Justice Beach in the Federal Court found that claims to methods of identifying cattle based on genetic analysis are patentable, noting in his reasoning Justice Gordon's comments on uncontested claims in *Myriad* to probes and diagnostic methods:

> *What then did Myriad do? It took the idea, concept or principle that specific mutations or polymorphisms in that sequence suggest a predisposition to breast cancer and ovarian cancer and moved to carry out that idea, concept or principle, or embody it in a manner of new manufacture, in claims 4–30. The validity of those claims is not in issue.*
>
> *Claim 4 may be taken as an example. In simple terms, it comprises a nucleic acid probe in which the nucleotide sequence is a portion of an isolated nucleic acid with the characteristic identified in claim 1 …*
>
> *The invention in claim 4 carried into effect the idea that specifically identified mutations or polymorphisms in a sequence of the BRCA1 gene suggest a predisposition to breast cancer and ovarian cancer by testing for the presence of one or more of the specifically identified mutations or polymorphisms. That is an invention.*[26]

20 *Ibid* at [28].
21 *Cargill Incorporated v Dow AgroSciences LLC* [2016] APO 43.
22 *Ibid* at [44].
23 *Academisch Ziekenhuis Leiden and BioMarin Technologies BV* [2018] APO 49.
24 *Ibid* at [99], [104] and [108].
25 *Meat & Livestock Australia Limited v Cargill, Inc* [2018] FCA 51.
26 *Ibid* at [430].

(e) *Methods of detecting cell free fetal DNA*[27]

In this Australian *Sequenom v Ariosa* dispute, Justice Beach in the Australian Federal Court again found that methods of diagnosis are patentable, consistent with the *Myriad* decision.[28]

There is therefore ample opportunity for obtaining patent protection in Australia for inventions based on nucleic acids. Whilst claims to an isolated nucleic acid *per se* having a naturally occurring sequence are unpatentable, claims to expression vectors, probes, functional polynucleotides such as iRNA or antisense oligonucleotides, or modified sequences such as codon-optimised sequences remain patentable. Importantly, diagnostic methods are clearly patentable in Australia.

4. Natural products

Given the narrow reading of *Myriad* in Australia, isolated natural products other than polynucleotides remain patentable. Central to the reasoning in *Myriad* was that the substance of the claim related to information which was represented in the genetic code. That information was found to be unpatentable. By contrast, isolated natural biological products such as proteins will most often have a functional capacity that has a practical effect, which is more than the theoretical, abstract quality of stored information.

5. Chemical arts

Following the narrow reading of *Myriad* in Australia, isolated small molecules other than polynucleotides also remain patentable. For example, a small molecule isolated from a plant extract, which inhibits the binding of a ligand to a cellular receptor may achieve the practical effect of blocking signaling via that receptor. There is no 'information' present in the small molecule that is central to its existence and its function. Instead, there is a function which has been identified as having a practical application.

6. Methods of treatment

The application of natural products in a field of economic endeavour is also patent eligible in Australia. Included in such applications are therapeutic methods of treatment of the human or animal body, whether they are conducted using natural or unnatural products. Unlike the legal position in jurisdictions such as Europe, Japan and New Zealand, the Australian High Court confirmed in *Apotex Pty Ltd v Sanofi-Aventis Australia Pty Ltd* [2013] HCA 50 (Apotex) that therapeutic methods of treatment are patentable in Australia. In considering a patent claiming a method of preventing or treating psoriasis using

---

27 *Sequenom, Inc v Ariosa Diagnostics, Inc* [2019].

28 *Ibid*, see, eg, [380]–[382].

the known drug leflunomide, the High Court recounted the development of common law in respect of the 'manner of manufacture' provision and clearly determined that:

> *Assuming that all other requirements for patentability are met, a method (or process) for medical treatment of the human body which is capable of satisfying the NRDC Case test, namely that it is a contribution to a useful art having economic utility, can be a manner of manufacture and hence a patentable invention within the meaning of s 18(1)(a) of the 1990 Act.*[29]

Included amongst the basis for this finding was that such methods are capable of being practically applied in commerce or industry. The same reasoning applies to methods of cosmetic treatment.

Swiss-type claims in the form 'Use of substance X in the manufacture of a medicament for the treatment of disease Y' are also patentable in Australia and have been determined as providing a different scope of protection to 'method of treatment' claims. In *Otsuka Pharmaceutical Co, Ltd v Generic Health Pty Ltd* (No 4) [2015] FCA 634, Justice Yates considered the historical development of such claims in Europe and characterised such claims as 'method' claims under Australian law.[30] The alternative scope of such claims in comparison to method of treatment claims was evident in *Mylan Health Pty Ltd v Sun Pharma ANZ Pty Ltd* [2020] FCAFC 116, where indirect infringement of a method of treatment claim was found, despite the finding of a lack of infringement of a Swiss-type claim. In that case, an absence of evidence that a medicament was manufactured for the claimed treatment precluded a finding of infringement of a Swiss-type claim; nevertheless, the supply of a medicament which was used in a claimed method of treatment was found to be an act of contributory infringement.

Given the permissibility of method of treatment and Swiss-type claims in Australia, it is recommended that both claim formats be included in Australian patent applications.

7. Hot topics

7.1 Artificial intelligence/machine learning (AI/ML) inventions

While there is no specific case law on the patentability of AI/ML inventions in Australia, current IP Australia practice adopts a similar approach as to how it assesses other types of computer implemented inventions. That is, where the substance of the invention resides in the application of AI/ML, for example, to provide a technical solution to a technical problem, or to provide an improvement in computer technology, AI/ML inventions are likely to be

29 *Apotex Pty Ltd v Sanofi-Aventis Australia Pty Ltd* [2013] HCA 50 at [286].
30 *Otsuka Pharmaceutical Co, Ltd v Generic Health Pty Ltd* (No 4) [2015] FCA 634 at [120].

considered to be patent eligible. On the other hand, where the substance of the invention is instead in the actual topology/structure of the AI/ML, IP Australia may raise an objection on the grounds that mathematical algorithms *per se* are not a manner of manufacture; however, careful claim drafting may assist in circumventing such objections.

As is well recognised, technical solutions provided by many machine learning type inventions rely largely on how they are trained to perform a specific application, and the data set used for the training. Although there have not been any decisions in Australia on sufficiency of disclosure or best method of performing the invention requirements in respect of AI/ML inventions, caution should be taken to ensure a sufficient specificity of the training and training data set is described in any patent application.

7.2 Personalised medicine

Given the clarity of Australian law on the patentability of diagnostic methods and methods of treatment as described above, and with the limited exception of claims to an isolated nucleic acid having a naturally occurring sequence, there remains significant scope for obtaining patent protection in the rapidly developing field of personalised medicine.

Canada

Graeme Boocock
Natasha Gulati
Beverley Moore
Jason Mueller-Neuhaus
Borden Ladner Gervais LLP

1. Background and executive summary

In Canada, patent-eligible subject matter is determined based on an assessment as to whether claimed subject matter falls within one of the 'statutory categories of invention' defined in the Patent Act,[1] as follows:

invention means any new and useful art, process, machine, manufacture or composition of matter, or any new and useful improvement in any art, process, machine, manufacture or composition of matter ...[2]

In addition, Subsection 27(8) of the Patent Act stipulates that:

No patent shall be granted for any mere scientific principle or abstract theorem.[3]

Certain judicially created exclusions to patentability also exist in Canada, for example, for higher life forms,[4] methods of medical treatment,[5] and methods requiring the exercise of professional skill,[6] with the Patent Appeal Board (PAB), Federal Court (FC) and the Federal Court of Appeal (FCA) often adding significant details to decisions of higher authorities. Due to this, the subject matter eligibility of medical 'use' claims is highly nuanced in Canada, and significantly different to corresponding practice in Europe and elsewhere.

During patent examination, subject matter eligibility is governed by examination policies set by the Canadian Intellectual Property Office (CIPO), many of which are summarised in CIPO's *Manual of Patent Office Practice* (MOPOP).[7] These policies are not always in strict agreement with the jurisprudence, and often extend into areas that remain formally untested in court.

Over the years, these examination policies have created significant challenges for certain categories of subject matter, including medical

1 Patent Act, RSC 1985, c P-4 ('Patent Act').
2 Patent Act, *supra* note 1, Section 2, *sv* 'invention'.
3 Patent Act, *supra* note 1, Section 27(8).
4 *Harvard College v Canada (Commissioner of Patents)* 2002 SCC 76 (*Harvard College*).
5 *Tennessee Eastman Co v Canada (Commissioner of Patents)* [1974] SCR 111 (*Tennessee Eastman*).
6 *Lawson v Commissioner of Patents* (1970) 62 CPR 101 (Ex Ct Can) (*Lawson*).
7 Canadian Intellectual Property Office, *Manual of the Patent Office Practice*, December 2020 update (Ottawa: Innovation, Science and Economic Development Canada, 2020) (MOPOP).

diagnostics and computer-implemented inventions. At the time of writing, newly published guidelines, resulting from a recent FC decision,[8] appear to have improved the situation substantially for diagnostics.

2. Electrical and computer arts

2.1 Introduction

In the electrical and computer arts, methods of all kinds fall generally into the categories of art or process, and devices (including computing devices) fall generally into the category of machine or manufacture. The Patent Act does not exclude from patent eligibility any particular category of technology.[9] As such, the principles to be applied when making such a determination are agnostic with respect to technology type, at least in theory.

In the case of inventions in the electrical and computer arts, how such principles are applied during examination depends largely on whether CIPO perceives the 'inventive contribution' to reside exclusively in data processing or information transformation, or instead requires interaction of physical agents and entities in order to produce the desired result.

2.2 Discussion of case law

(a) Basic requirements

As noted above, the Patent Act contains only a single categorical exclusion from patent eligibility, namely that "no patent shall be granted for any mere scientific principle or abstract theorem" ('the abstract ideas prohibition').[10] Thus, the courts have held that while a disembodied idea is not patent eligible, a practical method of application of the idea may be patent eligible.[11]

Canadian courts have found that calculations and mathematical formulae *per se* are encompassed by this prohibition, and that mental operations and processes,[12] plans or information transformations involving no change to underlying physical entities,[13] schemes or rules (including in relation to games) involving a conventional use of known equipment,[14] and computer programs *per se*[15] are also excluded from patentability due to subject matter.

The courts have held that, in general, subject matter is patent eligible if, when performed or employed, it involves some physical existence or

8 *Choueifaty v Canada (Attorney General)* 2020 FC 837 (*Choueifaty*).
9 Including so called 'business methods': see *Re Amazon.com Inc* 2011 FCA 328 at para 60 (*Amazon*).
10 Patent Act, *supra* note 1, Section 27(8).
11 See *Shell Oil Co v Canada (Commissioner of Patents)* [1982] 2 SCR 536 at para 40 (*Shell Oil*).
12 See *Schlumberger Ltd v Canada (Patent Commissioner)* [1982] 1 FC 845 at para 5 (FCA) (*Schlumberger*).
13 See *Lawson, supra* note 6, at para 60.
14 See *Progressive Games Inc v Canada (Commissioner of Patents)* (1999), 3 CPR (4th) 517 (FCTD).
15 See *Apple Computer Inc v Mackintosh Computers Ltd* [1987] 1 FC 173 at para 97, aff'd [1988] 1 FC 673 (FCA), aff'd [1990] 2 SCR 209.

manifestation of a discernible effect or change ('the physicality standard').[16] A computing device configured to perform an algorithm appears to meet this standard, since it has physical existence and performance of an algorithm by it typically manifests a discernible effect or change in at least some physical state of matter. The courts have also held, however, that performance of patent-ineligible subject matter (eg, calculations and mathematical formulae) by computing devices does not render the subject matter patent eligible.[17] Much of the uncertainty in the treatment of computer-implemented inventions thus involves how the courts and CIPO have attempted to reconcile these principles, particularly in connection with subject matter where the inventive concept resides in an algorithm which resolves ultimately to calculations and mathematical formulae.

(b) *Purposive construction*

Part of this attempt has involved 'purposive construction', a procedure performed prior to all determinations of validity or infringement, including determinations as to whether or not claimed subject matter falls within one of the statutory categories of invention.

'Purposive construction' was defined by the Supreme Court of Canada (SCC) in two companion cases.[18] Purposive construction aims to interpret words in the claim consistently with the intention of the inventor, as inferred from the context in which the words appear. The words chosen by the inventor will be read in the sense that the inventor is presumed to have intended, and in a way that is sympathetic to the accomplishment of the inventor's purpose, whether it is express or implicit in the text of the claims. In these cases, the Court held that claims are to be construed purposively rather than strictly adhering to the language, and formulated a test ('the *Free World Trust* test') for this determination. The test involves a determination as to whether each claim element is to be regarded as 'essential' or 'non-essential'. Determining the essential elements has been described as the "key to purposive construction".[19] The SCC has further explained this concept by stating that the "nonessential elements may be substituted or omitted without having a material effect on either the structure or the operation of the invention described in the claims".[20]

To this end, the *Free World Trust* test asks two questions: (1) whether it is clear based on a purposive construction of the words of the claim that the claim element at issue was clearly not intended to be essential, ie, that it was intended to be interpreted so as to include variants; or (2) whether a skilled person would

---

16 See *Amazon, supra* note 9, at para 71. See also *Lawson, supra* note 6, at para 29.

17 See *Schlumberger, supra* note 12, at para 5.

18 *Free World Trust v Électro Santé Inc* 2000 SCC 66 (*Free World Trust*) and *Whirlpool Corp v Camco Inc* 2000 SCC 67 (*Whirlpool*).

19 *Whirlpool, supra* note 18, at para 45.

20 *Free World Trust, supra* note 18, at para 20.

have understood that the invention would have worked in the same way whether it used the claim element strictly construed or the allegedly infringing variant (in other words, the claim element is 'functionally substitutable').

CIPO interpreted this test in such a way as to conclude that a functionally substitutable claim element could be found non-essential, and omitted, even if such a conclusion would be clearly contrary to the objective intention of the applicant.[21] On this basis, CIPO formulated examination guidelines[22] in 2013 that enabled a finding that claimed subject matter is patent ineligible, even if it meets the physicality standard, when the inventive concept resides in the implemented algorithm. These former guidelines employed a problem-solution approach, asking what 'problem' was addressed by the application, what 'solution' was taught by the application, and by identifying as 'essential' (within the framework of the *Free World Trust* test) only those claim elements required for that 'solution', with the remaining elements being deemed 'non-essential' and omitted. In practice, the former guidelines operated to isolate the inventive contribution from the claimed subject matter and assess only it against the statutory categories. In the case of inventions wherein the inventive contribution resided in an algorithm, the former guidelines typically resulted in the conclusion that the 'problem' was not a 'computer problem' when the computing device was used in a conventional way, that the 'solution' therefore did not require the device, and that it was instead a disembodied algorithm, or idea, not falling within one of the statutory categories.[23]

The former guidelines were overruled by the FC as contravening the governing jurisprudence.[24] In particular, the FC held that CIPO's employment of a problem-solution analysis was in error, as well as the effect of the guidelines to find claim elements non-essential despite the applicant's intention expressed or implicit in the text of the claims.[25]

While, as discussed below, CIPO subsequently issued replacement guidelines ('the Current Guidelines'),[26] there is as yet no case law which assesses their validity or otherwise provides guidance with respect to specific subject matter. It is credible to expect, however, that such replacement guidelines may be applied in such a way as to maintain at least some aspects of the former guidelines.

---

21 See *IGT, Re*, 2013 CarswellNat 5532 (Patent Appeal Board and Commissioner of Patents). Also available at the Canadian Patent Office website at https://brevets-decisions-patents.opic-cipo.gc.ca/pab-cab/p/en/item/467865/index.do?q=1346.

22 These guidelines were published by the Patent Office in 2013 as Practice Notices identified as PN2013-02 and PN2013-03, on the website of the Patent Office at www.ic.gc.ca/eic/site/cipointernet-internetopic.nsf/eng/wr03626.html and www.ic.gc.ca/eic/site/cipointernet-internetopic.nsf/eng/wr03627.html.

23 See MOPOP, *supra* note 7 at 12.02 concerning the Office's guidelines intended to implement the *Free World Trust* test, and also MOPOP, *supra* note 8 at 22 dealing with computer-implemented inventions.

24 In *Choueifaty v Canada (Attorney General)* 2020 FC 837 (*Choueifaty*).

25 *Choueifaty, supra* note 24, at paras 39-40.

26 See Canadian Intellectual Property Office, *Patentable Subject Matter under the Patent Act* (Ottawa: CIPO, 3 November, 2020) (*CIPO Guide*), available at www.ic.gc.ca/eic/site/cipointernet-internetopic.nsf/eng/wr04860.html#fn15-rf.

2.3 How are eligibility issues handled by the Patent Office?

(a) CIPO's current examination guidelines

MOPOP, CIPO's primary examination guidelines document, sets forth CIPO's position with respect to subject patent eligibility.[27] In view of the above-discussed overruling of CIPO's former examination guidelines with respect to the patent eligibility of computer-implemented inventions, CIPO issued replacement guidelines[28] which have not yet been integrated into MOPOP.

The Current Guidelines acknowledge, in accordance with the *Free World Trust* test, that claim elements cannot be found non-essential despite the applicant's intention as expressed in or implied by the text of the claims. They also repudiate the previous employment of any assessment of a 'contribution' of a claim, or of a "technological solution to a technological problem",[29] or of the use of the problem-solution approach in the identification of essential elements when applying the *Free World Trust* test.

Instead, the Current Guidelines employ the concept of an 'actual invention' consisting of either a single element or a combination of elements that provide a solution to a problem. According to the Current Guidelines, in order to be both patent eligible and not fall within the abstract ideas prohibition, claimed subject matter must be limited to or narrower than an 'actual invention' that meets the physicality standard and which relates to the manual or productive arts.

The Current Guidelines emphasise that while a claim element may be essential in accordance with the *Free World Trust* test, it may nevertheless have no material effect on the working of the 'actual invention', as in the case of a superfluous limitation or 'self-inflicted wound'. In a footnote, the Current Guidelines assert that if a claim is broader than the 'actual invention', then it would contravene a particular provision of the Patent Act generally asserted in connection with lack of clarity,[30] but also asserted in connection with exhaustive combinations where the claim exceeds the immediate and cooperating environment of the inventive contribution. The Current Guidelines seem to suggest, therefore, that where particular claim elements do not form an overall combination with remaining elements to produce new and unexpected results, then those particular claim elements may be found not to form a part of the 'actual invention', and the claim would be indefinite as defining an exhaustive combination.

---

27 Available at www.ic.gc.ca/eic/site/cipointernet-internetopic.nsf/eng/h_wr00720.html. The Office's guidelines with respect to 'purposive construction' and the *Free World Trust* test are set forth in MOPOP, *supra* note 7, at 12.02, and with respect to computer-implemented inventions are set forth in MOPOP, *supra* note 7, at 22.

28 *CIPO Guide, supra* note 26.

29 *Ibid.*

30 Patent Act, *supra* note 1, Section 27(4).

In connection specifically with computer-implemented inventions, the Current Guidelines assert that even if a computing device is an essential element in accordance with the *Free World Trust* test, it may not form a part of the 'actual invention'. The Current Guidelines assert that if the computing device is used merely in a well-known manner to perform an algorithm, and such performance does not solve any problem in the functioning of the device, then the device and algorithm will not be regarded to form a single 'actual invention', and the subject matter will be regarded to offend the abstract ideas prohibition.

While there have not yet been any decisions of the Commissioner of Patents to elaborate or provide insight as to how CIPO intends to apply the Current Guidelines in practice, examples are provided, which give a measure of clarification.[31] In particular, the examples seem to indicate that when a claim defines means or steps for data collection in the form of measurements of physical systems, and the collected data is processed by a computing device performing an algorithm, then the combination will be the 'actual invention', and the subject matter patent eligible. Similarly, when a claim defines processing of received data by a computing device performing an algorithm, and also defines performance of physical activity based on the processing results, then the combination will likewise be the 'actual invention', and the subject matter patent eligible. However, that conventional data receiving means or steps, or conventional output means or steps (such as a displaying step), would not form a part of the 'actual invention', and thus a claim defining performance of an algorithm by a computing device with only conventional data receiving and output or display steps and would offend the abstract ideas prohibition.

The Current Guidelines indicate, however, that when performance of an algorithm by a computing device solves a problem in the functioning of the device, then the algorithm-device combination will be the 'actual invention', as opposed to the algorithm alone, and thus constitute patent-eligible subject matter. A further example provided indicates that where a new algorithm requires fewer instructions than known methods, such that performance of the algorithm requires less processing power, then performance of the algorithm solves a problem in the functioning of the computing device, which will therefore form a part of the 'actual invention'. Thus, performance of the algorithm by the computing device will constitute patent-eligible subject matter even if only conventional data receiving and output or display steps are involved.

It is expected that elaboration of the principles set forth in the replacement

---

31 The examples are presented on the Canadian Patent Office's website at www.ic.gc.ca/eic/site/cipointernet-internetopic.nsf/eng/wr04861.html.

Guidelines will follow in the coming months as appeals of final rejections by patent examiners are adjudicated by the Commissioner of Patents.

(b) Special topics

MOPOP sets forth CIPO's position with respect to subject matter patent eligibility in connection with a number of special topics.

Graphical user interfaces: CIPO takes the position that a graphical user interface (GUI) is an arrangement of visual elements for display on a screen constituting information having purely intellectual or aesthetic significance which does not constitute patent-eligible subject matter, and thus claims to GUIs *per se* or of a computer-readable medium providing the GUI are typically found to be patent ineligible. A GUI integrated in a combination with otherwise patent-eligible subject matter may also be patent eligible, and thus a claim to a computing device configured with a GUI which interoperates with other functionality of the device to solve a problem related to computing function may be considered patent eligible.[32]

Data structures and databases: similarly, CIPO takes the position that a data structure or a database is a format for organising and storing a collection of related data items to suit a specific purpose, and in isolation is an abstract idea or plan for organising data items. As such, data structures and databases *per se*, and computer programs or computer-readable media implementing the same are typically found to be patent ineligible. If a particular data structure or database solves a problem related to computing function, however, which improves performance or resource consumption, then a claim to a method, device, or medium implementing a combination of the data structure and function may be patent eligible.[33]

Signals: CIPO takes the position that electromagnetic and acoustic signals and waveforms *per se* are forms of energy despite requiring a physical medium for transmission, and consequently regard them to be patent-ineligible subject matter. Moreover, CIPO considers signals to be transitory in nature, and therefore regards claims that define a physical medium storing a signal or a waveform to be indefinite.[34]

32 MOPOP, *supra* note 7, at 22.09.01.
33 MOPOP, *supra* note 7, at 22.09.02 and 22.09.03.
34 MOPOP, *supra* note 7, at 22.09.05.

3. Biological and pharmaceutical arts

3.1 Discussion of case law

(a) *Natural processes*

In the landmark *Pioneer Hi-Bred* decision,[35] the SCC confirmed that claims to a plant line produced by natural crossbreeding were not adequately supported by a specification that made reference to a deposited sample of seeds. The SCC drew a distinction between genetically manipulated plants and those produced by entirely natural processes, but chose to dispose of the appeal solely on the basis of insufficiency of disclosure, holding that a deposit of seeds did not adequately teach third parties how to make the claimed invention. While the SCC's finding of insufficiency appears to have been influenced by the involvement of a natural process, there has yet to be definitive instruction from the courts on the subject matter eligibility *per se* of natural processes.

(b) *Life forms*

Canada also has a judicially created prohibition on the patenting of so-called 'higher life forms', though there is little guidance from the courts on where the line between higher life forms and lower life lies. In Harvard College,[36] the majority of the SCC supported an arbitrary distinction concerning the patentability of lower and higher life forms, but called for legislative action in this matter:

> *Though this Court is not faced with the issue of the patentability of lower life forms, it must nonetheless address the respondent's argument that the line between higher and lower life forms is indefensible. As discussed above, I am of the opinion that the unique concerns and issues raised by the patentability of plants and animals necessitate a parliamentary response. Only Parliament has the institutional competence to extend patent rights or another form of intellectual property protection to plants and animals and to attach appropriate conditions to the right that is granted. In the interim, I see no reason to alter the line drawn by the Patent Office. The distinction between lower and higher life forms, though not explicit in the Act, is nonetheless defensible on the basis of commonsense differences between the two. Perhaps more importantly, there appears to be a consensus that human life is not patentable; yet this distinction is also not explicit in the Act. If the line between lower and higher life forms is indefensible and arbitrary, so too is the line between human beings and other higher life forms.*[37]

Almost two decades later, this legislative action has not yet occurred.

---

35 *Pioneer Hi-Bred Ltd v Canada (Commissioner of Patents)* [1989] 1 SCR 1623.
36 *Harvard College, supra* note 4.
37 *Harvard College, supra* note 4 at para 199. See also paras 202–206.

The impact of this majority decision on patent applicants was softened by a subsequent Supreme Court majority decision, *Monsanto v Schmeiser,*[38] which held that claims to chimeric genes and cells containing them were enforceable against and infringed by a grower of a plant comprising such chimeric genes or cells. The SCC in *Monsanto* acknowledged that its holding in *Harvard Mouse* included the finding that plants and seeds were found to be ineligible 'higher life forms'. However, the SCC analogised the chimeric genes and cells at issue in *Monsanto* with allowed and uncontested claims to plasmids and somatic cell cultures from *Harvard Mouse,* thus finding that claims to the chimeric genes and cells containing them were similarly valid.[39]

Beyond patents, Canada is also signatory to the International Union for the Protection of New Varieties of Plants (UPOV). The Plant Breeders' Rights Office, a division of the Canadian Food Inspection Agency, oversees the grant of plant breeders' rights, which offer protection for propagating material of new and distinct plant varieties.

(c) ***Methods of medical treatment and medical uses***

Canada has a judicially created exception to the patentability of methods of medical treatment. *Tennessee Eastman*[40] is a landmark 1972 decision of the SCC with respect to the non-patentability of medical and surgical methods. This decision turned on former Section 41(1) of the Patent Act, which established a general prohibition on patent claims to substances prepared or produced by chemical processes and intended for food or medicine. The method claims struck down by the SCC were presented in a format that circumvented this prohibition. This provision has long since been repealed, but the FCA accepted that *Tennessee Eastman* established that methods of medical treatment are non-patentable,[41] and the decision has subsequently been applied, interpreted, and arguably expanded by lower courts and by CIPO.

In 2002, claims to a new use for a previously known compound were affirmed by the SCC in *Wellcome.*[42]

These two strands of SCC jurisprudence concerning methods of medical treatment and medical uses are in tension with one another.

Subsequent decisions of the FC have established a further distinction between use claims that require or prevent the exercise of professional skill or judgement of a medical practitioner, and those that do not. The former have been held to be ineligible subject matter, and the latter eligible. The approach de-emphasises claim category in favour of scrutiny of a claim's technical

---

38 *Monsanto Canada Inc v Schmeiser,* 2004 SCC 34 (*Monsanto*).

39 *Ibid,* paras 21 to 23.

40 *Tennessee Eastman, supra* note 5.

41 *Imperial Chemical Industries Ltd v Canada (Commissioner of Patents)* [1986] 3 FC 40 (FCA) (*Imperial Chemical*).

42 *Apotex Inc v Wellcome Foundation Ltd* 2002 SCC 77.

features. For example, medical use claims comprising a dosage range have been interpreted as impermissible methods of medical treatment, even when no method *per se* is claimed. In some cases, the Federal Court appears to have been influenced in its decision making by a concern about inhibiting physicians from taking decisions in patient care.

In the 2006 *Axcan* decision,[43] the Court was asked to consider invalidity allegations with respect to a patent claiming the use of 13 to 15 mg of Ursodiol per kg of the patient's weight per day, for the treatment of primary biliary cirrhosis. The Court held that a patent claim over a dosage range of a known drug for a known use is not a vendible product and, therefore, is not patentable. The Court stated at paragraph 46:

> *It is up to the physician based on his or her knowledge of the patient's rate of metabolism and other factors to determine the appropriate daily dosage. I cannot, for a moment, contemplate that Axcan could claim exclusive property in the dosage and sue a physician for prescribing Ursodiol for the treatment of PBC at a dosage less than 13 mg/kg/day or greater than 15 mg/kg/day.*

Since the emphasis in the patent at issue was on the dosage range rather than on an actual dosage, the Court accepted the invalidity allegations.

Merck[44] stands in contrast to *Axcan*. Here, the Court upheld claims directed to a dosage form of alendronate monosodium trihydrate. The claim was for tablets with a strict dosing regime and the 'how and when' of administration were not part of the patent. The Court found that the claims covered a vendible product, and not a patent-ineligible method of medical treatment.

In the decision of the FC in *Janssen*,[45] the claims covered a use of galantamine to treat Alzheimer's disease in a specific titration regimen. In this case, galantamine was a known compound that had been previously used to treat Alzheimer's disease, and was to be provided to Alzheimer's subjects in lower dosages with an advantageous effect. The claims were held to be directed to a method of medical treatment. The Court stated at paragraph 26:

> *... a patent claim over a method of medical treatment that, by its nature, covers an area for which a physician's skill or judgment is expected to be exercised is not patentable in Canada. This would include the administration of a drug whereby the physician, while relying upon the dosage advice of the patentee, would still be expected to be alert and responsive to a patient's profile and to the patient's reaction to the compound.*

The Court stated at paragraph 52:

> *By attempting to monopolize an effective titration regimen for galantamine, the '950 Patent interferes with the ability of physicians to exercise their judgment in*

---

43 *Axcan Pharma Inc v Pharmascience Inc* 2006 FC 527.
44 *Merck & Co Inc v Apotex Inc* 2005 FC 755.
45 *Janssen Inc v Mylan Pharmaceuticals ULC* 2010 FC 1123.

the administration of generic versions of the drug. This is because, absent a license from Janssen, any physician attempting to administer a generic version of galantamine to treat Alzheimer's disease by the method claimed by the '950 Patent would infringe.

In another *Merck* case,[46] the patent claimed the use of 1.0 mg of the drug for the treatment of male baldness, which the Court construed as a daily dosage. The claims were held to be directed to a vendible product, and not a method of medical treatment. At paragraph 114, the Court stated:

... a distinction must be made between claims that rely upon the skill and judgment of a medial practitioner and those that deal with a vendible product, be it a scalpel, X-ray machine or 1 mg tablet that are to be used or prescribed for use by such practitioner. In the present case, we have a 1.0 mg tablet taken as a daily dose. No skill or judgment is brought to bear. It is a vendible product and not a method of medical treatment.

More recent FC decisions have generally followed the distinction set by earlier cases between claims involving dosage or timing ranges and those that do not.[47] At times, the approach has been quite nuanced, such that it was not apparent that a claim did or did not involve a timing range until specific terms within the claims were construed by the Court in light of expert evidence.[48]

3.2 How are eligibility issues handled by the Patent Office?

(a) Natural processes

During examination, CIPO will allow claims to methods that involve a natural process provided that there is sufficient technical intervention specified beyond the natural process itself, and provided that the results are reproducible.[49] For example, a method claim comprising a step of plant breeding will be allowed if it includes a prior step of transformation with an artificial gene expression construct and subsequent selection for progeny plants that comprise the construct.

(b) Life forms

Historically, CIPO has refused all patent claims to higher life forms. CIPO's position on higher life forms was confirmed by a majority decision of the SCC, discussed above.[50] However, there are significant disparities between the SCC

46 *Merck & Co v Pharmascience Inc* 2010 FC 510.
47 See *Sanofi-Aventis Canada Inc v Hospira Healthcare Corp* 2009 FC 1077 (*Sanofi-Aventis*); *Novartis Pharmaceuticals Canada Inc v Cobalt Pharmaceuticals Company*, 2014 FCA 17; *Abbott Laboratories (Bermuda) Ltd, Re* 2014 FC 1251 (*Abbott*).
48 See *Sanofi-Aventis, supra* note 46; *Abbott, supra* note 46.
49 MOPOP, *supra* note 7, at 23.02.02
50 *Harvard College, supra* note 4.

decision and CIPO's approach, with the latter being more restrictive and extending into areas untested by the courts.

For example, while the SCC found that a fertilised egg was a patentable composition,[51] CIPO's MOPOP states that animals at any stage of development are not patent-eligible subject matter. Consequently, claims to fertilised eggs and totipotent stem cells will be rejected during examination, whereas claims to multipotent or pluripotent stem cells are generally allowed. CIPO provides the following definitions:

> *Lower life forms include: microscopic algae; unicellular fungi (including moulds and yeasts); bacteria; protozoa; viruses; transformed cell lines; hybridomas; and embryonic, pluripotent and multipotent stem cells.*
>
> *Higher life forms include: animals, plants, mushrooms, fertilized eggs and totipotent stem cells … A plant part such as a cutting, callus, rhizome, tuber, fruit, or seed (regardless of whether the seed is coated) is also considered to be a higher life form.*[52]

CIPO also routinely rejects claims specified as being 'part of' a higher life form, as well as claims to tissues and organs.[53]

That said, a claim to a more generically defined 'cell' – plant or animal – will generally be accepted by CIPO as eligible subject matter.

Claims to recombinant genes and genetically modified plant cells comprising them have been held enforceable by the SCC.[54] Accordingly, applicants should consider converting claims to higher life forms to 'cell' format during examination, where appropriate, and should also consider including claims to relevant biopolymers (see section 3.2(c) below).

(c) Naturally occurring molecules

In Canada, the patentability of naturally occurring molecules has not been tested in court. During examination, claims to naturally occurring molecules, such as genes, mRNAs, polypeptides and proteins, are generally accepted as patent-eligible subject matter provided that they are claimed in something other than their naturally occurring state, and provided that other patentability criteria are met. Claiming such molecules in an 'isolated' form is often sufficient.

(d) Medical diagnostics

The patentability of diagnostic methods has been significantly impacted over the years by unfavourable examination policies set by CIPO. At the time of writing, CIPO's Current Guidelines appear to restore a more reasonable state of

51 *Harvard College, supra* note 4, at para 162.
52 MOPOP, *supra* note 7, at 23.02.01.
53 MOPOP, *supra* note 7, at 23.02.02.
54 *Monsanto, supra* note 37.

affairs for many inventions in this field. The Current Guidelines are discussed extensively above (see section 2.3(a) above).

Notably, the Current Guidelines also introduce the concept of an 'actual invention', which is different to what is claimed:

> *An element of a claimed invention that is identified as essential for establishing the fences of the monopoly under purposive construction is not necessarily part of the actual invention. For example, an element may be an essential element of a claim only because the applicant intended to limit the scope of the monopoly being claimed to less than what the applicant actually invented. An element may thus be an essential element of the claim because the applicant intended it to be essential even though it has no material effect on the working of the invention. Such an element would not form part of the actual invention because the fact that it has no material effect on the working of the invention means it does not cooperate with other elements of the claimed invention.*[55]

Under the Current Guidelines, it is CIPO's 'actual invention' that must meet subject matter eligibility requirements. Accordingly, the claims are construed to determine essential elements, but only the subset of elements deemed to be part of the 'actual invention' are assessed for subject matter eligibility.

There are several points of disparity between this approach and jurisprudence. For example, according to the SCC, a claim element is essential if its substitution or omission affects the working of the invention,[56] whereas CIPO appears to contemplate essential elements that do not have a material effect on the invention. CIPO's scrutiny of the 'actual invention' against subject matter eligibility requirements also seems to strike at the SCC's affirmation that valid patent claims can be based on a patent-ineligible abstract idea.[57]

Setting these problems aside, the practical result of the Current Guidelines appears to be favourable for diagnostic inventions but have yet to be tested in court. The Current Guidelines acknowledge that many diagnostic methods specify a physical step of testing or quantifying an analyte, and that this element may cooperate with other features, including a correlation, to form a single 'actual invention' that constitutes patentable subject matter. This contrasts markedly with CIPO's previous approach, which held such combinations to be non-cooperative aggregations.

Two example claims provided distinguish between a physical step of measuring an analyte (claim 1) and a step of merely receiving information about the analyte (claim 2):

1. A method of diagnosing whether a human subject is at risk for developing cancer, comprising:

---

55 *CIPO Guide, supra* note 26.
56 *Free World Trust, supra* note 18, at para 15.
57 *Shell Oil, supra* note 11, at 19.

a. measuring the level of X in a biological sample from the subject; and
b. comparing said level to the level of a non-cancerous reference sample, wherein an increase in the level of X relative to said reference indicates the subject is at risk for cancer.

2. A method of diagnosing whether a human subject is at risk for developing cancer, comprising:
a. receiving a report summarising the level of X in a sample from the subject; and
b. comparing said level to the level of a non-cancerous reference sample, wherein an increase in the level of X relative to said reference indicates the subject is at risk for cancer.

Claim 1 is said to relate to an 'actual invention' that comprises a physical step that renders it patentable subject matter. In contrast, the 'receiving a report' step of claim 2 is said not to provide the required physicality, resulting in a lack of eligible subject matter. The Current Guidelines thus appear to accept, as patentable subject matter, a diagnostics claim that certainly would have been objected to under previous practice.

It appears that claims to many diagnostics inventions would now meet CIPO's physicality requirement, and that many others could be amended to do so by making the step of collecting data more overtly active and physical. That said, diagnostic inventions that rely on data from biological signal collection could continue to face challenges, depending on how the physicality requirement is interpreted.

Much will be learned in the coming months, as CIPO examiners apply the new guidelines to various types of claims.

(e) Methods of medical treatment and medical uses

Canada's judicially created prohibition[58] on patentability of methods of medical treatment (see section 3.1(d) above) results in CIPO's routine rejection of such claims during examination. However, uses of a compound or composition (including new uses of a known compound or composition) for treatment of a condition are generally accepted, provided that they meet all other criteria for patentability.

Decisions from the Patent Appeal Board and the FC have established specific guidance as to whether or not particular methods are or are not impermissible methods of medical treatment. These determinations have been highly fact-dependent, and their practical significance has diminished in view of the availability of use claims.

Three main types of use claims are available in Canada: the Canadian-type use claim ('a use of X for treatment of Y'), the Swiss-type use claim ('a use of X

58 *Imperial Chemical, supra* note 40.

for preparation of a medicament for treatment of Y'), and the use-limited product claim ('a compound/composition X for use in treating Y') akin to the EPC2000 format. Commercial package and kit claims are also available and should be considered for these inventions.

CIPO's Current Guidelines for subject matter eligibility generally are much less prescriptive than its previous approach. For example, CIPO's former guidelines indicated that a new use for treatment of a patient subpopulation defined by genotype was always inherently anticipated by prior treatment of the wider population. This example has no counterpart in the Current Guidelines, and it is hoped that this signals a more favourable treatment of personalised and precision medical uses, in line with CIPO's revised handling of diagnostic methods.

As far as dosage and timing ranges are concerned, the Current Guidelines are consistent with jurisprudence insofar as an example claim comprising dosage and timing range features is said to impermissibly restrict, prevent, interfere with, or require the exercise of the professional skill and judgement of a medical professional. The claim is said to cover ineligible subject matter. However, the Current Guidelines also emphasise that mere presence of such features is not, by itself, determinative, and state that it is necessary for examiners to consider whether the exercise of professional skill and judgement of a medical professional is part of the actual invention.

During examination, applicants may be required to amend claims reciting dosage or timing ranges to instead specify discrete values. Canada has no excess claims fees and a flexible basis for amendment, and it is therefore usually possible to include several parallel independent claims reciting different discrete values.

4. Chemical arts

4.1 Discussion of case law

In Canadian practice, compounds, compositions, products, processes, systems, and kits, including polymers, agricultural chemicals, pharmaceuticals and cosmetics, are all patentable subject matter.[59] A compound is considered to be a composition of matter, and thus falls within the definition of an invention. Synthetic as well as naturally occurring compounds may be the subject of a patent claim, provided that other patentability criteria are met, as discussed above.

Prior to 1987, Canada's *Patent Act* contained a prohibition on a *per se* claim to a medicinal ingredient. However, this prohibition was removed when amendments were made to modernise the *Patent Act*.

---

59 Patent Act, *supra* note 1, Section 2.

4.2 How are eligibility issues handled by the Patent Office?

During examination, claims to naturally occurring chemical compounds must be claimed in something other than their natural state to meet CIPO's requirements, but otherwise tend not to be scrutinised for subject matter eligibility.

5. Statistics

In the last 15 years, the courts in Canada have considered statutory subject matter infrequently.

Canada has linkage proceedings for pharmaceuticals, which, until recently, were typically not subject to appeal, and, thus, were not considered as precedential as standard patent infringement and validity actions. Thus, the statistics have been separated.

Statutory subject matter has been considered at trial in three infringement or validity actions, and the relevant claims of the patent were invalidated in one. It was considered in 12 linkage proceedings and the invalidity allegations were successful in four.

It remains to be seen how patents issued under the Current Guidelines from CIPO will be considered by the courts.

The authors would like to thank articling students Sam Campbell and Mohit Sethi for their assistance with this chapter.

China

Chong He
Ping Luo
Cheng Wang
Wenwen Wang
Hui Yuan
Advance China IP Law Office

1. Background and executive summary

China follows a bifurcated approach for patent protection. On the one hand, the China National Intellectual Property Administration (CNIPA) is responsible for determining the eligibility/validity of patents in examining patent applications for grant or rejection, re-examining rejected patent applications upon request, and handling invalidation requests for granted patents. On the other hand, however, one may file an administrative lawsuit before the court against the re-examination or invalidation decisions made by CNIPA. The courts also handle patent infringement litigations and determine if patent infringement can be established, but the defendant, if questioning the validity of the patent right, shall file a request for invalidation with CNIPA rather than the court.

The Patent Law of the People's Republic of China (hereinafter referred to as 'the Patent Law', the latest amendments to which are the fourth, which will take effect on 1 June 2021) stipulates the types of patents and the subject matters that are eligible for patent granting. In addition, the Guidelines for Patent Examination of the People's Republic of China (hereinafter referred to as 'the Examination Guidelines') make abundant and detailed explanations regarding the specific examination standards of CNIPA.

In China, patent types include the invention patent (roughly equivalent to the 'utility patent' in the United States), the utility model patent, and the design patent. The latter two are subject only to preliminary examination (formality examination) rather than substantive examination. In this chapter, only subject matter eligibility related to invention patents will be discussed.

Under the Patent Law, provisions concerning the subject matter eligibility of invention patents mainly include:

- the definition of 'invention' patents and 'new technical solutions' under Article 2;
- the non-patentable subject matters that are contrary to the laws or social morality or that are detrimental to public interest, as under Article 5, paragraph 1;

- the non-patentable subject matters which were developed relying on illegal acquisition or illegal use of the genetic resources as under Article 5, paragraph 2; and
- the non-patentable subject matters under Article 25, paragraph 1, including;
  - scientific discoveries;
  - rules and methods of mental activities;
  - methods for the diagnosis or for the treatment of diseases;
  - animal and plant varieties (production methods thereof are patentable, though);
  - methods of nuclear transformation and substances obtained by means of nuclear transformation; and
  - designs of two-dimensional printing goods, made of the pattern, the colour or the combination of the two, which serve mainly as indicators.

The determination criteria of non-patentable subject matters will be explained by analysing specific case studies of various technical fields and providing suggestions in practice. Statistics of related re-examination and invalidation decisions made by CNIPA in the past three years will also be provided, and recent hot topics will be described briefly.

2. Electrical and computer arts

Patent applications relating to artificial intelligence, 'Internet +', big data, and blockchains, etc, generally involve algorithm features or business rules. With the rapid development of technology, some adjustments have been made to the examination of eligibility of such applications in recent years in the practice of patent examination in China. The patent-eligible subject criteria, cases, and practical suggestions in the electrical field will be discussed based on current examination practice in conjunction with the latest amendments to the Examination Guidelines.

2.1 Determination criteria

For a patent application including algorithm features or business rules, checks are made on whether the application belongs to the "rules and methods for mental activities" specified in Article 25, paragraph 1 of the Chinese Patent Law and whether it is a 'new technical solution' in the sense of Article 2, paragraph 2 of the Patent Law, as shown in Figure 1.

Figure 1. Flowchart of determination on eligibility

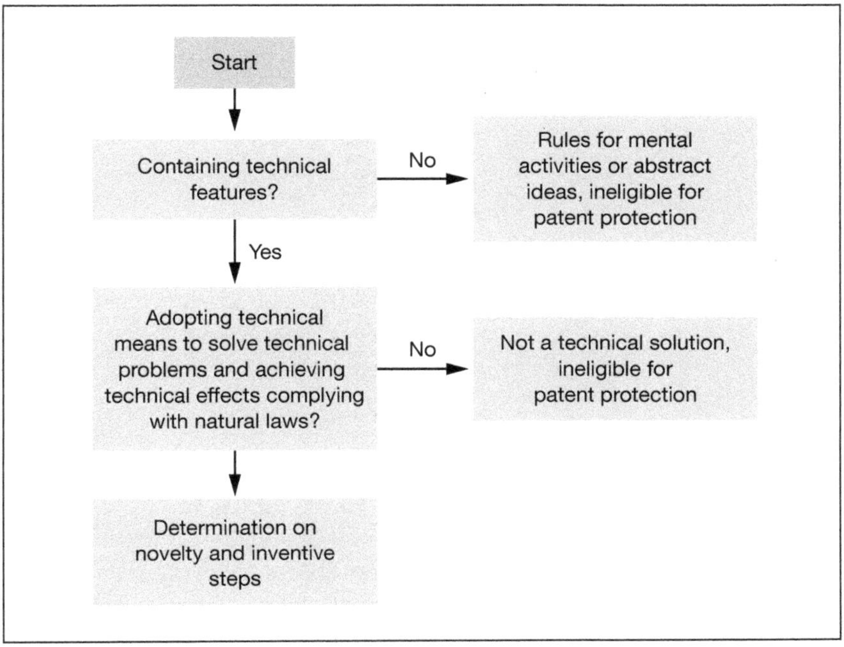

(a) Determination based on Article 25.1(2)

Article 25.1(2) provides that no patent right should be granted to rules and methods for mental activities.

It should be noted that, for the purpose of ruling out a solution from patentable subject matter, Article 25 is intended to determine whether there are NO technical features, rather than determining whether there are rules and methods for mental activities.

In this regard, the revision of the Examination Guidelines that took effect on 1 February 2020 sets out a clear determination principle that if a claim relates to an abstract algorithm or a simple business rule or method, and does not contain any technical features, the claim shall not be granted a patent right as being "rules and methods for mental activities" as set out in Article 25.1.2; whereas, in addition to the algorithm features or the method features of the business rules, the claim also contains technical features, then the claim as a whole is not considered a rule and method for mental activities, and the possibility of being granted a patent right should not be excluded by Article 25.1(2).

In view of this, few claims are generally rejected as rules and methods for mental activities. Even if such rejections are made, they are relatively easy to overturn by amending the claims to introduce technical features. Nevertheless, there are also cases where abstract mental activities are 'dressed up' with technical features and yet are rejected as essentially being rules and methods for mental activities. Such a case (Case 1) will be discussed in the case studies section.

(b) Determination based on Article 2.2

After passing the determination under Article 25.1(2), a claim is considered to have technical elements. However, technical elements alone do not render a claim eligible for patentability. It is also necessary to examine whether the technical elements of the claim amount to a technical solution under Article 2.2.

Specifically, a 'technical solution' eligible for patenting is defined as an aggregation of technical means applying natural laws to solve a technical problem, while technical means are embodied as technical features recited in a claim (Chapter 1, Part II of the Examination Guidelines).

Regarding whether a claim belongs to the technical solution, the latest Examination Guidelines in effect, as amended, provide that if the claim records technical means using natural laws to solve a technical problem, thus obtaining a technical effect complying with natural laws, the solution defined in the claim belongs to the technical solution as provided in Article 2.2 of the Patent Law. (Section 6, Chapter 9, Part II of the Examination Guidelines). While the Examination Guidelines do not provide any definition or explanation of 'natural laws', the term usually refers to objective laws in nature such as the laws of physics, chemistry or biology. The requirement that a technical solution must 'use natural laws', especially for inventions related to software or business methods, is usually cited to exclude those solutions that only use man-made rules, economic laws, or the like.

2.2 Case studies

(a) A patent application including algorithm features or business rules and method features falling within the scope of Article 25.1(2) is ineligible for patent protection

Case 1: Hefei University of Technology requested re-examination of patent application No CN201510981462.0 entitled "Improved Bitwise Substitution Method for Finding Inverse Matrix Module". The Re-examination Board (Re-examination Decision No 197084, 9 December 2019) upheld the final rejection. Claim 1, to which the final rejection was directed, is as follows:

1. *A module finding an inverse matrix of a matrix using an improved bitwise substitution method, comprising a boundary element acquiring unit, an inner element acquiring unit, a lower triangular matrix acquiring unit, an upper triangular matrix acquiring unit, and an inverse matrix acquiring unit;*

the boundary element acquiring unit is configured to acquire a boundary element of the reduced coefficient matrix N of the matrix to be inversed;
the matrix A to be inversed is an M-order square matrix that each order of principal subformulae is not 0;
a_{ji} *denotes an element at row j and a column i; i, j=1, 2, 3, ... , M...*

$$A=\begin{pmatrix} a_{11} & a_{12} & \cdots & a_{1i} & \cdots & a_{1M} \\ a_{21} & a_{22} & \cdots & a_{2i} & \cdots & a_{2M} \\ \vdots & \vdots & \cdots & \vdots & \cdots & \vdots \\ a_{j1} & a_{j2} & \cdots & a_{ji} & \cdots & a_{jM} \\ \vdots & \vdots & \cdots & \vdots & \cdots & \vdots \\ a_{M1} & a_{M2} & \cdots & a_{Mi} & \cdots & a_{MM} \end{pmatrix}$$

The applicant introduced the additional features in claim 2 into claim 1 at the time of filing the request for re-examination, modified claim 1 as "A module finding an inverse matrix of a matrix using an improved bitwise substitution method in an engineering computation, and the module is configured for finding inverse matrix of a matrix in the engineering computation", and submitted that the field of application was engineering calculation, which was implemented in an engineering computer or other computing chips, not merely an algorithm or a rule itself, and was therefore not merely a rule or method for mental activities. However, according to the Re-examination Board's final decision, the solution involved how to solve a mathematical problem of finding an inverse matrix of a matrix using an improved bitwise substitution method, in which the parameters involved only expressed abstract mathematical meaning without reflecting any actual physical meaning, the solution as a whole did not reflect any combination with any actual technical application field or solve any corresponding technical problem, and the acquisition process of each unit of the module still reflected an abstract mathematical calculation process. Therefore, the claimed solution in claim 1 belonged to the rules and methods for mental activities provided in Article 25.1(2).

The above is a typical case that dresses up rules and methods for mental activities with technical limitations. Although the algorithm is defined for use in engineering calculations, it just clarifies the body that executes the algorithm, ie, the engineering computer, and the claim is essentially the same as directly describing the implementation of the algorithm. Therefore, the dressed-up algorithm was still considered as a rule or a method for mental activities.

(b) ***A patent application containing algorithm features or features of a business rule and method which obtains a technical effect by using a technical means in order to solve a technical problem belongs to the technical solution provided in Article 2.2, and is therefore eligible for patent protection***

Case 2: Siemens Medical Solutions USA Inc requested re-examination of the patent application No CN201480050799.3, entitled "Method and System for Reconstructing Image of Target Object from Input Signal". The Re-examination Board (Re-examination Decision No 178940, 20 May 2019) revoked the final rejection. Claim 1, to which the final rejection was directed, is as follows:

1. *A computer-implemented method of constructing a model of a target object, the method comprising causing a computer to execute instructions for:*
   receiving …;
   selecting …;
   estimating …; and
   generating an output …

When requesting the re-examination, the applicant amended the title of claim 1 to "a computer-implemented method of constructing a model of a target object in image reconstruction", and further defined in claim 1 "and using the output for reconstructing the image".

The Re-examination board carried out the analysis on the 'three elements' of the technical problem, technical means, and technical effects. The board identified the technical problem as being that image data may be affected by noise. The technical means was that a computer-implemented method for constructing a model of a target object in image reconstruction is provided, in which the method is used for image reconstruction, and features such as reconstructing an image by using the output are not an arbitrary choice of a person, nor are the features changed according to a subjective desire of a person; natural laws are obeyed, and therefore a technical means complying with the natural laws is used. The technical effects were improvements of image quality and reducing radiation dose, which are technical effects following the natural laws.

Accordingly, the Re-examination Board found that the problem to be solved by solution of a claim belonged to a technical problem, a technical means was adopted, and technical effects were obtained, and concluded that the solution claimed in the claim is eligible for patenting.

It should be noted that, regarding the identification of the technical problem in claim 1 of the present application, in the substantive examination, the problem to be solved was the construction of the model itself, rather than the technical problem in the field of image reconstruction. By defining the field of application of claim 1 as 'image reconstruction' and introducing the limitation of using the output to reconstruct the image, the modelling method is closely combined with the technical field of image reconstruction, and therefore the problem to be solved is a technical problem.

Case 3: Beijing DiDi Infinity Technology and Development Co Ltd requested re-examination of the patent application No CN201710702596.3, entitled "Method and Apparatus for Order Processing, Server, and Computer-Readable Storage Medium". The Re-examination Board (Re-examination Decision No 209955, 21 April 2020) revoked the final rejection. Claim 1 to which the final rejection was directed is as follows:

1. *A method for processing online ride-hailing order, adapted for a server, comprising:*

    detecting if the order is queueing or queued upon receiving an order;

    when detecting that the order is queueing, determining a queue trigger threshold of the queueing according to a queue status of the queued; and

    determining whether to perform a queuing operation on the queueing according to the queue trigger threshold to switch to the queued when performing a queuing operation,

    wherein the queueing and the queued belong to a same automatic queuing area.

At the substantive examination stage, the examiner first determined that the technical problem to be solved by the claim was not a technical problem, but a service management problem of a commercial order. Then the examiner determined that the means adopted by the claim belonged to setting a commercial service management rule rather than a technical means applying natural laws, and the obtained technical effects thereof are also management effects rather than technical effects brought about by solving the technical problem by using the natural laws. The examiner also considered that although technical means such as a server and a network were used therein, it was not to solve the technical problem existing on the server and the network to improve the performance of a computer or a network.

The applicant did not amend the claims when requesting for re-examination, and submitted that "the technical problem to be solved by claim 1 was to alleviate traffic congestion, which was a technical problem"; the Re-examination Board upheld the rejection, and then the applicant amended claim 1 as:

1. *A method for processing online ride-hailing order, adapted for a server, comprising:*

detecting if the order is queueing or queued upon receiving an order;

when detecting that the order is queueing, determining a queue trigger threshold of the queueing according to a queue status of the queued; and

determining whether to perform a queueing operation on the queueing according to the queue trigger threshold to switch to the queued when performing a queueing operation, wherein the queueing and the queued belong to a same automatic queueing area; and ***in response to switching the queueing to the queued, closing the queueing operation based on an ON time and a length of a queue to release queue resources.***

The applicant argued that the technical problem to be solved by claim 1 was how to reasonably utilise queue resources. The technical means such as switching to queued by a server in response to queueing, closing a queueing operation based on an ON time and a length of a queue to release the queue resources were used. The technical effects of balancing supply and demand was achieved through scheduling available transportation resources to areas in need. The Re-examination Board accepted the argument and determined that:

the method for processing online ride-hailing order as defined in claim 1, by detecting and processing orders and performing queue management on pending orders through a server, can solve the problem of insufficient calculation resources and unreasonable utilization of queue resources, which was a technical problem in the field of computer technology.

(c) A patent application containing algorithm features or features of a business rule and method which does not solve a technical problem, or does not utilise a technical means, or does not achieve technical effects, does not belong to the technical solution provided in Article 2.2, and is therefore ineligible for patent protection

Case 4: Tsinghua University requested re-examination of patent application No CN201711327015.9, entitled "Method and System for Updating Credit Evaluation Model, Credit Evaluation Method and System". The Re-examination Board (Re-examination Decision No 196522, 26 November 2019) upheld the final rejection. Claim 1 to which the final rejection was directed is as follows:

1. *A method for updating a credit evaluation model, the method comprising: acquiring a new credit evaluation model inputted by a user;*

   determining a model matching degree of the new credit evaluation model based on an effective amount of information, model coverage, and model accuracy of the new credit evaluation model;

determining whether the model matching degree of the new credit evaluation model is greater than a model matching degree of the original credit evaluation model, and obtaining a first determination result;

replacing the original credit evaluation model with the new credit evaluation model when the model matching degree of the new credit evaluation model is greater than the model matching degree of the original credit evaluation model; and

when the model matching degree of the new credit evaluation model is less than or equal to the model matching degree of the original credit evaluation model, retaining the original credit evaluation model.

No claim amendments were made throughout the re-examination procedure. Finally, it was determined that the problem to be solved by the claimed solution of claim 1 was how to determine whether to update the updating criteria of the credit evaluation model, which did not constitute a technical problem; the adopted means was setting the updating condition by arbitrary rules, which was not a technical means; and the obtained effect was to determine whether to update the model according to arbitrary rules and was not a technical effect.

Case 5: NEC CORP requested re-examination of patent application No. CN201410101670.2 entitled "Method and Apparatus for Determining Relationship Model". The Re-Examination Board (Re-examination Decision No 172996, 4 March 2019) upheld the final rejection.

Claim amendments were made in the re-examination procedure and the final claim 1 is as follows:

1. *A method for determining a relationship model, the method comprising:*

   acquiring a logarithm likelihood, a regular term, and a logarithm of a variational distribution of each hidden variable determined according to sample data, at least two hidden variables and model parameters, each hidden variable being configured to describe a sample category to which the sample data belongs; wherein the sample date comprises client analysis data, bioanalysis data, or geographic analysis data;

   [...]

The Board considered that the problem to be solved was to determine a relationship model and perform clustering by using the relationship model. Although the claim defined that the sample data may be customer analysis data, bioanalysis data, or geographic analysis data, the solution may perform clustering by using the determined relationship model to perform customer analysis, biological analysis, or geographic analysis, yet it did not reflect a specific combination of a data analysis method and an application field; that is, the solution did not solve any specific technical problem. It was still essentially a mathematical analysis method, and no technical means complying with natural laws was used; the resulting effect was also merely an optimisation of the data modelling method itself and was not a technical effect following the natural laws. Therefore, the claimed solution of claim 1 did not constitute a technical solution and was not eligible for patent protection under Article 2.2 of the Patent Law.

It is clear from the examination of this case that a mathematical analysis method (for example, a mathematical modelling method, an optimisation method of a mathematical model, and the like) is still a mathematical method in nature. Only when the mathematical analysis method is combined with a specific application field to solve a specific technical problem in the specific application field, and a corresponding technical effect is obtained, then it is possible to constitute a technical solution.

2.3 Examination trends and suggestions

On 10 November 2020, CNIPA published 'Draft Amendments to the Patent Examination Guidelines (Second Draft for Comment)' (not yet finalised). It is worth noting that starting from the definition of the technical solution in Article 2.2, the determination of the technical solution is modified to the language of

> *... using technical means to solve the technical problem so as to obtain the technical effect complying with natural laws, and then this solution belongs to the technical solution provided in Article 2.2 of the Patent Law*
>
> and
>
> *... no technical means is used to solve the technical problem to obtain the technical effect complying with natural laws, and then this solution does not belong to the technical solution provided in Article 2.2 of the Patent Law.*

That is, the determination of the technical solution on the 'three elements' is first directed to determining whether any technical means is described, and the correlation among the three elements is reflected. This aims to highlight the role of the technical means in the determination of the three elements of the technical solution, to make the patent eligibility determination more objective, and to strengthen the protection of innovative achievements in new fields and in new forms.

In fact, cases observing such logic are not uncommon in the examination practice.

Beijing Yinfeng Xinrong Technology Development Ltd requested re-examination of the patent application No CN201610895616.9, entitled "Method for Monitoring Suspicious Capital Transactions Based on Capital Network". The examination idea reflected such logic.

Claim 1 to which the final rejection was directed is as follows:

1. *A method for monitoring suspicious fund transactions based on a fund network, comprising the steps of:*
   (1) *establishing a rule database and a multi-subject model database, wherein the rule database comprises suspicious money laundering rules provided in anti-money laundering laws and regulations, and the multi-subject model database comprises roles of a plurality of associated transaction subjects in specific money laundering cases, behaviour characteristics of each transaction subject, and suspicious money laundering rules violated by each transaction subject;*
   (2) *extracting information on the fund transaction, the extracted information comprising a client subject, a behaviour characteristic of the client subject, and a transaction object subject;*
   (3) *matching the behaviour characteristics of the client subject and the rule database after the information extraction, and identifying whether the fund transaction is a suspicious fund transaction;*
   (4) *monitoring other fund transactions associated with the suspicious fund transaction within a certain period of time in the future, starting from the client subject and the transaction object subject in the suspicious fund transaction, and constructing a fund network with the associated transaction subjects as points and with the fund transactions as sides, wherein each transaction subject in the fund network comprises the role of the transaction subject and the behaviour characteristics of the transaction subject;*

the specific steps for constructing a fund network are...

The main ground for rejection was that the problem to be solved by the solution of claim 1 was an economic problem in society, rather than a technical problem, and the effect thereof likewise did not belong to any technical effects; it was only a means for identifying suspicious fund transactions according to a rule set by man and did not conform to the natural laws, and therefore no technical means for utilising the natural laws was adopted.

The Re-examination Board determined that (Re-examination Decision No 173339, 11 March 2019) claim 1 uses a series of technical means such as establishing a database, extracting information, matching behaviour characteristics, and establishing a fund network by removing duplicates and combining data, thereby obtaining technical effects such as improving the accuracy and validity of monitoring suspicious fund transactions, and reducing the alarm rate. Although the suspicious fund transaction itself belongs to an economic problem in social activities, the process of monitoring and identifying the suspicious fund transaction does not belong to an economic activity, but a technical problem. The described means adopted for monitoring the suspicious fund transaction is a technical means following natural laws, and the resulting effect also belongs to technical effects.

In addition, as to how to determine the three elements starting from the technical means, the above-mentioned Draft Amendments also provided a guide: "When a solution of a patent application involving a computer program utilizes a computer-implemented technical means, it must be able to solve a technical problem and obtain technical effects." Regarding the determination of a technical means implemented by a computer, the Draft Amendments presented two examples:

> *Scenario 1, the solution describes contents of an information processing apparatus such as a computer, a network apparatus, and a programmable apparatus, and whereby a computer program is executed and control and processing are effected.*
>
> *Scenario 2, the solution does not include an information processing apparatus such as a computer, a network apparatus, or a programmable apparatus, nevertheless it describes contents that a computer program is executed and control and processing by a computer are effected.*

Of course, the above revisions are not yet finalised. Still, it can be concluded that the determination of the technical solution focuses on the technicality of the solution. Accordingly, for patent applications in the electrical and computer arts that include rules and methods such as algorithm features or business rules and methods, it is advisable to do the following.

- Describe the solution down to the machine level rather than from the perspective of a user or an operator. This includes emphasising the technicality of the problem to be solved, the data processing at the machine level as well as the technicality of the corresponding effect. For example, for inventions involving business activity rules, the solution might be intended to solve business or social problems, but there is still supposed to be a corresponding technical problem at the machine level, the implementing means should have data processing at the machine level, and there should be corresponding technical effects.
- Demonstrate the specific internal effects, such as improvements to the performance of the computer itself. Generally, describing that the solution is implemented to 'improve efficiency' or 'save resources' may not be sufficient to persuade the examiner that the solution has brought about 'extra' effects in addition to benefits attributable to the performance of the computer itself. A good way is trying to describe specific technical effects such as increased storage capacity or reduced resource consumption of graphic display.
- Demonstrate external effects, such as effecting a collaboration between

computer and/or other objects, as mentioned in the Draft Amendments: 'control and processing are effected'. The Examination Guidelines provided the following example: a solution describes implementing a series of controls at each stage of the industrial process, measurement or test process by executing an industrial process, measurement or test process control program, or performing a series of technical processes on the technical data by executing a technical data processing program, or implementing a series of internal settings or adjustments to the various components of the computer system by executing a system internal performance improvement program.

- Illustrate specific and actual application scenarios instead of intermediate results only. Many so-called abstract concepts, in fact, may overcome the rejection of mental activity rules if they are combined with specific application scenarios.

3. Biological, chemical and pharmaceutical arts

The non-patentable subjects related to biological and medical fields according to the Chinese Patent Law include: those that are contrary to the law or social morality or are detrimental to public interest under Article 5, paragraph 1; those developed based on genetic resources obtained or used contrary to the laws or administrative regulations under Article 5, paragraph 2; or those considered as scientific discoveries, rules and methods for mental activities, methods for the diagnosis or treatment of diseases, animal and plant varieties under the first paragraph of Article 25.

3.1 Methods for diagnosis or treatment of diseases

Rejection of subject matter involving "methods for the diagnosis or for the treatment of diseases" (Art 25.1(3)) has long been a hot topic in this field. According to the official website of the Re-examination Board, methods for diagnosis/treatment account for more than 95% of the re-examination and invalidation decisions in the past ten years related to non-patentable subject matter in the biological and medical technologies.

(a) Determination criteria

As defined in the Examination Guidelines (Section 4.3, Chapter 1, Part II), methods for the diagnosis or for the treatment of diseases refers to "the processes of identifying, determining, or eliminating the cause or focus of diseases which are practised directly on living human or animal bodies".

A diagnostic method (Section 4.3.1, Chapter 1, Part II of the Examination Guidelines) is further defined as "the processes of identifying, studying, and determining the cause or focus of diseases on living human or animal bodies". To determine that a subject matter is a "diagnostic method" the following conditions must both be met: (1) the method is practised on a living human or animal body; and (2) the immediate purpose is to obtain the diagnostic result of a disease or health condition.

A method of treatment (Section 4.3.2, Chapter 1, Part II of the Examination Guidelines) is further defined as "the processes of intercepting, relieving, or eliminating the cause or focus of diseases so that the living human or animal bodies may recover or gain health or relieve pain". Similarly, the following conditions must both be met: (1) the method is practised on a living human or animal body; and (2) the immediate purpose is to block, alleviate or eliminate the cause or focus of the disease.

(b) Case studies

There are many types of biological and medical inventions that may involve methods for disease diagnosis and treatment, such as medical uses of substances, methods of *in vitro* sample detection, or use or methods for use of medical devices or auxiliary systems. For medical technology spawned with the development of computers, big data and artificial intelligence, subject matter eligibility further involves an analysis of the computer-related subject matter.

Diagnostic and therapeutic uses of substances (medicine, cosmetics, etc): the medical uses of Chinese and Western medical substances or materials for diagnosis or treatment are unpatentable, but such substances and materials in themselves and their uses in preparing medicines (Swiss-type claim) are patentable in China.

For products that are not typically for 'medical purposes' (such as cosmetics), whether their uses or methods (such as cosmetic methods) are patentable depends on whether therapeutic purposes can be clearly excluded.

Mary Kay Co Ltd requested re-examination of a patent App No 201280000499.5 entitled "Cosmetic Composition" after the application was rejected. The Re-examination Board (Re-examination Decision No 129361, 22 August 2017) upheld the rejection, finding that the following claim 16 was a treatment method:

> 16. *A method of treating skin for non-therapeutic purposes, comprising topically applying the composition according to any one of claims 1 to 15 to the skin in need of treatment, wherein topical application of the composition reduces the activity of hyaluronidase in skin, increases the production of hyaluronic acid in skin, and increases the production of fibronectin and laminin in skin.*

The Re-examination Decision pointed out that increasing the production of hyaluronic acid, fibronectin, and laminin in the skin could facilitate the repair of skin barrier function, preventing and treating skin diseases, while a variety of diseases to be treated were described in the specification such as dermatitis, sunburn, burns, and open wounds. Accordingly, it was believed to be a method of prevention and treatment of skin diseases directly implemented on living humans or animals with intervention. Even if claim 16 defined the method as having a "non-therapeutic purpose", the therapeutic effect of the method was, in fact, inseparable from the cosmetic effect.

However, it is still possible to patent the use of cosmetics if one can clearly exclude any therapeutic use. For example, Fuzhou Melalyn Biotechnology Co Ltd filed an invalidation request of the invention patent No 2003380104016.7 entitled "Anthranilic acid amides and the derivatives thereof as cosmetic and pharmaceutical agents" from Symrise Gmbh And Co KG in 2019, with one of the grounds being that claim 1 was essentially a method of treating diseases. Claim 1 was finally invalidated for lacking inventiveness, but the Board supported its subject matter eligibility under Art 25.1(3):

1. *Use of compound of Formula I or a mixture of two or more different compounds of Formula I,*
   ... (Formula I omitted)
   as a cosmetic agent for inhibiting release of histamine from mast cells that is induced by substance P
   or
   for the preparation of a medicament for inhibiting release of histamine from mast cells that is induced by the substance P.

The patentee provided evidence including the Chinese Regulations on Administration of Cosmetics Labelling to argue that cosmetic agents had different definitions and uses from drugs and that claim 1, by listing the uses of cosmetics and drugs in parallel, was in itself sufficient to distinguish the use of the invention as cosmetics from the use as drugs. The Re-examination Board supported this argument and concluded that the claim language of parallel recitation was explicit enough to separate the use as cosmetic agents from drugs and such cosmetic use should not be considered as having therapeutic purposes or as overlapping with the category of drugs.

***In vitro* detection methods on isolated samples:** an invention of methods for *in vitro* detection on isolated (*in vitro*) samples will be regarded as a diagnostic method if the sample is obtained from a living human or animal body and the 'immediate purpose' of the *in vitro* detection is to obtain a diagnostic result or to determine the health status of the human or animal body. The invention will not be considered a diagnostic method only if the information obtained from the sample is merely an 'intermediate result', based on which (and in view of common knowledge) one cannot directly derive a diagnostic result or insight into a health condition.

Patent App No 201710242893.4 of Chengdu Knowledge Vision Technology Co Ltd, entitled "A method for detecting cell mitosis in breast cancer scoring system" was rejected for involving diagnosis and treatment methods for disease, yet the Re-examination Decision (No 184402, 19 July 2019) reversed the rejection. Claim 1 was set out as follows:

1. *A method for detecting cell mitosis in a breast cancer scoring system, including the following steps:*
   A. *annotating manually by a pathologist the ROI area in a digital slice of breast cancer to obtain an image of cell mitosis;*
   B. *reading the digital slice file image and cut the image into small pieces; by querying the information in the pathologist's annotation file, determining whether the small piece of image contains mitosis information, and marking the position of mitosis to obtain two types of sample sets, namely: mitosis samples and non-mitosis samples;*
   C. *designing a cell mitosis generation model;*
   D. *using the non-mitosis samples as a simulation training set to simulate mitotic cell samples; and*
   E. *using simulated mitosis samples as training samples and the mitotic samples marked by the pathologist as a verification sample to start a CNN neural network, initiate training and allow the network to automatically learn characteristics of mitosis to establish a recognition model; wherein ... (omitted) ...*

The examination department insisted that the specification stated that "the number of mitotic cells is an important indicator for breast cancer rating, because it evaluates the spread and aggressiveness of the tumor" so that one can evaluate breast cancer status via the number of mitotic cells, rendering the invention a method of disease diagnosis. However, the Re-examination Board held that the technical solution was essentially the use of samples to train a recognition model of cell mitosis for image recognition, with the "breast cancer scoring system" only indicating the application scenario of the detection method, wherein the detection method essentially only involved the identification model for obtaining the intermediate result of the "number of mitotic cells" and did not draw any diagnostic conclusions.

Similarly, Royal Philips Electronics Co Ltd's patent application No 200980109532.6 entitled "Cartridge for assays with magnetic particles" had its claim 14 (a method for detecting a target component in a liquid sample) rejected at first but supported during the re-examination. The Re-examination Board similarly determined that its immediate purpose was only used to detect intermediate results (that is, whether the body fluid contains certain particles and the concentrations thereof) rather than to obtain disease diagnostic results or health status, and revoked the rejection (Decision No 106854, 14 March 2016).

Methods and uses of medical devices and treatment-related auxiliary systems: medical devices and treatment-related auxiliary systems are patentable as product inventions, but the eligibility of their related methods and uses usually depends on the 'immediate purpose'.

Wenzhou Medical University applied for an invention patent with App No of 201510115104.1 originally entitled as "A method of intelligent intraoperative error correction and interruption recovery for laser therapy instrument", which was rejected as a method for disease diagnosis and treatment and upheld by the Re-examination Board (Re-examination Decision No 160840, 4 September 2018).

During the re-examination process, the applicant deleted the word "intraoperative" in the title and revised claim 1 to be

1. *A method of intelligent error correction and interruption recovery for laser therapy instrument, including the following steps:*
   a. *identifying incorrect surgical parameters, and monitoring the laser energy and laser working status of the instrument through a working status detection module and identifying incorrect surgical parameters when laser emission interruption is detected;*
   b. *updating new surgical parameters, and obtaining new surgical parameters through a graphical user interface;*
   c. *determining whether previous operations based on the incorrect parameters are all completed; and*
   d. *performing a compensation operation on the incorrect surgical parameters to recalculate a laser pulse sequence Q set, wherein ... (omitted) ...*

The applicant argued that the invention related to software applied to a laser treatment instrument, with the technical problem solved being the automatic recovery method of the laser treatment instrument, rather than the laser surgery itself, wherein the parameters involved were operating parameters of the laser treatment instrument rather than of the surgery itself. However, the Re-examination Board held that the method included steps of obtaining parameters during the operation which accompanied, and were inseparable from, the surgical process, rendering the method a surgical method for treating disease.

However, when Jinan Zhibang Electronic Technology Co Ltd was rejected for the same reason and requested re-examination for the patent App No 201410009845.7 entitled "A medical intravenous transfusion alarm", the rejection was successfully revoked (Re-Examination Decision 111373, 23 June 2016):

1. *A detection method for a medical intravenous transfusion alarm, the intravenous transfusion alarm comprises:*
   ... (omitted);

the detection method of the medical intravenous transfusion alarm is realized by the following steps:
a) ... (omitted) ... d) collecting voltage signals in real time and, during the transfusion of the patient, the microcontroller collecting the voltage value of the output terminal of the detection device in real time; ... (omitted) ... h) sending an alarm signal, and the microcontroller controlling the alarm circuit to send out one or more of voice, flashing and vibrating alarm signals to remind patients, medical staff or accompanying persons that the transfusion is complete.

The Re-Examination Board held that, although the detection method of the medical intravenous transfusion alarm was used in the drug injection process, the information collected merely reflected whether there was still liquid flowing through the transfusion tube, so as to determine whether the drug liquid was empty and to send an alarm for transfusion completion accordingly, wherein the detected information did not reflect the patient's status, nor did it control the transfusion process according to the patient's status. Therefore, this method did not target a living human or animal body and was not related to the treatment process.

Methods for diagnosis and treatment of diseases related to computer programs: to determine the subject matter eligibility of an invention involving methods for diagnosis or treatment of diseases in computer-based medical technology, it is necessary to first determine whether the computer-related subject matter belongs to a 'product' or a 'method'. After the revision of the Examination Guidelines that took effect on 1 April 2017, it was clarified that computer programs could be used as a component of a device claim. Based on this, an invention involving a method for disease diagnosis and treatment that relies entirely on a computer program process, if written as a method claim for the behavioural process of disease diagnosis and treatment by the computer executing corresponding program processes, is regarded as a method for disease diagnosis and treatment, ie, unpatentable. However, if it is written as a device claim, it is regarded as a product claim and no longer belongs to 'methods' for diagnosis or treatment of disease.

For example, the invention patent application of Shanghai United Imaging Medical Technology Co Ltd with App No 201511031048.X entitled "A method and equipment for determining dose distribution and optimizing radiotherapy plan" was rejected as being a method for disease treatment:

1. *A method for determining dose distribution in a radiotherapy plan, comprising: discretizing a beam and a region of interest into multiple beam elements and multiple voxels, respectively, and determining a contribution value of each beam element to each voxel; determining a continuous distribution of a cumulative dose on each voxel according to the dose contribution value; and,*

calculating the dose distribution at the current blade position according to the continuous distribution.

During the re-examination process, the applicant amended claim 1 to be the following device claim, which included processors and other hardware and was further defined by computer program flow:

1. *A device for determining dose distribution in a radiotherapy plan, comprising: a processor configured to discretize a beam and a region of interest into multiple beam elements and multiple voxels, respectively, and determine a contribution value of each beam element to each voxel; determine a continuous distribution of a cumulative dose on each voxel according to the dose contribution value; and, calculate the dose distribution at the current blade position according to the continuous distribution.*

The Re-examination Board (Re-examination Decision No 168292, 25 December 2018) determined that it was a product claim and thus not a method for disease treatment.

In another example, the invention patent application of the Affiliated Hospital of Southwest Medical University with App No of 201610529290.8 entitled "Method of constructing a mathematical model for predicting absorbed dose of organs at risk in intensity modulated radiotherapy" was rejected as a method for disease treatment:

1. *A method for constructing a mathematical model for predicting absorbed dose of organs at risk in intensity modulated radiotherapy, comprising following steps: (1) dividing the organ at risk into n sub-organs, ... (omitted) ...; (2) according to a IMRT treatment plan, obtaining a normalized absorbed dose Dn10~n100 of the organ at risk, ... (omitted)...; (3) and, according to ... (omitted) ..., obtaining a predictive mathematical model.*

During the re-examination process, the applicant amended claim 1 to the following system claim that was completely consistent with the method claims reflecting the computer program process. It was then determined to be a product claim eligible for patenting (Re-examination Decision No 201216, 20 December 2019):

1. *A system for predicting absorbed dose of organs at risk in intensity-modulated radiotherapy, comprising a sub-organ generation module, an intensity-modulated treatment plan analysis module, and a prediction model generation module; (omitted) ...*

(c) ***Practical tips***

Generally speaking, the ineligible subject matter of method for diagnosis and treatment of disease is strictly examined during patent examination in China.

For foreign applicants, especially US applicants, it is important to incorporate additional eligible subject matters into the specification, such as treatment-related substances, equipment, computer program devices, and use of diagnosis and treatment methods in the preparation of related drugs.

To avoid having a claim interpreted as involving a method for disease diagnosis/treatment and thus ineligible for patent protection, at least one of the following conditions must be met: (1) the target is not a living human or animal body; or (2) the method's direct purpose is not to obtain diagnostic results or health status, nor to block, alleviate or eliminate the cause or focus of a disease.

Method/Process inventions that may have both therapeutic and non-therapeutic uses, such as the use, or method of use, of cosmetics, can usually become eligible by limiting the claim to 'non-therapeutic purposes'. However, this is not a 'panacea' and the invention may still be deemed ineligible if the examiner believes that the technical effect of the invention cannot exclude or be separated from therapeutic effect (see the aforementioned Re-examination Decision No 129361).

For *in vitro* detection methods involving *in vitro* samples, emphasis should be made that the 'immediate purpose' of the detection is only to obtain 'intermediate results' instead of diagnostic results or health status. Specifically, the information obtained from the test sample, can only be regarded as an 'intermediate result' if one skilled in the art, in view of common knowledge, cannot directly get to the diagnostic result or health status (see the aforementioned Re-examination Decision No 184402). Similarly, for the use, or method for use, of medical devices, it should be noted that the 'immediate purpose' is not to diagnose or treat a living body. Otherwise, the method will be considered a method for diagnosis or treatment of disease (see the aforementioned Decision No 111373).

For methods for diagnosis and treatment of disease involving computer programs, attention should be paid to the way of drafting. If it is drafted as a method claim, it is often not ineligible. But if it is written as a device claim with an architecture of program modules or with program features, or as a claim of 'medium-plus-computer program flow', the claim will become a product claim that is patentable, ie, by defining a device or equipment capable of executing the computer program flow to realise corresponding functions of diagnosis and treatment, or a medium capable of storing the computer program flow (see the aforementioned Re-examination Decision No 168292 and No 201216).

Finally, it is worth noting that in Section 4.3.1.2 "Invention not belonging to method for diagnosis", Chapter 1, Part II of the Draft Amendments to the Patent Examination Guidelines published on 10 November 2020, a new item was entered as:

> *(4) an information processing method implemented by a computer or other device with information processing capabilities, the immediate purpose of which is*

not to obtain diagnostic results or health conditions, but only to obtain intermediate results.

And in a relevant explanation, the "information processing method" was interpreted as:

in order to improve the accuracy of information processing and facilitate the identification, storage and transmission of information, with the core technical means adopted usually involving algorithms, information statistical analysis, information interconnection and intercommunication, artificial intelligence and other technologies. The results provided by computers are usually only for doctors to accurately diagnose diseases and formulate treatment plans.

This, once in effect, will further clarify the criteria of 'intermediate results' in computer program-related treatment methods.

3.2 Animal and plant varieties

(a) Determination criteria

The Examination Guidelines (Section 4.4, Chapter 1, Part II) define animal varieties as "animal embryonic stem cells, animal individuals and their various stages of formation and development such as germ cells, fertilized eggs, embryos, etc" and plant varieties as "individual plants capable of survival using photosynthesis to synthesize carbohydrates and proteins from inorganic substances such as water, carbon dioxide and inorganic salts, and their propagation materials (such as seeds)". Such animal and plant varieties are not eligible subject matter. It is worth noting that new varieties of genetically modified animals or plants are also non-patentable animal and plant varieties.

(b) Case study

Monsanto Technology Company's patent application No 200980138582.7 entitled "Soybean transgenic event mon87705 and methods for detection thereof" was rejected due to lack of inventiveness and ineligible subject matter of plant variety. The re-examination decision (No 108644, 22 April 2016) upheld the rejection. The following claim 1 was rejected due to ineligible subject matter (plant variety):

1. *A soybean plant cell comprising a DNA molecule containing a polynucleotide having two or more sequences selected from SEQ ID NOs: 1, 2 and 18 or a sequence complementary to the sequences.*

The Re-examination Board believed that, if a plant cell had the ability to develop and form photosynthetic plants capable of using this ability to maintain their growth and survive, then it belonged to the category of 'plant varieties'. As the specification disclosed that the soybean plant cell could produce a complete transgenic plant, it was considered a propagation material of the plant, ie, a plant variety.

The Scripps Research Institute's application No 201410347355.8 entitled "Generation and maintenance of stem cells" was rejected partially for ineligible subject matter of animal varieties with the rejection upheld during re-examination (Decision No 156029, 11 July 2018). The original claims rejected for being animal varieties were as follows:

18. *A culture of pluripotent mammalian cells, which comprise sufficient amounts of: a. MEK inhibitor; and b. GSK3? inhibitor; to allow at least one cell passage while conserving cell pluripotency, wherein the pluripotent mammalian cells are not embryonic stem cells.*
29. *An isolated pluripotent animal cell obtained by the method of any one of claims 1-17, provided that the isolated pluripotent animal cell is not an embryonic stem cell (ESC).*

The claims were amended as follows but still determined to be 'animal varieties' during the re-examination:

17. *A culture of pluripotent mammalian cells, which comprise sufficient amounts of: a. MEK inhibitor; and b. GSK3? inhibitor; to allow at least one cell passage to produce a cell population comprising pluripotent passage cells, wherein the pluripotent mammalian cells and the pluripotent passage cells (1) are cells capable of forming all three germ layers and (2) are not embryonic stem cells.*
28. *An isolated passaged pluripotent animal cell obtained by the method of any one of claims 1-16, provided that the isolated passaged pluripotent animal cell (1) can form a cell of any layer of the three germ layers and (2) is not an embryonic stem cell (ESC).*

The Re-Examination Board held that claims 17 and 28 failed to exclude induced pluripotent stem cells (iPSc), which could develop into individuals of transgenic animals and thus were cells at an initial stage of formation and development of an animal individual, ie, an animal variety. The specification discloses that the cells of the present invention may include iPSCs and that "[L]ike mESCs, the cells of the present invention have the ability to give rise to all cell types *in vitro*, and contribute to an entire animal *in vivo*, including germline, when placed back into blastocyts." In addition, Examples 1 and 5 have demonstrated formation of hybrid animals using the riPSCs prepared.

(c) ***Practical tips***

Plant or animal tissues and even cells, if having a potential to develop into complete animal or plant individuals as disclosed by the specification, will be considered as animal and plant varieties.

New plant varieties, although they cannot be granted as patents, can be granted rights of new plant varieties through the State Forestry Administration Office for the Protection of New Varieties of Plants.

3.3 Microorganisms (patentable)

Microorganisms do not belong to plants or animals and therefore are excluded from the ineligible subject matter of 'animal and plant varieties' (Section 4.4, Chapter 1, Part II and Section 9.1.2.1, Chapter 10, Part II of the Examination Guidelines). Microorganisms that exist in their natural state in nature are considered as scientific discoveries and therefore unpatentable under Article 25.1(1). However, microorganisms isolated into pure cultures and related inventions with industrial applicability are patentable.

3.4 Gene sequences (patentable)

A gene sequence is regarded as a chemical substance and, when existing in its natural state in nature, a scientific discovery unpatentable under Article 25.1(1) (Section 9.1.2.2, Chapter 10, Part II of the Examination Guidelines). However, a gene sequence is an eligible subject matter for patent if it is isolated or extracted from nature for the first time, accurately characterised, and has industrial applicability.

One of the cases for reference is Zheng Minjun's invalidation request of CJ Cheil Jedang's patent No 200910266085.7, entitled "Promoter nucleic acid, expression cassette and vector, host cell and method of using the sample to express genes" (Invalidation Decision No 46582, 20 October 2020).

4. Statistics

We performed a search using the Incopat database and statistical analysis for re-examination and invalidation decisions made by CNIPA (including the Patent Re-examination Board) from 2018 to 2020 on cases involving non-patentable subject matters.

The retrieved results show 179 decisions regarding re-examination cases and 29 decisions regarding invalidation cases between 2018 and 2020. Among them, the rejection of claims in 111 re-examination cases (62%) were upheld and the claimed subject matter was declared ineligible for patent protection in one invalidation case (6.9%). It can be seen from Figures 2 and 3 that, in the re-examination cases, the proportions for rejections to be upheld are 65%, 84% and 51.4% respectively for rejections according to Article 2.2 (the definition of 'invention' patents and 'technical solutions'), Article 5 (ineligibility due to laws, social morality and public interest) and Article 25.1 of the Patent Law (list of non-patentable subject matters) (see Figure 2). In the invalidation cases, although the number of cases is relatively small, almost all cases resulted in a finding that the claimed subject matter was patentable (see Figure 3).

Figure 2. Results of re-examination decisions involving eligible subject matters made from 2018 to 2020 (comparison between Article 2.2, Article 5 and Article 25.1)

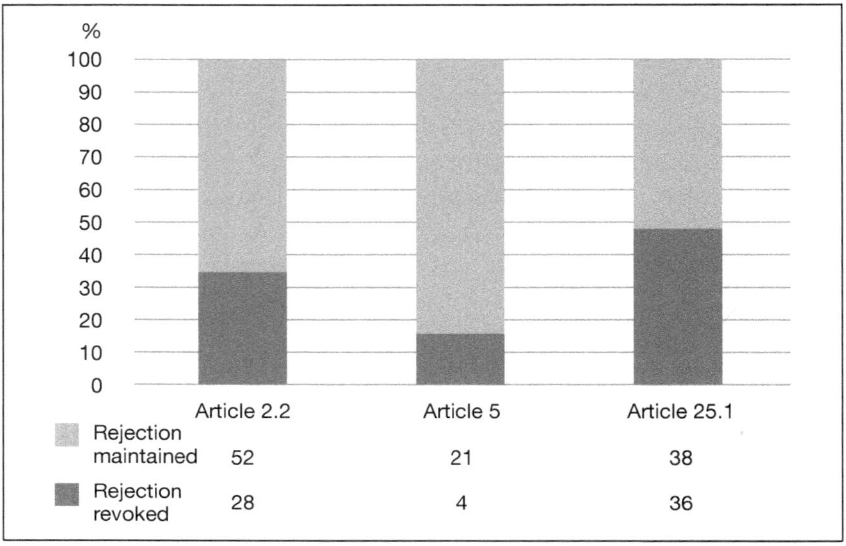

Figure 3. Results of invalidation decisions involving eligible subject matters made from 2018 to 2020 (comparison between Article 2.2, Article 5 and Article 25.1)

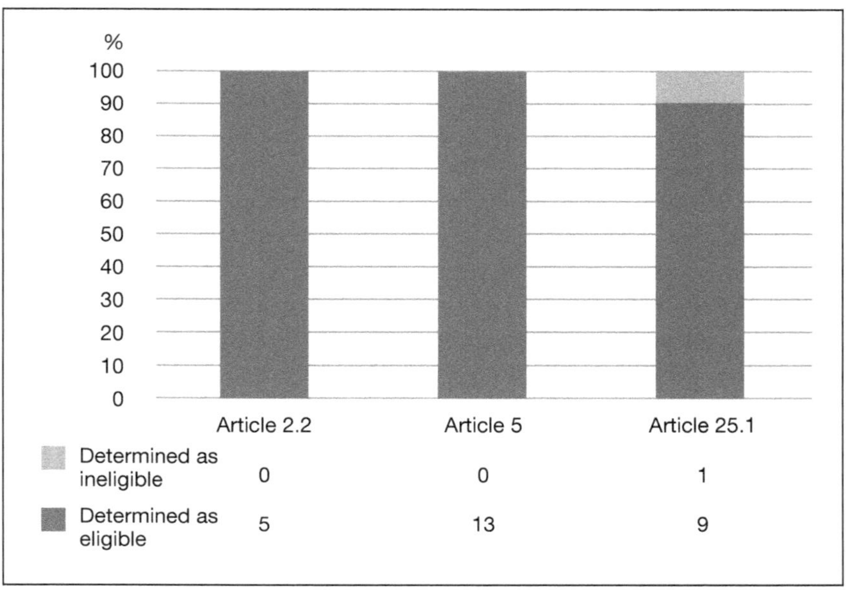

There is often a misconception that the Chinese patent office favours domestic applicants in patent re-examination and invalidation over foreign applicants. We therefore also compared the results of Chinese applicants versus foreign applicants defending rejections or challenges to subject matter eligibility. In re-examination cases, 135 were requested by Chinese applicants, 98 of which were upheld as rejected with a probability of 72.6%, while the other 44 cases came from foreign applicants, 13 of which were upheld as rejected with a probability of 29.5% (Figure 4). In invalidation cases, 22 are in the name of Chinese patentees and seven in the name of foreign patentees. Only one case from the foreign patentees was invalidated due to subject matter (Figure 5).

Figure 4. Results of re-examination decisions involving ineligible subject matters made from 2018 to 2020 (comparison between Chinese and foreign applicants and/or patentees)

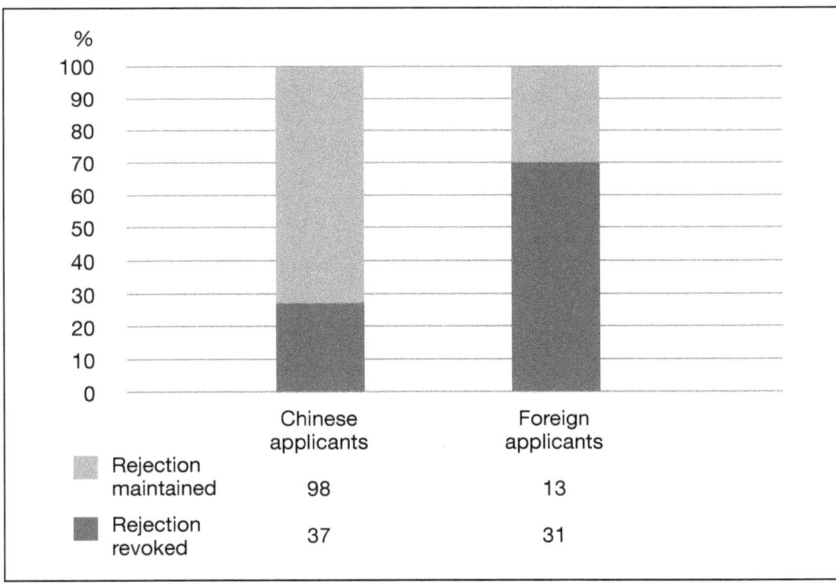

Figure 5. Results of invalidation decisions involving ineligible subject matters made from 2018 to 2020 (comparison between Chinese and foreign applicants and/or patentees)

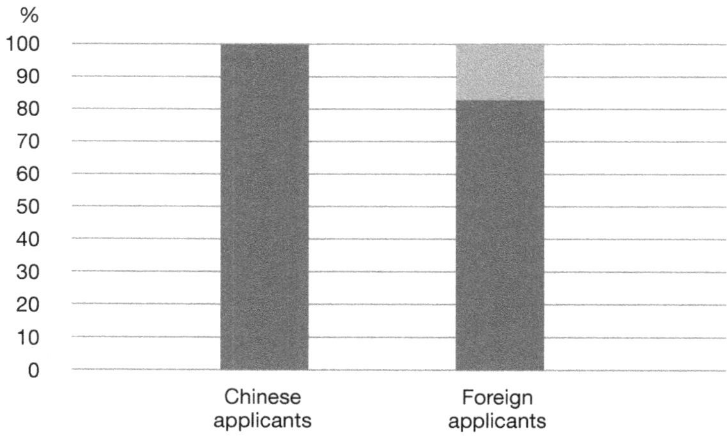

	Chinese applicants	Foreign applicants
Determined as ineligible	0	1
Determined as eligible	22	5

5. Hot topics

5.1 Human embryonic stem cells

For social ethics reasons, "human bodies at various stages of formation and development", including human embryos, are deemed as non-patentable subject matters for being "contrary to social morality" under Article 5.1 of the Patent Law. With the development of human embryonic stem cell technologies, the Examination Guidelines made amendments in 2019 to exclude "human embryonic stem cells" from the scope of "human bodies at various stages of formation and development", and to exclude the invention "using a human embryo that has not undergone *in vivo* development and within 14 days of fertilisation to isolate or obtain stem cells" from the non-patentable subject matters which are "contrary to social morality". Therefore, such kind of inventions may be granted patent rights in China if they meet the relevant requirements.

5.2 Artificial intelligence

The previous practical tips for electrical and computer arts also apply to new artificial intelligence technologies. Generally speaking, technical solutions involving artificial intelligence may be about improvements to artificial intelligence technologies or may be the application of artificial intelligence to some specific areas such as medical treatment.

Technical solutions as an improvement of artificial intelligence technology may have different applications and it may be a problem that the protection scope of the invention may be narrowed significantly when limiting the technical solution to specific application areas or when describing specific technical effects. Therefore, it is recommended that the description includes sufficient embodiments and different application areas with corresponding technical effects when providing a more general protection scope in the generic claims.

We thank the authors for their respective contributions to this chapter: Mr Chong He and Dr Wenwen Wang for "1. Background and executive summary" as well as review and finalisation of the whole chapter; Ms Cheng Wang and Mr Ping Luo for "2. Electrical and computer arts"; Dr Wenwen Wang for "3. Biological, chemical and pharmaceutical arts"; and Ms Hui Yuan for "4. Statistics". We also thank Ms Kang Fu and Ms Yan Li for their insightful advice and comments on the draft.

European Patent Office

Victoria Barker
Nicholas Fox
Yelena Morozova
Maeve O'Flynn
Finnegan Europe LLP

1. Statutory basis

Questions of subject matter eligibility before the European Patent Office (EPO) are determined by reference to Articles 52 and 53 of the European Patent Convention (EPC) and the associated implementing regulations.

Article 52 EPC states that:

(1) European patents shall be granted for any inventions, in all fields of technology, provided that they are new, involve an inventive step and are susceptible of industrial application.

(2) The following in particular shall not be regarded as inventions within the meaning of paragraph 1:

(a) discoveries, scientific theories and mathematical methods;

(b) aesthetic creations;

(c) schemes, rules and methods for performing mental acts, playing games or doing business, and programs for computers;

(d) presentations of information.

(3) Paragraph 2 shall exclude the patentability of the subject-matter or activities referred to therein only to the extent to which a European patent application or European patent relates to such subject-matter or activities as such.

For computer-implemented inventions, the meaning and scope of the exclusions and the term 'as such' are of great importance and have generated significant amounts of jurisprudence at the EPO. This case law is discussed in detail in section 2 of this chapter.

For patent applications in the life sciences and chemistry fields, the most important considerations are whether the invention is capable of industrial application (Article 52(1) EPC) and whether the invention is a discovery 'as such' (Article 52(2)(a) EPC). These considerations are discussed in section 3 of this chapter.

In addition to the exclusions listed in Article 52(2) EPC, Article 53 EPC prohibits patents from being granted in respect of certain types of subject matter.

Article 53 EPC states that:

European patents shall not be granted in respect of:

(a) inventions the commercial exploitation of which would be contrary to "ordre public" or morality; such exploitation shall not be deemed to be so contrary merely because it is prohibited by law or regulation in some or all of the Contracting States;

(b) plant or animal varieties or essentially biological processes for the production of plants or animals; this provision shall not apply to microbiological processes or the products thereof;

(c) methods for treatment of the human or animal body by surgery or therapy and diagnostic methods practised on the human or animal body; this provision shall not apply to products, in particular substances or compositions, for use in any of these methods.

These additional exclusions are rarely relevant in the software and electronics field. However, each of these subclauses is highly relevant to inventions in the chemical and biological fields. Questions of morality under Article 53(a) EPC arise in the context of animal-based research and inventions requiring the use of embryos and embryonic tissues. The wording 'essentially biological processes' and how Article 53(b) EPC is applied in practice, have been highly contentious in recent years. These issues, as well as the EPO approach to inventions relating to methods of treatment of the human and animal body, are also discussed in section 3 below.

A series of flowcharts (Figures 4–7) assisting attorneys with the application of these rules is annexed to the end of this chapter.

2. Computer-implemented inventions

2.1 Historical background

(a) *Vicom*

Judicial consideration of the relationship between the EPC exclusions from patentability and computer-implemented inventions began with the EPO Boards of Appeal decision T208/84 *VICOM/Computer related invention.*

The invention in *Vicom* was directed to a method of digitally processing images. The Board had to consider whether such methods were excluded from patentability on the grounds that they were mathematical methods 'as such'.

The Board initially observed that any processing operation on an electric signal could be described in mathematical terms.

The Board then established the existence of a 'technical effect' as the basis for distinguishing between a patentable mathematical method and an unpatentable mathematical method 'as such', stating:[1]

A basic difference between a mathematical method and a technical problem can

1 *Vicom*, Reasons for decision, paragraph 5.

be seen, however, in the fact that a mathematical method or mathematical algorithm is carried out on numbers ... and provides a result also in numerical form, the mathematical method or algorithm being only an abstract concept prescribing how to operate on the numbers. No direct technical result is produced by the method as such. In contrast thereto, if a mathematical method is used in a technical process, that process can be carried out on a physical entity ... and provides as its result a certain change in that entity.

The Board continued in its reasoning:[2]

Generally speaking, an invention which would be patentable in accordance with conventional patentability criteria should not be excluded from protection by the mere fact that, for its implementation, modern technical means in the form of a computer program are used. Decisive is what technical contribution the invention as defined in the claim when considered as a whole makes to the known art.

Vicom settled EPO practice on patent eligibility of computer-implemented inventions through to the early 2000s. The key to distinguishing between patentable and unpatentable subject matter was the existence of a 'technical effect'. In other words, whether a claimed invention provided a technical solution to a technical problem. If it could be established that a claimed invention provided such an effect, then the EPO would not reject claims on the grounds that it related to unpatentable subject matter under Article 52(2) EPC and would proceed to examine the claims for novelty and inventive step.

(b) *Pension benefits*

Although the test established in *Vicom* served the EPO well for many years, there were two issues associated with the test for determining the existence of a 'technical effect': a practical one and a theoretical one.

The practical issue was one of duplication. The EPO's 'problem-and-solution approach' for determining inventive step[3] involves an assessment of whether a claimed invention provided a non-obvious technical solution to a technical problem. This meant that the EPO assessed computer-implemented inventions for existence of a technical effect twice: once when assessing patent eligibility and then again when assessing inventive step.

The theoretical issue flowed from this duplicate test. The *Vicom* test for establishing whether a claimed invention related to patentable subject matter requires a comparison of the claimed invention with the prior art to establish the 'objective technical problem' an invention may be said to solve. However, in contrast to novelty and inventive step, the EPC does not provide a definition of the state of the art for the assessment of patentable subject matter.[4]

2 *Ibid*, Reasons for decision, paragraph 16.

3 Discussed in section 2.2 below.

4 The state of the art for the purposes of assessment of novelty is defined in Article 54(2) & (3) EPC. For the purposes of assessment of inventive step only prior art under Article 54(2) is considered.

The EPO began to amend its approach with the decision in T931/95 *PBS Partnership/Pension Benefits*, which concerned a method of controlling a pension benefits program. The application described in detail a method of managing pension contributions and proceeded to state, albeit without any technical details, that management of the pension system could be implemented by a computer.

The Board of Appeal initially rejected the method claims in the application, which were directed to a method of managing a pension system, on the grounds that they did not relate to technical subject matter, stating that:

All the features ... of this claim are steps of processing and producing information having purely administrative, actuarial and/or financial character ... the invention as claimed does not go beyond a method of doing business as such and, therefore, is excluded from patentability under Article 52(2)(c) in combination with Article 52(3) EPC; the claim does not define an invention within the meaning of Article 52(1) EPC.[5]

The Board then considered the apparatus claims, stating that:

In the Board's view a computer system suitably programmed for use in a particular field, even if that is the field of business and economy, has the character of a concrete apparatus in the sense of a physical entity, man-made for a utilitarian purpose and is thus an invention within the meaning of Article 52(1) EPC ... This means that, if a claim is directed to such an entity, the formal category of such a claim does in fact imply physical features of the claimed subject-matter which may qualify as technical features of the invention concerned and thus be relevant for its patentability.

Therefore the Board concludes that:

an apparatus constituting a physical entity or concrete product suitable for performing or supporting an economic activity, is an invention within the mean of Article 52(1) EPC.[6]

However, when assessing inventive step, the Board concluded that:

... the invention according to the application is an essentially economic one, i.e. lies in the field of economy, which, therefore, cannot contribute to inventive step. The regime of patentable subject-matter is only entered with programming of a computer system for carrying out the invention.

The assessment of inventive step has thus to be carried out from the point of view of a software developer or application programmer, as the appropriate person skilled in the art, having the knowledge of the concept and structure of the improved pension benefits system and of the underlying schemes of information processing as set out for example in the present method claims.[7]

---

5 *Pension Benefits*, reasons, section 3.
6 *Ibid*, reasons, section 5.
7 *Ibid*, reasons, section 8.

The concrete character approach adopted in the *Pension Benefits* case solved the two issues with the previous *Vicom* test. It replaced the double assessment of 'technical effect' with a simple test of concrete character, ie, whether a claimed apparatus was directed to a physical man-made entity, and the existence of a technical effect was reserved for the assessment of inventive step.

(c) Hitachi

The Boards of Appeal extended the new approach established by *Pension Benefits* to method claims in T258/03 *Hitachi/Auction method.*

The invention in the *Hitachi* case concerned a computerised implementation of a Dutch auction, a type of auction which is frequently used for trading financial products such as futures and derivatives. In a Dutch auction the price paid by a successful bidder is determined by the timing of when a bid is received. *Hitachi*'s invention addressed this sensitivity to the timing of bids by modifying the bidding process so that prices could be determined based on either the timing of a bid or a bid value included in a bidding instruction.

When assessing patentable subject matter, the Board initially applied the test established in *Pension Benefits* to the apparatus claims in the application and concluded that the apparatus claims were not excluded under Article 52(2) because they comprised: "clearly technical features such as a 'server computer', 'client computers' and 'a network.'"[8]

The Board then proceeded to consider the method claims and extended the concrete character test of *Pension Benefits* to cover such claims, stating:

> *What matters having regard to the concept of 'invention' within the meaning of Article 52(1) EPC is the presence of technical character which may be implied by the physical features of an entity or the nature of an activity, or may be conferred to a non-technical activity by the use of technical means. In particular, the Board holds that the latter cannot be considered to be a non-invention 'as such' within the meaning of Article 52(2) and (3) EPC. Hence, in the Board's view, activities falling within the notion of a non-invention 'as such' would typically represent purely abstract concepts devoid of any technical implication.*[9]

And the Board concluded that:

> *A method involving technical means is an invention within the meaning of Article 52(1) EPC.*[10]

Having ruled that neither the apparatus claims nor the method claims lacked concrete character and hence were not purely abstract, the Board then considered novelty and obviousness, taking into account only the 'technical

---

8 *Hitachi*, reasons, paragraph 3.7.
9 *Ibid*, reasons, paragraph 4.5.
10 *Ibid*, reasons, paragraph 4.7.

features' in the claims. In doing so, all the technical features of the claims were found to be anticipated by the prior art and the only novel features were non-technical business features. The application was therefore rejected on the grounds that the claimed invention lacked inventive step, as the only problems which the invention could be said to solve were solely within the business realm and the only novel technical aspects of the invention were limited to the mere automation of a novel business system.

2.2 Obviousness and inventive step

Although an assessment of technical character is no longer a part of the EPO's test for patentable subject matter, the EPO complements its test for patentable subject matter with a test for assessing inventive step that focuses on the technical contribution made by an invention. This can be of particular importance when evaluating computer-implemented inventions.

The approach adopted by the EPO is known as the 'problem-and-solution' approach, which involves the following steps:

- determining the closest prior art;
- establishing the 'objective technical problem', the technical problem any differences between the claimed invention and the closest prior art may be said to address;
- considering whether the claimed invention, starting from the closest prior art and the objective technical problem, would have been obvious to the skilled person.[11]

The 'closest prior art' is the single prior art reference that discloses the combination of features which constitutes the most promising starting point for a development leading to a claimed invention. In selecting the closest prior art, the first consideration is to select the art that belongs to the same or a closely related technical field as the invention as claimed.[12] Often, this will be the prior art which requires the fewest structural and functional modifications to arrive at the claimed invention.[13]

Once the closest prior art has been identified, any technical advantages which follow from the differences between an invention as claimed and the closest prior art are used to establish the 'objective technical problem', which defines the technical problem that the invention as claimed attempts to solve with respect to the closest prior art. In deriving the 'objective technical problem', only the differences which provide a 'technical effect' or lend an invention 'technical character' are considered.[14]

---

11 Guidelines for Examination in the European Patent Office, Part G, Chapter VII, section 5.
12 Guidelines for Examination in the European Patent Office, Part G, Chapter VII, section 5.1.
13 T606/89 *Unilever/Detergent composition.*
14 T931/95 *PBS Partnership/Pension Benefits*, discussed in section 2.1(b) above.

Non-technical features and non-technical benefits are ignored.[15] This is achieved by formulating the 'objective technical problem' from the perspective of a person skilled in the art, who is aware of the 'non-technical' aspects of an invention. For example, if the invention is a computer-implemented business scheme, the 'objective technical problem' can be formulated from the perspective of a computer programmer who is made aware of the content of the proposed 'non-technical' business scheme and is seeking to implement the same as a computer program. In practice, for many computer-implemented inventions, assessment of what is and what is not 'technical', and hence which features of a claimed invention are excluded from assessment of inventive step, is determinative of the success of a patent application.

Having formulated the 'objective technical problem', the final step of the 'problem-and-solution approach' involves assessing the prior art as a whole and determining whether or not the prior art would cause a skilled person to adapt the closest prior art to solve the objective technical problem in the manner that would cause the skilled person to arrive at the claimed invention.

2.3 The modern approach

Since *Hitachi*, the EPO Boards of Appeal have consistently applied a concrete character test to both method and apparatus claims, combined with an assessment of obviousness which considers only the obviousness of the technical aspects of the claims.

Thus, for example, in T154/04 *Duns Licensing/Estimating sales activity*, the Board held that, in examining the patentability of a claimed invention, the claim must be construed to determine the technical features of the invention. The Board stated that it is legitimate to have a mix of technical and 'non-technical' features appearing in a claim, and even that the non-technical features may form a dominating part of the claimed subject matter. Assessment of inventive step is, however, based only on technical features, which must be clearly defined in the claim. This is because non-technical features, which do not interact with the technical subject matter of the claim, are considered incapable of solving a technical problem, and thus do not provide a technical contribution over the prior art. Thus, non-technical features are ignored in assessing inventive step.

This approach was implicitly endorsed by the Enlarged Board of Appeal in 2010 in the G3/08 *Presidential Reference/Patentability of programs for computers* decision and has now been explicitly endorsed by the Enlarged Board of Appeal in G1/19 *Bentley/Pedestrian simulation*.

The G3/08 *Presidential Reference/Patentability of programs for computers* decision arose in the context of the then President of the EPO making use of her power

15 T641/00 *Comvik/Two identities*.

under Article 112(1)(b) EPC to refer questions of law to the Enlarged Board of Appeal where different opinions of the Boards of Appeal existed. When the referral by the President came up for consideration, the Enlarged Board rejected the referral as invalid on the grounds that, contrary to the suggestion of the President, there was no divergence of opinion in the jurisprudence. Rather the development of the case law through decisions such as *Vicom*, *Hitachi* and *Pension Benefits* represented the natural development of the law and that the Boards of Appeal had been consistent in applying the law as it developed.

The Enlarged Board finally expressly considered issues regarding the patentability of computer-implemented inventions in their 2021 decision in G1/19 *Bentley/Pedestrian simulation.*[16]

In G1/19, the Enlarged Board of Appeal extensively referred to the prior case law and described the EPO's approach as a 'two-hurdle approach' stating that in relation to patentability:

> *... the first hurdle, is to be assessed under Article 52 EPC without considering the prior art, i.e. without regard to whether computers existed at the priority date of the invention. The use of a computer in the claimed subject-matter therefore makes it eligible under Article 52 EPC.*
>
> *For the second hurdle, the prior art is to be considered. Inventive step is based on the difference between the prior art and the claimed subject-matter. The requirement that the features supporting inventive step contribute to a technical solution for a technical problem means that the invention, understood as a teaching based on existing prior art, has to be a "technical invention". The use of a general-purpose computer always constitutes prior art in this context. The invention to be assessed under this provision needs to be "technical" beyond the use of a general-purpose computer ... In general terms, features that can be considered technical per se may still not contribute to inventive step if they do not contribute to the solution of a technical problem ... In line with this principle, a technical step within a computer-implemented process may or may not contribute to the problem solved by the invention.*[17]

The modern approach of the EPO is therefore to apply a low-level test for the assessment of patentable subject matter under Article 52(2) based solely on the presence of a physical feature in a claim, balanced by a requirement to demonstrate that an invention provides a technical solution to a technical problem (in other words, whether the invention solves a technical problem in a technical field) when assessing inventive step under Article 56 EPC.

This modern approach to assessing computer-implemented inventions is summarised in the EPO Guidelines for Examination,[18] which state that:

---

16 Discussed in section 2.4(a) below.
17 G1/19, at paragraphs 78 and 79.
18 Guidelines for Examination, Part G, Chapter II, 3.6.

Computer programs are excluded from patentability under Art. 52(2)(c) and (3) if claimed as such. However, following the generally applicable criteria for Art. 52(2) and (3) (G-II, 2), the exclusion does not apply to computer programs having a technical character.

In order to have a technical character, and thus not be excluded from patentability, a computer program must produce a "further technical effect" when run on a computer. A "further technical effect" is a technical effect going beyond the "normal" physical interactions between the program (software) and the computer (hardware) on which it is run. The normal physical effects of the execution of a program, eg, the circulation of electrical currents in the computer, are not in themselves sufficient to confer technical character to a computer program (T 1173/97 and G3/08).

Examples of further technical effects which confer technical character to a computer program are the control of a technical process or of the internal functioning of the computer itself or its interfaces (see G-II, 3.6.1).

The presence of a further technical effect is assessed without reference to the prior art. It follows that the mere fact that a computer program serving a non-technical purpose requires less computing time than a prior-art program serving the same non-technical purpose does not on its own establish the presence of a further technical effect (T1227/05, T1784/06, T1370/11). Likewise, comparing a computer program with how a human being would perform the same task is not a suitable basis for assessing if the computer program has a technical character (T1358/09). If a further technical effect of the computer program has already been established, the computational efficiency of an algorithm affecting the established technical effect contributes to the technical character of the invention and thus to inventive step (eg, where the design of the algorithm is motivated by technical considerations of the internal functioning of the computer; see also G-II, 3.3).

A computer program cannot derive a technical character from the mere fact that it has been designed such that it can be automatically performed by a computer. "Further technical considerations", typically related to the technical considerations of the internal functioning of the computer, going beyond merely finding a computer algorithm to perform a task are needed. They have to be reflected in claimed features that cause a further technical effect (G 3/08).

2.4 Individual exceptions to patentability

The individual exceptions to patentable subject matter remain important when determining what does or does not constitute 'technical subject matter' that might be said to address a 'technical problem', and hence what claimed features are evaluated during the assessment of inventive step.

(a) Mathematical methods and mental acts

One of the most important subject matter exclusions for the patentability of computer-implemented inventions and particularly when considering the patentability of artificial intelligence inventions, is the express exclusion in Article 52(2) EPC of mathematical methods and mental acts.

The general approach of the EPO is that AI algorithms constitute mathematical methods which lack technical character. Such mathematical methods then only contribute to the technical character of an invention if the method serves a technical purpose by its application to a field of technology,[19] or alternatively if the algorithm itself is adapted to a specific technical implementation.[20]

Fields which the EPO consider 'technical' and where patentable subject matter issues are unlikely to arise include:

- image classification;[21]
- medical systems;[22] and
- detection of faults in physical systems.[23]

Whereas, non-technical applications, where such issues are much more likely to arise, include:

- text classification;[24] and
- e-commerce recommendation systems.[25]

The exclusion of mathematical methods and mental acts from patentability follows from the general principle that purely abstract or intellectual methods are not patentable. Thus, abstract mathematical methods, such as a shortcut method of division, would not be patentable. However, the application of such methods to solve technical problems are patentable. By way of example, methods of encrypting/decrypting or signing electronic communications may be and routinely are regarded as technical methods, even if they are essentially based on mathematics.[26]

A claim directed to a technical process in which a mathematical method is restricted to a particular technical field, is not considered to be directed to a mathematical method 'as such'. For example, the EPO Examination Guidelines[27] describe a method of encoding audio information in a communication system with the aim of reducing distortion induced by channel noise as an example of

19 See for example T1784/06 or T1358/09 – examples of abstract AI classification systems rejected due to lack of technical application.
20 See for example, T2330/13 (method of checking the consistency and completeness of selection conditions of a configurable product – allowed), T22/12 (classification and identification of spam e-mails – rejected) and T1358/09 (classification of text documents – rejected).
21 Cf T1286/09.
22 Cf T1285/10 and T161/18.
23 Cf T1175/09 and T1255/08.
24 Cf T1558/09 and T22/12.
25 Cf T306/10 and T1869/08 discussed in section 2.4(b).
26 See for example, T1326/06 *Giesecke/RSA Schlüsselpaarberechnung*.
27 Guidelines for Examination, Part G, Chapter II, 3.3.

a patentable invention. Similarly, in T1326/06 *RSA Schlüsselpaarberechnung*, the Board of Appeal held a method of encrypting/decrypting or signing electronic communications to be a technical method, even though it was essentially based on a mathematical algorithm, as it was implicit that the claimed method had to be implemented by technical means as the processing in question was not of the type which could be undertaken other than by an appropriately programmed computer.

Historically, before the change in approach in *Pension Benefits* and *Hitachi*, the mental acts exclusion was applied to exclude automation of pre-existing processes from patentability. This was demonstrated by a series of appeals involving IBM in the late 1980s in the context of word processing. The common theme running through all these cases was that in each case the applicant was attempting to obtain a monopoly on the automation of a process previously undertaken manually, rather than a specific implementation or approach to such automation.

For example, in T22/85 *IBM/Document abstracting*, the Board of Appeal assessed the patentability of a method for automatically abstracting and storing an input document in an information storage and retrieval system and a corresponding method for retrieving a document from the system. Rejecting the application, the Board stated that the mere setting out of the sequence of steps necessary to perform the activity in terms of functions or functional means to be realised with the aid of conventional computer hardware elements did not import any technical considerations and could therefore neither lend technical character to the activity nor to the claimed subject matter considered as a whole, any more than solving a mathematical equation could be regarded as a technical activity when a conventional calculation machine is used.

In T38/86 *IBM/Text processing*, the Board assessed the patentability of an invention which involved automatically replacing difficult expressions in a text with simpler expressions to improve the understandability level of the text. Again, the Board rejected the application, ruling that the use of technical means for carrying out a method for performing mental acts, partly or entirely without human intervention, is excluded from patentability if the use of technical means does not involve a contribution to the art outside a field excluded from patentability. In *IBM/Text processing*, the technical implementation of the method involved no more than the straightforward application of conventional techniques, and therefore was considered obvious to a person skilled in the art. A claim to an apparatus did not specify any technical features beyond those already comprised in the corresponding method claim, and only defined the apparatus in functional terms corresponding to the steps of that method, and thus similarly the method claim was also not allowable.

Similarly, in T121/85 *IBM/Spelling checking* and T65/86 *IBM/Text editing* relating to the automatic detection and replacement of homophones, the

Boards of appeal concluded that the claimed word processing systems failed to make any contribution in a technical field, and hence were not allowable.

Under the modern approach, the inventions the subject of these early appeals would most likely have been rejected on the grounds of lack of inventive step rather than lack of patentable subject matter because they all related to the mere automation of methods which had previously been performed manually. However, these early decisions of the Boards are still of relevance as they form the basis of the EPO's current approach to assessing the patentability of artificial intelligence inventions, and particularly the EPO's current view that linguistic or textual analysis of documents is a non-technical field and hence not patentable.

By way of example, in T22/12 *Microsoft/spam classification*, the Board of Appeal upheld the decision of the Examining Division that a method claim defining linguistic analysis using a mathematical algorithm lacked inventive step. The Board of Appeal held that such linguistic analysis was non-technical, and articulated its view that:

the classification of messages as a function of their content is not technical per se. In this regard, it is immaterial whether the messages are electronic messages, because, even though an email has technical properties, it is the content of the email that is classified. Furthermore, mathematical methods as such are not technical and the application of a mathematical method as such in a non-technical analysis of message content does not change that.[28]

The Board then considered arguments that a technical effect could reside in the fact that the claimed approach simplified the training process for the classification of emails, and rejected such an argument, commenting that:

... the Board does not consider that reducing the complexity of an algorithm is necessarily a technical effect, or evidence of underlying technical considerations. That is because complexity is an inherent property of the algorithm as such. If the design of the algorithm were motivated by a problem related to the internal workings of the computer, e.g. if it were adapted to a particular computer architecture, it could, arguably, be considered as technical ... However, the Board does not see any such motivations in the present case.[29]

A similar approach was adopted by the Board of Appeal in T1358/09 *BDGB Enterprise/Classification method* which concerned the classification of text documents based on building a 'classification model'. After stating that a mathematical algorithm contributes to the technical character of a computer-implemented method only insofar as it serves a technical purpose, the Board rejected the proposal that textual analysis could provide such a purpose, commenting that:

---

28 Reasons for the decision, paragraph 2.2.
29 Reasons for the decision, paragraph 2.8.

> *Classification of text documents is certainly useful, as it may help to locate text documents with a relevant cognitive content, but in the Board's view it does not qualify as a technical purpose. Whether two text documents in respect of their textual content belong to the same "class" of documents is not a technical issue.*[30]

Where an invention concerns the interaction of a computer with the physical world, ordinarily the mathematical and mental act exclusions will be easy to overcome and cases where applications are rejected on this ground are rare.

T914/02 *General Electric Company/Nuclear Core loading* is a rare example of an invention which was found to fall purely within the mental act exclusion. The claims of the application in T914/02 were directed to a method for designing a nuclear core loading arrangement. Considering these claims, the Board rejected the application on the grounds that the claimed method neither specified use of technical means or measures of a technical nature nor included the provision of a physical entity as the resulting product but rather were purely abstract in nature. Therefore, the claimed method could be carried out mentally and was found entirely lacking in technical character.

Had, instead, the claims in T914/02 *General Electric Company/Nuclear Core loading* been directed to something of concrete character, the result would likely have been different as is demonstrated by the decision in T453/91 *IBM/VLSI chip design*. The application in T453/91 *IBM/VLSI chip design* included product claims to a VLSI chip and a claim to a method of designing the chip itself. Similar to the decision in T914/02, the Board considered a method of designing a chip to be a purely abstract matter and thus fall within the mathematical methods and mental acts exclusion. However, in contrast, product claims to a chip designed in a particular way were held to be novel and inventive.

The Boards have also had to consider the boundaries of patentable subject matter in the context of computer simulations.

T1227/05 *Infineon/circuit simulation* concerned a computer-implemented method with mathematical steps for simulating the performance of a circuit subject to 1/f noise. In that case, the Board concluded that the simulation of 1/f noise by feeding suitable random numbers into a circuit model had technical character because it was necessarily computer-implemented. Turning then to features which might be considered for the purposes of assessing inventive step, the Board was persuaded that the simulation of noise in a circuit was itself an adequately definite technical problem which could be said to be solved by the invention, and hence all features addressing that problem could be considered when assessing obviousness.

In 2021, the Enlarged Board of Appeal endorsed this approach in G1/19 *Bentley/Pedestrian simulation*, a case concerning a computerised simulation of

30 Reasons for the decision, paragraph 5.2.

movement of individuals through a building. In that case the Enlarged Board ruled that a computer-implemented simulation of a technical system or process will be considered 'technical' if it gives rise to a technical effect beyond mere implementation of the simulation on a computer. That a simulation is based, in whole or in part, on technical principles underlying the simulated system or process is not sufficient to make that simulation 'technical'. Rather, exactly as with other computer-implemented inventions, to be considered 'technical' a computer simulation has to address a 'technical problem', and if it does, then it will be considered to relate to patentable subject matter.

(b) *Business methods*

How the EPO deals with patents in the business field is dependent upon a characterisation of where the EPO perceives the benefits and advantages of an invention lie.

That an invention arises in a business context is not fatal to an application. This was clearly established by the Board of Appeal in T769/92 *Sohei/General Purpose Management System.*

The invention in the Sohei case concerned a computer system for managing financial and inventory data. The claimed system facilitated management of different types of data separately and independently. All data was inputted into the system through a single 'transfer slip' displayed on the computer screen. The Board accepted that although financial and inventory management would normally fall under the 'doing business' exclusion in Article 52(2) EPC and despite references to financial and inventory management appearing in the independent claims, the application was allowable. In reaching that conclusion, the Board considered that the references to business data appearing in the independent claim were merely labels and considered the patentability of a generalised claim where different types of data were input via a single interface and then managed separately – in other words, the Board considered the patentability of the system independently from the type of data that was input and processed. Managing data in the manner claimed was considered to be a technical problem, which was solved by the claimed invention, and hence the application was found allowable.

An invention involving both physical and business considerations is more likely to find favour with the Boards of Appeal. For example, in T767/99 *Pitney Bowes/System for processing mail*, a sorting machine configured to sort mail based on the timing of pick-up and deliveries was considered to be allowable. The Board accepted that the timing of deliveries was largely a business decision but considered that the claimed invention improved efficiency of the mail delivery process, which was held to be technical, and thus constituted a technical invention in the field of mail sorting.

In contrast, the Board of Appeal in T641/00 *Comvik/Two identities* rejected an application directed towards a novel SIM card having two different SIM identities, which facilitated billing for mobile phone use on two different accounts. Reviewing the application, the Board identified that the only benefits arising from the novel features in the claimed invention were exclusively business benefits, and hence the claimed invention did not provide a technical solution to a technical problem.

In T1670/07 *Nokia/Shopping with mobile device*, the Board of Appeal summarised three arguments that applicants frequently advance unsuccessfully to argue in favour of patentability:

- the 'technical leakage fallacy', in which the intrinsic technical nature of the implementation is argued to leak back into the intrinsically non-technical nature of the problem. Use of technical means to solve a non-technical problem does not render an invention patentable;
- the 'broken technical chain fallacy', in which a chain of steps from providing information to its use in a technical process is broken by the intervention of a user. The possible final technical effect brought about by the action of a user cannot be used to establish an overall technical effect because it is conditional on the mental activities of the user; and
- the 'non-technical prejudice fallacy', in which non-technical aspects are invoked as a reason for not modifying the prior art, whereas these non-technical aspects cannot in fact contribute to inventive step.

In T1755/10 *TRILOGY/Software structure* and T1834/10 *EBAY/Image selection*, the Boards identified a further 'fallacy' which the Boards have subsequently referred to as "the software implementation fallacy" which seeks to suggest that "modified software causes a modified behaviour of the computer and should for that very reason be considered as a technical implementation".

T1755/10 *TRILOGY/Software structure* concerned a method of determining commissions to be paid to recipients based on a data model which included quotas and allocation rules. In the view of the Board, the combination of a data model with a commission engine was a known general software concept. In the absence of a 'further' technical effect, the fact that a computer might have to be programmed in a specific way to arrive at the claimed invention did not amount to a technical implementation. The applicant argued that a different way of programming changes the internal operation of the computer, and thus should be considered a technical implementation. The Board rejected the argument, reasoning that accepting the applicant's argument as valid would result in any software being a technical implementation, and thus would effectively remove computer programs from the list of the excluded subject matter under Article 52(2)(c) EPC.

T1834/10 *EBAY/Image selection* concerned the automated selection of images for inclusion in an e-commerce website. The Board's view was that such a selection did not serve a technical aim, but merely related to a presentation of information driven by the needs of an online shop manager. The applicant argued that the claimed invention in the form of a single software instruction conveying both the number and locations of images enabled a simple and efficient regeneration of a web page. Rejecting such an argument, the Board stated that a piece of software serving a non-technical purpose (presentation of information) could not be considered a technical implementation absent the demonstration of any further technical effect beyond the elementary interaction between software and hardware.

The application of artificial intelligence systems in a business context was considered in T306/10 *Yahoo!/Relationship discovery* and in T1869/08.

T306/10 concerned the use of an AI system to make user-specific recommendations on e-commerce websites based on selections made by users. The computer-based analysis sought to improve the accuracy and relevance of such recommendations, by accounting for the relative popularity of different product selections. In assessing the inventive step of the claimed algorithm, the Board could not identify any 'technical purpose' for the algorithm and rejected arguments that improvements in saving user time when performing a search constituted a technical effect that could form the basis for a valid argument for inventive step. The Board commented that:

> *While making "good" or "bad" recommendations may lead to different user reactions and thereby, in the end, to different technical results (the user might for example play more or fewer songs, or issue more or fewer search queries in order to find other songs), such results do not qualify as a technical effect of the recommendations, as they depend on subjective choices made by the user.*[31]

The Board of Appeal considered a similar system for generating user recommendations in T1869/08. There, the Board rejected arguments that use of 'recommendations generated for' third parties as opposed to 'recommendations given by' third parties was a technical distinction between the claimed invention and prior art. Although such a modification resulted in a simplified algorithm for generating recommendations, the Board was not convinced that this kind of simplification would result in any appreciable reduction in computation overhead or improvement in reliability. The Board was not persuaded because within the context of the claimed invention 'reliability' would be understood as being a recommendation better matched to the subjective taste of a user, which could not constitute a technical effect.

(c) Scheme, rule or method for playing a game

Video games have given rise to several patent applications where the Boards of Appeal have ruled on the scope of the 'method for playing a game' exception.

31 Reasons for Decision, paragraph 5.2.

For video games, a fundamental distinction is made between game rules and game design which improves playability or player interest.

T336/07 *IGT/Electronic Poker* is an example of a patent application rejected on the grounds that it was directed solely to gaming rules. The Board ruled that gaming rules "defining the regulatory framework agreed between [or with] players concerning conduct and conventions and conditions that are meaningful only in a gaming context" were not patentable. Similarly, in T2127/09 *BANDAI Game apparatus*, the Board refused an application directed to a novel form of Tetris game because the only novel features in the game concerned the addition of a new gaming rule as to when blocks disappeared, which was a feature entirely devoid of technical considerations.

In contrast, where innovations in the gaming field extend beyond being mere rules of the game being played, the EPO will frequently allow applications to proceed to grant.

For example, in T928/03 *KONAMI/Video game*, the Board of Appeal considered the patentability of the game mechanics of a video game involving the display of a ring-shaped guide mark at the foot of an active character and using a visual indicator at the edge of the screen to highlight the relative position of an off-screen character. The Board ruled that using a visual indicator on a display screen to indicate the relative position of an off-screen character contributed to the objective technical function of the display, and that the functional quality was not affected by the fact that the visualised information was to be relied upon by a user playing a game. In reaching this conclusion, the Board emphasised the distinctions made in the earlier *Comvik* decision between technical and non-technical features of a claim. Whereas non-technical aspects of a claim could be utilised in the formulation of a technical problem, the actual contributions of any features having technical character had to be considered when assessing inventive step.

The EPO has also allowed applications based on consideration of the underlying structure or narrative of a game. This occurred in T717/05 *Labtronix Concept Inc/Auxiliary Game*, where the Board of Appeal had to consider the patentability of a gaming apparatus that periodically caused a player to access an auxiliary game. Ruling that the application was allowable, the Board expressed the view that game design directed at maintaining a player's interest was a technical problem in that it was directly linked to the purpose of the gaming apparatus itself. Thus, the implementation of an auxiliary game and the way progress towards that game was displayed to a user was relevant for the assessment of inventive step.

A similar result was achieved in T12/08 *NINTENDO/Game machine and storage medium* which concerned a video game where a player navigates around a gaming environment and randomly encounters other characters with whom the player interacts. The invention concerned a novel way of improving the unpredictability of interacting with characters in the game. Again, the Board distinguished between gaming rules, and the mechanics of a game to make the game more interesting. The Board ruled that the mechanism for making game play more unpredictable was considered to provide a technical solution to the technical problem of maintaining player interest.

(d) Presentation of information

When interpreting the presentation of information exclusion, the EPO distinguishes between the semantic content of information and any technical benefits a particular type of presentation might achieve. Presentation of information solely defined by its content or semantic meaning is not patentable, regardless of the manner or form in which the information is presented. In contrast, the EPO accepts that if a particular arrangement or manner of presentation can be identified as having some form of technical effect, then that is potentially patentable.[32]

For example, in T1749/06 *Nokia/Three-dimensional icons for graphical user interface* an icon with alternating light and dark stripes conferring a three-dimensional appearance was considered potentially patentable, since the claimed design of icon solved the technical problem of how to provide a two-dimensional icon with a three-dimensional appearance. The Board noted the distinction between 'what is displayed' and 'how something is displayed', commenting that the claimed effect was independent of the cognitive content of a specific icon.

A similar distinction was found in T887/92 *IBM/On-line help facility*, which concerned making a help facility in an interactive information handling system more user friendly. Approving the application, the Board held that providing visual indications about the internal conditions of an apparatus or system was a technical problem. Within the context of the application, displaying only valid commands in a help panel had technical character because the content of the help panel reflected the status or condition of the system. Hence, a computer program which implemented such an invention would constitute technical means for carrying out a technical invention.

In T336/14 *Presentation of operating instructions/GAMBRO*, a claim relating to "a user interface for an extracorporeal blood treatment machine" was deemed to be an example of a 'mixed type invention'. When assessing inventive step, the Board concluded that the distinguishing features of: "data comprising operating instructions for readying the machine for use" and "at least two images being pictographs which represent configurations of the machine correlated to the operating instructions" related to the content of information (ie, 'what' was presented) rather than to the manner in which the information

32 Practical application of this approach is illustrated in Figure 3 at the end of this chapter.

was presented (ie, as to 'how'). Therefore, the Board held that these features constituted "presentations of information as such". The distinguishing claim features were therefore not taken into account when assessing inventive step.

In contrast, where a particular manner of presentation is itself associated with a technical advantage, such a presentation is a valid basis for an invention and this can extend to the form of a signal or a data carrier itself. Thus, for example in T163/85 *BBC/Television signal,* a colour television signal characterised by technical features of the system in which it occurred was considered to be patentable.

2.5 Practical considerations

Most subject matter eligibility issues may be avoided by appropriate claim drafting. Claims for computer-implemented inventions need to be directed to concrete subject matter that provides a technical solution to a technical problem. It is therefore imperative to draft a patent application so that it describes an invention in concrete technical terms. This is best achieved by describing a computer-implemented invention in terms of the data structures and processing undertaken by a computer rather than in terms of human interaction with a computer. Further, it needs to be clear from the description that features of a claimed invention are grounded in some form of physical reality such as blocks of programming code or other data stored in a physical machine.

Novel aspects of an invention should be described in terms of structure, function, and advantage. If an element is solely described in terms of its structure, problems may arise when attempting to generalise the described structure to obtain broad claim language which covers alternatives that achieve the same result. Conversely, describing an invention solely in terms of advantages or benefits risks a description being found too abstract. Claim language derived from such a description may be open to objection on the grounds that it claims a result to be achieved, rather than the means for achieving a result.

Advantages should be specific to the invention claimed. Mere boiler-plate language stating that a particular algorithm is more efficient is unlikely to be sufficient to support a technical argument. An examiner will be interested in knowing why an advantage arises and how a claimed invention achieves this. Experimental data is not essential. However, such data can be helpful, particularly in cases where the purpose or effect of a particular form of processing would not otherwise be apparent.

Applicants should take care in their use of non-technical language. Although it is not necessary to obscure the fact that an invention arises within a business context,[33] it is preferable that references to non-technical aspects of

33 See, for example, T769/92 *Sohei/General Purpose Management System.*

an invention are minimised, to avoid detracting from technical issues. The focus of an application should always be on the technical implementation and the technical advantages which arise from that implementation.

The onus is on the applicant to convince an examiner that an application relates to a patentable invention. It is not sufficient merely to argue that an examiner's objections are not fairly based. Applications need to be written as persuasive documents highlighting the technical advantages and benefits arising from an invention in order to demonstrate that an application provides a non-obvious technical solution to a technical problem.

At the inventive step analysis stage, an applicant is generally allowed to define or redefine an objective technical problem in view of the cited art. However, the Boards of Appeal, and consequently the Examining Divisions, will focus on identifying the actual motivation behind the claimed invention when evaluating whether it amounts to a technical implementation and recent decisions by the Boards of Appeal[34] suggest that the EPO may not accept the newly defined or redefined technical problem if the application lacks a corresponding technical story. When an application indicates that the actual motivation is non-technical and is silent about addressing any technical problems, an applicant is unlikely to persuade the EPO otherwise after the fact. Therefore, drafting a patent application to reflect the motivation behind the claimed invention in the terms of seeking a technical solution to a technical problem is imperative for successful prosecution of applications directed to computer-implemented inventions. If an invention in a potentially problematic area (eg, in a business context) does indeed solve a technical problem, it is preferable to indicate that fact in the content of the application itself.

When drafting applications which potentially engage the presentation of information exclusion, it is recommended to identify if the presentation of information causes any objective physiological effects in a user. The existence of such a physiological response will be independent of the semantic qualities of the information presented to a user and may therefore support a technical effect argument.

Similarly, if the purpose of the presentation of information is to convey information about the state of an underlying system, then this should be highlighted in the application, as this has been found to be a valid technical effect.

The EPO Guidelines are a useful resource. To assist applicants, the EPO maintains a dedicated webpage[35] with an index of the sections of the Guidelines as they apply to computer-implemented inventions to which applicants should

34 See, for example, T1755/10 *TRILOGY/Software structure*, T1834/10 *EBAY/Image selection*, and T22/12 *Microsoft/spam classification*.

35 www.epo.org/law-practice/legal-texts/html/guidelines/e/j.htm.

refer. The Guidelines are periodically reviewed and updated with best practice tips in respect of emerging technologies.

3. Life sciences and chemical inventions

For readers approaching this chapter from a US perspective, the subject matter eligibility requirements at the EPO will probably seem much less restrictive than their US counterparts. Indeed, aside from some specific explicitly excluded inventions, it is generally possible to find a way to claim the inventive concept underlying most biotechnological and chemical inventions at the EPO, although this may require a different claim format to other countries. Moreover, practitioners familiar with US practice may be relieved to hear that the EPO has generally adopted a consistent approach to the case law (although not completely without U-turns) providing greater reassurance for applicants and patentees alike.

In the following, inventions explicitly excluded from patentability by the EPC are first considered before moving on to the following classes of inventions: plant and animal varieties; medical and surgical methods; diagnostic methods; and natural products. In each of these sections, we include 'practice points' with practical advice and tips when drafting patent applications in any of these specific subject areas.

3.1 Ethical exclusions

As noted in the introduction, certain inventions are excluded from patentability at the EPO. Article 53(a) EPC prohibits the patenting of inventions considered contrary to *'ordre public'* or morality when commercially exploited. This is strictly an ethical consideration, and the legality of the invention in some or all of the contracting states is irrelevant.

In T356/93, the Board of Appeal defined both *'ordre public'* and 'morality'. The case in question related to genetic manipulation of plants and seeds, rendering them resistant to a particular class of herbicides so that they could be selectively protected against weeds and fungal diseases. The objection raised was that exploitation of the invention was likely to cause serious damage to the environment.

The Board defined the concept of *'ordre public'* as covering the protection of public security and the physical integrity of individuals as part of society. It also encompassed the protection of the environment. Accordingly, inventions that could cause significant harm to the environment were to be excluded from patentability as being contrary to *'ordre public'*.

The Board also clarified that, for the purposes of Article 53(a) EPC, the culture in question was the culture inherent in European society and civilisation, and that inventions that were not in conformity with the conventionally accepted standards of conduct pertaining to this culture were to be excluded from patentability as being contrary to morality. Opinion poll evidence on what the public did and did not find objectionable was considered to be of very limited value, as there are many drawbacks to such data collection methods.

In the specific case of T356/93, the Board held that, although there was some evidence that the invention could lead to environmental hazards, there was insufficient evidence that the exploitation of any of the claimed subject matter would seriously prejudice the environment. So, the objection that the invention was contrary to the *'ordre public'* was rejected. Moreover, the Board held that the invention was not objectionable on moral grounds either, since selective breeding techniques could achieve a similar effect, and such techniques had no moral objections.

Of interest here is whether a similar result would be found by a Board of Appeal sitting today, some 25 years later, at a time when environmental concerns are higher on the social and political agenda. Since the term of a patent is 20 years, it seems possible that the question of whether an invention meets the requirements of Article 53(a) EPC could change during a patent's lifetime. This was recognised by the Board of Appeal in T315/03, where it was noted that compliance with Article 53(a) EPC must be assessed at the filing or priority date of the patent.

More concrete guidance on subject matter excluded from patentability on the ground of *'ordre public'* is provided by Rule 28(1) EPC, which states that:

(1) Under Article 53(a), European patents shall not be granted in respect of biotechnological inventions which, in particular, concern the following:

- *(a) processes for cloning human beings;*
- *(b) processes for modifying the germ line genetic identity of human beings;*
- *(c) uses of human embryos for industrial or commercial purposes;*
- *(d) processes for modifying the genetic identity of animals which are likely to cause them suffering without any substantial medical benefit to man or animal, and also animals resulting from such processes.*

There is no case law relating to Rules 28(1)(a) and (b) EPC, although it is noted that these provisions only extend to humans and do not apply to animals.

The EPO's approach to Rule 28(1)(c) EPC regarding the patentability of human embryos has been controversial since EPO case law on this issue has in the past conflicted with case law of the Court of Justice of the European Union (CJEU). However, differences have been resolved and, in EPO Board of Appeal decision T385/14, the Board held that an objection under Article 53(a) EPC and Rule 28(1)(c) EPC cannot be raised in respect of an application pertaining to human pluripotent stem cells, including human embryonic stem cells, uses thereof or products derived therefrom if (i) the application has an effective date (ie, a valid priority date or, if no priority is claimed or the priority is not valid, a filing date) on or after 5 June 2003, and (ii) its technical teaching can be put into practice using human embryonic stem cells derived from parthenogenetically activated human oocytes.

The relationship between Rule 28(1)(d) EPC and Article 53(a) EPC was considered by the Boards of Appeal in T315/03. The claims related to methods for producing a transgenic non-human mammalian animal by insertion of an activated oncogene, and to the animals themselves (so-called 'onco-mice'). The Board of Appeal noted that the insertion of the oncogenes made the animals abnormally sensitive to carcinogenic substances and consequently prone to develop tumours, which caused suffering. The Board, however, considered that the requirement of a balance between the suffering of the animals and the benefit to mankind was met, given the benefits to using such mice in medical research.[36]

Provided that the requirements of Rule 28(1) EPC are met, it is rare for applications to be rejected on the grounds of Article 53(a) EPC. While there may be moral or ethical objections to some inventions (such as euthanasia drugs) these can frequently be overcome by providing a positive benefit for society (in this case, ending suffering). If the application falls into a moral 'grey area' it may therefore be worth emphasising any such benefits when drafting.

Aside from patentability considerations, it is noted that the 20-year term of the patent at issue in T315/03 expired before the decision was published. The large number of opponents (particularly anti-vivisection groups) prolonged proceedings and pushed up costs for the parties. Other forms of intellectual property protection may therefore be worthwhile considering, such as trade secrets, if there is a risk that third parties might raise objections under Article 53(a) EPC.

3.2 Plant and animal varieties

Article 53(b) EPC prohibits patenting of plant and animal varieties or essentially biological processes for the production of plants or animals. Article 53(b) EPC does, however, specifically note that this provision shall not apply to microbiological processes or the products thereof.

The term 'plant variety' is defined by Rule 26(4) EPC as:

any plant grouping within a single botanical taxon of the lowest known rank, which grouping, irrespective of whether the conditions for the grant of a plant variety right are fully met, can be:

(a) defined by the expression of the characteristics that results from a given genotype or combination of genotypes,

---

36 There is little recent case law in this area. The application of Article 53(a) EPC and Rule 28(d) EPC was discussed in detail in the preliminary opinion for T682/16. However, before the hearing could take place, the patentee abandoned certain claims such that the final decision of the Board does not provide further insight on this issue.

(b) distinguished from any other plant grouping by the expression of at least one of the said characteristics, and
(c) considered as a unit with regard to its suitability for being propagated unchanged.

The leading case law in this area is G1/98, which held that a claim wherein specific plant varieties are not individually claimed is not excluded from patentability under Article 53(b) EPC, even though it may embrace plant varieties and that the exception to patentability in Article 53(b) EPC applies to plant varieties irrespective of the way in which they were produced. Therefore, plant varieties containing genes introduced into an ancestral plant by recombinant gene technology are excluded from patentability.

The *Onco-Mouse* examination appeal[37] considered Article 53(b) EPC in detail, as the Examining division construed this as prohibiting the patenting of animals as such. The Board of Appeal, however, disagreed, noting that Article 53(b) EPC did not exclude patents granted to subject matter which is not covered by any of the terms 'animal varieties', '*races animales*' ('animal breeds') or '*Tierarten*' ('animal species').[38] This means that a patent cannot be granted for a single animal variety (or breed or species) but could be granted if varieties might fall within the scope of its claims.

The meaning of the term 'essentially biological processes' and what exactly this term excludes from patentability has been the subject of much debate at the EPO in recent years. The debate arose due to an apparent conflict between the Rules and Articles of the EPC. In particular, Rule 28(2) EPC, introduced following the implementation of Directive 98/44/EC of the European Parliament and of the Council of 6 July 1998 (the Biotech Directive[39]), refers back to Article 53(b) EPC and specifies that:

European patents shall not be granted in respect of plants or animals exclusively obtained by means of an essentially biological process.

Rule 26(5) EPC further specifies that:

A process for the production of plants or animals is essentially biological if it consists entirely of natural phenomena such as crossing or selection.

How these provisions should be interpreted has been the subject of fierce debate at the EPO for several years, although there does appear to now be some clarity on this issue.

In 2015, Enlarged Board of Appeal decisions G2/12 *Tomato II* and G2/13

37 T19/90; related to T315/03 discussed above.

38 The three terms arise from the three official languages of the EPC – English, French and German – and the slightly different terminology used in each language.

39 As its colloquial name suggests, the Biotech Directive relates to the patent protection of biotechnological inventions and was intended to harmonise the laws of EU Member States regarding the patentability of biotechnological inventions, including plant varieties and human genes. While the EPO and the EU operate through separate governance systems, certain provisions of the Directive were carried over into the EPC Implementing Regulations in June 1999, with the addition of new Rules 26–29 EPC.

Broccoli II held that the non-patentability of essentially biological processes for the production of plants or animals under Article 53(b) EPC did not extend to products that are exclusively obtained by means of an essentially biological process. In other words, prior to the implementation of the Biotech Directive, Article 53(b) EPC did not prohibit patenting of plants and animals obtained by essentially biological processes. The technical Board of Appeal followed these decisions when deciding on T1063/18, indicating that new Rule 28(2) EPC had no impact on the interpretation of Article 53(b) EPC. This led to a referral to the Enlarged Board of Appeal (G3/19) to decide which took precedence – the Rules or the Articles of the EPC.

The Enlarged Board of Appeal decided in May 2020 that plants and animals exclusively obtained by essentially biological processes are not patentable after all – contrary to G2/12 and G2/13. Thus, Article 53(b) EPC prohibits product claims and product-by-process claims directed to plants, plant material or animals if the claimed product is exclusively obtained by means of an essentially biological process or if the process features define an essentially biological process.

The EPO Boards of Appeal have in the past adopted a more lenient approach when considering whether a process for the production of animals is 'essentially biological'. For example, in both T19/90 and T315/03, the Board held that genetic manipulation to form transgenic animals was not an essentially biological process. These decisions are consistent with the findings of G3/19, and it therefore seems unlikely that the EPO will change its approach in this area. Consequently, animals obtained by genetic manipulation seem likely to remain patentable, but animals obtained via selective breeding methods will not.

In general, the EPO is more lenient when considering the patentability of animal varieties and essentially biological processes for the production of animals than plant varieties since, as noted in T19/90, no other provisions exist for protection of animal varieties. For plant varieties, registration with the Community Plant Variety Office provides a viable alternative to patent protection in Europe, although registration with the Community Plant Variety Office only encompasses EU member states, and not all EPC contracting states.[40]

While G3/19 overturns previous decisions of the Enlarged Board, G3/19 does not have retroactive effect. Therefore, G3/19 only affects applications with a priority or application date on or after 1 July 2017, the date on which Rule 28(2) EPC entered into force. Patent applications for products derived from essentially biological processes with priority or application dates prior to 1 July 2017 will continue under the provisions of G2/13 and G3/13.

40 At the time of writing, there are 27 EU member states, and 38 EPC contracting states (as well as an additional six EPC extension and validation states).

It is noted that Article 53(b) EPC expressly indicates that microbiological processes or the products thereof are not excluded from patentability. While the Boards of Appeal have defined the term 'microbiological' broadly to include essentially all generally unicellular organisms, the Board is clear that 'technical processes including a microbiological step' cannot be equated with 'microbiological processes'.[41] Thus, simply including a microbiological step in an otherwise unallowable claim does not render the claim patentable.

3.3 Medical and surgical methods

Article 53(c) EPC prohibits the patenting of methods of medical treatment on the human or animal body by surgery or therapy, and diagnostic methods practised on the human or animal body. Article 53(c) EPC does, however, permit 'composition or compound for use' claims. Therefore, a US-style 'method of treating cancer by administration of compound x' claim can be rewritten as 'compound x for use in treating cancer'. This redrafting is required for compliance with Article 53(c) EPC and does not add matter, despite the omission of the 'administration' step.

While medications prescribed by a physician might be expected to be provided for a therapeutic use, the EPO's definition of a therapeutic indication is somewhat narrower. For example, treatment of disease states to cure or alleviate the symptoms of that disease are considered to be therapeutic, as are prophylactic treatments to avoid disease states.[42] However, while the treatment of pain is considered to be therapeutic,[43] reducing muscle fatigue in athletes is not.[44] Reducing fatigue associated with a disease or as a side-effect of a drug would, however, be patentable as a therapeutic indication.

Contraceptive methods are not considered to be therapeutic since, as noted in T1635/09, as pregnancy is not an illness, its prevention is not a therapeutic method, not even when done prophylactically.[45] In T74/93, a claim relating to a contraceptive, requiring the use of a compound for applying to the cervix of a female capable of conception was rejected by the EPO for lacking industrial applicability under Article 52 EPC.

Article 52 EPC requires that an invention must be susceptible of industrial application. Article 57 EPC defines 'susceptible of industrial application', noting that "[A]n invention shall be considered as susceptible of industrial application if it can be made or used in any kind of industry, including agriculture". This is a low barrier and as such it is rare for applications to be refused on the grounds of lack of compliance with Article 52 EPC. In T74/93, however, the Board

41 T365/93.
42 T144/83 and G5/83.
43 T81/84.
44 T469/94.
45 T820/92, Reasons for decision 5.2 ff, confirmed in T74/93, Reasons 2.2.3.

considered that application of a contraceptive directly to the cervix was a purely personal use carried out in private, and therefore not 'an industrial activity'.

This does not mean, however, that inventions related to private medical activities and/or contraceptives are necessarily excluded from patentability at the EPO. For example, in T1165/97, a claim to a method of using a vaginal discharge collector and disposing of the collector after a single use was allowed since such a method might not be limited to purely personal needs but may be used to collect a diagnostic sample on the instructions of a doctor.

There are inventions that encompass both therapeutic and non-therapeutic methods. One recent example was discussed in T1916/19, which included method claims encompassing an antimicrobial composition. This could be therapeutic (ie, removal of pathogenic bacteria) and non-therapeutic (ie, removal of odour-causing bacteria) or mixed. In this case, the Board only allowed the method claims that included a proviso that the method was non-therapeutic. This follows G1/07, which found that cosmetic methods are not therapeutic and are therefore patentable.

Veterinary 'therapies' have similar considerations to those discussed above for human patients. There is, however, a further class of invention relating to methods that improve a desirable characteristic, typically of livestock, for example, methods relating to increased milk yields. Such methods are not strictly therapeutic as they do not treat or prevent a disease, but neither are they cosmetic as they do not relate to appearance. In T774/89 the Board recognised this problem when considering claims relating to the use of efomycins to improve milk production. In this case, the claims were allowed with the addition of a disclaimer that the use was 'non-therapeutic', with the Board noting that it was evident that the success of the treatment did not depend on the animals' state of health, and the insertion of the disclaimer excluded any therapeutic effects of the medication.

Following G1/07, surgical methods are defined as those that include:

an invasive step representing a substantial physical intervention on the body which requires professional medical expertise to be carried out and which entails a substantial health risk even when carried out with the required professional care and expertise.

At first glance, this would appear to only exclude what might be thought of colloquially as 'major surgery'. However, this is not the approach adopted in the case law. For example, in T1075/06, venipuncture of blood donors and the extraction of blood from a donor's body was considered to be a substantial physical intervention on the body, since blood was generally collected from the median cubital vein, and consequently carried significant health risks such as infection, bleeding and hematoma, secondary vein perforation, phlebitis, tendon injury, and nerve irritation and injury. While the Board acknowledged that such risks were low, they were 'undoubtedly substantial', and the claims were rejected under Article 53(c) EPC.

In T1695/07, it was held that blood manipulation involving the continuous removal of blood from a patient, its subsequent flowing through a circulating line of an extracorporeal circuit and its re-delivery to the patient is a method of treatment of the human body by surgery excepted from patentability under Article 53(c) EPC. The Board followed this decision in T1927/16 when refusing an application directed towards a dialysis method, noting that blood is an organ and that therefore removal of blood from the body is manipulation of an organ carrying potentially significant health risks.

When drafting, it is recommended to include basis for a first or second medical use claim, as such claims are allowed by Article 53(c) EPC (for example, 'a substance or composition for use in a surgical method/method of treating disease X'). Alternatively, claims may be included that relate to methods for operating a device. Such claims are allowable provided that they do not include any functional link between the claimed method and the effects produced by the device on the body (see T245/87 and T789/96).

G1/07, referring to G1/03 and G2/03, indicates that disclaimers may be introduced into claims to delimit against subject matter that is otherwise prohibited from patentability by Articles 52 to 57 EPC (see Headnote 2.1). One example of such a disclaimer might be adding the term 'non-therapeutic' or 'non-surgical' to the preamble of a claim. This approach should, however, be treated with caution. Claims incorporating so-called 'undisclosed disclaimers' are particularly vulnerable to post-grant attacks on the grounds of added subject matter. A preferred approach is therefore to include basis for disclaiming any surgical steps when drafting an application.

It is relatively rare for applications to be rejected on the grounds of lacking industrial applicability under Article 52(1) EPC. Following T74/93, however, it may be easier to obtain broader claims if there is a risk of rejection for lack of industrial applicability. For instance, if the impugned claim in T74/93 had referred to application to 'the female body' rather than specifically to the cervix, it seems less likely to have been rejected.

3.4 Diagnostic methods

As noted above, Article 53(c) EPC prohibits the patenting of diagnostic methods practised on the human or animal body. The leading case law in this area is Enlarged Board of Appeal decision G1/04, which held that diagnostic methods practised on the human or animal body are excluded only if they include all of the following method steps:

- an examination phase, involving the collection of data;
- the comparison of these data with standard values;
- the finding of any significant deviation, eg, a symptom, during the comparison; and
- the attribution of the deviation to a particular clinical picture, ie, the deductive medical or veterinary decision phase resulting in diagnosis.

The presence of additional, intermediate, steps is irrelevant, and claims will be rejected if they contain at least the above listed steps.[46] However, all the above steps must be present for a claim to be excluded from patentability under Article 53(a) EPC. For example, in the case at issue in T1232/15, the claims relate to the use of adhesive and haptic strips to form an aid for the blind to enable the line-by-line scanning of areas of skin that encompass the breasts of a female human body. As a result, surface areas of the human body to be scanned are provided with a tactile orientation and coordinate system that can be felt by the blind. The Board held that the claims therefore related to an aid for a diagnostic method, but not to a diagnostic method *per se*. In particular, the claims did not contain any steps resulting in a diagnosis based on palpation of lumps. The constitutive steps for making the diagnosis, namely the examination phase with the collection of data (performing the palpation), the comparison of these data with the normal values, and the determination of a significant deviation in this comparison were also not claimed.

G1/04 also indicates that who carries out the method is irrelevant when deciding whether or not a claim relates to a diagnostic method. Thus, the participation of a medical or veterinary practitioner is irrelevant.

Although not explicitly recited in Article 53(c) EPC, to be excluded from patentability a diagnostic method must be carried out on a living human or animal body. Post-mortem methods are therefore not excluded by Article 53(c) EPC.

Diagnostic methods carried out on samples obtained from a human or animal body are not excluded from patentability. However, methods of obtaining the samples may be excluded from patentability as surgical methods (see eg, discussion relating to venipuncture above).

Since diagnostic method claims are only excluded from patentability if they include all four of the steps required by G1/04, patentable claims can be drafted by excluding one of these steps. The most commonly excluded step is arguably the data collection step. For example, allowable claims can be drafted by indicating that the diagnostic method is carried out on an *in vitro* tissue sample, or by specifying that a sample is 'provided' (rather than 'obtained'). Alternatively, claims may be drafted such that they provide information but not a final diagnosis. Use claim format (eg, 'A substance or composition for use in a diagnostic method') can also be considered.

3.5 Natural products

The EPC does not specifically exclude applications directed towards natural products from patentability. Instead, Article 52(2)(a) EPC states that discoveries are not patentable. In everyday English, a 'discovery' is something new that has

46 T143/04.

been detected for the first time and so might be expected to encompass natural products. This definition is not how the term is used within the meaning of the EPC, however, and 'new things' (including newly identified natural products) that have been detected for the first time may nevertheless be patentable if they have a technical effect. In a similar vein, 'new uses for known things' are also patentable if there is a clear technical effect.

The requirement of a technical effect is key here, as emphasised by the Enlarged Board of Appeal in G2/88. In this decision, the Board held that, "the fact that the idea or concept underlying the claimed subject matter resides in a discovery does not necessarily mean that the claimed subject matter is a discovery 'as such'". The Board emphasised that "the essential first step" in determining whether an invention is a discovery or not requires a consideration of the technical features of a claim.[47] Thus, so-called 'second non-medical uses' are patentable, provided that the new use provides a technical benefit.

In the biological sphere this means that if, for example, a natural product isolated from nature can be shown to produce a technical effect, it may be patentable. The EPO Guidelines for Examination 2019 gives the example of a substance occurring in nature which is found to have an antibiotic effect. Since an antibiotic effect is a technical effect, such a substance may be patentable.[48]

The requirement for a technical effect is particularly important for claims relating to gene sequences, as laid down by Rule 29 EPC which states that:

(1) The human body, at the various stages of its formation and development, and the simple discovery of one of its elements, including the sequence or partial sequence of a gene, cannot constitute patentable inventions.

(2) An element isolated from the human body or otherwise produced by means of a technical process, including the sequence or partial sequence of a gene, may constitute a patentable invention, even if the structure of that element is identical to that of a natural element.

(3) The industrial application of a sequence or a partial sequence of a gene must be disclosed in the patent application.

As used in Rule 29(3) EPC, 'industrial application' simply means the purpose or effect of the gene sequence and is intended to prohibit wholly speculative patent applications. Thus, the EPC allows the patenting of gene sequences, even those isolated from the human body, provided that they have a clear technical effect. It is important however that the technical effect of the gene sequence is recited in the application. While this is not a formal requirement for other classes of claims, applications that do not include a clear technical effect are vulnerable to objections on the grounds of a lack of plausibility, inventive step and/or sufficiency.

---

47 G2/88, Reasons of decision, paragraph 8.

48 Guidelines for Examination in the European Patent Office, Part G, Chapter II, section 3.1.

While it is always tempting to file applications early, it seems necessary to wait until at least some data is available to demonstrate industrial applicability for gene sequences. For other technical fields, filing without data may be less problematic for compliance with Article 52(2)(a) EPC, although the other requirements of the EPC may not be met (particularly Article 83 EPC). If early filing of a priority application cannot be avoided due to disclosure of the invention, applications should at the very least include a proposed technical effect with adequate reasoning. Data showing the technical effect could then be included in a subsequent filing.

4. Statistics

Figures 1 and 2 illustrate the relative frequency with which different patentable subject matter objections are mentioned in the decisions of the Boards of Appeal and the frequency with which different provisions of the EPC are cited by the Boards when considering subject matter patentability.

Figure 1

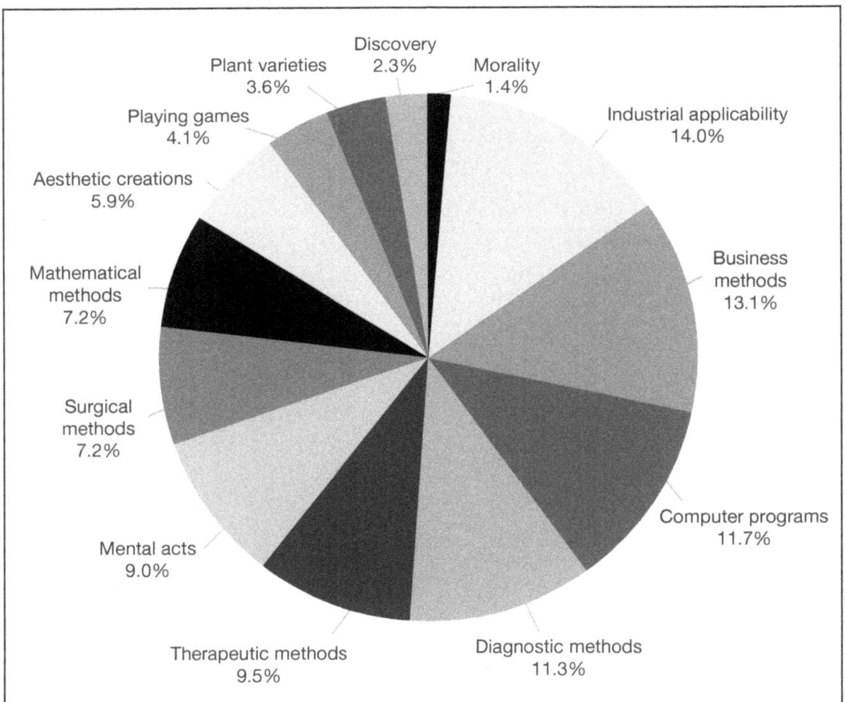

Figure 2

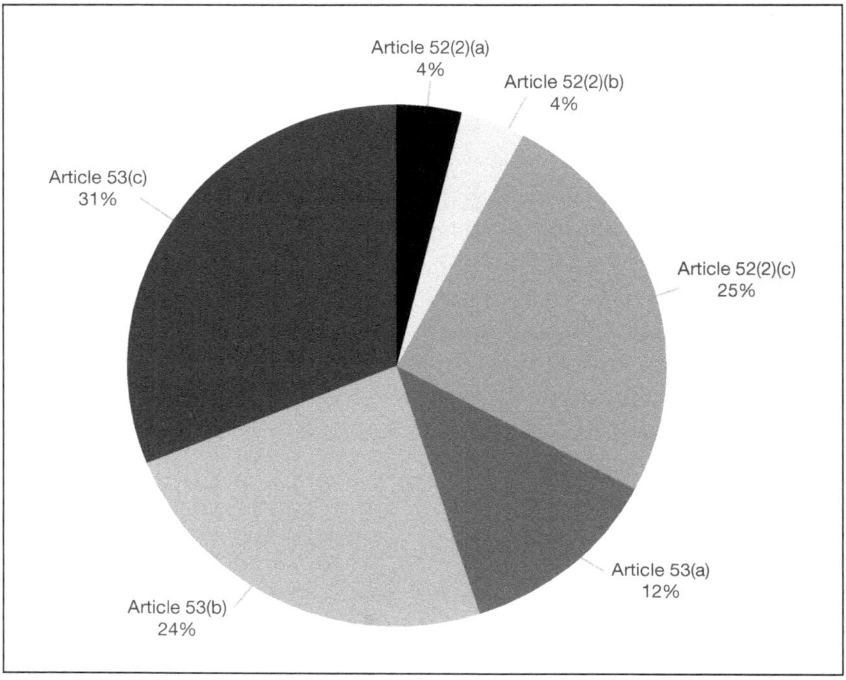

When patentable subject matter objections are raised, they are overturned or rejected slightly more often than they are upheld, with the Boards finding that patentable subject matter is present in 52.3% of cases and not present in 47.7% of cases in which the issue has arisen. There is, however, a significant variation on whether or not patentable subject matter has been found to be present depending on the ground of objection raised in the proceedings. Figure 3 illustrates the allowance rate broken down by ground of objection.

Figure 3. Allowance rate when objection raised

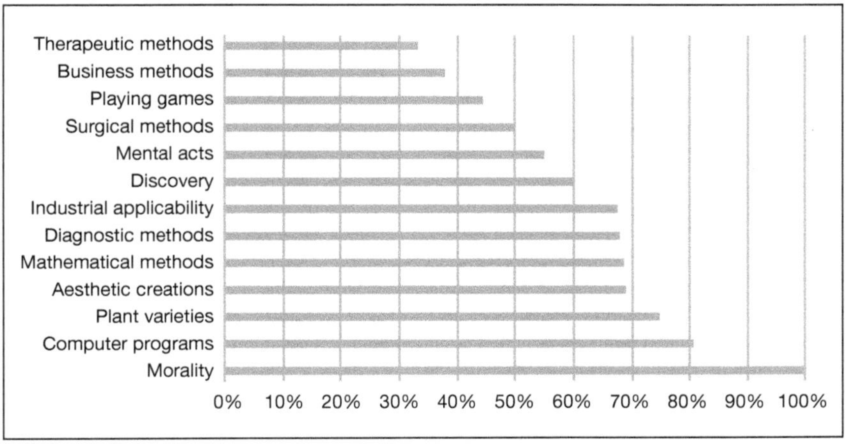

As can be seen above, to date, no objections based on the morality objections have been upheld. This will in part be because the matter is raised very infrequently in cases before the Boards of Appeal. In contrast, two-thirds of cases where objections based on an invention being a therapeutic method are mentioned have resulted in a patent or patent application being refused or revoked.

It should be noted that the numbers of cases where patentable subject matter objections are raised before the Boards of Appeal are relatively small as most such objections are resolved earlier in examination or opposition proceedings. However, the above statistics do indicate the relative likelihood of a patent or patent application surviving a challenge if such an objection is raised in the context of an appeal.

Finally, the above statistics only relate to cases where the Boards of Appeal cite a particular article or keyword. As explained earlier in this chapter, many computer-implemented inventions are rejected as lacking inventive step due to the lack of any technical effect. These cases are not included in the above figures. Hence, the relatively high allowance rates of cases which refer to the computer programs (81%) and mathematical methods (69%) exceptions may present an overly positive picture of the likelihood of success for the patentability of computer-implemented inventions before the EPO.

The authors would like to thank their colleagues Luigi Distefano and Harrison Chang for their assistance in drafting this chapter.

Figure 4. Overview for subject matter patentability

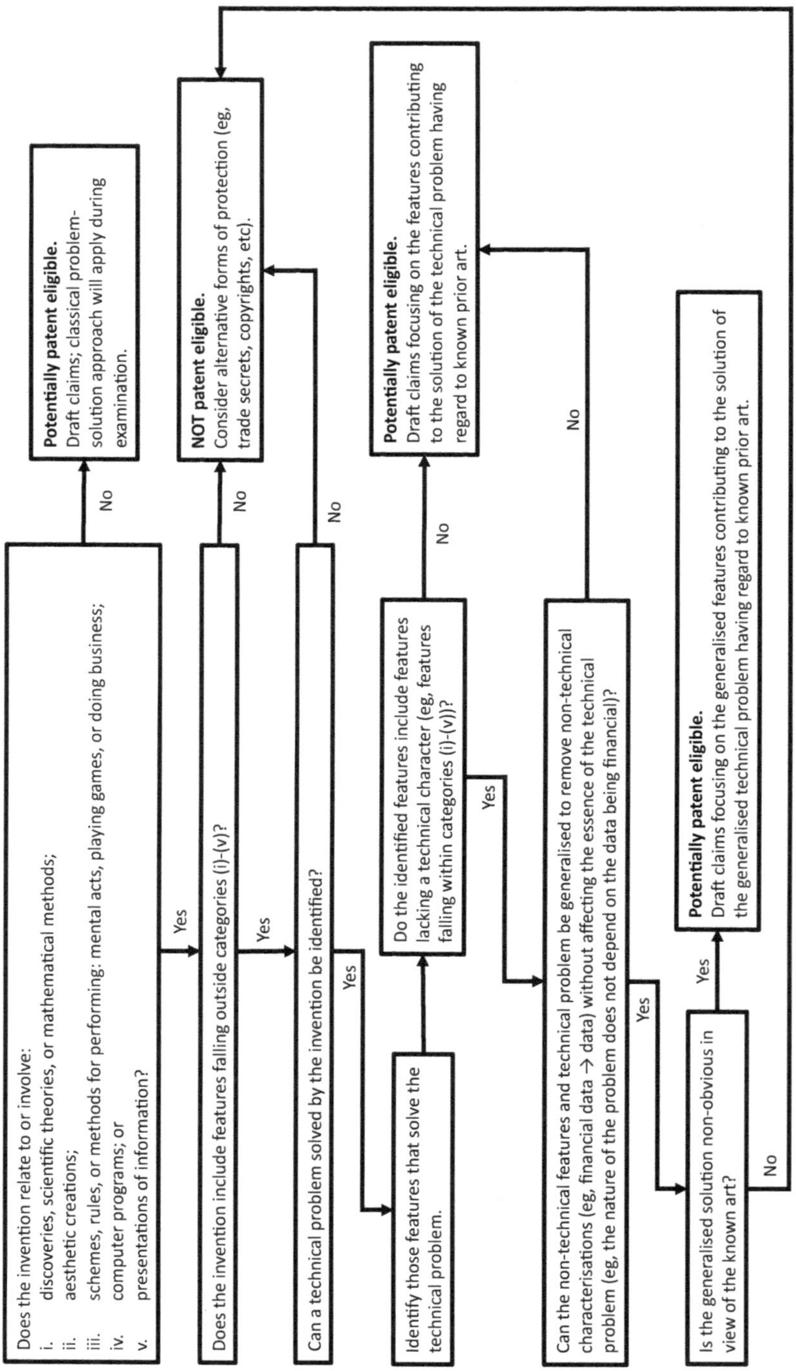

Figure 5. Computer-implemented inventions

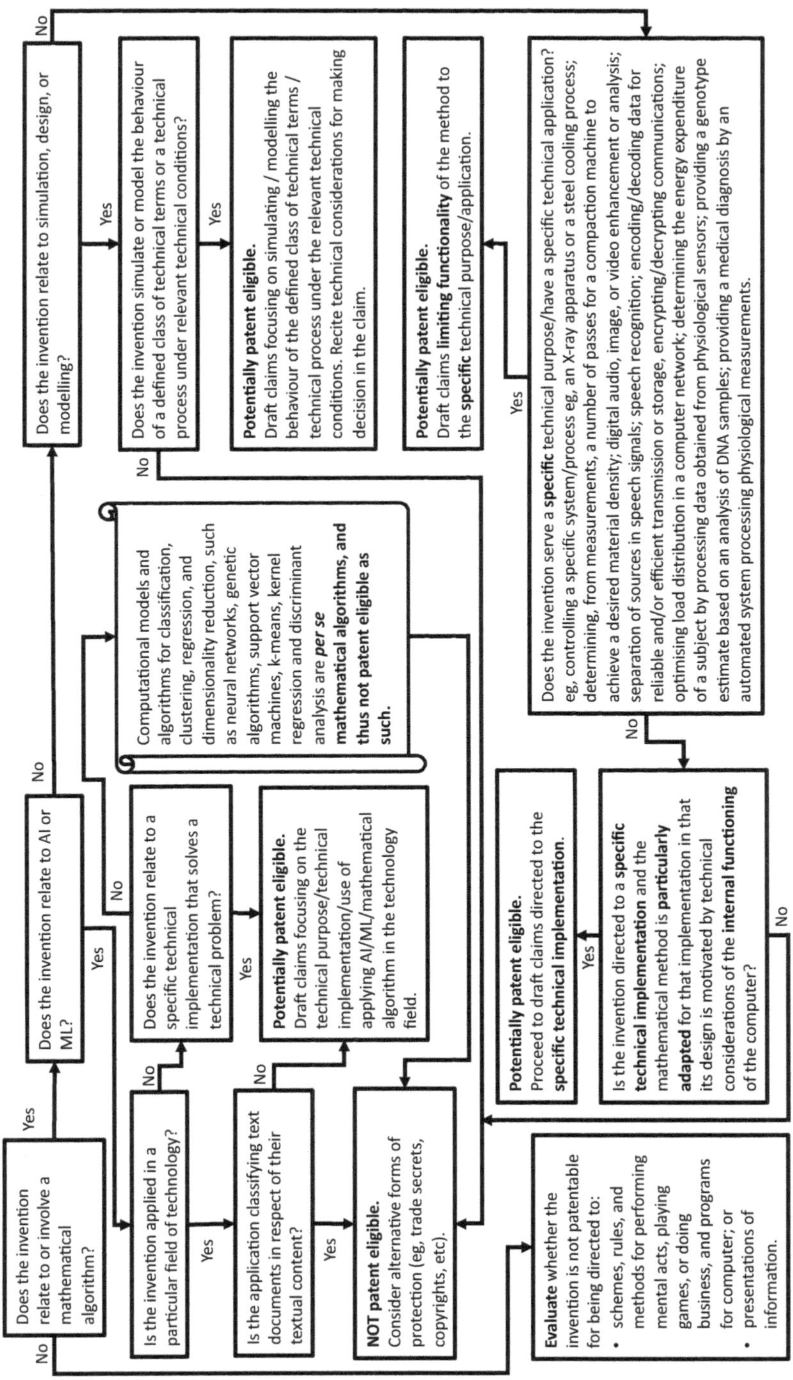

Figure 6. Presentation of information – computer-implemented inventions

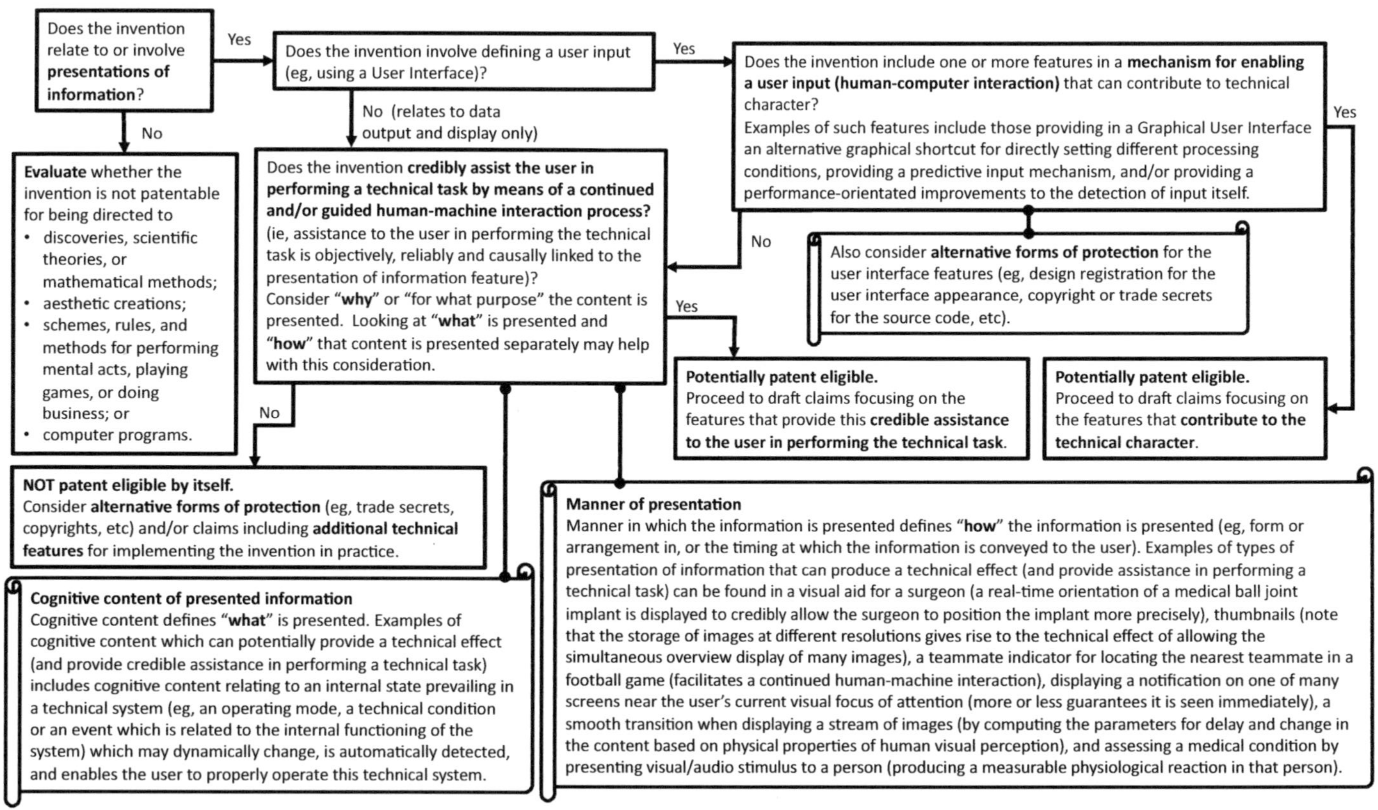

Figure 7. Biotech and chemical inventions

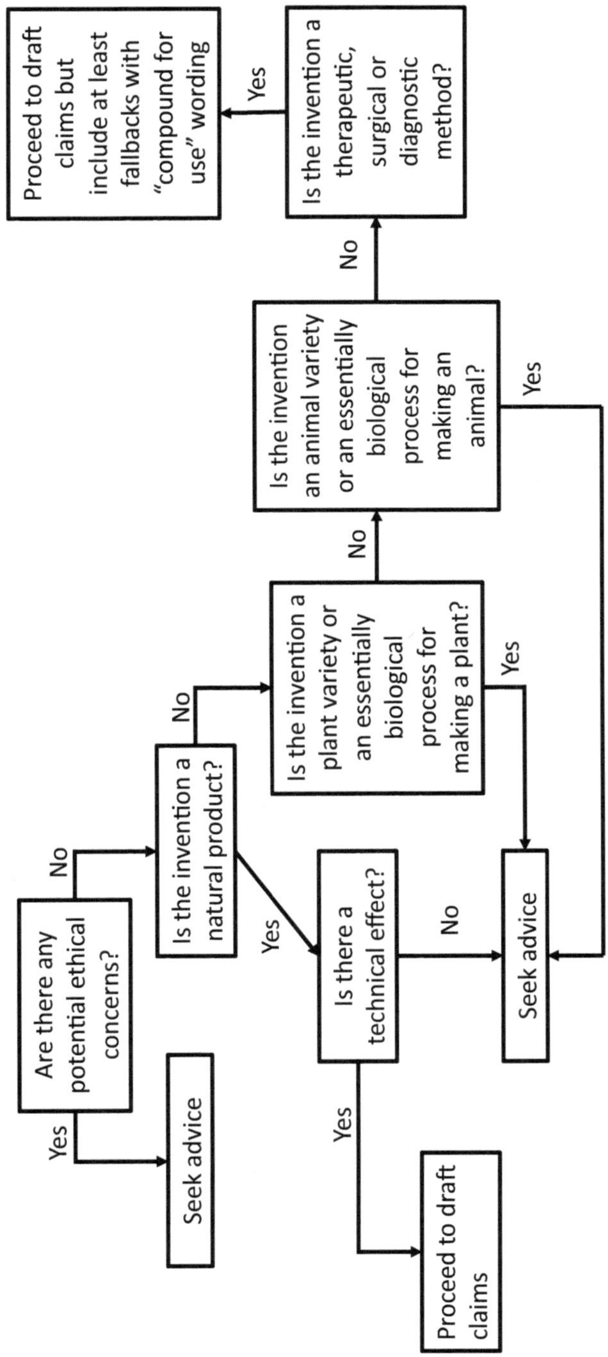

France

Anne Buchet
Gaëtan Lassere
Vincent Pons
Laurent & Charras

1. Background and executive summary

Industrial property matters in France are administered by the National Institute for Industrial Property (INPI), while the Court of Justice (TJ) of Paris, formerly the High Court (TGI) of Paris, handles litigation.

Books VI of the legislative and regulatory parts of the Intellectual Property Code (CPI) define the protection of inventions and technical know-how (patents of invention, utility certificates, and supplementary protection certificates based on a patent).

In application of the CPI, the INPI has the particular task of administering the patent prosecution, from filing the patent application to grant of the patent. The INPI also administers keeping the patents in force upon the payment of an annual fee and, since the PACTE law (Action Plan for Business Growth and Transformation) of 22 May 2019, it handles opposition proceedings.

Opposition proceedings, which can be initiated within a period of nine months following the grant of a French patent, pertain only to the French patent. It does not concern the French part of a European patent. The Director General of the INPI terminates the opposition proceedings by issuing a decision which is open to appeal before the Court of Appeal (CA) of Paris.

Any third party can contest the validity of a French patent or of the French part of a European patent by initiating a nullity action before the Paris TJ. Article L615-8-1 CPI, which has come into force since the PACTE law, states that: "[T]he nullity action of a patent is not subject to any limitation period." In principle, therefore, it is possible to initiate a nullity action throughout the lifetime of the patent.

Since this chapter concerns the conditions for patentability in France, we will not go into the details, but we would point out that the grounds for opposition are the same as in Europe.

Articles L611-10 to L611-19 CPI define the nature of inventions which are patentable or excluded from patentability. More precisely, according to Article L611-10 (paragraph 1) CPI:

1. *In all technical fields, novel inventions involving an inventive step and which are capable of industrial application are patentable.*

Although the CPI does not provide a definition of an invention, the "Patents and utility certificates"[1] guidelines from the INPI (Section C, Ch VII, 1) state that:

The invention must have a technical character, it must provide a solution with technical features to a technical problem, it must therefore contain the technical features stated in the form of claims defining the matter for which protection is sought.

In paragraph 2 of Article L611-10, the CPI provides a negative definition of an invention:

2. *The following in particular shall not be regarded as inventions within the meaning of the first paragraph of the present article:*
   (a) discoveries, as well as scientific theories and mathematical methods;
   (b) aesthetic creations;
   (c) schemes, rules and methods for performing mental acts, playing games, in the field of economic activities, as well as programs for computers;
   (d) presentations of information.

Paragraph 3 of Article L611-10 states that:

3. *The provisions of paragraph 2 of the present article exclude the patentability of the elements referred to therein only to the extent to which the patent application or patent relates to one of these elements as such.*

The first three paragraphs of Article L611-10 CPI are therefore in agreement with Article 52 of the European Patent Convention (EPC).

It should also be noted, in relation to section 3 of this chapter, that biological material is not excluded from patentability: paragraph 4 of Article L611-10 CPI states:

4. *Subject to the provisions of articles L. 611-16 to L. 611-19, inventions pertaining to a product wholly or partially constituted by biological material or to a process allowing biological material to be produced, processed or used, are patentable under the conditions envisaged in paragraph 1.*

   Material which contains genetic information and which can reproduce or be reproduced in a biological system is regarded as biological material.

In practice, the Director General of the INPI can rely on the provisions of Article L61110 CPI (paragraph 1) to reject an application for a patent by application of Article L612-12 CPI (paragraph 7). Since the PACTE law, inventions which do not involve an inventive step can also be rejected; previously, only a blatant lack of novelty could constitute grounds for a rejection. In this regard, the INPI guidelines (Section C, Ch VII, 5.4) recommend the problem-solution approach, in the same way as the European Patent Office. However, in the case of a nullity action, the approach taken by French judges may differ from that applied by INPI.

---

1 INPI – Grant – Guidelines for patent and utility certificate applications – May 2020, available at www.inpi.fr/fr/directives.

With the aid of specific examples, sections 2, 3 and 4 of this chapter highlight the details of French law in patentability matters and, if appropriate, where it differs from practice before the European Patent Office.

2. Electrical and computer arts

Every year, the INPI Awards highlight and reward businesses and centres for innovative research which distinguish themselves by the exemplary nature of their industrial property strategies.[2] In 2020, in the patent category, the three laureates were in technologies in the fields of electronics and computing. In fact, the three inventions spotlighted by the INPI concern the design of tools for the maintenance of railroad infrastructures using innovative electronic sensors (4NRJ), automated tethered drones for surveillance and tactical communications (Elistair), and home automation solutions connected together in order to optimise the management of energy and buildings (Delta Dore – runner-up).

Thus, there are great expectations for inventions in the fields of electronics and computing and numbers have been increasing for a number of years.

There are, however, a few specific aspects to the patentability of inventions in these technical fields.

First, the law has introduced limitations to subject matter which can be protected; Article L611-10 CPI, paragraph 2 states in particular that the following shall not be regarded as inventions:

- methods for performing mental acts, playing games or in the field of economic activities;
- programs for computers; and
- presentations of information.

This paragraph 2 of Article L611-10 CPI is immediately limited by paragraph 3 of that same Article, which states that paragraph 2 excludes patentability of those elements, which are claimed only as such.

Secondly, if the patent application or the patent passes this examination as regards the inventive concept, the requirements for novelty and inventive step are also examined in a specific manner when the claims contain technical and non-technical features.

In this section, we shall study recent case law on the interpretation of the inventive concept for the various exceptions to patentability and on the analysis of patentability. Comments will then be provided on practice within the INPI from our standpoint as practitioners. Finally, a flowchart illustrates in summary how one may determine whether an invention in the fields of electronics and computing can satisfy the requirements for patentability.

---

2 www.INPI.fr/fr/trophees-INPI-2020.

2.1 Discussion of case law

(a) Exceptions to patentability

Schemes, rules and methods in the exercise of mental acts: regarding the exception to patentability for inventions pertaining to methods in the exercise of mental acts, the *Infomil* decision against Atos[3] was in the favour of the patentee.

In fact, patent FR 9708712 from Infomil concerns a "[D]evice for automatic delivery of discount coupons when customers call a store cash desk".

This device uses a number of files and employs a programmed control server in order to:

- allow articles corresponding to a purchase to be registered;
- compare information relative to the purchase, carried out with allocation conditions;
- compare information relative to the identity of the customer with allocation conditions; and
- deliver the coupon allocated to the customer if the purchase satisfies the allocation conditions.

In response to the action for infringement initiated by Infomil, Atos pleaded for annulment of patent FR 9708712 for lack of validity under Article L611-10 CPI on the grounds that the invention was in respect of "a scheme, rule or method in the exercise of mental acts", that it was devoid of technical character because it only concerned the contents of particular files and that it solely pertained to economical and commercial matters.

The Court of Appeal found that the method and the device described a computer system which could deliver coupons offering commercial advantages to store customers after having passed through the cash desks, the collection system incorporating this method and allowing data contained in critical files, customer files and discount files to be compared. Thus, the aim of the invention was not to protect the content of the files, but in fact a structure which constituted a computer system, the protectable nature of which was not in dispute. Finally, it was of little importance that the result was to provide a commercial advantage and to participate in the marketing of a store, since it was the proposed computer system which was protected.

As a consequence, the Court affirmed the validity of the patent FR 9708712 on that ground. This decision shows that it is possible to protect a structure of a computer system even if the destination of that structure is a field which is excluded from patentability.

---

3 CA Paris, 20 November 2007, *Infomil v Atos*.

Similarly, the decision of the Paris Court of Appeal in the *Bull* case against the decision of the Director General of the INPI[4] was also in favour of the patentee.

Patent application FR 1600894 from Bull concerns transportable terminals used in the field of military operations. Claim 1 encompasses a "terminal for establishing communications by broadcasting within a group" comprising different technical means such as a microprocessor, a storage means, a communications interface and a screen. These technical means interact with each other to allow each combatant of a military unit to have an overall view of a situation by means of a display of data on a single screen.

The Director General of the INPI rejected the patent application on the grounds that the proposed solution, despite the designations in the claims, did not include any specific technical features but merely disclosed a method for conducting intellectual operations carried out by generic computational means and that as a consequence the subject matter of the claims concerned a method for carrying out mental acts which could not be considered to be a patentable invention.

The Court judged that the technical problem posed was that of an overall visualisation, on one screen, of a situation for a unit comprising several soldiers and not that of performing mental acts during a stressful combat situation, which is a problem of a cognitive nature. By completely or partially excluding human intervention, the use of technical means for carrying out a method in the exercise of mental acts could endow that method with a technical nature and thus allow it to be considered as an invention. In fact, the subject matter of the main claim included different technical means interacting with each other, and thus the invention did not concern a method in the field of mental acts *per se*, and thus for this reason was not excluded from patentability.

In conclusion, in assessing the exception to patentability concerning the exercise of mental acts, it is vital to describe technical means for carrying out the method. Furthermore, the question of knowing whether the claimed subject matter falls within the non-patentable inventions exception has to be examined independently of the question regarding novelty and inventive step.

Computer programs: regarding the exception to patentability for inventions pertaining to computer programs *per se*, the *Cafetel* decision against Index Multimedia[5] was in favour of the patentee.

French patent FR 0101336 from Cafetel concerns a "[M]ethod for adding sound via a telephone network to a page of data that can be remotely consulted via a communication network". The method according to claim 1 combines

4 CA Paris, 22 November 2019, *Bull v Director General of the INPI.*
5 TGI Paris, 20 July 2006, *Cafetel v Index Multimedia.*

establishing telephonic communications with a visitor connected to the site and transmission to this visitor, via the telephone communication, of sounds the emission of which is triggered by navigation to the site. A website can then broadcast good quality sound without any surcharges from the communications network used for access to the site, that communications network only being used to transfer text or images.

In response to the action for infringement instigated by Cafetel, Index Multimedia claimed nullity of this patent on the grounds that carrying out the invention was in reality essentially based on the execution of a computer program or software which did not provide any technical effect in respect of the description and the claims, and that the invention therefore in fact concerned a computer program which is excluded from patent protection by Article L611-10c) of the Intellectual Property Code.

The Court rejected these grounds, considering that while computer programs were in principle excluded from the field of patentability, a method cannot be devoid of patentability for the sole reason that one or more of its steps were carried out by a computer that has to be controlled by a program. This is the case here, since the patented method requires the use of software in one of its stages, which cannot in any way reduce the invention to a 'simple' computer program and that furthermore, each step of the method requires physical means such as a voice server, an internet server, a computer terminal, a telephone, etc, and involves technical considerations such as emitting sound over the telephone triggered by a navigation action.

Thus, although computer programs are not patentable *per se*, the French courts acknowledge the patentability of a method comprising one or more steps carried out in accordance with a computer program where physical technical means are claimed.

In the *Orange* decision, in contrast to the previous decision, the Court[6] considered that certain claims of the patent from Orange concerned a computer program *per se*.

In this case, Orange accused Free in particular of having infringed its European patent EP 2044797 pertaining to "switching of multimedia sessions from a mobile terminal to equipment of a local home network", allowing multimedia content stored on a remote hard disk to be viewed on a mobile terminal.

Part of the judgment dealt with the question of knowing whether the subject matter defined in claims 12, 14 and 15 of the French part of European patent EP 2044797 from Orange were excluded from patentability.

Claim 12 required a "[C]omputer program product which is downloadable from a communications network and/or stored on a computer-readable support and/or which can be executed by a microprocessor of a mobile terminal".

---

6 TGI Paris, 18 June 2015, *Orange v Free*.

Claim 13 required a "[C]omputer program product which is downloadable from a communications network and/or stored on a computer-readable support and/or which can be executed by a microprocessor of a domestic portal in combination with a plurality of pieces of domestic equipment in a domestic local area network".

Claim 15 required "[A] storage support on which the program in accordance with one of claims 12 to 14 is stored".

For the Court, claims 12 to 14 clearly concerned a computer program *per se* and did not involve an inventive concept. According to the author's analysis, these claims 12 to 14 must effectively be considered to be non-patentable inventions because the technical means for downloading or reading are not claimed.

Concerning claim 15, the Court indicated that the storage support did not provide any particular technical features and that it was simply a "presentation", which meant that the exclusion to patentability concerning computer programs, which are excluded from patentability, was not circumvented.

The decision of the Court concerning the recording support type claim was more surprising because this claim concerned a storage support and thus should not have been excluded *"per se"*.

This decision shows that the French courts can adopt a more severe position than the EPO on inventive concept. However, the description of technical means in the claims should allow the conditions for an invention to be fulfilled even if the claims contain one or more steps carried out by a computer program.

Presentation of information: the exception to patentability for inventions pertaining to a presentation of information follows the same logic.

On appeal, following a rejection decision by the Director General of the INPI considering that the invention pertained to a presentation of information associated with a mathematical method, Thales later obtained an annulment of the rejection decision.[7]

The claim of patent FR 10049947 from Thales related to:

A method for displaying stages of a mission of an aircraft on a screen [...], characterised in that the various stages are displayed in a first graphical window comprising a time scale or "timeline" (TL), the various stages being displayed opposite a schedule of time indications corresponding to their accomplishment, the length of the "timeline" being greater than the length of the first graphical window, the graphical window then displaying only a part of the "timeline", the part being imposed by the user of the display device.

Considering that the characteristics of the 'timeline' describe a distinct

7 CA Paris, 21 May 2019, *Thales v Director General of the INPI.*

technical means for the information content itself, helping the pilot to select from those that are the most pertinent, the Court judged that claim 1 taken as a whole was not excluded from patentability.

Thus, the 'technical' features of a claim are not necessarily physical elements such as a processor or a server but could correspond to technical means of a non-technical element such as a graphical interface.

The lack of 'technical' means in a claim which concerns an exception to patentability is thus a ground for annulment of a patent, as adjudged in *Exalead v Sinequa*.[8]

In this case, claims 1 and 14 of patent EP 1182581 from Exalead respectively pertain to a tool and a unified search method using keyword categories, ie, an internet search engine. Sinequa requested annulment of these claims on the grounds that they constituted a presentation of information obtained from a database.

Claim 1 envisaged the following functional steps in response to the first request from a user:

- searching in the database for entries and sending entries in response to the query;
- selecting categories from said set of categories as a function of the entries returned by said query;
- dynamically selecting keywords associated with the entries returned by said query; and
- displaying said selected categories and said selected keywords to the user;
- in response to activation by the user of one from said displayed categories and said displayed keywords, launching a second query which refines the first query.

Thus, in claim 1, reference is made to a database and to a server for interpreting the queries. However, the Court considered that the database was not claimed as a static memory configuration but as a pre-existing structure enabling the execution of the steps described by claim 1. In addition, the Court adjudged that the reference to a 'server' which functioned to carry out the search and display the results drawn from a database did not endow the invention with a technical character, since the server was a basic and usual search tool and the operations of searching and displaying were basic computing operations.

Considering that claims 1 and 14 were not characterised technically, the Court decided that they were not patentable. Thus, the Court annulled the patent for lack of patentability, basing its arguments on a lack of invention.

In conclusion, if an intellectual method, a computer program, or a

8 CA Paris, 16 December 2016, *Exalead v Sinequa*.

presentation of information is claimed with technical means, it should not be excluded from patentability.

(b) *Patentability of inventions comprising technical and non-technical features*

When a patent application contains an inventive concept, the three conditions for patentability may be examined: novelty, inventive step and industrial application. For inventions in the field of electronics and computing, it is difficult to imagine an invention which does not satisfy the demand for industrial application. However, the assessment of inventive step frequently requires a distinction to be drawn between technical and non-technical features.

As indicated in the INPI guidelines (Section C, Ch VII 1.5.4), in order to assess the inventive step of claims comprising both technical features and non-technical features, only the features contributing to a technical character of the invention are taken into account.

Thus, in the *Bull* case against the decision by the Director General of the INPI,[9] discussed above regarding the inventive concept, the Director General of the INPI assumed that updating as a function of user input constituted an intellectual comparison of non-technical data. Furthermore, the Director General of the INPI also considered that adapting the display to a screen was not further characterised by the technical data but was solely in respect of the graphical properties.

For these reasons, the Director General of the INPI opined that the means that were mentioned (memories, microprocessor, screen) were only characterised by functions which derived therefrom and consisted of the management of information stored in a generic programmable memory which was technically non-specific, concerning basic and usual computing tools.

In its decision, the Court annulled the decision of the Director General of the INPI on the grounds that these arguments were not grounds for rejecting a patent application on the basis of a lack of invention or a lack of novelty.

In fact, these arguments for removing the claimed non-technical features that are claimed are pertinent, but only to the analysis of inventive step.

2.2 How are eligibility issues handled by the Patent Office?

Until May 2020, the examiners at INPI could not reject an application for lack of inventive step. Thus, in order to reject inventions in the fields of electronics or computing, a large number of patentability objections were formulated on the basis of lack of invention, ie, by showing that the claimed subject matter was not an invention because it involved an exception to patentability as listed in Article L611-10 CPI. This represents a major divergence from examination carried out by the EPO.

9 CA Paris, 22 November 2019, *Bull v Director General of the INPI.*

On 22 May 2020, the new PACTE law introduced the examination of inventive step into the French proceedings.

Because of the change to the law, the precision of the INPI guidelines and the convergence of the case law, it may now be hoped that the practice of examiners of the INPI will more closely adhere to the limits to patentability which have been described above, and that some of the objections previously raised regarding the inventive concept will henceforth be based on an inventive step approach which distinguishes technical features from non-technical features.

2.3 Summary flowchart

Figure 1 illustrates how a claim in the fields of electronics or computing may be analysed.

Figure 1. Acceptance test for a claim in electronics or computing fields

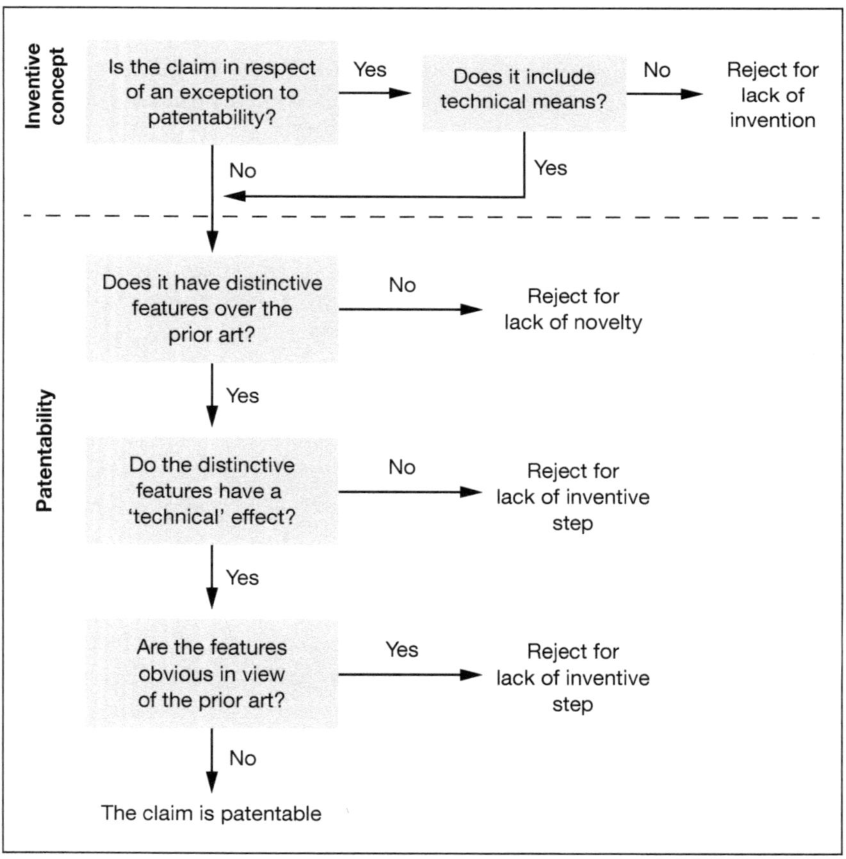

3. Biological and pharmaceutical arts

3.1 Discussion of case law

Articles L611-16 to L611-19 CPI are the relevant articles in relation to biological and pharmaceutical arts:

L611-16: *Shall not be patentable methods for treatment of the human or animal body by surgery or therapy and diagnostic methods practised on the human or animal body; this provision shall not apply to products, in particular substances or compositions, for use in any of these methods.*

L611-17: *Shall not be patentable inventions the commercial exploitation of which would be contrary to human dignity, "ordre public" or morality; such exploitation shall not be deemed to be so contrary merely because it is prohibited by law or regulation.*

L611-18: *The human body, at the various stages of its formation and development, and the simple discovery of one of its elements, including the sequence or partial sequence of a gene, cannot constitute patentable inventions.*
Only an invention constituting the technical application of a function of an element of the human body may be protected by a patent. Such a protection only covers the element of the human body in so far as it is necessary to the realisation and exploitation of that particular application. Said application must be disclosed in a concrete and precise manner in the patent application.
In particular, the following shall not be patentable:
a) processes for cloning human beings;
b) processes for modifying the genetic identity of human beings;
c) uses of human embryos for industrial or commercial purposes;
d) sequences or partial sequences of a gene as such.

L611-19:
I. – The following shall not be patentable:
1° Animal breeds
2° Plant varieties as defined by Article 5 of Council Regulation (EC) No 2100/94 of 27 July 1994 on Community plant variety rights
3° Essentially biological processes for the production of plants or animals; this provision applies to processes which exclusively rely on natural phenomena such as crossing or selection
3° bis Products exclusively obtained by means of an essentially biological process as defined in 3°, including the elements constituting said products and the genetic information contained therein
4° Processes for modifying the genetic identity of animals which are likely to cause them suffering without any substantial medical benefit to man or animal, and also animals resulting from such processes.

II. – Notwithstanding the provision of I above, inventions relating to plants or animals shall be patentable if the technical feasibility of the invention is not limited to a particular plant or animal variety.

III. – The provision of I-3°above shall not apply to inventions relating to technical processes, especially microbiological processes, or the products thereof; A microbiological process relates to any process using or producing biological material or involving an intervention on said matter.

In relation to biological and pharmaceutical arts, the INPI basically applies the same approach as the EPO. As an example, non-human living organisms are patentable with the proviso recited in the law:

- cells, with the exception of human embryonic cells obtained by embryo destruction (Article L611-18 CPI), and microorganisms (Article L611-19 III CPI). The complete characterisation of such an organism can require its deposit according to the Budapest Treaty. In France, the depository institution is the Collection Nationale des Cultures de Micro-organismes (CNCM), Institut Pasteur, 28 rue du Dr Roux, 75724 PARIS CEDEX 15; and
- plants or animals as long as they are not plant varieties nor animal breeds and are not obtained by essentially biological processes. For transgenic animals, a further condition is that the medical benefit is superior to the pain (Article L611-19 I and II CPI).

However, two specificities of the French practice should be noticed, one concerning the scope of protection conferred by gene claims and the other concerning the impossibility to protect a dosing regimen.

(a) Biological arts, patentability of genes

In Europe, the patentability of biological matter is set out in Directive 98/44/CE, the European Union Directive on the legal protection of biotechnological inventions. This directive defines biological matter as being matter containing genetic information and which is self-reproducing or reproducible in a biological system. It states that an element isolated from the human body or otherwise produced by a technical procedure, including the sequence or partial sequence of a gene, is patentable, even if the structure of that element is identical to that of a natural element, provided that the industrial application of that genetic sequence is fully disclosed in the patent application. As a consequence, a gene sequence that is merely isolated is not patentable (considered as a discovery of one element of the human body), whereas a gene sequence for which a therapeutic or diagnostic use is reported is patentable (if novel and inventive).

The provisions of this directive have been transposed into French law in Article L611-18 CPI (see above). French law is more restrictive with regard to protection, as the directive specifies that "only an invention constituting the technical application of a function of an element of the human body may be protected by patent" and that "this protection only covers the element of the human body in so far as this is necessary to the realisation and exploitation of that particular application".

In practice, and contrary to the spirit of the European Directive, this means that a French patent would merely confer a protection on a given application of a gene sequence (as demonstrated in the patent) and not to the sequence as such, regardless of its further applications. Unfortunately, and for the time being, this inconsistency has not been clarified nor its interpretation confirmed by case law.

(b) Pharmaceutical arts, medical use claims

One major difference between the American and European patent systems concerns the patentability of methods of treatment. While such wording is acceptable according to USPTO practice, it is rejected by the EPO and by the INPI. However, and according to European and French practices, the patentability of a first or second medical use is acknowledged and results from the combination of Articles L611-16 and L611-11 CPI.

Article L611-16 (see above) provides that, unlike methods for surgical or therapeutic treatment or for diagnosis, products for implementing such methods are patentable.

Article L611-11, relating to novelty, indicates, in paragraphs 4 and 5, that the first medical use of a known substance or composition and the second medical use of a known therapeutic substance or composition are patentable.

In practice, the following may be patentable in France:

- a first medical use of a product known from the prior art for a non-medical use ("Substance X for use in medicine");
- a second medical use, whether or not the first use was successful ("Substance X for use in the treatment of disease Y"). The former Swiss-type claims ("Use of substance X for the manufacture of a medicament for the treatment of disease Y") are not allowed by the INPI since January 2011;
- an invention characterised in that it relates to a new patient group; and
- an invention characterised in that it relates to a novel technical effect.

However, in France and contrary to the EPO practice (see Decision G02/08 by the Enlarged Board of Appeal), claims relating to a posology (dosage) are not permitted according to some decisions of case law, and are systematically rejected by the INPI.

Indeed, this opposite position was first adopted by the Court of First Instance,[10] which considered that the French national courts were not bound by

10 TGI Paris, 28 September 2010, *Actavis v MSD*.

the EPO decisions and that a specific posology constituted as such neither a first nor a second medical use.

According to the Court's interpretation, a posology is defined by the physician, freely and under his responsibility, and would therefore be comparable to a therapeutic treatment method excluded from the field of patentability (Article L611-16 CPI). In this case, claim No 1 was drafted as follows:

use of X for the preparation of a medicament for oral administration useful for the treatment of androgenic alopecia in a person and wherein the dosage amount is about 0.05 to 1.0 mg (former Swiss-type claim).

This position was confirmed by the subsequent decision handed down by the Court,[11] in which the Court considered that dosage regimens are excluded from patentability since it is up to the physicians to assess the doses and the number of administrations required for the treatment of their patients.

More recently, the same position was adopted by the Court of First Instance,[12] and further confirmed by the Court of Appeal.[13]

Noticeably, the position of the TGI of Paris in the *Activis* case was reversed by the Paris Court of Appeal.[14] However, the patent was considered not valid for a lack of novelty in the absence of any technical effect linked to the claimed dosages.

However, the INPI relies on this decision to reject claims whose subject matter is a medicament posology, on the grounds that it constitutes a therapeutic treatment method. The INPI guidelines (Section C, Ch VII, 2.1.2.b) indicate: "the following are thus likely to be rejected [...] a claim concerning the dosage of a medical product", the reference to the decision of 28 September 2010 appearing in the margin as a reference.

It should be noted that in most of the decisions regarding patents relating to a second medical use these patents were judged to be invalid either for:

- insufficiency of disclosure;[15]
- lack of novelty;[16] or
- lack of inventive step.[17]

In particular, it appears from a number of decisions that the requirement of sufficiency of disclosure in the pharmaceutical field has a meaning other than in the other technical fields. In particular, it requires that the description mentions the existence of research studies and of results.

---

11 TGI Paris, 20 March 2012, *Teva v Eli Lilly.*

12 TGI Paris, 19 June 2015, *Mylan v Richter.*

13 CA Paris, 3 March 2018, *Mylan v Richter.*

14 CA Paris, 30 January 2015, *Merck v Acatavis.*

15 TGI Paris, 6 October 2009, *Teva v Sepracor.* TGI Paris, 9 November 2010, *Teva v Merck.*

16 CA Paris, 22 September 2006, *Laboratoire de contactologie appliqué v Alcon.* CA Paris, 30 January 2015, *Actavis v MSD.*

17 TGI Paris, 20 March 2012, *Teva v Eli Lilly;* CA Paris 12 March 2014.

3.2 How are eligibility issues handled by the Patent Office?

When the INPI considers that a claim relates to an exclusion from patentability, a deficiency notification is issued and the applicant is invited to correct the non-compliant claim before examination of the application (ie, before the search report is established).

As an example, a claim reciting "wherein the composition is administered orally" would be objected to. A way to overcome such an objection is to reformulate it by reciting "wherein the composition is under a form suitable for oral administration". Of course, such a claim does not confer the same scope of protection and such a reformulation is acceptable when it merely concerns a dependent claim, ie, a secondary aspect of the invention. However, an application dealing with a specific posology (eg, route and number of administrations, doses, etc) should be rejected by the INPI as relating to an exclusion from patentability.

As noted above, it emerges from the study of the case law that most of the decisions handed down since 2004 acknowledge the patentability of a second medical use but that the examination of the validity of these patents results virtually systematically in the nullity thereof, especially for insufficiency of disclosure or lack of inventive step.

4. Chemical arts

4.1 Discussion of case law

In the field of chemistry, there are no major differences between the INPI and EPO as regards the assessment of patentability. In fact, in both cases, the following inventions in particular are recognised as being patentable:

(a) Inventions of selection

Inventions residing in specific ranges of values, isolated compounds or experimental conditions for a process such as the temperature or pressure are recognised as being novel. However, the disclosure of a single value belonging to a specific range of values of the invention destroys the novelty of that invention.

French judges appear to consider that the motivation for making a selection involves an inventive step. Thus, it is necessary to prove that:

- the sub-set of compounds or the specific range of values brings about a particular effect; and
- the person skilled in the art would not be motivated to make this selection.

As an example, the Court of Appeal of Paris has recognised the novelty of a composition based on the specific amounts of active components. However, since the novel range of values was not associated with a novel effect, the CA considered that the composition was obvious in view of the prior art.[18]

(b) *New uses of a known substance*

The novel function of a known substance constitutes a novel and inventive application of known means. Accordingly, the CA of Lyon acknowledged that using known components in other applications is indeed a novelty.[19] On the other hand, patentability was not recognised (lack of inventive step) for the use of a known steel in the field of fencing, because this new use did not provide a novel function.[20]

(c) *Inventions of combination*

An invention corresponding to a combination of known elements is novel if the prior art does not explicitly disclose that combination. In particular, an inventive step can be recognised for an invention the combined elements of which belong to a technical field (blood sample collecting or medical fluid injecting) which is different from that of the invention (dentistry) and which seeks to achieve a different objective.[21] Furthermore, an inventive step has also been recognised for an invention (storage and distribution device for parts such as rivets) corresponding to a combination of elements belonging to different technical fields and seeking different objectives (device for conveying pipes, parts cleaning, post-treatment of containers, parts packaging).[22]

(d) *Product by process inventions*

Claims of the 'product by process' type are accepted when it is not possible to characterise a product other than by its production process. However, these claims are only admissible in the case in which the product is novel and involves an inventive step.

(e) *Intermediate product inventions*

Intermediate product inventions are patentable, provided that:

> *the structure of the intermediate product and the final product is sufficiently similar to conclude that the intermediate product has been specifically designed for the sole purpose of carrying out the process for the manufacture of the final product* (INPI guidelines, Section C, Ch VI, 3.1).

---

18 CA Paris, 31 October 2003, *Crea v Eurexim Securiflame.*
19 CA Lyon, 14 November 2002, *GS v Application des Gaz.*
20 TGI Paris, 9 November 1990, *Saarstahl Volklingen v Hostin.*
21 CA Paris, 13 June 2017, *Produits Dentaires Pierre Rolland v Itena Clinical.*
22 Cass Com, 17 March 2015, *Brotje Automation v Ateliers de la Haute Garonne Établissements Auriol.*

(f) ***Chemical products***

Chemical products (compounds defined by their structure or name, or compositions) are patentable as long as they are novel, inventive and capable of industrial application. Accordingly, regardless of their natural or synthetic origin, chemical products are patentable if they have been identified and isolated for the first time and if they exhibit a technical effect. A composition comprising a mixture of naturally occurring compounds is also patentable.

(g) ***Nuclear energy***

There are no particular provisions or derogations in relation to patentability in the nuclear energy field, in particular atomic nuclear energy.

(h) ***Pharmaceuticals***

While inventions relating to the pharmaceutical field have not been patentable in the past, since 1960 this has no longer been the case and all inventions, with the exception of the provisions of Article L611-16, which exclude surgical or therapeutic treatment methods for the human or animal body and diagnostic methods applied to the human or animal body from patentability, are now patentable. Thus, products, in particular substances or compositions, for carrying out these methods that are excluded from patentability, can be protected by a patent.

(i) ***Inventions by result***

On the other hand, inventions said to be inventions by result are not patentable. In fact, claiming a technical effect without specifying the essential technical features for arriving at it is not patentable insofar as it corresponds to a result to be achieved. The TGI of Paris affirmed the nullity (insufficient disclosure) of a patent covering a device for creating an ornamental cascade for use in an aquarium since the description did not specify the means to carry out the invention and to afford the desired result.[23]

4.2 How are eligibility issues handled by the Patent Office?

As we have already indicated, the INPI can reject a patent application on one of the following grounds in particular: novelty, inventive step, industrial application.

The analysis of novelty is generally in agreement with practice before the EPO. "An invention is considered to be novel if it is not included in the state of the art" (Article L611-11 CPI; INPI guidelines, Section C, Ch VII, 4).

Furthermore, it will be recalled that the INPI guidelines (Section C, Ch VII, 5) recommend the problem–solution approach for assessing the inventive activity criterion.

---

23 TGI Paris, 15 June 1999, *TRAN NGOC v Rochepierre.*

However, only French patent applications filed from 22 May 2020 are subject to this regime. Thus, it is too early to analyse the INPI's practice in this regard.

5. Statistics

In general, the number of lawsuits concerning French patents is relatively low compared with other European states. Because of the current low number of lawsuits, it is difficult to highlight any particular tendencies. As an example, a study of the impact of the PACTE law shows fewer than 40 actions for annulment as the principal matter, ie, cases which are not linked to an infringement action. Assuming that this small number of cases results from the costs and the slow nature of the proceedings, the legislature introduced a simple and rapid administrative procedure, in point of fact the opposition proceedings which came into force with the PACTE law. However, the French part of European patents is not involved in these opposition proceedings, and it is not certain that this produces the desired effect in terms of the number of actions which are initiated.

The introduction of opposition proceedings and the consideration of inventive step of the invention during examination of French patent applications will certainly modify the data of previous years.

For information, in cross-actions for annulment following an infringement action over the period 2010–16,[24] French judges rejected patents for lack of inventive step (54%), for lack of novelty (32%), for insufficiency of the description (13%) and for lack of industrial application (1%). On the other hand, French patents were annulled more often than the French parts of European patents (41% as opposed to 23%).

The validity of French patents filed after the PACTE law came into force should be strengthened because inventive step can now be considered to be grounds for rejection and because of the opposition proceedings. The rejection rate should thus draw close to that of the French parts of European patents.

6. Hot topics, including emerging technology

There is no unanimous agreement as to what constitutes 'emerging technologies', but when this subject is mentioned, the initial thoughts turn to technologies coming out of computing and, more specifically, those linked to artificial intelligence (AI).

AI raises many questions in the context of intellectual property; most recently, the International Association for the Protection of Intellectual Property (AIPPI) discussed the following: can AI be an inventor in the context of patent rights? The position of the French group was divided on this question

---

24 S Agé/Véron & Associés, AAPI CNCPI seminar, 15 June 2017.

because in our opinion, there has not as yet been an invention which has been entirely made by AI and it is difficult to anticipate the capabilities which AI known as 'strong' AI will have.

Recently, we have noted a willingness of the INPI to standardise the work of examiners by adding a specific section to the guidelines for dealing with inventions linked to AI (Section C, Ch VII, 1.3.2). This part of the guidelines in particular combines examples of AI applications and inventions considered to be technical or non-technical for these categories.

- Computerised visualisation, such as the processing, recognition and/or classification of images and/or videos. Examples that are considered to be technical are:
  - the recognition of the environment of an autonomous vehicle from data obtained with the aid of sensors; and
  - the use of artificial intelligence for the analysis of digital images with a view to the recognition of an event such as a tumour in a series of images or for the detection of a movement within a video sequence.
- Speech recognition and/or man-machine dialogs. An example that is considered to be technical is the use of artificial intelligence with the aim of analysing human language by a dedicated robot, word data being acquired via audio sensors and converted into language data via speech recognition software in order to decide upon and output the gestural and vocal behaviours of the robot.
- Robotics and/or control/command processes. Examples that are considered to be technical are:
  - real-time control of a drilling tool from physical properties measured in the drilling environment via training of a neural network; and
  - the classification of traffic at nodes of IP (Internet Protocol) networks using automatic learning in order to improve traffic management on the IP network.
- Predictive analysis. As an example, a method using artificial intelligence to predict stock exchange prices was judged to be non-technical. In contrast, the use of a neural network in heart monitoring apparatus for detecting irregular heartbeats makes a technical contribution.
- Text processing. As an example, the use of a tool to extract commercial keywords from content to allow their identification and indexing using artificial intelligence was judged to be non-technical.

In common with inventions in the fields of electronics and computing, it is thus often possible to anticipate acceptance or rejection of inventions linked to AI by the INPI even if those inventions are often much more complicated to defend than inventions in the mechanical field, for example.

In addition, protection by the patent mechanism necessitates a clear and complete disclosure of the invention so that a person skilled in the art can reproduce it. However, certain inventions implemented by computers are difficult to detect if these computing processes can be sliced up into a plurality of functions carried out on a plurality of servers and/or implemented at different locations on the planet. This is particularly the case with processes carried out by AI.

Thus, inventions linked to AI may encounter difficulties with protection by the patent mechanism and difficulties in providing evidence of infringement, while the obligation of disclosure may become discriminatory in respect of the return on investment anticipated for the patent mechanism.

Furthermore, in the computing field, and more particularly that of AI, the cost of developing novel solutions is more and more closely linked to the cost of constituting and updating one or more databases. In fact, a large number of AI algorithms are now available, and the intelligence of the proposed solutions often resides in the reference elements used to teach the AI.

In order to secure investment into the development of novel solutions linked to AI, a re-emergence of policies of secrecy has been observed, as well as the use of protection mechanisms which differ from the patent of invention.

In contrast to other technical fields, there are a large number of legal protection mechanisms which could cover an invention linked to the field of computing. Before being coded, a computing solution generally comprises an interface and the ergonomics of that interface can be protected in France both by copyright and by models. The code itself can also be protected by the copyright mechanism to cover the manner in which the computing functions are written.

It is also possible to protect a database by copyright and the database producer's right to protect the investments made to create the database. A database is defined by the CPI as a collection of works, data or other independent materials arranged in a systematic or methodical way and individually accessible by electronic means or other means. The database producer's right, which was formalised in the mid-1990s following the development of electronic commerce and the first data processing technologies, derives from the Community Directive of 11 March 1996, transposed into the French intellectual property law by the Law of 1 July 1998.

This database producer's right is far from perfect because it concentrates on the creation of the database and not on its use,[25] but it is anticipated that database rights will develop over the forthcoming years in order to protect databases developed in the context of the development of AI as well as all the 'Big Data' type data which is currently stored.

25 www.INPI.fr/fr/valoriser-vos-actifs/le-mag/le-droit-des-producteurs-de-bases-de-donnees-l-heure-du-big-data.

Furthermore, in the face of climate change, we can also expect more and more development in inventions linked to green technologies. This development is apparently already burgeoning, since in 2019 one-third of all patent applications filings were identified as being linked to green technologies, while only 7% of filings were counted in 2000 for this type of technology. In fact, between 2000 and 2009, filings linked to solar energy tripled, those linked to wind energy or hydraulic energy were up fourfold and those linked to alternative propulsion for modes of transport increased two-and-a-half times.[26]

A number of changes are being discussed in order to promote the emergence of these green technologies and these changes to patent law in this regard can be expected in the forthcoming years. In fact, changes have been noted in various jurisdictions with accelerated procedures for patents linked to green technologies, being seen in particular before the British, South Korean, Australian, Japanese, American, Israeli, Canadian, Brazilian and Chinese offices.

For now, in France, the INPI has not yet put specific programmes for patent applications linked to green technologies in place because, until now, examination before the INPI was particularly fast since grounds for rejection did not include the question of inventive step. With the application of the new PACTE law, the French procedure will be extended and discussions regarding accelerated grant procedures will certainly come up again.

In addition to the questions of inventions linked to green technologies, in view of recent events, it can also be expected that measures will be taken to administer innovations linked to pandemics, such as the COVID-19 crisis, as rapidly as possible.

The authors thank Ms Isabelle Chan-Piu and Mr Eric Denjean (Laurent & Charras) for fruitful discussions.

26 C Ducruet, *Les technologies vertes concentrent un tiers des demandes* [Green technologies make up one third of applications], *Les Echos*, 23 March 2010. G Henry, *Technologies vertes et propriété intellectuelle* [Green technologies and intellectual property](LexisNexis, 2013).

Germany

Thomas Becher
Hoffmann Eitle Dusseldorf
Markus Georg Müller
Andreas Stefferl
Hoffmann Eitle Munich

1. Introduction

Germany has been a signatory of the General Agreement on Tariffs and Trade (GATT) since 1951 and an EU member country since 1958. It is also a signatory of the 1963 and 1971 versions of the Convention on the Unification of Certain Points of Substantive Law on Patents for Invention (commonly termed the Strasbourg Convention, which entered into force in 1980), and a member of the World Trade Organization (WTO) which it joined in 1995. Germany has also adopted measures to incorporate the EU's Directive on the legal protection of biotechnological inventions ('Biopatent Directive') into national law in order to achieve the objectives set by the directive. Many of the statutes rendering subject matter non-eligible for patent protection are therefore harmonised with the other member states of the WTO, and, most notably, the other EU member states.

There are three major fields which are affected by the statutes on patent eligibility:

- the electrical and computer arts, where software, business methods, and presentation of information are most prominently discussed;
- the biological and pharmaceutical arts, where technical interventions in the human genome and genetic modifications of plants and animal varieties have received significant attention; and
- medical procedures, where treatments of the human or animal body by surgery or therapy on the one hand, and diagnostic methods practised on the human or animal body on the other hand, are regularly discussed by the courts.

It should be noted for the sake of completeness that aesthetic creations as well as schemes, rules and methods for performing mental acts and playing games are also not eligible for patent protection. However, these have not played a major role in recent German patent invalidity proceedings.

In the period from 2009 to 2019, a total of 4,511 actions for invalidity of patents, both German national and European patents,[1] were filed with the German Federal Patent Court (FPC). Of these, only 1,750 (about 39%) resulted in a reasoned decision on the merits by the FPC. The others were disposed of without a decision on the merits, for instance because of settlements. Of the cases with a reasoned decision, 797 (46%) resulted in a complete revocation, 601 (34%) in a partial revocation of the patent, and 352 (20%) in a dismissal of the action for invalidity. There were 1,131 (65%) appeals of FPC decisions, but only 524 appeals (30%) resulted in a decision from the Federal Court of Justice ('FCJ'). Upon appeal, the FCJ confirmed 273 (52%) of the first instance decisions and reversed or amended 251 (48%). The ultimate outcome after the appeal instance was that 192 patents (37% of the cases decided by the FCJ) were revoked over their entire scope, 188 (36%) over part of their scope, and 129 (25%) in a dismissal of the action for invalidity.[2]

In Germany, law is primarily and predominantly derived from the wording and the purpose of the relevant statutes. The courts will seek to interpret the statutes in as much as this is needed for the individual case at hand. Case law is not viewed as a binding precedent. In principle, any court may deviate from the decisions issued by another court, even one of higher instance.[3] From a dogmatic and purely legal point of view, even the decisions from the highest instance are therefore not 'law', and so are not binding for other cases. However, the persuasive power of a sufficiently well-developed reasoning issued from a court with authority may well have a binding effect beyond the individual case in which the reasoning was issued.[4] Once a sufficient number of courts follow its reasoning, a decision may thus turn into practically binding guidance.

Therefore, in the following sections, both the relevant statutes and some of the case law for the three major fields identified above will be discussed.

2. Electrical and computer arts

Advances in electrical engineering and computer science (EECS) have strongly impacted our daily life and economy in the past decades. For example, the fast-moving electronics and telecommunications industries have provided means for data access anywhere at any time. The ongoing integration of daily appliances in the Internet of Things, 'connected cars', artificial intelligence, big data etc, will lead to smart devices in a connected world, where standards and patents will play an important role. Patent-eligibility issues in the EECS space particularly arise with respect to computer programs, user interfaces and algorithms to name a few. This section provides guidance on eligibility issues affecting the EECS space in Germany.

1 When assessing the merits of actions for revocation of German national patents, the courts are to apply the German Patent Act (GPA) and related statutes, whilst they are to apply the European Patent Convention (EPC) when assessing the merits of actions for revocation of European patents.

2 Fifteen cases are listed with 'other outcome'.

3 Federal Constitutional Court, 1 BvR 1243/88 of 3 November 1992, marginal note 15 with further references, BVerfGE 87, 273.

4 Federal Constitutional Court, 1 BvR 779/85 of 26 June 1991, marginal notes 41, 42, BVerfGE 84, 212.

The basic legal framework for patenting EECS inventions at the German Patent and Trademark Office (GPTO) is the German Patent Act (GPA), which, together with related case law interpreting its sections, will be addressed below. The developments in the case law of the Federal Court of Justice (FCJ) are also reflected in GPTO's Guidelines for Examination which are regularly updated.

Of particular relevance for patent eligibility in Germany is GPA, Section 1, essentially corresponding to the German text of Article 52(1), (2) and (3) EPC, showing that the GPA and the European Patent Convention (EPC) have been aligned. Similar to several other statutes on patents, including the EPC, the GPA does not provide a positive definition of inventions but instead defines some properties that an invention shall have.

According to Section 1 I, patents shall be granted for any inventions, in all fields of technology, provided that they are new, involve an inventive step and are susceptible of industrial application. This implies that they must also have technical character or 'technicity',[5] which according to the case law is generally the case if the invention contains teachings for achieving a result following clear causal steps by controlling natural forces.[6] It is not necessary that the causal result is obtained by the direct application of controllable natural forces, but an invention can also have technical character if it is characterised by knowledge based on technical considerations and by the realisation of this knowledge.[7]

Exceptions to patentability in the EECS space are laid out in GPA, Section 1, III, IV. Pursuant to Section 1 III, the following are not regarded as inventions within the meaning of Section 1:

- discoveries as well as scientific theories and mathematical methods;
- aesthetic creations;
- schemes, rules and methods for performing mental acts, playing games or doing business as well as programs for computers; and
- presentations of information.

However, GPA Section 1 IV clarifies that subsection III shall exclude patentability only to the extent to which protection is being sought for the subject matter or activities referred to as such. Accordingly, (computer) program-related inventions, for example, which are not limited to a pure computer program, eg, including also a computer or processor, are not excluded from patent protection. Further, these exceptions to patentability generally only apply to methods but not to apparatuses.[8]

---

5 It is noted that the German courts often use the German term '*Technizität*', which can be considered as a term coined to underline that it specifically refers to technical character of inventions in the sense given by the case law. Here, the term has been translated into 'technicity' (sometimes also translated as 'technicality').

6 FCJ X ZB 15 67, *rote Taube*, 27 March 1969 – GRUR 1969, 672.

7 FCJ X ZB 11/98, *Logikverifikation*, 13 December 1999 – GRUR 2000, 498.

8 FCJ X ZB 11/17, 27 March 2018.

2.1 The FCJ's approach to eligibility to patent protection

The above-mentioned principle that patents shall have technical character has been confirmed by case law over several decades. One of the first decisions of the FCJ, called *Seitenpuffer* (Page Buffer), clarified already in 1991[9] that the question of whether a teaching has technical character has to be considered separately from the requirements of novelty and inventive step. Further, it was noted that a teaching related to a program is technical if it relates to the functionality (in the sense of operational capability) of a data processing system as such and thus enables direct interaction between its elements. Here, the method comprised instructions to directly use the elements of the data processing system in operation in a particular manner. Accordingly, the special interaction of these elements could be regarded as technical means solving the technical problem of making better use of the RAM of the computer and providing shorter access times.

The requirement of technicity as well as the requirement that a technical problem needs to be solved are particularly found in case law to exclude some subject matter such as plain computer programs for business methods from patentability. Accordingly, one may separate software related inventions into business methods embodied in a computer program and computer-implemented inventions (CII), for example, related to computer programs controlling or being adapted to technical processes. The discussion below will focus on the latter. Indeed, the general concept of a business method should not be patentable, because it will not be regarded to be in a field of technology even if it were, in circumvention of GPA, Section 1 III no 3, directed to a system and not a method. However, a specific technical implementation of a business method using technical means, such as a specifically configured computer network, solving a technical problem may still be eligible for patent protection.

2.2 The FCJ's three-stage examination approach

Based on the case law with respect to GPA, with Sections 1, 3 and 4 a formal three-stage approach for the examination of program-related inventions has been developed. According to the Guidelines for Examination, program-related inventions are those where the implementation involves the use of a computer, computer network or other programmable apparatus and which comprise at least one feature which is realised wholly or partly by means of a computer program. Such inventions are often also referred to as computer-implemented inventions. Although computer programs are referred to in the exception to patentability in Sec 1 III no. 3 and most decisions concern program steps, the same three-stage approach is applicable for other exceptions including mathematical methods (Section 1 III no 1), rules or methods for doing business

9 FCJ X ZB 13/88, *Seitenpuffer*, 11 June 1991 – GRUR 1992, 33.

(Section 1 III no 3) or the presentation of information (Section 1 III no 3). Thus, apparatuses making use of such teachings are not excluded from patentability.

The first stage of the examination relates to the question mentioned in the above *Seitenpuffer* decision, namely whether the subject matter of the invention has technical character (GPA, Section 1 I). The execution of method steps using electronic data processing fulfils this first technicity requirement if it at least implicitly teaches the use of computer components and thus provides a technical teaching. This is also the case if the method relates to the processing, storage or transfer of data by means of a technical device or concerns the direct interaction of the elements of a computer system.[10] An apparatus, such as a computer, has technical character merely due to its concrete physical nature regardless of whether it contributes to the state of the art or not. In the FCJ decision *Sprachanalyseeinrichtung*,[11] the patent application was directed to a dialogue-type speech analysis device having the means of processing and analysing text and it was considered that a device that is technically configured by program in a certain way has a technical character even if only text processing is performed.

In the second stage, the examination is whether the invention as such is excluded from patentability (GPA, Section 1 III and IV) based on the above-mentioned exceptions 1 to 4. That is, patent protection is not available for a method simply because it uses data processing or a program to control a computer to achieve a desired result. In particular, whether or not a technical problem is solved by technical means needs to be examined. In the FCJ decision *Suche fehlerhafter Zeichenketten*,[12] the contested claim was directed to a digital storage medium, in particular a disk, with electronically readable control signals, which can interact with a programmable computer system such that a method according to claim 1 is performed. The decision notes that the essential instructions of the claimed teaching must contribute to the solution of a concrete technical problem. Under this condition, subject matter is eligible for patent protection even if claimed as a computer program or storage medium, such as a data carrier used by a computer. In essence, the exceptions to patentability pursuant to Section 1 III do not apply if at least part of the teaching is based on a specific technical problem. When answering the question as to whether a teaching includes instructions that assist to solve a specific technical problem by technical means, it is necessary to properly determine the technical problem, which is also relevant for the examination in the third stage. The determination of the technical problem underlying an invention is part of the interpretation of the claims, wherein the technical problem must be derived from what is actually achieved by the invention.

---

10 FCJ Xa ZB 20/08, *Dynamische Dokumentengenerierung*, 22 April 2010 – GRUR 2010, 613.
11 FCJ X ZB 15/98, *Sprachanalyseeinrichtung*, 11 May 2000 – GRUR 2000, 1007.
12 FCJ X ZB 16/00, *Suche fehlerhafter Zeichenketten*, 17 October 2001 – GRUR 2002, 143.

The first and second stage can thus be considered as a test for eligibility for patent protection carried out independent of the relevant prior art before novelty and inventive step are examined in the third step.

In the third stage, the examination of the solution to a specific technical problem with regard to novelty and inventive step pursuant to GPA, Sections 3 and 4 is carried out. That is, a patent on a program-related invention can only be granted if the solution of the specific technical problem is new and involves an inventive step. In the same way as with all other inventions, the claimed subject matter is examined with respect to the prior art, wherein only instructions determining or at least influencing the solution of a specific technical problem by technical means can support an inventive step. In other words, only technical features can contribute to an inventive step, while non-technical features cannot.

According to the above, the FCJ's three-stage examination approach may be summarised in the flowchart in Figure 1:

Figure 1: The FCJ's three-stage examination approach

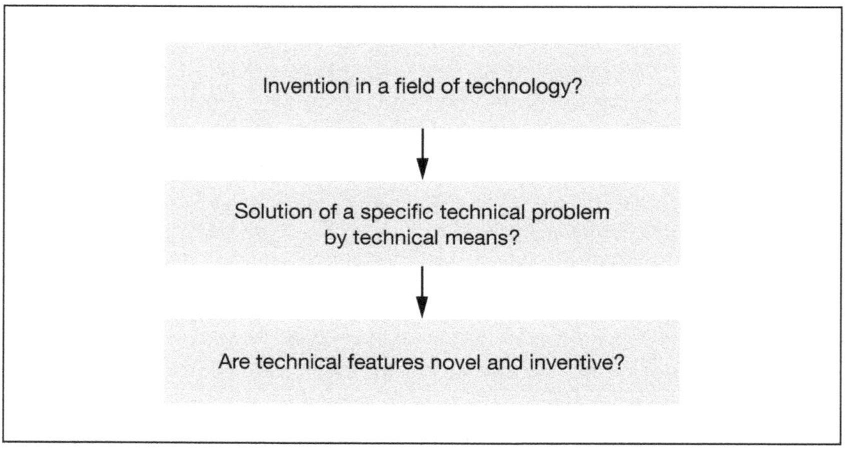

2.3 Examples of inventions related to the presentation of information (Section 1 III no 4)

While the discussion above focused on computer programs which as such are considered ineligible for patent protection due to the exclusion in Section 1 III no 3 but may be eligible if they are not claimed as such, two FCJ decisions related to the presentation of information (Section 1 III no 4) are briefly touched on below.

The FCJ decision *Fahrzeugnavigationssystem*[13] (Vehicle Navigation System)

13 FCJ X ZR 27/12, *Fahrzeugnavigationssystem*, 23 April 2013 – GRUR 2013, 909.

related to a vehicle navigation system for use in a vehicle, the system also comprising a central processing unit. According to the patent, voice guidance in a navigation system is particularly useful since in dangerous traffic conditions the driver's eyes can remain on the street and there is no need to look at a navigation display. Conventional navigation systems allegedly did not include street names in their voice guidance. Although the invention was eligible for patent protection, since it did not relate to the presentation of information as such, inventive step was not acknowledged. The decision found that instructions to a skilled person to consider certain detailed information (in this case, street names) during the voice output of a navigation message under certain conditions, concerns the content of the information optically or acoustically output by the navigation system and is not to be considered for the examination of the technical teaching of the patent with respect to inventive step, thus failing the third stage of examination.

The FCJ decision *Bildstrom*[14] (Image Stream) also concerned the requirements of obtaining patent protection for man-machine-interfaces. The problem underlying the invention was that the frame display rate of images from a camera of an endoscopic capsule cannot be chosen arbitrarily high, as an individual frame must be visible for a certain minimum time in order to ensure that the medical professional reviewing the image stream would be able to recognise a pathology with sufficient certainty. The solution was to divide the original image stream into two partial image streams and then display the two partial image streams simultaneously in respective windows next to each other thereby increasing the individual frame display time. The FCJ found that instructions contribute to the solution of a technical problem by technical means if said instructions relate to the (visual) transmission of information, where the main issue is not, however, the conveyance of certain content or the conveyance thereof using a certain get-up, but rather the presentation of image content in such a manner that takes the physical circumstances of human perception and intake of information into account. Thus, in contrast to the decision *Fahrzeugnavigationssystem* which according to the FCJ concerned merely the presentation of the content of information that did not contribute to a technical effect, the FCJ considers the manner of presentation to be able to contribute to an inventive step.

Finally, it is important to note the FCJ's acknowledgement[15] that the GPA was deliberately harmonised with Article 52(2)(c) and (3) EPC and that the interpretation as to what is eligible for patent protection or not should be left to legal practice. Starting from considerations that the field of computer programs was at the time of drafting the EPC a relatively new field of technology, the Court notes that protection shall not indefinitely expand to cover fields that

14 FCJ X ZR 37/13, *Bildstrom*, 26 February 2015 – GRUR 2015, 660.
15 FCJ X ZB 16/00, *Suche fehlerhafter Zeichenketten*, 17 October 2001 – GRUR 2002, 143.

traditionally do not belong to technology, merely because of the fact that they are realised or automated by means of a computer. On the other hand, it would appear not justified to deny protection to teachings characterised by technical processes or considerations merely because they are performed with the help of a computer. In practice, deviations in case law between the FCJ and EPO's Boards of Appeal in this field appear to be small which is especially important for legal certainty because the FCJ regularly decides as the appeal court on the validity of European patents granted for Germany.

3. Biological and pharmaceutical arts

Biotechnology is an area characterised by rapid developments and worldwide competition among public and private research organisations and industry. The number of patent applications in this field has increased tremendously over the past decades, with a growing impact on health care and agricultural industry. The aim of this section is to provide guidance on eligibility issues affecting the biotechnology sector in Germany.

The primary legal framework for patenting biotechnological inventions at the German Patent and Trademark Office (GPTO) is the German Patent Act (GPA), which is the focus of the present discussion. Other legislation that may impact the practising of biotechnology-related inventions in Germany, such as the German Embryo Protection Act (defined in GPA, Section 2), the German Stem Cell Act and the German Plant Variety Act are not the focus of this discussion. Of particular relevance for eligibility requirements for bio(techno)logical inventions are GPA, Sections 1 III 1, 1a I, 2 and 2a I. Supplementary means of interpreting the GPA are provided by the EU Biotechnology Directive 98/44/EC which was implemented into German National Law in 2005 and is explicitly cross-referenced in the GPA. Furthermore, a broad scope of established or emerging case law that shapes our understanding of patent eligibility, notably considering public health, safety, environmental protection, animal welfare, the preservation of genetic diversity and compliance with ethical standards are now being looked at. Key decisions considered on eligibility issues for bio(techno)logical inventions are discussed below.

3.1 Inventions versus bio(techno)logical discoveries under GPA, Section 1 III no 1

The GPA distinguishes between technical inventions and mere 'discoveries' in Section 1 III no 1. As far back as 1969, the Federal Court of Justice (FCJ) had to define the dividing lines between the mere discovery or identification of a (biological) substance or law of nature, which cannot be defined as an invention (GPA, Section 1 III no 1), and the methodical and repeatable utilisation of natural biological forces which is not excluded from patent protection.[16] In the

16 FCJ X ZB 15 67, *Rote Taube*, 27 March 1969 – GRUR 1969, 672.

case decided, a breeding method for red doves was rejected as lacking reproducibility, but not technicity. The court reasoned that harnessing biological reactions to obtain predictable and controllable results falls within the ambit of harnessing natural phenomena to achieve technical results. In a number of follow up decisions, the FCJ opened an avenue to substance protection of, for example, a microorganism such as yeast or a virus if means are provided to reproduce the patented microorganism or the microorganism had been deposited and is available to the public.[17]

3.2 Elements of the human body under GPA, Section 1a I

According to GPA, Section 1a I, the human body at its various stages of formation and development and the simple discovery of one of its elements such as DNA sequences do not constitute a patentable invention. GPA, Section 1a II, on the other hand, provides patent protection for elements produced by technical means, including sequences or partial sequences of a gene.

This potential tension between an excluded 'simple discovery' and an eligible invention is addressed in a more recent FCJ decision,[18] dealing with claims directed to nucleic acid encoding a human protein as a substance and a method for detecting said nucleic acid. The case was based on the finding that certain genetic modifications occur in leukaemia and can be utilised in the diagnosis thereof.

In line with its case law reaching back to the 'red dove' decision, the FCJ stressed that a technical teaching on the use of a discovery to bring about a certain success may be eligible for patent protection irrespective of whether the teaching contains an 'inventive added value' beyond the use of the naturally occurring correlation discovered. Hence, German practice does not preclude patents based on finding 'rules of nature', provided they can be put to technical use. The same decision clarifies that claims directed to nucleic acid molecules as a product may be patentable under the GPA, even if they encode human proteins. The decision also sheds light on the practical implementation of GPA, Section 1a III, according to which the industrial application of a sequence must be specifically disclosed by indicating the function fulfilled by the sequence in the specification.

In a recent decision the Federal Patent Court[19] drew a line when a patent claim is not intended to protect technically modified blood cells or blood cells obtained by a technical process but instead is directed to native human blood stem cells as they occur naturally in the human body. According to the Patent

---

17 FCJ X ZB 4/74, *Bäckerhefe*, 11 March 1975 – GRUR 1975, 430. FPC 16 W (pat) 45/76, *Lactobacillus bavaricus*, 5 April 1978 – GRUR 1978, 586. FCJ X ZB 4 86, *Tollwutvirus*, 12 February 1987 – GRUR 1987, 231. FPC 16 W (pat) 64/75, *Naturstoffe*, 28 July 1977 – GRUR 1978, 238.

18 FCJ X ZR 141/13, *Rezeptortyrosinkinase*, 19 January 2016 – GRUR 2016, 475.

19 FPC 14 W (pat) 41/12, *Stammzellen aus Eigenblut*, 18 March 2016 – BeckRS 2016, 7052.

Court, such a claim is excluded from patent protection under GPA, Section 1a I. One can see a parallel in this decision with older German case law on naturally occurring substances, which can be patented if produced by technical means, but not as a mere discovery of something existing in nature. A further parallel exists to case law that DNA-sequences isolated from natural sources do not represent a mere discovery.[20]

3.3 Processes for cloning or heritable modification of human beings and use of human embryos under GPA, Section 2 II

Inventions are excluded from patent protection if they stand in unambiguous contradiction to the widely accepted ethical and social standards in our society, guaranteeing the integrity and dignity of individuals. Specifically, under German practice, patents cannot be granted for processes for cloning human beings, for modifying the heritable genetic identity or use of human embryos for commercial purposes (GPA, Section 2 II 1–3; Embryo Protection Act).

The latter became relevant in a patent rights dispute between a German stem cell researcher, Oliver Brüstle, and Greenpeace eV. In 1999, Brüstle was granted a patent on isolated and purified neural precursor cells, methods for their production from embryonic stem cells (ESCs), and the use of these neural precursor cells for the therapy of neural defects (for example, Parkinson's disease). After Greenpeace had successfully sought annulment of the German patent,[21] Brüstle appealed against that judgment to the German FCJ. The FCJ submitted several questions for judgment to the Court of Justice of the European Union (CJEU), particularly to the definition of an 'embryo' and whether the human ESCs which serve as starting material for the patented methods constitute 'embryos' within the meaning of Article 6(2)(c) of Directive 98/44/EC.[22] In the so-called *Brüstle* decision, the CJEU ruled that any human ovum capable of commencing the process of development of a human being is regarded as a human 'embryo'. That classification includes human ovum after fertilisation but also non-fertilised human ovum, for example, into which a cell nucleus from a mature human cell has been transplanted or whose division and further development have been stimulated by parthenogenesis.[23] Following this guidance, the German FCJ decided that the claimed methods for production of neural precursor cells from ESCs comprise the destruction of human 'embryos'. The fact that it may be executable without the destruction of human embryos was considered irrelevant because the general description of the patent in suit gives the impression that the claimed subject matter may be executed in such a

---

20 Discussed, for example, in Schrell, *et al*, *Biotechnology Patenting Policy in the European Union – as Exemplified by the Development in Germany* (Springer-Verlag, 2007), doi: 10.1007/10_2007_049.

21 FPC 3 Ni 42/04, *Neurale Vorläuferzellen I*, 5 December 2006 – BeckRS 2007, 10014.

22 CJEU C-34/10 *Oliver Brüstle v Greenpeace eV* – BeckRS 2011, 81505 (*Brüstle*).

23 *Brüstle*, recital 35ff.

way.[24] The FCJ confirmed that a patent must not give the impression that a teaching contrary to morality is approved by the state.

In light of current scientific knowledge, the CJEU ruled differently in 2014.[25] A non-fertilised human ovum whose division and further development had been stimulated by parthenogenesis was not included in the classification of a human 'embryo'.[26] As the judges did not consider the ability to develop into a human being likely for pluripotent ESCs, claims to human pluripotent ESCs obtained in ways that do not destroy human embryos are not excluded from patentability.

In summary, a comprehensive ban on patenting subject matter relating to human embryonic stem cells which some had hoped for and others feared was not pronounced by the CJEU and German FCJ in these rulings. Rather, as at the EPO, research in the field of embryonic stem cells may still be awarded patent protection within the German legal framework.

Furthermore, under German and European patent law practice, patents cannot be granted for processes for modifying the genetic identity of animals or for animals resulting from such processes when a likelihood of suffering is established and not balanced by a medical benefit (GPA, Section 2 II 4; Article 53(a) and Rule 28(1) EPC). In view of rapidly emerging technology such as CRISPR/Cas genome editing, and its reported use of heritable human genome editing (HHGE) in 2018,[27] this legal area is evolving at pace. For example, the European patent EP 2 800 811 by Jennifer Doudna, Emmanuelle Charpentier, *et al* is currently under appeal after revocation by the court of first instance.[28] It remains to be seen if the Board of Appeal will be convinced by the arguments that the inclusion of possible unlawful embodiments does not render an invention unpatentable. For claims broadly directed at generating animal models by genetic modification, a critical legal question will be whether the mere hypothetical possibility of unnecessary animal suffering is sufficient to trigger the lack of patentability, or whether there must be concrete evidence that the claimed genome editing method inevitably will result in suffering. While therapeutic CRISPR/Cas genome editing is still in the early stages of development, CRISPR-based clinical trials are underway in five treatment areas: blood disorders, cancers, eye disease, chronic infections, or protein-folding disorders.[29] Importantly, all trials are restricted to edit specific target cells or tissues without affecting the patient's germline.

---

24 FCJ X ZR 58/07, *Neurale Vorläuferzellen II*, 27 November 2012 – GRUR 2013, 272.

25 C-364/13 *International Stem Cell Corporation v Comptroller General of Patents, Designs and Trade Marks* 18 December 2014 – GRUR 2015, 156 (*International Stem Cell Corporation*).

26 *International Stem Cell Corporation*, recital 38.

27 The Royal Society, National Academy of Sciences, *et al*, *Heritable Human Genome Editing* (National Academies Press, 2020), DOI: 10.17226/25665.

28 BoA, T1087/20, pending.

29 Hope Henderson, "CRISPR Clinical Trials: A 2021 Update", 3 March 2021, Perspectives, https://innovativegenomics.org/news/crispr-clinical-trials-2021/.

3.4 Plant or animal varieties under GPA, Section 2a I 1

Since 2013 any process for breeding plants or animals based entirely on natural phenomena such as crossing or selection are excluded from patent protection in Germany (GPA, Section 2a I 1, III 3). This practice is in line with a number of EPO Enlarged Board of Appeal decisions, culminating in the recent decision G3/19[30] according to which plant or animal varieties exclusively obtained by non-technical, ie, essentially biological processes are excluded from patentability. However, all European patents granted prior to 1 July 2017 and those applied for until that date are not covered by the new practice and may still be patentable at the EPO. It remains to be seen how such 'old' cases will be treated by German courts.

The exclusion of plants and animal varieties does not apply to plants or animals originating from a technical process or characterised by a technical intervention in the genome (for example, by CRISPR/Cas).

On-going lawsuits concerning genetically modified plants wherein said modification increases, for example, resistance to herbicides or plant viruses confirm that the German public discourages the cultivation of genetically modified (GM) crops to the extent possible within the already stringent EU legislation on genetically modified organisms (GMOs).[31] For example, patent EP1962578 by the applicant Monsanto on virus-resistant melons was challenged by several German parties and revoked on the basis that said resistance was already detected in indigenous melon varieties in India. The appeal of the decision is currently pending.[32] In addition, recent inventions such as patent EP 1965658 by an Australian company on salmon fed in such a way that they have an increased content of omega-3 fatty acids and fish oil thereof are currently being challenged by the German activist group 'No Patents on Seeds'.[33] Hence, to what extent these decisions will depart from existing case law such as the *Monsanto* case on plants having enhanced glyphosate herbicides tolerance[34] and might impact on the patentability of plants or animals originating from a technical process remains to be seen.

4. Medical procedures

According to GPA, Section 2a I 2, patents shall not be granted in respect of methods for treatment of the human or animal body by surgery or therapy and diagnostic methods practised on the human or animal body. However, there is an exception to this exception in that this provision shall not apply to products, in particular substances or compositions, for use in any of these methods.

---

30 G3/19, *Pepper* (follow-up to *Tomatoes II* and *Broccoli II*), decision of 14 May 2020.

31 "Restrictions on Genetically Modified Organisms: Germany", 24 July 2020, www.loc.gov/law/help/restrictions-on-gmos/germany.php.

32 BoA T1045/16-3.3.04, pending.

33 No Patents on Seeds!, www.no-patents-on-seeds.org/de/patentfaelle/archiv.

34 BoA T0179/01, *EPSPS/Monsanto*, decision of 6 April 2005.

As in the European Patent Convention, the statute excluding such medical procedures from the realm of patentability had been coupled to the requirement for industrial applicability. Once the changes brought about with the EPC 2000[35] were implemented into German law,[36] this was no longer the case. Thus, whilst older decisions may prominently discuss industrial applicability, and implications such as the requirement for certain procedures to be carried out by a professional such as a doctor,[37] when determining patent eligibility of medical procedures, this typically has become less relevant. It still serves as a rebuttable indication for the severity of an intervention with the human or animal body, with the boundary between sufficiently severe interventions, which would then be deemed to constitute surgery, and less severe interventions being fuzzy.

Non-eligibility of medical procedures is not, and has never been, an exclusion because of lack of technicity.[38] In accordance with today's understanding, the exclusion of medical procedures rather exists for socio-ethical and health policy reasons and has the purpose to maintain the freedom of medical personnel to decide, also on short notice, on measures for eliminating illnesses or diseases, or to decide on methods for examining the human or animal body so as to identify such illnesses or diseases.[39] Also, the patient's freedom to choose a medical professional ought not to be affected by the professional's freedom to practice medical methods depending on whether they are patented.[40]

In keeping with this distinction of the non-eligibility of non-technical subject matter, the test for the eligibility of medical procedures is then not a multi-stage approach in which the courts determine eligible and non-eligible aspects of the claimed subject-matter, to then assess patentability over the prior art of the eligible aspects only. It is a single test in which the courts determine whether any aspect of the claimed subject matter is non-eligible. If so, the entire claim will be deemed to fail the eligibility requirement.

The statute on the non-eligibility of medical procedures does not expressly recite if the human or animal body must be alive. The requirement that the body must be alive, however, has been added by case law.[41] Put differently, any medical method practised on a corpse or cadaver would be patent eligible.

---

35 Formally speaking the Act revising the Convention on the Grant of European Patents (European Patent Convention) of 29 November 2000.

36 Effected with the German Act on Ratification of the EPC 2000 dated 24 August 2007 (BGBl. I S. 2166), with effect as of 13 December 2007.

37 The EU Directive on Recognition of Professional Qualifications (2005/36/EC) defines (liberal) professions as "those practised on the basis of relevant professional qualifications in a personal, responsible and professionally independent capacity by those providing intellectual and conceptual services in the interest of the client and the public". In this context, a profession is not an industry.

38 Krasser and Ann, *Patentrecht*, 7th Ed, (CH Beck, 2016), §14 II, margin note 53 with reference to Moufang in GRUR Int 1992, 17, 21.

39 FCJ X ZB 20/99 *Endoprotheseeinsatz* in GRUR 2001, 321.

40 Krasser and Ann, *Patentrecht*, 7th Ed (CH Beck, 2016), §14 II, margin note 53.

41 Generally accepted.

In accordance with German case law, methods for treatment of the human or animal body are deemed to be methods for treatment by therapy if they have the purpose to heal. Healing is contrasted with purely cosmetic purposes. Remedying illnesses, diseases or injuries, the reduction of health disorders, be they caused by a medical condition or a natural condition such as menstruation, age, fatigue, or headaches, the alleviation of infirmity, the removal or correction of physical defects are all embraced by the purpose to heal.[42] Combating hair loss is not, unless it is done by means of hair transplantations.[43] Ancillary procedures such as anaesthetics, the administration of antihypertensive agents, and hypothermia (cold therapy) are likewise not patentable.[44] For pharmaceutical inventions based on an active ingredient and its administration by conventional means, the exclusion of therapeutic methods from patentability is, in practical terms, more a question of correct claim wording than a hard barrier of eligibility. The FCJ in principle accepts claims directed to 'extended' medical use claims as patent eligible, even when the invention lies not in the active substance but in particular ways of administering it to a patient.[45]

Although it seems to be a generally accepted requirement for methods for treatment of the human or animal body to qualify as surgery that the human or animal body be kept alive,[46] the distinction between methods having a purpose to heal and those that do not is less helpful when determining the eligibility of such methods.[47] The courts ought to consider the type of treatment more than the purpose.[48] Once the type of treatment involves a sufficiently severe interaction with the human or animal body, it is deemed to be of a surgical nature. The FPC, for instance, has found[49] the taking of a blood sample to lack the required severity. In an *obiter dictum* the court noted that both invasive and non-invasive interactions may well qualify as surgery, and mentioned as examples the alignment of broken bones, the resetting of dislocated joints, operating with a scalpel, laser and other beams, or with high frequency currents. The court equally noted that the piercing of ears, the administration of injections and tattooing would also lack the required severity, but ultimately left open the degree of severity that is necessary to render subject

42 Mellulis in Benkard, *Commentary on the Patent Act*, 11th Ed (CH Beck, 2015), section 2a, margin note 57.

43 FCJ Ia ZB 1/65 *Glatzenoperation* in GRUR 1968, 142.

44 Keukenschrijver in Busse, *Commentary on the Patent Act*, 9th Ed (de Gruyter, 2020), Sec 2a, margin note 49.

45 FCJ X ZB 5/13 *Kollagenase I*, 25 February 2014 – GRUR 2014, 461. FCJ XZB 6/13 *Kollagenase II*, 25 February 2014 – GRUR 2014, 464.

46 Krasser and Ann, §14 II, Rn 78.

47 Krasser and Ann, §14 II, Rn 73. Keukenschrijver in Busse, *Commentary on the Patent Act*, 9th Ed (de Gruyter, 2020), Sec 2a, margin note 45.

48 See fn 45.

49 FPC 21 W (pat) 68/04, obtainable at http://juris.bundespatentgericht.de/cgi-bin/rechtsprechung/document.py?Gericht=bpatg&Art=en&sid=715dd28816a2473898e1feef773cebe1&nr=3001&pos=0&anz=1&Blank=1.pdf.

matter non-eligible. The decision was issued in an *ex parte* appeal. It has been given weight by a citation in one of the leading commentaries of the GPA.[50]

Ancillary procedures such as the sterilisation of instruments, the disinfection of the operating theatre or of the surgical personnel[51] are eligible.[52] In a landmark decision[53] concerning a method for supporting the targeted navigation of a catheter invasively inserted into a hollow organ of the human or animal body (for example, blood vessels) to a pathological location by means of imaging, the FCJ ruled that the claimed method was directed to the imaging rather than the catheter navigation, and that the imaging is not subject to the surgical exclusion because the exclusion does not embrace the patenting of methods which are carried out in conjunction with, and in support of, the actual surgical procedure. In this decision, the FCJ aligned its case law with the decisions of the EPO's Enlarged Board of Appeal by reference to the EPO decisions G1/04[54] and G1/07.[55]

Method claims embracing both a treatment of the human or animal body which is considered therapy or surgery, and a treatment that is not, are not allowable. Such claims can generally be amended to be limited to the non-therapeutic or non-surgical aspects, provided that the subject matter of the amended claim is directly and unambiguously derivable from the application as filed as one potential embodiment of the invention. The amendment can also be effected by means of a disclaimer, even if the wording for the disclaimer is not to be found in the application as filed. However, disclaiming the entire content of the application as filed is deemed to result in the amended claim extending beyond the content of the application as filed and therefore not allowable.[56]

In accordance with EPO case law,[57] diagnostic methods have a sequence of necessary phases, namely:

- the examination phase, involving the collection of data;
- the comparison of the data with standard values;
- the finding of any significant deviation, ie, a symptom, during the comparison; and
- the attribution of the deviation to a particular clinical picture, ie, the deductive medical or veterinary decision phase (diagnosis for curative purposes *stricto sensu*).

---

50 Mellulis in Benkard, *Commentary on the Patent Act*, 11th Ed (CH Beck, 2015), section 2a, margin note 67.
51 As opposed to the patient.
52 See fn 42.
53 FCJ X ZB 9/09, *Bildunterstützung bei Katheternavigation*, 31 August 2010 – GRUR 2010, 1081.
54 G1/04 Diagnostic methods in EPO OJ 2005, 334.
55 G1/07 (Treatment by surgery/MEDI-PHYSICS) of 15 February 2010 – GRUR Int 2010, 333.
56 FPC 21 W (pat) 17/05 *Verfahren zur passiven Gymnastik* in GRUR 2008, 329.
57 See fn 54.

The German Federal Patent Court[58] and the Federal Court of Justice[59] have agreed with that finding. A claim must recite all four phases for it to be directed to a diagnostic method. If one of the phases is not claimed, for instance the final phase (attribution of the deviation to a particular clinical picture), there is a good likelihood under German law that the subject matter of that claim is eligible.[60]

This is confirmed by a recent decision from the Federal Patent Court.[61] It concerned a method for the detection of the presence of foetal nucleic acid in a serum or plasma sample taken from a pregnant woman. The Federal Patent Court dealt with the question whether the patented method is subject to the exclusion of medical methods. The FPC ruled that the claimed method concerned a non-invasive prenatal diagnosis wherein maternal serum or plasma samples are tested *in vitro* for the presence of foetal nucleic acids. For this purpose, a blood sample had to be taken from the pregnant woman. Taking a blood sample does not constitute a surgical procedure as it is regularly carried out by medical assistants and (similar to the administration of, for example, an X-ray contrast medium) does not correspond to a therapeutic treatment of the human body within the meaning of GPA, Section 2a I 2. The mere fact that a physician may, on the basis of the data obtained from the blood analysis, decide on the further procedure is not sufficient for the exclusion of the diagnostic method as claimed. Hence, the FPC has clarified that not every diagnostic method is excluded from patentability. This approach is similar to the stance the EPO is taking on the matter.

Patent applications which are drafted with the non-eligibility of medical procedures in mind thus have significantly better prospects of proceeding to being granted if they contain examples of an application of the claimed method in a non-surgical or non-therapeutic context. These may include practising the method on a dummy or on a cadaver, for instance, for testing or calibration purposes. Diagnostic methods ought to be claimed without the final step of attributing the deviation between collected data and standard values to a particular clinical picture, and the application as a whole ought not to leave the reader with the impression that this final step is essential for the invention to work. To the extent that it does, the GPTO may have basis to object.

As mentioned at the beginning of this section, there is an exception to the exception of medical methods from being patented. The double exception means that products for use in any of the non-eligible methods, in particular substances or compositions, are eligible. The exception to the exception may

58 FPC 23 W (pat) 55/04 *Auswertung diskreter Messwerte* in GRUR 2007, 133.
59 FCJ X ZB 9/09, *Bildunterstützung bei Katheternavigation*, 31 August 2010 – GRUR 2010, 1081.
60 See fn 58.
61 FPC 3 Ni 68/16 (EP), *Nichtinvasives Verfahren zum Nachweis fötaler Nukleinsäuren*, 24 April 2018 – BeckRS 2018, 24732.

become relevant when, for instance, a claimed bodily tissue or fluid has been extracted from a living human or animal body. If such tissue or fluid is permanently extracted and used outside of the human or animal body, it ought to be patent eligible. If, conversely, the tissue or fluid is recirculated, as is normally the case for fluid in an extracorporeal circuit,[62] the fluid is non-eligible.

5. Hot topics: new technologies including artificial intelligence

In general, it can be stated that the German Patent Act and the GPTO Guidelines for Examination do not distinguish between different technologies related to the electrical and computer arts, such as computer-implemented inventions. As outlined above with respect to inventions in the electrical and computer arts section 2, the law and relevant case law provides for abstract approaches fitting to a plethora of scenarios and/or technologies instead of providing specific approaches tailored to just a single specific scenario and/or technology, the same will most likely hold true for emerging technologies, such as artificial intelligence (AI). In particular, it appears reasonable to consider that certain exceptions to patentability mentioned in GPA, Section 1 III will also play a role for AI inventions, such as 'mathematical methods', 'schemes, rules and methods for performing mental acts' and 'programs for computers'.

Established case law by the FCJ and the GPTO's present practice have established a general procedure for examining inventions containing a mix of features, including features that are considered to be 'technical' as well as features that are considered to be 'non-technical'. All inventions related to computer-implemented inventions and mathematical models as well as those related to business methods and other subject-matter which is excluded from patentability if claimed as such generally fall under this procedure.

The Guidelines for Examination at the GPTO and case law provide such generality that the actual technology to which they are applied does not require any changes to the procedure as such. That is to say that whether an invention is based on relatively established technologies like simulations assisting a production scheme or newer technology such as neural networks, deep learning, artificial intelligence, Internet of Things, etc has relatively little influence on the general route taken during the examination. In each of these cases, the GPTO will consider the three-stage examination approach outlined in part B above. In fact, these emerging technologies have already reached the GPTO and GPTO's established examination approach seems reflected in the latest GPTO office actions.

Of course, the specific details of the application under examination will always matter, but generally an applicant is always advised to provide a good explanation in the application of how the invention solves a specific technical

62 Mellulis in Benkard, *Commentary on the Patent Act*, 11th Ed (CH Beck, 2015), section 2a margin note 77.

problem by technical means which is expected to remain the core of the examination.

In other words, it is expected that emerging technologies will – at least in the short term – be handled in a very similar manner compared to the recent advances in the field of computer-implemented inventions and it is not to be expected that the GPTO will deviate substantially from case law developed in this field over several decades.

India

Himanshu Chawla
Durgesh Mukharya
K&S Partners

1. Background

India, the sixth largest economy in the world, is fast becoming an important global player, as far as intellectual property (IP) is concerned. As is the case with any rapidly growing nation, an increase in purchasing power of the population gives rise to a steady increase in demand for quality products and services, which in turn allows for healthy competition amongst organisations to cater to the rising needs. This provides them with an opportunity to innovate and put forth best technologies to create a strong customer base and build on it, especially when the potential market is that of the second most populous country in the world. It is therefore no surprise that companies that hold important patents are seen as key differentiators in this race for success.

Patent protection in India is driven by the Indian Patents Act 1970, (hereinafter 'the Act') which, amongst other important provisions, provides for the definition of an invention and its requisites through Section 2(1)(j) and lists inventions that are not considered to be patent eligible in India under its Sections 3 and 4.

2. Definition of 'invention' and 'inventive step'

Before getting into the details of patent-eligible subject matter, it is important to understand the basic premise of an invention in India, which is defined by Section 2(1)(j) of the Act as "a new product or process involving an inventive step and capable of industrial application".

Noteworthily, the definition only recognises products and processes to be inventions within the ambit of the Act, and leaves out their uses or applications. This position is further emphasised by Section2(1)(ac) of the Act which defines the said term 'capable of industrial application' in the context of an invention as that which is capable of being made or used in an industry. Thus, in terms of claim categories, the Indian patent law only recognises products and processes as inventions, and a patent application carrying claims merely for their use or application as such will be considered to fall outside the purview of an invention in India. Additionally, a product-by-process[1] claim is also challenging in India as it must define a novel and unobvious product as such. The patentability of such a claim cannot depend on the novelty and non-obviousness of the process limitations alone.

Secondly, the Act explicitly defines 'inventive step' through its Section 2(1)(ja) as "a feature of an invention that involves technical advance as compared to the existing knowledge or having economic significance or both and that makes the invention not obvious to a person skilled in the art". Thus, from the Indian context, emphasis is given on both, technical advancement or the surprising effect of an invention and on how the invention is non-obvious to a person skilled in the art. This is essential to note as for some patent offices, non-obviousness over the prior art alone is good enough to comply with inventive step requirement.

For defending inventive step, some approaches seem to work better than others at the Indian Patent Office (IPO). These include:

- Appropriate data points – the following can be most helpful:
  - comparison of how the present invention fares versus the closest prior art(s); and/or
  - negative data on how deviations (of specific elements/ parameters/conditions) from the present invention do not lead to the desired results.

While it is best that these data points are included in the as-filed specification, presenting them at the time of prosecution is also acceptable to most examiners.

- Problem-solution approach – examiners in India, like their European counterparts, generally appreciate getting a perspective of a problem, a challenge or an issue which an industry or consumers were facing, and how the invention in question is trying to solve it. This cuts across industries and showcasing the technical effect of an invention to solve real life practical problems goes a long way in making a positive impression in the mind of the examiners.
- Hindsight approach – describing how a person skilled in the art would not be motivated to combine certain prior art documents (perhaps because of their differing objectives or modes of reaching the solution or otherwise) or the fact that they are combined only in hindsight, also lays a good foundation for a successful argument.

As objections pertaining to inventive step are raised in almost all applications filed at the IPO, keeping these aspects in mind helps one negotiate with them more easily.

---

1 Intellectual Property Appellate Board OA/11/2009/PT/DEL (Order No. 200/2012) *The Research Foundation Of State University Of New York Vs Assistant Controller Of Patents* [42].

3. Inventions not patentable (Section 3)

While proving novelty and inventive step of an invention in India drives you closer to getting a patent, an invention also needs to steer past the questions of patent eligibility by overcoming the thresholds set by Sections 3 and 4 of the Indian Patents Act.

While the check for patent eligibility is a routine step to ensure compliance with provisions which exclude certain inventions from patentability in respective countries, India treads a slightly different and somewhat more complex path on this. Section 3 of the Indian patent law not only bars inventions from patentability in sync with Article 27 of the TRIPS agreement and in alignment with most other patent laws across the globe; for specific kinds of inventions, it also creates a separate threshold on top of the novelty and inventive step criteria for making them patentable in India. While in some cases, the reasons through which one addresses an inventive step rejection overlap with the manner in which a Section 3 objection is overcome, for all practical purposes these two should be dealt with separately during prosecution of a patent application, and for the satisfaction of the examiners at the IPO.

Historically, the introduction of Section 3 is attributed to the reforms in patent law based on recommendations first by a 1949 committee under Justice Bakshi Tek Chand and later by the 1957 committee under Justice N Rajagopala Ayyangar, which set out to improve the preceding Patent Act of 1911, introduced by the British prior to independence. General perception of what little the Act of 1911 did to promote domestic interests led to the setting up of committees post-independence which in turn recommended the barring of patents on inventions which were a) globally recognised to be outside the purview of patents, and b) related to chemical inventions, food, medicine and agriculture. The impetus for the latter particularly came from the need to encourage development and exploitation of new inventions for industrial purposes in the country. One of the ways to achieve this was to prevent inventions which were expected to be merely incremental, spurious, and did not seem to promote research, innovation and industrial progress, or were detrimental to national health and well-being. These recommendations were ultimately adopted by the new Patents Act of 1970 and refined through subsequent amendments to their current form under Section 3.

Section 3 is defined under Chapter II of the Act which recites 'inventions not patentable' and is reproduced here:

> *3. What are not inventions.—The following are not inventions within the meaning of this Act,—*
>
> *(a) an invention which is frivolous or which claims anything obviously contrary to well established natural laws;*
>
> *(b) an invention, the primary or intended use or commercial exploitation of*

which would be contrary to public order or morality or which causes serious prejudice to human, animal or plant life or health or to the environment;

(c) *the mere discovery of a scientific principle or the formulation of or discovery of any living thing or non-living substance occurring in nature;*

(d) *the mere discovery of a new form of a known substance which does not result in the enhancement of the known efficacy of that substance or the mere discovery of any new property or new use for a known substance or of the mere use of a known process, machine or apparatus unless such known process results in a new product or employs at least one new reactant.*

Explanation.—For the purposes of this clause, salts, esters, ethers, polymorphs, metabolites, pure form, particle size, isomers, mixtures of isomers, complexes, combinations and other derivatives of a known substance shall be considered to be the same substance, unless they differ significantly in properties with regard to efficacy;

(e) *a substance obtained by a mere admixture resulting only in the aggregation of the properties of the components thereof or a process for producing such substance;*

(f) *the mere arrangement or re-arrangement or duplication of known devices each functioning independently of one another in a known way;*

[Clause (g) omitted by Act 38 of 2002, Section 4]

(h) *a method of agriculture or horticulture;*

(i) *any process for the medicinal, surgical, curative, prophylactic, diagnostic, therapeutic or other treatment of human beings or any process for a similar treatment of animals to render them free of disease or to increase their economic value or that of their products;*

(j) *plants and animals in whole or any part thereof other than micro-organisms but including seeds, varieties and species and essentially biological processes for production or propagation of plants and animals;*

(k) *a mathematical or business method or a computer programme per se or algorithms;*

(l) *a literary, dramatic, musical or artistic work or any other aesthetic creation whatsoever including cinematographic works and television productions;*

(m) *a mere scheme or rule or method of performing a mental act or method of playing game;*

(n) *a presentation of information;*

(o) *topography of integrated circuits;*

(p) *an invention which, in effect, is traditional knowledge or which is an aggregation or duplication of known properties of traditionally known component or components.*

Although these clauses independently restrict patentability of different subject matters across technologies, more than one clause can be applicable to the same claim or invention. Thus, a general guidance on their applicability to common claim types within a realm of technological art and possible rebuttal positions can be valuable to traverse objections from the IPO. The next three sections accordingly help in providing an analysis of how specific subject matters from electrical and computer arts, biological arts and pharmaceutical, chemical, material and metallurgical arts, would be looked at through the prism of Section 3.

3.1 Patent eligibility for inventions belonging to electrical and computer arts

Innovations in electrical and computer arts are driven by various technologies such as basic electronics, analogue integrated circuits, digital integrated circuits, telecommunication, networking, software, data structure, hardware, machine learning, artificial intelligence, neural networks, etc. Accordingly, a vast array of subject matter results from these technological areas which are potentially patentable in India. However, as is the case with geographies like the United States and Europe, electrical and computer inventions tread a fine line as far as patent eligibility is concerned, even in India.

Of the 15 clauses of Section 3, the most important ones for inventions belonging to electrical and computer arts are provided below. Appropriate reasoning on their applicability as well as some handy practice pointers are provided to help navigate through them.

Table 1. Exclusions related to electrical and computer arts

Relevant clause of Section 3:	Prohibited subject matter is directed to:
Section 3(k)	mathematical method or business method or computer programme *per se* or algorithm
Section 3(m)	a mere scheme or rule or method of performing mental act or method of playing game
Section 3(n)	presentation of information
Section 3(o)	topography of integrated circuits

The Indian Patent Office (IPO) issued "Guidelines for examination of computer related inventions (CRIs)" on 30 June 2017.[2] The guidelines provide

2 Guidelines for examination of computer related inventions available at www.ipindia.nic.in/writereaddata/Portal/IPOGuidelinesManuals/1_86_1_Revised__Guidelines_for_Examination_of_Computer-related_Inventions_CRI__.pdf.

guidance in respect of patentability of CRIs and pointers to be followed by the Indian Examiners while examining applications related to CRIs.

The following differentiates allowable and non-allowable subject matter with respect to each of the clauses indicated above.

(a) Section 3(k): Mathematical method

The following are not allowed:	**The following may be allowed:**
• claim exclusively solving a mathematical problem, eg, a method of multiplying two numbers	• claim providing technical solution to a technical problem and not a mathematical problem
• end result of a claim being a numerical value having no practical utility	• claim exhibiting practical application (utility) in real world
• claim relating to act of mind or mental thought/ contemplation	• a novel multiplier device defining hardware components

It is to be noted that a claim purely solving a mathematical problem by defining a mathematical expression may attract the provisions of mathematical method. For example, a method of multiplying two numbers, comprising the steps of inputting two numbers (A and B) and performing the operation of multiplication (A x B) would be considered a mental method rather than a technical method. Also, this type of method may not be considered as providing any utility/application to industry.

On the other hand, if the claimed method includes mathematical expressions and is directed towards technical subject matter and solves a technical problem, the same may not attract the provisions of mathematical method. For example, such a claim might involve mathematical expressions for solving a technical problem relating to a technical field such as encoding/ decoding.[3]

This approach has also been acknowledged by the Delhi High Court in *Telefonaktiebolaget Lm Ericsson v Lava International Ltd.*[4] The Delhi High Court in this case held that inventions which result in technical advancement and have practical implementation or physical representation are patentable and not mere theoretical or abstract algorithms or mere mathematical or mental methods or even computer programmes *per se*.

---

3 *Ibid*, pp15–16.

4 *Telefonaktiebolaget Lm Ericsson v Lava International Ltd* dated 10 June 2016 available at https://indiankanoon.org/doc/100117737/, [89-94].

(b) ***Section 3(k): Business method***

The following are not allowed:	The following may be allowed:
• claim relating to commercial activity, for example, transaction of goods and/or services • claim relating to business, trade, financial activity • claim relating to addressing an administrative problem	• claim providing a technical solution to a technical problem and not a business problem • invention outcome not focusing on increase in revenue or administrative solution

A claim defining a business method in substance would be rejected under section 3(k). For example, a claim relating to delivering advertisements to a user which results in increase in revenue for the advertiser would be interpreted as intended to enhance business, which is purely administrative and non-technical in nature.

On the contrary, if the claimed subject matter defines an online share trading terminal comprising means for optimising network bandwidth, the claim may not be considered as a business method and may be allowed. This is because the intent of the claim may be understood as optimising network resources rather than enhancing business/revenue, which is purely technical in nature. Therefore, it is important to note that if the objective of the claimed invention is to solve a technical problem, even if the claimed subject matter defines business related terms, the claim may be considered patentable.

(c) ***Section 3(k): Computer programme* per se**

The following are not allowed:	The following may be allowed:
• set of instructions expressed in words/codes/schemes • means plus function claims • Beauregard claims (computer readable media) • functionally worded product claims (device/apparatus/system)	• novel hardware not required • novel function implemented on a conventional hardware leading to technical advancement over existing technology • claim having real world effect • claim defining physical interaction and functional interrelationship leading to technical advancement

Computer programs as such are excluded from patentability. This is clear from the fact that clause (k) defines the exclusion as computer program *per se*. *Per se* was added to clause k of Section 3 to ensure that genuine inventions developed based on computer programs are not refused patents. Thus, if the claimed subject matter defines a piece of code in any programming language (C/C++, etc), the same may be considered as a program *per se* and not patentable. On the other hand, if the claimed subject matter defines the functionality associated with a computer program and said functionality involves technical character (provides technical advancement over the prior art), the same may not attract the provisions of a program *per se* and be considered patentable.

This approach has also been acknowledged by the Intellectual Property Appellate Board (IPAB) in *Ferid Allani v Assistant Controller of Patents & Designs*. In this case, the board acknowledged that, if an invention provides technical contribution to the state of art and possesses a technical effect, it is patentable even though the invention is based on a computer program.[5]

Some important issues are:

- means plus function claims – as per Indian patent practice, means plus function claims in respect of computer related inventions are generally not allowed. This is because the term 'means' is interpreted to include components (software, hardware, firmware or combination) that can perform the claimed function and can be envisaged by a person skilled in the art but not necessarily restricted to the specification. Thus, the Indian Examiners opine that means plus function claims are very broad and provide undue protection. These claims may be allowed by replacing 'means' with tangible components defined in the specification;
- Beauregard claims (Computer readable media) – as per Indian patent practice, conventional storage medium, for example, a CD/DVD storing novel software/code/data structure is not allowed. Indian Examiners opine that medium *per se* must exhibit novel changes in structure to qualify as patentable subject matter; and
- functionally worded product claims (Device/Apparatus/System) – according to Indian patent practice, a functionally worded device/apparatus/system claim may not be allowed. For example, "a processing device programmed/configured to perform the steps of the method..." may not be allowed. The Indian Examiners opine that a device/apparatus/system claim should define one or more machine components, functional details of one or more machine components, functional interrelationship, and physical interaction between one or more machine components to qualify as patentable subject matter.

5 *Ferid Allani v Assistant Controller of Patents & Designs*, 20 July 2020 available at www.ipab.gov.in/ipab_orders/delhi/OA-17-2020-PT-DEL.pdf.

(d) Section 3(k): Algorithms

The following are not allowed:	**The following may be allowed:**
• method steps or rules or procedures expressed as instructions for solving a problem • underlying principle for a software developer	• claim carrying out a technical process for achieving technical output/effect • claim defining implementation tool (machine components carrying out method steps) to achieve real world function

An algorithm is generally categorised as a theoretical concept not resulting in direct technical result. In other words, an algorithm is a theoretical construct which exists only on paper and which does not have any practical implementation or realisation. To the contrary, if the claimed subject matter is capable of being implemented in the real world for creating a practical effect, the claim may be deemed patentable.

For example, consider a telecommunication method in a telecommunication network, comprising: transmitting, by a transmitter, a plurality of packets over a physical channel to a base station; and receiving, by a receiver, an acknowledgement from the base station over the physical channel. In this example, transmission/reception of data packets over a physical channel clearly establishes functionality in the real world. A person skilled in the art would understand and appreciate that transmission/reception of data in a telecommunication network requires a physical set up involving physical systems such as transmitters, receivers, antennas, modulators, de-modulators, etc. Such establishment of network devices, which interact with each other in the real world, cannot be construed as abstract.

This approach has also been acknowledged by the Delhi High Court in *Telefonaktiebolaget Lm Ericsson v Lava International Ltd*. The Delhi High Court in this case held that inventions which result in technical advancement and have practical implementation or physical representation are patentable and not mere theoretical or abstract algorithms or mere mathematical or mental methods or even computer programs *per se*.[6]

6 Note 4, *supra*.

(e) Section 3(m): Method of performing mental act

The following are not allowed:	The following may be allowed:
• abstract ideas • process or act performed merely by mental skill of a human being • outcome of process or act arises from mental thought process which does not manifest any physical changes in the real world	• process solving a technical problem • involvement of tool (machine components) • real world effect

It is to be noted that any process or method may be performed/implemented in the following manner:

1) purely by a machine without substantial involvement of a human being;
2) by a combination of human being and machine; and
3) purely by a human being (a process which requires involvement of mind alone).

The claimed subject matter defining a process implemented according to point 3 above may attract the provisions of a mental act. Such process does not manifest any physical changes in the real world, ie, such process does not have any industrial and real world applications. Also, such process can be easily infringed mentally, for example, a method of teaching or a method of playing chess.

On the other hand, any process implemented at least partially by a machine indicates an application in industry. Such process is not abstract and may be considered as patentable, for example, a method of communication between a mobile device and a base station.

(f) *Section 3(n): Presentation of information*

The following are not allowed:	The following may be allowed:
• claim relating to mere presentation/display of information, eg, a sign board • claim focusing on what is displayed rather than how it is displayed • no technical problem • non-existence of technical solution and technical effect in claim	• claim directed towards technical subject matter such as process or apparatus of presenting information leading to technical effect

If the claimed subject matter is directed to mere presentation/display of information, for example, a method of conveying directions on a sign board that merely defines the directions, the claim may be considered to be directed to the presentation of information. This presentation of information is considered as an abstract idea that is non-technical in nature. In other words, mere presentation of directions on a sign board does not solve any technical problem, hence does not involve a technical character.

On the other hand, if the claimed subject matter includes technical features for presenting or conveying information, the same may be considered patentable. For example, take a method of presenting advertisements to a user device from a content server based on the user's interest and preferences. This type of method involves technical features such as interaction between the user device and the content server for filtration of advertisements based on one or more criterion before presenting information (advertisements) to the user device.

(g) *Section 3(o): Topography of integrated circuits*

The following are not allowed:	The following may be allowed:
• layout design or mask work • three-dimensional illustration of different circuit elements on a substrate to manufacture or to produce an integrated circuit	• integrated circuit *per se* • constructional novelty in integrated circuit • solution (technical in nature)

The Act does not define topography or layout of integrated circuits. The definition is provided in the Semiconductor Integrated Circuits Layout-Design Act 2000.[7]

Section 2(h) of the Semiconductor Integrated Circuits Layout-Design Act 2000 gives the following definition of 'layout design':

> *'Layout-design' means a layout of transistors, and other circuitry elements and includes lead wires connecting such elements and expressed in any manner in a semiconductor integrated circuit.*[8]

In view of the above definition, unless the claimed subject matter defines a layout of circuit elements (active and passive) and a layout of lead wires connecting the layout of active and passive circuit elements, the claim may not be rejected under Section 3(o).

Further guidance differentiating layout designs and patentable subject matter is provided by the World Intellectual Property Organization (WIPO). It is stated that:

> *layout designs of integrated circuits are normally not patentable inventions, because making them usually does not involve an inventive step, although it does require a great deal of work by an expert. The subject matter of layout design protection does not extend to the inventive nature or function of a product or a process of making a product, but it does cover the original designs of a three-dimensional disposition, which is the result of an intellectual effort.*[9]

Thus, it may be understood that if an invention relating to integrated circuits involves inventive step, ie, achieves technical advancement over the existing art, the same may be considered as a patentable invention and not 'layout design' within the meaning of Section 3(o).

3.2 Patent eligibility for inventions belonging to mechanical arts

In reference to mechanical arts, the exclusions from eligibility are mainly governed by Section 3(f) of the Act.

Table 2. Exclusion related to mechanical arts

Relevant clause of Section 3:	Prohibited subject matter is directed to:
Section 3(f)	mere arrangement or rearrangement or duplication of known devices each functioning independently of one another in a known way

7 Semiconductor Integrated Circuits Layout-Design Act 2000 available at http://sicldr.gov.in/Resources/SICLD-Act-English.pdf.
8 *Ibid*, p2.
9 www.wipo.int/patents/en/topics/integrated_circuits.html.

The following differentiates allowable and non-allowable subject matter in respect of clause (f) of section 3.

The following is not allowed:	The following may be allowed:
• a mere juxtaposition of known devices in which each device functions independently	• claim clearly establishes interdependency and synergy among different components which are not functioning independently of each other

A mere juxtaposition of known devices, in which each device functions independently, may implicate the provisions of Section 3(f). However, if the known devices, when placed together, have some working interrelationship, then there may be patentable subject matter in the idea of the working interrelationship brought about by the connection of the devices.

For example, a claim which is directed towards an umbrella with a fan where both umbrella and fan are operating independently of each other may be held unpatentable under Section 3(f). This is because both the umbrella and fan elements are known devices and function independently to achieve independent functions. On the other hand, consider a claim that is directed towards a device comprising an umbrella and a fan connected and functioning in a manner that the fan operates (starts rotating) in response to the umbrella being opened. This type of arrangement may not implicate the provisions of Section 3(f), as the functioning of one element (umbrella) affects the functioning of the other element (fan). In other words, the operation and functioning of the fan is interdependent and interrelated with the operation and functioning of the umbrella.

3.3 Patent eligibility for inventions belonging to biological arts

The term 'biological arts' is a fairly broad term that encompasses a spectrum of simple to complex innovations based in disciplines such as biotechnology, biochemistry, cell biology, genetics, immunology, microbiology and molecular biology. Accordingly, a vast array of subject matter results from these domains. However, as is the case with geographies like the US, biological inventions tread a fine line as far as patent eligibility is concerned, even in India.

Out of the 15 clauses of Section 3, below are the most important ones for inventions belonging to biological arts. Appropriate reasoning on their applicability as well as some handy practice pointers are provided to help navigate through them.

Table 3. Exclusions related to biological arts

Relevant clause of Section 3:	Prohibited subject matter is directed to:
Section 3(b)	products and processes that cause any prejudice to life forms
Section 3(c)	naturally occurring elements or organisms
Section 3(d)	new form of a known substance or mere discovery of any new property or new use or mere use of a known process
Section 3(e)	compositions without synergy between their components
Section 3(h)	agricultural methods
Section 3(i)	medical use, intervention or supervision
Section 3(j)	plants or animals or their parts, or naturally occurring biological processes
Section 3(p)	products and processes that utilise traditional knowledge

(a) *New biological product, molecule or entity claims*

Subject matter claimed:	**Common Section 3 objection(s) and reasoning:**
• new biological molecules/entities ◦ nucleic acids/proteins ◦ organisms/cells ◦ genetic constructs/elements ◦ biochemical compounds/constituting extracts	Section 3(c) – for ensuring that a claim is not directed to naturally occurring molecule/entity Section 3(d) – for checking if any modification to a molecule/entity creates a derivative or new form of the corresponding parent molecule/entity Section 3(j) – for checking if a claim is directed to a plant/animal, their parts or cells (native or recombinant)

Examples of allowable claims are:

- a polynucleotide or polypeptide sequence or recombinant protein or biological extract or biochemical compound defined by specific sequence ids. or structural characteristics; and
- a recombinant microorganism or prokaryotic cell or plasmid or vector or gene construct defined by specific sequences or genetic elements or structural characteristics.

Practice tip: from the perspective of Section 3(c), the claimed sequence must be a synthetic sequence or structurally different from its naturally occuring counterpart. Human intervention must be demonstrated, beyond the usual step of isolation. A simple action of attaching an artificial tag or probe or marker to a naturally occurring sequence can take the claim outside the purview of Section 3(c). If the claim is directed to a microorganism, it must also not be naturally occurring and should be a recombinant microorganism. Similarly, a claim to a vaccine would be patent eligible as long as it comprises an attenuated or mutated organism or its part, not the naturally occurring organism *per se*.

Importantly, mere use of the term 'isolated' does not make a sequence or genetic element patent eligible, as structural difference is a must.

From the perspective of Section 3(d), while objections under Section 3(d) should ideally be restricted to chemistry-based inventions, examiners do tend to levy this section to biological inventions as well. Non-applicability of Section 3(d) to such inventions must be argued. For example, biological or chemical modification to an insulin polypeptide to arrive at a different polypeptide, cannot be equated with a structural modification in a chemical substance to arrive at its derivative. This is supported by the *Novartis*[10] judgment, where the Supreme Court of India clarified that the evolution of Section 3(d) clearly suggests its applicability for chemical substances and pharmaceutical products.

Even then, if the examiner is adamant, comparison of efficacy of the previously known substance with the invented molecule to show improved results (in the purpose recognised to be fulfilled by the known substance) would be helpful.

From the perspective of Section 3(j), claim language must specify that the cell is a prokaryotic cell, as mere use of the term 'recombinant host cell' will be considered patent ineligible under Section 3(j) for contemplating cells of higher organisms. Similarly, a claim on a transgenic organism (except microorganism) will not be allowed under this section.

(b) Composition, formulation, kit or extract claims

Subject matter claimed:	**Common Section 3 objection(s) and reasoning:**
• compositions, formulations, kits or extracts	Section 3(e) – for ensuring that a claim is not directed to additive effect of the constituting components and displays a synergistic effect Note: If a claim has elements that attract other clauses of Section 3, such as use of stem cells or all components being naturally occurring or recombinant cells or traditionally known, objections under other sections may be additionally raised

An example of an allowable claim is:

- A composition or formulation or kit or extract comprising specific components.

Practice tip: from the perspective of Section 3(e), a synergistic relationship between the components must be demonstrated. Comparing the effect of the

10 Supreme Court of India Civil Appeal No 2706-2716 of 2013 *Novartis AG v Union of India*, [103].

individual components and the effect of the combination to show a surprising or synergistic effect over an expected or additive effect by the components would be helpful.

Where demonstrating synergy between the constituting components is difficult, one could also consider establishing the importance of other parameters, such as concentrations, amounts, ratios, pH, temperature and other conditions, to establish how they play a role, in the context of synergy. For example, one can show how two components provide the desired results only when mixed at specific concentrations or ratios, and not otherwise. Such data points can help in overcoming objections under this section.

However, Section 3(e) is applicable only when the components of the composition are all known or in the prior art.[11] The section will not be applicable if at least one component in the composition is novel. Non-applicability of Section 3(e) can be argued accordingly, as also confirmed by the *Stempeutics*[12] decision of the Intellectual Property Appellate Board (IPAB), where it was held that a product or composition comprising a novel ingredient cannot fall under the ambit of Section 3(e).

From the perspective of Section 3(c) and 3(j), it is also important to keep in mind that a composition where all the constituting ingredients are naturally occuring together in nature would not be allowed under Section 3(c) of the Act. Further, the composition must not have a eukaryotic cell as its main component along with one or more routine ingredients such as pharmaceutically acceptable carriers, as this would bring the claim under the purview of Section 3(j) of the Act.

---

11 Office of the CGPDTM, "Guidelines for Examination of Biotechnology Applications for Patent", March 2013 (p13).

12 Intellectual Property Appellate Board OA/03/2017/PT/CHN *Stempeutics Research Pvt Ltd v The Assistant Controller of Patent & Designs* [17].

(c) Manufacturing or bio-processing claims

Subject matter claimed:	Common Section 3 objection(s) and reasoning:
• methods or processes for obtaining or producing or processing or employing a biological product	Section 3(b) – for ensuring that a claimed method or process does not involve any step that would be contrary to public order or morality or causes prejudice to life forms Section 3(d) – for ensuring that a claimed method or process does not employ a previously known set of steps without any new reactant to arrive at the same product Section 3(h) – for ensuring that a claimed method or process is not directed to a conventional agricultural or horticultural practice

An example of an allowable claim is:

- a method of isolating a micro-organism from culture medium or a fermentation process for preparation of alcohol or method of introducing or detecting mutation in an organism or a cell or biological sample or method for preparing or processing or employing any of the abovementioned products.

Practice tip: from the perspective of Section 3(b), that section can be raised against claims which use stem cells or lead to harmful effects on the atmosphere, for example, a process for preparing seeds that might cause adverse environmental impact or a process for isolating embryonic stem cells from an embryo that causes destruction of the embryo as such. For stem cell related inventions, defining the source of the stem cells in the specification to confirm that the invention does not destroy any embryos or life forms would be helpful. This is equally applicable for product and process claims that employ or comprise stem cells.

From the perspective of Section 3(d), at least one step of the claimed method or process or the product formed must be novel, to take the claim outside the purview of Section 3(d).

From the perspective of Section 3(h), that section can be raised against claims which relate to any method in the field of agriculture or horticulture, for example, a method of growing leguminous plants as inter-cropping for improving fertility of soil by augmenting nitrogen content of the soil. Showing that the claimed method is not a standard or traditional method which would be carried out by a farmer or agriculturist and rather employs an unconventional, unique and non-obvious step would be helpful.

(d) Medical, therapeutic or diagnostic use claims

Subject matter claimed:	**Common Section 3 objection(s) and reasoning:**
• method – medical or therapautic or diagnostic use/application • medicinal methods • surgical methods • curative methods • prophylactic methods • diagnostic methods • therapeutic methods	Section 3(i) – for ensuring that a claim is not directed to subject matter that requires intervention or supervision of a medical expert

No claims are allowed: no claims directed to therapeutic use or method of treatment are allowed in India regardless of the format they are in. Thus, converting a claim to Swiss format, purpose limited product claim format or any other format does not make any difference from the Indian perspective.

Claims that are passive in their action, such as a method of preventing a disease or passive immunisation by adminsitration of a vaccine are also not allowed. Further, claims directed to a specific dosage or treatment regimen or population-specific administration are also barred from patentability in India.

Practice tip: mechanism of action – while the Indian Patent Office does not allow medical use or method of treatment claims in any form or shape, one can try to modify the claims to reflect the underlying mechanism of action, without referring to the final disease outcome. For example, a method of treating a disease A by administering a compound X may be redirected to a method of inhibiting Y by contacting it with compound X (where Y is an underlying biomolecular target that causes the disease A). Having said that, in most cases, the Indian Patent Office is still likely to reject such a claim as the examiners usually recognise it to be a disguised form of the original method or use claim. This strategy is therefore recommended for matters of strategic importance.

***In vitro* use:** for claims directed to identification of biomolecules or biomarkers or diagnosis of a disease, while the Indian Patent Office is fairly stringent on these as well, increasingly it is becoming accepting of claims to methods that are performed outside the human body, and a limitation to that effect proves helpful. For example, a method of detecting or diagnosing a disease A by measuring biomarker expression or levels of certain biomolecules or chemicals comprising certain steps, may be redirected to an *in vitro* method of measuring biomarker expression or biomolecule or chemical level in a biological sample comprising the steps modified to suit said *in vitro* conditions.

Cosmetic treatment: methods that are purely cosmetic and do not require intervention or supervision of a medical expert are allowed by the Indian Patent Office.

(e) ***General application or industry specific use claims***

Subject matter claimed:	**Common Section 3 objection(s) and reasoning:**
• industrial or agriculturaluse/application • new use/application of existing compounds, molecules or organisms	2(1)(j) and Section 3(d) – while use or application claims are not considered as inventions as per Section 2(1)(j), Section 3(d) also further prevents patenting of new property or new use of a known substance

No claims are allowed: no claims directed to use or application of a product are allowed in India, regardless of whether the product is previously known in the prior art, or the subject matter of the invention in question. Because the grant of a product claim confers rights against any use or application of the product by an infringer, separate use or application claims are not allowed in India.

Practice tip: method claims – it may be possible to redirect a typical use claim to project it as a method claim as some examiners at the Indian Patent Office find that acceptable. For example, use of a composition for reducing or enhancing activity of a substance can be redirected to a method for reducing or enhancing activity of a substance, said method comprising employing or contacting the composition with the substance.

3.4 Patent eligibility for inventions belonging to pharmaceutical, chemical, material and metallurgical arts

While pharmaceuticals, chemistry, material sciences and metallurgy (PCMM) are distinct technical disciplines, the types of claims most often seen in these domains overlap significantly. Consequently, the scrutiny of claims with respect to patent eligibility is also similar between these fields.

Out of the 15 clauses of Section 3, the most important ones for inventions belonging to these arts are set out in Table 4. Appropriate reasoning on their applicability as well as some handy practice pointers are provided to help navigate through them.

Table 4. Exclusions related to PCMM arts

Relevant clause of Section 3:	Prohibited subject matter is directed to:
Section 3(c)	naturally occurring compounds or agents
Section 3(d)	new form of a known substance or mere discovery of any new property or new use or mere use of a known process
Section 3(e)	compositions without synergy between their components
Section 3(i)	medical use, intervention or supervision

As has been done for other arts, a breakup of how these clauses apply to various subject matter and claim types, along with relevant examples of allowable claims in each category is provided in this section.

(a) New products, compounds or molecules

Subject matter claimed:

- chemical entities
  - chemical compounds (specific or Markush structure)
  - derivatives
  - pure form of compounds
  - metallic compounds
  - polymers

Common Section 3 objection(s) and reasoning:

Section 3(c) – for ensuring that a claim is not directed to naturally occurring compounds

Section 3(d) – for checking if any modification to a molecule/entity creates a derivative or new form of the corresponding parent compound

Example of an allowable claim: a compound or a specific chemical form or a derivative or an analogue or a polymer defined by specific formula or structure X, where the compound represents a specific compound or a generic class of compounds through a Markush structure, or an elemental metallic powder having metal content of at least about X%.

Practice tip: from the perspective of Section 3(c), the compound must be a synthetic compound or structurally different from a naturally occuring counterpart. Human intervention must be demonstrated. A mere use of the term 'isolated' does not make the compound patent eligible, as structural difference is a must.

From the perspective of Section 3(d), the compound must be a new chemical entity and not a mere derivative or new form of a known compound. Section 3(d) defines salts, esters, ethers, polymorphs, metabolites, pure form, particle size, isomers, mixtures of isomers, complexes and combinations as new forms, which are derived after appropriate modifications to a known parent compound. It must therefore be shown that the claimed compound is not a result of a minor modification aimed at an incremental innovation to achieve the same or similar end result.

It is essential to remember that, often, an objection under Section 3(d) is also levied for new chemical entities which are not derived from an existing compound. In such cases non-applicability of Section 3(d) must be argued by showing that the invented compound is not a derivative of any known parent compound.

However, in cases where the invention does relate to a new form, unless disclosed by the specification of the invention, the onus of identifying such a known parent compound with respect to the invented new form lies on the examiner at the Indian Patent Office. Thereafter, the applicant can rebut on:

- how the choice of the examiner is flawed, and a different compound needs to be considered as the closest or known parent compound; and
- how the new form possesses better efficacy when compared to said closest or known parent compound, identified by the examiner or shown by the applicant.

This efficacy must be considered with respect to the purpose for which the known parent compound was used. Thus, the known parent compound must also possess an efficacy of its own (known efficacy), against which the efficacy of the new form must be compared. In case of a medicinal product, this efficacy is 'therapeutic efficacy', ie, a direct correlation must be shown between the new form and its ability to cure a disease condition better. It must be emphasised here that for a new form capable of 'therapeutic' effect, regardless of the improvement in properties, such as solubility, bioavailability, etc, an explicit relationship with respect to the disease outcome is critical and must be established by research data.[13]

For non-therapeutic or industrial compounds, the test of efficacy depends on the purpose for which the known parent compound was used. This position of law was also confirmed by the *Novartis*[14] decision, where the Supreme Court of India clarified that the test of efficacy would depend upon the result the product under consideration is desired or intended to produce. In other words, the test of efficacy would depend upon the function, utility or the purpose of the product under consideration.

(b) Composition, formulation, kit or extract claims

Subject matter claimed:	**Common Section 3 objection(s) and reasoning:**
• compositions, formulations, composites, alloys, reagents, kits or extracts	Section 3(e) – for ensuring that a claim is not directed to additive effect of the constituting components and displays a synergistic effect Note: If a claim has elements which attract other clauses of Section 3, such as use of components which are all naturally occurring, objections under other Sections may be additionally raised

Example of an allowable claim: a composition or formulation or composite or alloy or reagent or kit or extract comprising specific components.

Practice tip: from the perspective of Section 3(e), a synergistic relationship between the components must be demonstrated. Comparing the effect of the individual components and the effect of the combination to show a surprising or synergistic effect over an expected or additive effect by the components would be helpful.

Formulations: in pharmaceuticals, arriving at a formulation of a chemical compound with routine or conventional excipients or additives is fairly

13 *Supra*, note 2, [189].
14 *Supra*, note 2, [180].

common. It would again be required to demonstrate how bringing these components together results in a synergistic effect. One way of doing so would be to show how one or more of the specific excipients or additives is critical for arriving at a particular dosage form, without which the chemical compound itself cannot be utilised or administered or be industrially applicable.

Where demonstrating synergy between the constituting components is difficult, one could also consider establishing the importance of other parameters, such as concentrations, amounts, ratios, pH, temperature and other conditions, to establish how they play a role, in the context of synergy. For example, one can show how two components provide the desired results only when mixed at specific concentrations or ratios, and not otherwise. Such data points can help in overcoming objections under this section.

Further, combination inventions which bring together two independently functioning drugs or chemicals will not be allowed, for example, combination of an antidiabetic drug and an anticholesterolemic drug. Since the therapeutic effect of such a combination is likely to come from an overlap in the peak of their activities upon administration, it will fall under the methods defined by Section 3(i), and hence will not be allowed.

Importantly, Section 3(e) is applicable only when the components of the composition are all known or in the prior art.[15] The section will not be applicable if at least one component in the composition is novel. Non-applicability of the Section 3(e) can be argued accordingly, as also confirmed by the *Stempeutics*[16] decision of the Intellectual Property Appellate Board (IPAB), where it was held that a product or composition comprising a novel ingredient cannot fall under the ambit of Section 3(e).

From the perspective of Section 3(c), a composition where all the constituting ingredients are naturally occuring together in nature would not be allowed under Section 3(c) of the Act.

15 *Supra*, note 3.
16 *Supra*, note 4.

(c) Synthesis, preparation, production or processing claims

Subject matter claimed:	Common Section 3 objection(s) and reasoning:
• methods or processes for chemical synthesis or production of chemical compounds or compositions, or processing of a pharmaceutical, chemical or polymeric product	Section 3(d) – for ensuring that a claimed method or process does not employ a previously known set of steps without any new reactant to arrive at the same product

Example of an allowable claim: a method of preparing or synthesising or processing chemical compounds, nanoparticles, compounds of specific formula or features, compositions or formulations, or metal alloys.

Practice tip: from the perspective of Section 3(d), at least one step of the claimed method or process or the product formed must be novel, to take the claim outside the purview of Section 3(d).

(d) Medical, therapeutic or diagnostic use claims

Subject matter claimed:	Common Section 3 objection(s) and reasoning:
• method – medical or therapautic or diagnostic use/application ◦ medicinal methods ◦ surgical methods ◦ curative methods ◦ prophylactic methods ◦ diagnostic methods ◦ therapeutic methods	Section 3(i) – for ensuring that a claim is not directed to subject matter that requires intervention or supervision of a medical expert

No claims are allowed: please see the corresponding advice on such claims as provided for biological arts in the previous section.

(e) General application or industry specific use claims

Subject matter claimed:	Common Section 3 objection(s) and reasoning:
• industrial use/application • new use/application of existing chemical substances, compounds and formulations	2(1)(j) and Section 3(d) – While use or application claims are not considered as inventions as per the Section 2(1)(j), Section 3(d) also further prevents patenting of new property or new use of a known substance

No claims are allowed: please see the corresponding advice on such claims as provided for biological arts in the previous section.

In conclusion, while the examiners at the Indian Patent Office usually levy a Section 3 objection in almost all patent applications, the legitimacy of such an objection must be assessed by the applicant on a case-to-case basis. In a lot of cases, one can successfully argue non-applicability of the respective Section 3 objection as the first line of argument. For example, when a composition claim comprises at least one novel component, applicability of Section 3(e) can be argued. When a product is not a derivative of a known substance or when the examiner fails to identify a corresponding known parent compound, applicability of Section 3(d) can be argued. Similarly, when a claim relates to a pesticide rather than a method of agriculture, validity of an objection under Section 3(h) can be challenged, as would also be a case to rebut a Section 3(j) related objection when a claim relates to processing of the cell in a method claim rather than the cell itself. However, where the objection seems reasonable, relevant data or arguments must be highlighted as mentioned above, for overcoming the objection and establishing patent eligibility of a claim.

Objections under section 3(f) may be dealt with by highlighting that the elements of the claim are interacting in function and operation, ie, the elements of the claim exhibit constructional interaction and functional inter-relationship. Like in biological arts, the examiners in electrical and computer arts usually levy a Section 3(k) objection in almost all patent applications. The objections under Section 3(k) are mainly triggered by the presence of mathematical equations, business related terms and software related terms in the claims/specification. To deal with the objections under Section 3(k), the most important point is to analyse the essence of the invention defined in the claim rather than the way the claim is worded. If the essence lies in technical subject matter, objections under Section 3(k) may be argued even though the claim specifies mathematical equations or business-related terms or software related terms.

3.5 New advances/emerging technologies

Biological sciences, chemical businesses and pharmaceutical industries are slated to see exponential innovation in the next few years. From a healthcare perspective, personalised medicine, genetic tests for predisposition to diseases, cell and gene therapy for medicinal and cosmetic purposes, and gene editing and designing of effective expression systems for better control over production of therapeutic products such as antibodies and vaccines are going to be of prime importance. Improvements in crop survival and productivity along with nutrition quotient will continue to drive developments in the agriculture sector, whereas the need for curbing pollution and finding eco-friendly alternatives to existing chemicals will keep the chemists busy. Similarly, the electronics sector is also poised to see a multi-fold rise in patent applications in the emerging technologies such as artificial intelligence, machine learning, deep learning, artificial neural networks, virtual reality, augmented reality, autonomous vehicles, etc. In light of these emerging technologies, challenges with respect to patent-eligible subject matter in India are likely to increase. While one does not anticipate any significant change in law in the near future, there seems to be a constant endeavour to improve understanding of the technologies and their nuances by the examiners at the Indian Patent Office, which will help them examine the applications better. This is likely to continue and a culture of education and persistent effort driven by the patent offices collectively across the world can ensure that ultimately it's the ecosystem which benefits, by granting patents which are worthy of their salt, and rejecting those that are spurious. An important contribution in this exercise must also come from the government and the scientific community to ensure that they keep the patent offices updated from time to time about newer technologies and ensure that the patent specifications are written in a manner which complements that effort. With the current understanding of the patent-ineligible subject matter in India being fairly mature, it is now possible for patent specifications to be written keeping in mind the potential questions and challenges which are expected during prosecution, and hence ensuring that some of the issues are resolved at the drafting stage itself.

4. Inventions relating to atomic energy not patentable (Section 4)

In addition to Section 3, any invention which relates to atomic energy is also considered patent ineligible in India. Section 4 governing such inventions is recited as follows:

> *No patent shall be granted in respect of an invention relating to atomic energy falling within sub-Section (1) of Section 20 of the Atomic Energy Act, 1962 (33 of 1962).*

As can be seen, Section 4 in turn makes a reference to Section 20 of the Atomic Energy Act, which states that no patents shall be granted for inventions which in the opinion of the Central Government are useful for or relate to the production, control, use or disposal of atomic energy or the prospecting, mining, extraction, production, physical and chemical treatment, fabrication, enrichment, canning or use of any prescribed substance or radioactive substance or the ensuring of safety in atomic energy operations.

Thus, if the examiner at the Indian Patent Office believes that an invention relates to atomic energy, he/she is likely to refer the application to the Central Government for direction as to whether the invention is one within the purview of the Atomic Energy Act. Once referred, the patent application would proceed based on the decision of the Central Government, which could either be to allow the patent application to go through, or to reject the application for falling under Section 20 of the Atomic Energy Act.

Israel

Uri Fruchtman
Intellectual property lawyer
Ephraim Heiliczer
Pearl Cohen

1. Executive summary

Israeli patent law contains two forms of subject matter restrictions. Section 3 of the Patent Law limits patent-eligible subject matter to "an invention, whether a product or process, in any field of technology, which is novel and useful, can have an industrial application, and involves an inventive step".[1] For the purpose of subject matter eligibility, the significant term in Section 3 is the 'any field of technology' requirement, which has been interpreted to require a tangible invention.[2] As discussed below, this requirement has a particular impact on computer patent applications (eg, algorithms and software).

Section 7(1) of the Patent Law excludes methods of treatment of the human body from patentability. This is of particular importance in pharmaceutical patent applications. The EPC 2000 claim formulation ('composition for use' format) is effective in overcoming most method of treatment rejections in Israel. However, there is no means for patenting methods, such as surgery (except for certain types of cosmetic surgery), under Israeli law. Finally, Section 7(2) of the Patent Law excludes plant and animal varieties, except for microbiological organisms not produced naturally. This exception will be discussed in relation to biological patents.

Final rejections[3] for lack of subject matter eligibility are minimal for computer patents rejected under Section 3 and plant and animal varieties under Section 7(2). Rejections of pharmaceutical and medical patents under Section 7(1) are more common; however, the vast majority of applicants are able to overcome initial rejections by amending the claims to the appropriate format under Israeli Practice.

---

1 Patent Law 1967, Section 3.

2 The term 'industrial application' is considered synonymous with the technological field and utility requirements. Since this term is redundant, the Israeli Patent Office recently asked for public comments on whether the term 'industrial application' should be deleted from the law (Public Comment Request, November 2020, Section 8). Utility, another element of Section 3, is beyond the scope of this review.

3 The term final rejection as used in this article means a rejection in the last office action prior to an application's withdrawal or the issuance of a notice of refusal by the Israeli Patent Office.

2. Computer patents

Computer patent applications are often rejected under Section 3 of the law as not being part of a 'field of technology'. The Israeli courts have interpreted the 'field of technology' requirement to require a tangible technological process.[4] Tangibility requires "an expression of physical properties on something on which the invention is operated or on the manner of the product's or process's operation".[5] This rule effectively excludes all abstract ideas and non-technical processes from patentability even if these processes are conducted using a computer.[6] These ideas, excluded from the Israeli patent system, can be protected under copyright law.[7]

Israeli practice has tempered the tangibility rule to allow for the patenting of inventions that include abstract ideas or non-technical processes if combined in a computerised process that provides tangibility to the invention. The tangibility rule evaluates the invention as a whole without deconstructing the invention into different components. The second part of the rule then evaluates the invention's quantifiable contribution to the art in comparison to the state of the art. This contribution to the art can be a subjective contribution to the art over the background information presented by the applicant in the specification, and an objective contribution (eg, inventive step analysis) is not required.[8]

Applications that involve physical expressions, beyond the mere use of a computer or that equip the computer with new capabilities (eg, improved speed, accuracy, storage), are usually considered inventive. In this regard, claims directed to data carriers are allowable if they are included in claims directed to a patentable invention (ie, the claim without the data carrier element is inventive). Also, automatisation can be inventive if the automatised process is substantially different from the manual process.[9] However, only when the computer program is an integral and required part of the physical computer system is the invention patent eligible. In short, the core invention must be the physical computer system.[10]

A more stringent interpretation of tangibility taken in some cases by the patent office emphasises that merely using a computer to undertake a process

---

4 CA (Jerusalem District) 23/94 *United Technologies v Patent Authority.*

5 Israeli Patent Examiner's Guidelines, Appendix B (10 February 2020), p5.

6 See Patent Application 131733, decision dated 21 September 2006. This rule also makes business methods unpatentable in Israel.

7 See Patent Application 142049, decision dated 28 December 2005.

8 See Patent Application 171773, decision dated 10 December 2012; Israeli Patent Examiner's Guidelines Appendix B (10 February 2020), p5. In IL 171773 the Patent Commissioner found that an apparatus for generating social assignments for a plurality of subscribers using databases did not offer an inventive contribution over the prior art described in the application. Conversely, the Patent Commissioner found that a contribution that involved an improved process of selecting files and mixing their sound (audio mixing) was an inventive contribution over the prior art described in the application and subject matter eligible (see Patent Application 190125, decision dated 17 February 2014).

9 Israeli Patent Examiner's Guidelines Appendix B (10 February 2020), p5.

10 See Patent Application 131733, decision dated 21 September 2006. This rule also makes business methods unpatentable in Israel.

does not make an invention patentable. Rather, the invention must have an inventive quality that is not solely derived from the computerisation of the process.[11] Using this interpretation, a method of internet searching and presentation of results in which the process for obtaining and presenting the results was not indicated in the specification was found not to fall within a patent-eligible technological field.[12]

The Patent Office has also emphasised that merely automating work previously done manually does not render an invention patentable. In this regard, a toll collection system using a card reader and a transmitter that computerised a previously manual activity was not patentable. This ruling specifically refused to grant an Israeli patent,[13] despite the applicant's petition for allowance based on a corresponding granted US patent.[14] Similarly, the Patent Commissioner ruled that a 'hybrid invention', involving the use of computers to bill cars for parking, was not patentable, since the core of the invention was considered a business method and not within a technological field.[15] However, computerisation of an activity previously undertaken manually that in practice is substantively different from the manual activity, and thereby makes the manual activity impractical, is evidence of subject matter eligibility.[16]

However, a system for facilitating access to multiple audio layer items, accessed using a communication network with a subscriber application that allows for user selections and has a mixing module for creating a remix digital audio signal, was found patentable. According to the Patent Commissioner, this was because the invention is not merely an abstract application of a thought process or a business method, but rather involved the linkage of different technological components and each component providing a definite action. Thus, the invention was found to be a tangible technology and was not merely automation of a manual function.[17]

Finally, the Israel Patent Commissioner has emphasised that, unlike Article 52 of the EPC, there are no strict categories under Israeli law for determining whether an invention is within a technological field.[18] Therefore, the Israeli

---

11 See Opposition to Patent Applications 126864 and 125755, decision dated 16 April 2009.

12 See Patent Application 142049, decision dated 28 December 2005.

13 See Patent Application 179203, decision dated 21 May 2013. Claim 1 in this application claimed, "a method of collecting tolls on a high occupancy toll lane comprising:
Detecting a count of driver's licenses inserted into a card reader located in a vehicle using the high occupancy toll lane; and transmitting the count of driver's licenses to a roadside transceiver for a determination of a toll amount for the vehicle based on the count of driver's licenses".

14 Under Section 17c of the Patent Law, an applicant can petition for immediate allowance based on a foreign patent granted in one of several jurisdictions (eg, EPO, US). Cases examined in this manner usually do not undergo substantive examination for novelty, inventiveness, unity and support. However, cases allowed under Section 17c are examined for subject matter eligibility (Sections 3 and 7 of the law).

15 See Revocation Proceedings for Patent Application 118898, decision dated 19 August 2008.

16 Israeli Patent Examiner's Guidelines, Appendix B (10 February 2020), p6.

17 See Patent Application 190125, decision dated 17 February 2014.

18 See Patent Application 171773, decision dated 10 December 2012. In this case the Patent Commissioner compared Israel, US and EP law on the subject.

Patent Guidelines[19] provide several examples of computer related patent applications that either comply or run afoul of its subject matter tangibility rule. The following examples were found to comply with the tangibility rule:

- a computer trace unit attached to a processor that was capable of altering a compilation based on the trace signals, thereby improving the computer's activity;
- an index that allowed for accurate use of the functional (DLL) library in a computer by multiple programs, thereby improving the function and activity of the computer;
- simultaneous data gathering, monitoring, and analysis of multiple patients' conditions was considered unique and complex and, therefore, complied with the tangibility rule;
- methods of classifying images or processing data that can only be done on a computer;
- a machine learning method for identifying objects; and
- use of a neural network in a manner impractical without use of a computer.

Conversely, the following examples were found not to comply with the tangibility rule, and considered ineligible subject matter:

- a method of optimising the display of content was considered mere automatisation of the graphic design process, which did not involve any additional contribution beyond creating a computer program;[20]
- methods of computer data processing, including the use of algorithms that do not require use of a computer; and
- use of artificial intelligence in a manner not unique from human intelligence.

The Israeli patent office issued initial Section 3 rejections in about 3% of cases in 2020. Over the last three years, there has been a progressive increase in rejections from 1.25% in 2018 to 2.01% in 2019, and 3.12% in 2020. However, the amount of Section 3 rejections in subsequent office actions was three to four times lower than those issued in the initial examination.[21] These figures indicate that at the present time, Section 3 rejections for computer patents are not widespread in Israel.

---

19 Israeli Patent Examiner's Guidelines, Appendix B (10 February 2020).

20 However, methods relating to more than the mere display of information, but also the combination of information from multiple storage units with unique displays for each storage unit, with recording capabilities, were found to be a tangible technological process.

21 Based on figures provided by the Israeli Patent Office in January 2021. The initial figures exclude life sciences applications, figures including life sciences applications were 0.85% in 2018, 1.2% in 2019, and 1.9% in 2020. The figures for subsequent Section 3 rejections were 0.37% in 2018 and 2019, and 0.70% in 2020.

3. Pharmaceutical and medical patents

Section 7(1) of the Patent Law excludes methods of treatment of the human body from patentability.[22] The statutory exclusion of methods of treatment of the human body is based on the determination that a monopoly (ie, a patent) related to the human body is immoral. In this regard, Israeli patent law is aligned with European patent law.[23]

Subject matter ineligible methods of treatment of the human body include those directed to treatment, prophylactic treatment, repair, relief (eg, pain relief), alleviation, or prevention of worsening of either mental or physical symptoms, functional impairments, addictions, or deficiencies.[24] Further, claims relating to the use of a medical device for the treatment of the human body are also subject matter ineligible.[25]

Despite the general prohibition on method of treatment claims, EPC 2000 style claims are allowable under Israeli practice. Thus, claims formulated as 'Product X for use in treatment of Y' or 'Compound X for use as a medicament' are patentable.[26] However, under present Israeli practice, use claims are considered to be impermissible treatments of the human body.[27]

Claims directed to treatment regimens are allowable under Israeli law. This is because treatment regimens are considered guidelines for manufacturers as opposed to guidelines directed to treating physicians.[28] Further, functional claims directed to serum levels of a sustained release formulation are patentable and are not considered treatment of the human body.[29] Additionally, claims directed to combinations of two active pharmaceutical drugs have also been found to be subject matter eligible.[30]

---

22 Significantly, this section also prevents filing for allowance based on a granted foreign patent that contains method of treatment claims. Method of treatment claims must be removed before filing for allowance on the basis of such a foreign patent (eg, US).

23 CA 244/72 *Plantex Ltd v Wellcome Foundation*; CA 5768/94 *Ashir Import Export and Distribution v Device and Consumption Forum*. Methods of treatment *per se* can, however, still be protected as trade secrets.

24 Israeli Patent Examiner's Guidelines Appendix C (10 February 2020), pp1–2, 6–7. Addiction treatment is considered a medical treatment since treatment is undertaken under the guidance of medical professionals. Prevention of sexually transmitted diseases is considered unpatentable prophylactic treatment. However, treatment to prevent pregnancy is not a treatment of the human body since pregnancy is not considered a disease. Treatments for obesity (eg, appetite suppression) are allowable if restricted to cosmetic uses (see below regarding the cosmetic method of treatment exception).

25 Israeli Patent Examiner's Guidelines Appendix C (10 February 2020), pp2–4, 7. In this regard, claims directed to use of a medical device to remove foreign objects from blood are not patentable. Claims to processes that impact the activity of implants in the body are also unpatentable. However, claims directed to assembly of a modular implant outside the human body prior to implantation are patentable (see below regarding *in vitro* methods of treatment).

26 Israeli Patent Circular 034/2017, Section 11; Israeli Patent Examiner's Guidelines Appendix C (10 February 2020), pp5–6. For example, "an implantable material ... for use in a method of treating [a specified disease or impairment] in a patent comprising ..." is patentable under Israeli practice.

27 Israeli Patent Examiner's Guidelines Appendix C (10 February 2020), p6. Claims formulated as 'Use of X in the treatment of disease Y', 'Use of X in the manufacture/preparation of Y', or 'Use of substance X in the manufacture of a medicament to treat Y, the treatment comprising ...' are all not patentable under present Israeli practice.

28 See Patent Application 153109 decision dated 5 August 2010. Accordingly, this interpretation prevents generic manufacturers from marketing their pharmaceuticals with the claimed dosage instructions.

29 See Patent Application 136294 decision dated 30 September 2014.

30 See Patent Application 210616 decision dated 15 March 2020; also see Patent Application 178141 decision dated 4 January 2017.

Non-human methods of treatment are allowable under Section 7(1). However, Israeli practice requires that claims directed to treating an animal or *in vitro* methods of treatment expressly indicate that human treatment is excluded. Thus, claims directed generally to subjects or animals are often rejected, and applicants must amend the claims to explicitly state that they are directed to 'non-human animals' or '*in vitro* methods'.[31] In addition, processes generally undertaken outside the human body, even including activities such as isolating antibodies from a human subject, are subject matter eligible.[32]

Despite not allowing method of treatment claims *per se*, Israeli patent practice does allow claims directed to diagnostic and cosmetic methods. For example, a claim directed to a method of cosmetic breast surgery that involves inserting a skeleton into a breast to improve 'breast projection' is subject matter eligible under Section 7(1) of the law. Other types of cosmetic treatments, such as skin strengthening techniques, are also patentable. Significantly, only cosmetic surgeries are subject matter eligible, and corrective surgeries, such as corrective breast surgery after mastectomy are ineligible. However, if treatments similar to the breast surgery mentioned above are utilised for some patients in need of cosmetic treatment and other patients in need of restorative treatment, the treatment is patentable if the claim is expressly limited to cosmetic treatment.[33]

The subject matter eligibility of mixed claims, for example claims that relate to both methods of treatment *per se* (eg, non-cosmetic surgery) and diagnostic methods or cosmetic treatment, is determined based on the object of the method and its substantive nature. The determination is made by interpreting the claims in view of the specification, and if the specification does not offer a basis for considering the treatment to be a method of human treatment, the claim is considered subject matter eligible. For example, a method of measuring treatment efficacy that involves administering the treatment and evaluating the response necessarily involves medical treatment and is impermissible. Similarly, claims directed to cosmetic treatment, such as teeth whitening using an antibiotic, are impermissible, since again the treatment is necessarily medical in nature. In contrast, a claim that is directed to an imaging method (eg, CAT/PET Scan), that requires administration of certain compounds (eg, radiopharmaceuticals) to improve or allow for imaging, is allowable.[34] Further,

---

31 Israeli Patent Examiner's Guidelines Appendix C (10 February 2020), pp2–3. Israeli practice usually requires these types of disclaimers to be at the beginning of a claim (eg, "An *in vitro* method ..."). Unsupported disclaimers are rejected for lack of sufficiency under Section 13 of the law.

32 Israeli Patent Examiner's Guidelines Appendix C (10 February 2020), pp2–3, 7. Patentable claims of this nature cannot include the specific claim formulations directed to methods of treatment or methods of administration. However, terms such as immunising are allowable in such claims. For example, claims directed to *in vitro*, but not *in vivo*, human fertility methods are allowable.

33 Israeli Patent Examiner's Guidelines Appendix C (10 February 2020), pp2–5.

34 Israeli Patent Examiner's Guidelines Appendix C (10 February 2020), pp2–4.

the same standard is also used to evaluate the patentability of mixed claims directed to the treatment of the human body using computerised methods.[35]

The Israeli patent office issued initial Section 7(1) rejections in about 11% of cases in 2020. Over the last three years there has been a progressive decrease in rejections from 13.4% in 2018 to 11.7% in 2019, and 10.9% in 2020. The number of applications abandoned due to initial Section 7(1) rejections was 25% of the initially rejected applications in 2018. The amount of Section 7(1) rejections in subsequent office actions decreases significantly to under 1%.[36]

The reason for the high comparative rate of Section 7(1) rejections is that applications are often entered into the Israeli National Phase with US style method of treatment claims. Following the initial office action, applicants amend the claims to conform with Israel practice (ie, EPC 2000 style claims). The reason for the recent reduction in initial Section 7(1) rejections appears to be due to more applicants streamlining prosecution by amending the claims at filing or in response to notices before examination.

4. Biological (plant and animal varieties) patents

Section 7(2) of the Patent Law excludes plant and animal varieties, except for microbiological organisms not produced naturally. Natural plant and animal varieties are eligible for plant variety protection, and, therefore, their exclusion from patentability prevents a situation of dual IP right protection. Significantly, Section 7(2) only relates to plants and animals, and does not relate to the subject matter eligibility of other organisms. Thus, the patentability of bacteria, fungi, viruses and other similar organisms is not restricted under Section 7(2) of the Patent Law.[37]

Israeli patent law does not prevent the use of *per se* product terms (eg, plant, seed, transgenic animal) in claims directed to subject matter eligible as microbiological plant or animal organisms. Further, claims directed to processes related to plants and animals are also subject matter eligible under Section 7(2).[38]

Rejections under Section 7(2) are very uncommon in Israel. Only two applications were rejected under Section 7(2) in the last three years.[39]

---

35 Israeli Patent Examiner's Guidelines Appendix C (10 February 2020), pp7–9. For example, a computer model using imaging to assist a doctor during surgery or in pre-surgery planning is patentable. This is because, although the model is directly associated with surgery, the model is only a surgery accessory. Also, there is no direct contact between the computer imaging device and the human body. Similarly, robotic assistance in gripping a surgical instrument is also patentable. In contrast, a robotic method of inserting a catheter is an impermissible method of treatment. Also, computer activation of IV drug delivery is considered treatment of the human body since it involves an activity that directly influences the medical treatment of the patient's body.

36 Based on figures provided by the Israeli Patent Office in January 2021. Figures for abandonment after initial Section 7(1) rejections declined over the last two years, to 18.6% in 2019 to 10.9% in 2020. However, this apparent reduction is somewhat misleading because it does not include cases of passive abandonment due to a lack of response for applications initially rejected in 2019 and 2020. Subsequent Section 7(1) rejections were 0.68% in 2018, 0.98% in 2019, and 0.59% in 2020.

37 Israeli Patent Examiner's Guidelines Appendix C (10 February 2020), pp11–12.

38 Israeli Patent Examiner's Guidelines Appendix C (10 February 2020), pp11–12.

39 Based on figures provided by the Israeli Patent Office in January 2021. One application was rejected in 2018 and another in 2019. Only one of the two applications was rejected a second time under Section 7(2).

5. Hot topics

The main question will be whether any changes in subject matter eligibility are on the horizon in Israel. Recently, the Israeli Patent Office asked for public comments on potential amendments to both Section 3 and Section 7. The deadline for submitting comments was March 2021.[40]

40 Public Comment Request November 2020, Sections 8, 36–42.

Japan

Tsuyoshi Miura
Masaru Nakajima
Seiwa Patent & Law

---

1. Background and summary

Under the Japanese patent system, 'eligibility' issues relate to the body of Article 29, paragraph 1 of the Patent Law,[1] which stipulates that a person who has made an industrially applicable invention is entitled to obtain a patent for that invention. This article prescribes that a patentable invention must comply with two requirements, ie:

- eligibility as a statutory 'invention' (or 'subject matter eligibility'); and
- industrial applicability.

The sections that follow will outline the criteria for judging the subject matter eligibility requirement and the industrial applicability requirement on the basis of the Examination Guidelines for Patent and Utility Model in Japan[2] and the Examination Handbook for Patent and Utility Model in Japan[3] (hereinafter referred to as the 'Examination Guidelines' and the 'Examination Handbook' respectively), both prepared and disclosed by the Japan Patent Office (JPO), and give an overview of the main issues involved in these requirements (Sections 2 and 3). Sections 4 and 5 will focus on two specific technical fields which require special consideration, ie, the electrical and computer fields and the chemical, pharmaceutical, and biological fields.

However, first, the general flow of judgment of subject matter eligibility and industrial applicability under Japanese examination practice are summarised in Figure 1, which also indicates the section of this article in which each topic is discussed.

---

1 "Article 29 Conditions for Patentability
(1) Any person who has made an invention which is industrially applicable may obtain a patent therefor, except in the case of: ... [omitted]."

2 www.jpo.go.jp/e/system/laws/rule/guideline/patent/tukujitu_kijun/index.html.

3 www.jpo.go.jp/e/system/laws/rule/guideline/patent/handbook_shinsa/index.html.

Figure 1. General flowchart for judging subject matter eligibility and industrial applicability under Japanese examination practice

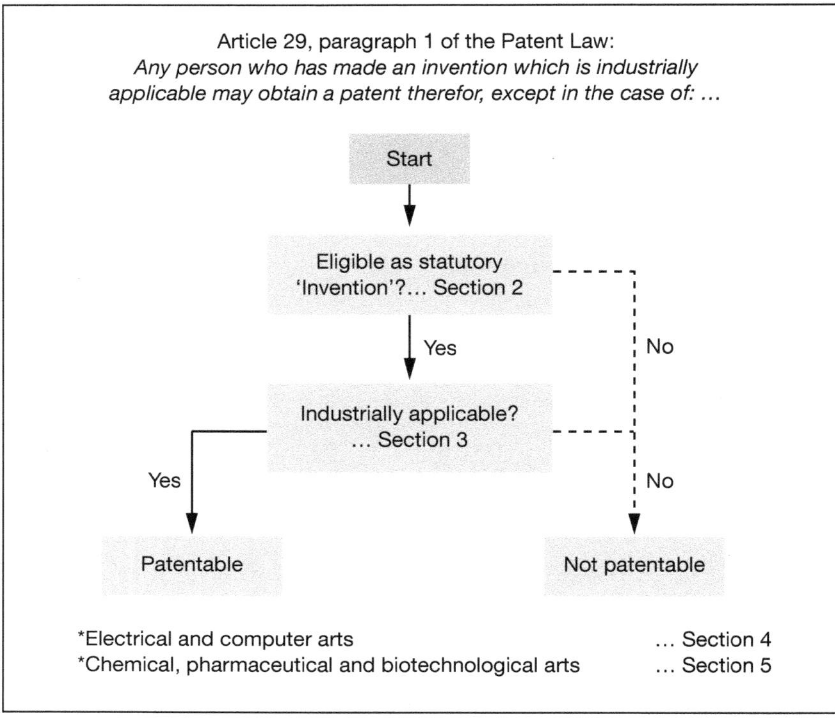

2. Subject matter eligibility

2.1 Summary

In order for an invention claimed in a patent application to be patentable, it must meet the statutory definition of an 'invention' (ie, subject matter eligibility). Judgment as to whether a claimed invention corresponds to a statutory 'invention' is made according to the procedure specified in Part III, Chapter 1, Section 2 of the Examination Guidelines: "Determination on Requirements of Eligibility for Patent."

Article 2, paragraph 1 of the Patent Law[4] defines an 'invention' as "a highly advanced creation of a technical idea utilising a law of nature". This means that in order for a claimed invention to be eligible as a statutory 'invention', the invention is required at least to:

4 "Article 2 Definitions
(1) 'Invention' in this Law means the highly advanced creation of technical ideas by which a law of nature is utilised."

- utilise a law of nature;
- be based on technical ideas; and
- involve a creation (Figure 2).

Figure 2. Flowchart for judging eligibility of a claimed invention as a statutory 'invention' (subject matter eligibility)

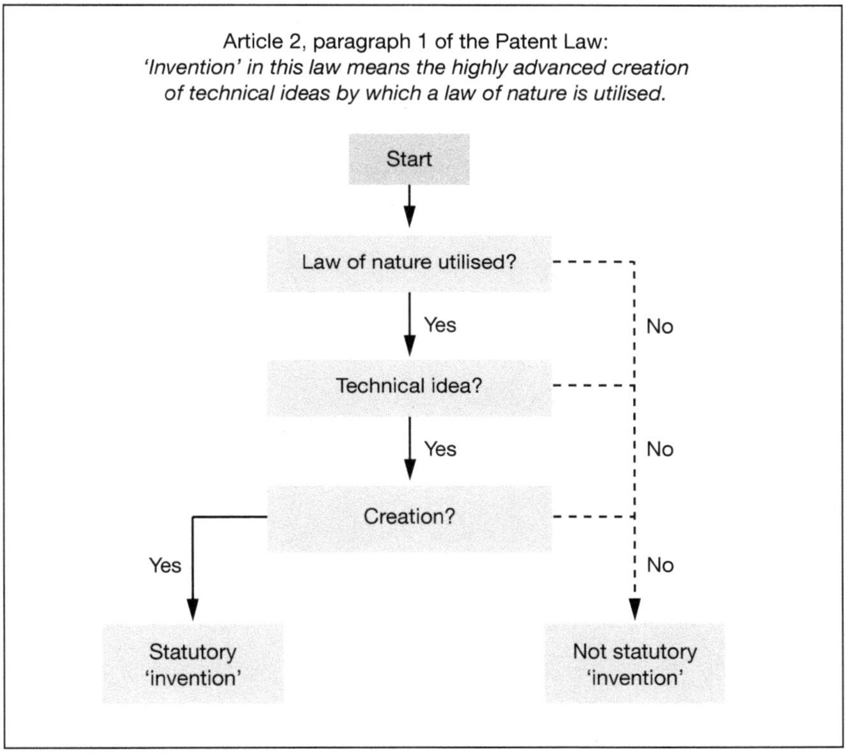

Based on this definition, the Examination Guidelines list six categories which do not meet the statutory definition of 'inventions' (see Part III, Chapter 1, Section 2.1 of the Examination Guidelines):

(i) laws of nature as such;
(ii) those which are not creations but mere discoveries;
(iii) those which are contrary to the laws of nature;
(iv) those which do not utilise a law of nature;
(v) those which are not regarded as technical ideas; and
(vi) those based on means which are alleged to solve the problem but are actually not capable of doing so.

If the claimed invention is deemed to fall under any of categories (i) to (vi) stated above, then the Examiner shall determine that the claimed invention does not meet the requirement of subject matter eligibility (see Part III, Chapter 1, Section 2 of the Examination Guidelines).

The criteria for judging the subject matter eligibility is discussed in this section, except for the criteria specifically applied to software-related inventions, which we will discuss in section 4 "Electrical and computer arts").

2.2 Utilisation of laws of nature

(a) Summary

A statutory 'invention' is required to utilise a law of nature. The utilisation of a law of nature in this context means utilisation of a law of causation underlying a natural phenomenon. According to the prevailing view, however, this requirement has very little positive meaning, and should be interpreted as merely excluding mental activities as such, pure and simple academic principles, artificial arrangements, etc, from statutory 'inventions'.[5]

(b) Laws of nature

If the claimed invention is deemed to fall under any of the following categories (i) to (v), then the claimed invention does not utilise a 'law of nature', and is therefore not a statutory 'invention' (see Part III, Chapter 1, Section 2.1.4 of the Examination Guidelines):

(i) laws other than the laws of nature (eg, economic laws);

(ii) arbitrary arrangements (eg, a rule for playing a game as such);

(iii) mathematical formula;

(iv) mental activities of humans;[6] and

(v) those utilising only any of (i) to (iv) above (eg, methods for doing business as such).

(c) Utilisation of a law of nature

If the claimed invention is a mere law of nature (such as the law of energy conservation or the law of universal gravitation), then the invention is not deemed to 'utilise' a law of nature, and therefore does not correspond to a statutory 'invention' (see Part III, Chapter 1, Section 2.1.1 of the Examination Guidelines).

Whether a claimed invention utilises a law of nature must be determined by

---

5 Nobuhiro Nakayama, *Patent Law*, 3rd ed, (Law Lectures Series, Koubundou Publishers Inc, 2019), p101.

6 See the IP High Court decision on 5 December 2012, Case 2012 (Gyo-ke) 10134, "Energy Saving Action Sheet", which ruled that even if the creation of technical ideas made for the purpose of solving a certain problem is concrete, beneficial, and useful, as long as the problem-solving process solely uses a principle or law involving mental activities, a principle or law in the field of social science, an artificial arrangement, or a mathematic formula, etc, and does not involve any laws of nature, such creation of technical ideas may not be regarded as a statutory 'invention'.

considering the claimed invention as a whole. Specifically, even if one or more of the features defining a claimed invention utilise a law of nature, the claimed invention as a whole can be deemed not to utilise a law of nature. On the other hand, even if one or more of the features defining a claimed invention does not utilise a law of nature, the claimed invention as a whole can be deemed to utilise a law of nature.[7] The characteristics of the technology to which the claimed invention belongs should be considered in determining whether the claimed invention as a whole utilises a law of nature (see Part III, Chapter 1, Section 2.1.4 of the Examination Guidelines).

If at least one of the features defining a claimed invention involves any means contrary to a law of nature (eg, a so-called 'perpetual motion' machine, which is contrary to the law of conservation of energy), then the claimed invention is not a statutory 'invention' (see Part III, Chapter 1, Section 2.1.3 of the Examination Guidelines).

(d) Technical ideas

Summary: the statutory 'invention' involves a 'technical idea'. The word 'technical idea' in this context refers to an idea of a technical means which can solve a certain problem with feasibility and repeatability. Accordingly, the 'technical idea' must be concrete and objective, while any idea lacking concreteness and objectivity does not comply with the definition of a 'technical idea'. The Examination Guidelines list typical examples which do not correspond to 'technical ideas' and are therefore not deemed to be statutory 'inventions' (see Part III, Chapter 1, Section 2.1.5 of the Examination Guidelines).

Personal skills: mere personal skills do not involve 'technical ideas' and are therefore not deemed to be statutory 'inventions'. The 'personal skill' in this context means a skill which can be acquired through personal experience and cannot be shared with others as knowledge due to lack of objectivity (eg, a method of throwing a split-fingered fastball characterised by the way of holding the ball in the fingers and throwing the same).

Mere presentations of information: mere presentations of information do not involve 'technical ideas' and are therefore not deemed to be statutory 'inventions'. The 'mere presentation' in this context refer to one which is characterised only by the contents of the information and is intended mainly

---

7 See the IP High Court decision on 17 October 2018, Case 2017 (Gyo-Ke) 10232, *Steak providing method*, which ruled that even if a claimed invention involves a technical feature by which a law of nature is not utilised, the claimed invention may correspond to a statutory 'invention' if the invention as a whole can be considered as a creation of technical ideas by which a law of nature is utilised.

to present the information. In other words, a presentation of information characterised by any feature relating to the presentation (eg, the presentation as such, the means of presentation, the method for presentation, etc) is not a mere presentation of information and therefore can be considered a 'technical idea'.

Mere aesthetic creations: mere aesthetic creations do not involve 'technical ideas' and are therefore not deemed to be statutory 'inventions'.

(e) ***Creativity***

The statutory 'invention' must be a 'creation' of technical ideas. Accordingly, mere discoveries of, eg, naturally occurring products (eg, ore) or natural phenomena, which have not been created by a person with intention, are not deemed to be statutory 'inventions'. On the other hand, products which have been artificially isolated from naturally occurring products, such as chemical substances or microorganisms, are deemed to have been created with intention and therefore are statutory 'inventions' (see Part III, Chapter 1, Section 2.1.2 of the Examination Guidelines).

(f) ***Highly advanced***

The statutory 'invention' must be a 'highly advanced' creation of technical ideas. This requirement was intended to distinguish an 'invention' subject to a patent under the Patent Law from a 'device' (small invention) subject to a utility model under the Utility Model Law. However, this requirement has lost practical meaning since the Utility Model Law was revised in 1993 such that utility models are registered without undergoing substantive examination. Accordingly, the JPO Examiners do not judge whether the claimed invention is 'highly advanced' (see Part III, Chapter 1, Section 2 of the Examination Guideline).

(g) ***Completion of an invention***

Although not explicitly stated in the law, the statutory 'invention' must be embodied and objectified to the extent that a person skilled in the art can repeatedly work the invention and thereby achieve its intended technical effect. In other words, an invention which has not been embodied and objectified to that extent is deemed incomplete, and therefore does not fall under the statutory definition of an 'invention'.

Based on this idea, the practice in the past, especially in the chemical and biological fields, was that if the effects of a claimed invention were not sufficiently supported by the examples and/or any other parts of the disclosure, a reason for rejection was issued on the grounds that the invention is incomplete and therefore does not comply with the requirement prescribed in the body of Article 29, paragraph 1 of the Patent Law.

This practice has almost disappeared recently, and such an objection due to incompleteness of the claimed invention is rarely issued. Insufficiency of support for the claimed invention is now usually treated as non-compliance with description requirements such as enablement, support and clarity. As an exception, when the claims recite technical means which are alleged to solve the problem but are actually not capable of doing so, a reason for rejection due to incompleteness of the invention may be issued under the body of Article 29, paragraph 1 of the Patent Law.

3. Industrial applicability

3.1 Summary

In order for an invention claimed in a patent application to be patentable, it is necessary for the claimed invention not only to fall under the statutory definition of an 'invention' (subject matter eligibility requirement) but also to be industrially applicable (industrial applicability requirement). Judgment as to whether a claimed invention is industrially applicable is made according to the procedure specified in Part III, Chapter 1, Section 3 of the Examination Guidelines: "Determination on Industrial Applicability Requirements".

According to the Examination Guidelines, 'industry' in this context is interpreted in a broad sense, including manufacturing, mining, agriculture, fishery, transportation, telecommunications, etc. Based on this definition, the Examination Guidelines list three categories of inventions which are not industrially applicable (see Part III, Chapter 1, Section 3.1 of the Examination Guidelines):

(i) inventions of methods of surgery, therapy or diagnosis of humans;
(ii) commercially inapplicable inventions; and
(iii)obviously impracticable inventions.

If the claimed invention is deemed to fall under any of categories (i) to (iii) stated above, then the Examiner shall determine that the claimed invention does not meet the requirement of industrial applicability (see Part III, Chapter 1, Section 3 of the Examination Guidelines).

3.2 Inventions of methods of surgery, therapy or diagnosis of humans (medical treatments)

The 'methods of surgery therapy or diagnosis of humans' are normally practised by medical doctors (including those who are directed by medical doctors), and have been typically termed 'medical treatments' (see Part III, Chapter 1, Section 3.1.1 of the Examination Guidelines). Inventions relating to such "methods of surgery, therapy or diagnosis of humans" (medical treatments) are considered as lacking industrial applicability (see Part III, Chapter 1, Section 3.1.1 of the Examination Guidelines).[8]

Since inventions falling under this category usually belong to the pharmaceutical and biological fields, we will explain this category in a later section (5. "Chemical, pharmaceutical and biological arts").

3.3 Commercially inapplicable inventions

Inventions falling under either category (i) or (ii) below are deemed to be 'commercially inapplicable inventions' and therefore lack industrial applicability:

(i) inventions applicable only for personal use (eg, a method of smoking); and

(ii) inventions applicable only for academic or experimental purposes.

Even if the claimed invention is applicable for personal use or academic or experimental purposes, the claimed invention may not be deemed a 'commercially inapplicable invention' if it involves a marketable or tradable subject matter (see Part III, Chapter 1, Section 3.2.2 of the Examination Guidelines). For example, a 'method of waving hair' which can be used for a commercial purpose in the beautician field as well as being for personal use, is not deemed to be an 'invention applied only for personal use' as indicated in item (i) above. Likewise, a 'kit for scientific experiments', which is used in experiments at school, is not deemed to be an 'invention applicable only for academic or experimental purposes' indicated in item (ii) above. Therefore, these inventions are not deemed to be 'commercially inapplicable inventions'. However, it is not necessary for a patent applicant to include in the original specification an explanation that the claimed invention involves marketable or tradable subject matter; it is possible to present this evidence either during prosecution of the patent application and/or during litigation of the resulting patent.

3.4 Obviously impracticable inventions

Inventions which cannot be practically implemented are deemed to be 'obviously impracticable inventions' and therefore lack industrial applicability. For example, if the claimed invention relates to a method for preventing an increase in ultraviolet rays associated with the destruction of the ozone layer by

---

8 There have been arguments on why inventions relating to methods of surgery, therapy, or diagnosis of humans (so-called 'medical treatments') fall under the category of 'inventions that cannot be worked as a business'. In this regard, the Tokyo High Court decision on 11 April 2002 in Case 2000 (Gyo-Ke) 65, the *Medical act* case, ruled that even though medical treatments by a medical doctor should be exempted from constituting infringement of a patent, no special measures are taken in the Patent Law for protecting medical doctors against such patent infringement, which means that the only possible interpretation is that medical treatments are not considered industrially applicable inventions.

covering the whole earth's surface with an ultraviolet ray-absorbing plastic film, then the claimed invention is deemed to be an 'obviously impracticable invention' and therefore lack industrial applicability (see Part III, Chapter 1, Section 3.1.3 of the Examination Guidelines).

4. Electrical and computer arts

4.1 Summary

Various discussions have been held in Japan regarding the determination of subject matter eligibility and industrial applicability of inventions using a computer or software (hereinafter referred to as 'software-related inventions'). The discussions have been particularly active in recent years, as software-related inventions have been created not only in the electrical and computer field but also in many other technical fields, with the rise of new technologies such as the Internet of Things (IoT) and artificial intelligence (AI), in order that examiners and users in various technical fields can clearly understand the method for judging subject matter eligibility.

It is our opinion, however, that in general, the JPO's stance in judging subject matter eligibility and industrial applicability of software-related inventions is less strict than those taken in other jurisdictions. In our experience, objections relating to subject matter eligibility and/or industrial applicability are not often raised by the JPO during prosecution and, if raised, can be overcome relatively easily in most cases by modifying the claim language slightly.

Specifically, when judging subject matter eligibility of software-related inventions, the JPO applies special criteria set forth in Chapter 1 of Annex B to the Examination Handbook. On the other hand, there are no special criteria for judging industrial applicability of software-related inventions; the industrial applicability of software-related inventions are examined in accordance with the same criteria as those applied to other technical fields.

Accordingly, the following description will focus on the special criteria for judging subject matter eligibility of software-related inventions, along with summaries of two major court precedents in which the subject matter eligibility of software-related inventions were contested.

4.2 Subject matter eligibility

(a) *Basic criteria for judging subject matter eligibility*

The basic criteria for judging subject matter eligibility of software-related inventions are stipulated in Part III, Chapter 1 of the Examination Guidelines: "Eligibility for Patent and Industrial Applicability".

Those utilising a law of nature as a whole and being considered as a 'creation of a technical idea utilising a law of nature', such as those corresponding to examples (i) and (ii) shown below, are deemed to correspond to statutory 'inventions' without being examined from a viewpoint of computer software, even though they utilise computer software[9] (Part III, Chapter 1, Section 2.2(1) of the Examination Guidelines):

(i) those concretely controlling an apparatus (eg, a rice cooker, washing machine, engine, hard disk drive, chemical reaction apparatus, or nucleic acid amplifier) or processing with respect to the control; and

(ii) those concretely processing information based on technical properties, such as physical, chemical, biological, or electric properties, of an object (eg, the rotation rate of an engine, the temperature for metallic rolling, the relationship between a gene sequence and the expression of a trait resulting from the gene in a living body, or the physical or chemical binding relationship between substances).

If a method of executing a series of steps using a computer corresponds to a 'creation of a technical idea utilising the laws of nature' and thus constitutes a statutory 'invention', various products derived from the method are also deemed statutory 'inventions', including:

- a computer program for causing a computer to execute the series of steps;
- a medium for storing the computer program; and
- a computer for executing the series of steps in response to the instructions by the computer program installed therein.

The subject matter of a claimed invention is determined not only based on the language of the preamble of the claim, but also taking into consideration the entire disclosure of the application along with the technical common knowledge at the time of filing. Specifically, even when any other word than a 'program' (eg, 'module', 'library', 'neural network', 'support vector machine', or 'model') is used in the preamble, the claimed invention is deemed a 'program' if it is clear in consideration of the entire disclosure of the application and the technical common knowledge at the time of filing that the claimed invention substantially relates to a 'program' (Chapter 1, Section 1.2.1.2 of Annex B to the Examination Handbook).

Even if the claimed invention is drawn to a subject matter which does not

---

9 The term 'computer software' herein refers to a program related to the operation of a computer or any other information equivalent to a program that is to be processed by a computer.
The term 'program' herein refers to a set of instructions given to a computer which are combined in order to produce a specific result (Article 2, paragraph 4 of the Patent Law).
The phrase 'equivalent to a program' herein refers to an entity which does not issue direct instructions to a computer and therefore cannot be called a program, but which has properties similar to those of a program in terms of prescribing computer processing. For example, 'data structure' (a logical structure of data expressed by correlations between data elements) can be deemed to be an entity 'equivalent to a program' if the structure of data prescribes information processing to be performed by a computer.

fall under category (i) or (ii) stated above, such as a method for doing business, a method for playing a game, or a method for calculating a mathematical formula, it can be deemed to be a 'creation of a technical idea utilising a law of nature' if it is developed as an applied computer software as a whole, such as a software for doing business, for playing a game, or for calculating a mathematical formula. The examiner shall examine whether such an invention is to be deemed to be a 'creation of a technical idea utilising a law of nature' from a viewpoint of a computer software. In other words, the examiner shall examine an invention utilising a computer software from this viewpoint, since it can correspond to a 'creation of a technical idea utilising a law of nature' if 'information processing by the software is concretely realised by using hardware resources'.[10]

(b) Specific flowchart for judging subject matter eligibility

The Examination Handbook also includes a flowchart showing the specific procedure for judging subject matter eligibility of software-related inventions, which is reproduced in Figure 3 (on the next page) with some modifications.

The examiner first reviews whether or not the claimed software-related invention is a 'creation of a technical idea utilising a law of nature', based on Part III, Chapter 1 of the Examination Guidelines, "Eligibility for Patent and Industrial Applicability" (step (a) of Figure 3) (Chapter 1, Section 2.1.1 of Annex B to the Examination Handbook).

For example, those described below normally fall under category (i) stated above (ie, "[t]hose concretely controlling an apparatus ... or processing with respect to the control") and are deemed to be 'creations of a technical idea utilising a law of nature' (Step (a1) of Figure 3) (Chapter 1, Section 2.1.1(1) of Annex B to the Examination Handbook).

(i-1) Those performing control of a target apparatus, based on a structure, system component, composition, action, function, nature, property, operation, etc., of the control target apparatus, or any other apparatus related to the control target apparatus

(i-2) Those performing control in a way that realises operations according to the purpose of an apparatus

(i-3) Those performing integrated control of a whole system comprising multiple related apparatuses.

In addition, those described below normally fall under the category of the above (ii) ("[t]hose concretely performing information processing based on the

10 The term 'hardware resource' herein refers to a physical device or a physical element that is used in processing, operation, or implementation of a function. Examples include a computer as a physical device, and components of a computer, such as a CPU, memory, input device, output device, or other physical devices connected to a computer.

Figure 3: Flowchart for judging subject matter eligibility for software-related inventions

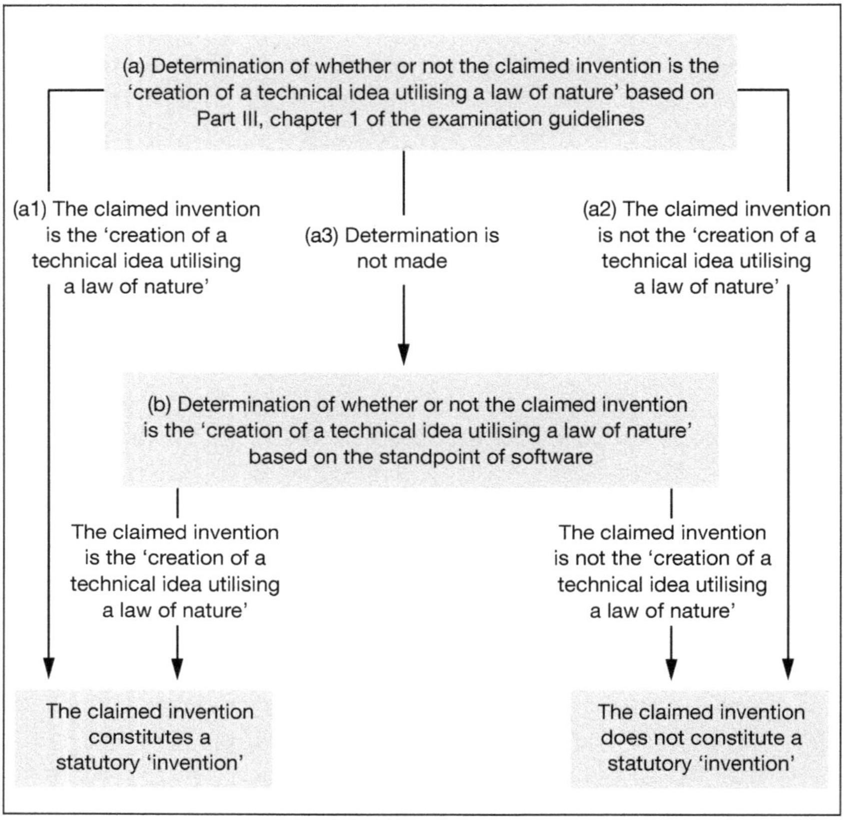

Source: Adapted from the flowchart in Chapter 1, Section 2.1.1 of Annex B to the Examination Handbook)

technical properties such as physical, chemical, biological or electric properties of an object") and are considered as the 'creation of a technical idea utilising a laws of nature' (Step (a1) of Figure 3) (Chapter 1, Section 2.1.1(1) of Annex B to the Examination Handbook).

(ii-1) Those obtaining intended numerical values, images, etc., by calculation or processing of numerical values, images, etc. showing the technical properties of an object, which is performed according to said technical properties

(ii-2) Those performing information processing by utilising a technical correlation between a state of an object and a phenomenon corresponding thereto.

When the claimed software-related invention falls under any of the categories stated in Section 2 above (and indicated again below), then the claimed invention is deemed not to correspond to a 'creation of a technical idea utilising a law of nature' (Step (a2) of Figure 3 above) (Chapter 1, Section 2.1.1(2) of Annex B to the Examination Handbook).

(1) Those in which a law of nature is not utilised, ie:
  (i) laws of nature as such;
  (ii) those which are not creations but mere discoveries;
  (iii) those which are contrary to the laws of nature;
  (iv) those which do not utilise a law of nature;
  (v) those which are not regarded as technical ideas; and
  (vi) those based on means which are alleged to solve the problem but cannot actually solve the problem.

(2) Mere presentation of information (where the feature resides solely in the content of the information, and the main object is to present information).

If whether the claimed software-related invention corresponds to a 'creations of a technical idea utilising a law of nature' cannot be determined according to the general criteria prescribed in Part III, Chapter 1 of the Examination Guidelines, "Eligibility for Patent and Industrial Applicability" (Step (a) of Figure 3 above), then the examiner shall move on to a second determination step according to special criteria for software-related inventions prescribed in Part III, Chapter 1, Section 2.1.2 of Annex B to the Examination Handbook (Step (b) of Figure 3 above).

If, according to the special criteria for software-related inventions, the claimed software-related invention is deemed one in which 'information processing by the software is concretely realised by using hardware resources', then the examiner shall determine the claimed invention to be a 'creation of a technical idea utilising a law of nature' (Chapter 1, Section 2.1.2(1) of Annex B to the Examination Handbook).

The requirement that 'information processing by the software is concretely realised by using hardware resources' herein means that a specific information processor or an operation method thereof suitable for the intended purpose is constructed via cooperation between the software and hardware resources (Chapter 1, Section 2.1.2(2) of Annex B to the Examination Handbook). Accordingly, the examiner shall determine whether or not the claimed invention is designed to achieve calculation or processing of information specific to the intended purpose by concrete means or procedures implemented by cooperation between the software and hardware resources.

Specifically, in order for a claimed software-related invention to be a 'creation of a technical idea utilising the law of nature' according to the special criteria for software-related inventions, it is required to explicitly recite, in the claims:

- hardware resources (eg, a computer as a physical device, and components of a computer, such as a CPU, memory, input device, output device, or other physical devices connected to a computer); and
- the relationship between the information processing made by the software and the hardware resources instructed by the processed information.

(c) Court precedents

IP High Court decision handed down on 24 September 2014 on Case No 2014 (Gyo-Ke) 10014 (*Knowledge base* case): this case relates to a patent application claiming a database system using a computer characterised by storing and displaying a set of specific data in a certain manner. The collegial body of trial examiners of the JPO rejected the application, on the ground that the claimed invention is not eligible as a statutory 'invention'. The applicant appealed to the IP High Court, which maintained the JPO's trial decision.

In this decision, the IP High Court decided that the claimed invention did not comply with the subject matter eligibility according to the general criteria, since the claimed invention merely utilised a computer in a conventional manner and did not recite any specific instructions to cause the computer to execute desired operations, so that the claimed invention as a whole should be interpreted as an abstract idea or an arbitrary agreement. The IP High Court further decided that the claimed invention also did not comply with the subject matter eligibility according to the special criteria for software-related inventions, since the data processing to be achieved by the claimed invention was not concretely realised by using hardware resources.

Thus, this court decision provides a basis for the two-step procedure for judging subject matter eligibility of software-related inventions (Steps (a) and (b) of Figure 3).

IP High Court decision handed down on 25 May 2009 on Case No. 2008 (Gyo-Ke) 10151 (*Accounting system* case): this case relates to an invalidation trial against a patent claiming an accounting system characterised by carrying out a series of specific operations using a computer, but also involving additional operations to be carried out manually. The collegial body of trial examiners of the JPO decided to maintain the patent, on the ground that the claimed invention was eligible as a statutory 'invention'. The appellant in the invalidation trial appealed to the IP High Court, which maintained the JPO's decision.

In this decision, the IP High Court decided that the claimed invention complied with the subject matter eligibility according to the general criteria, since the claimed invention was characterised by specific instructions which caused a computer to execute desired operations, and therefore corresponded to a 'creation of a technical idea utilising a law of nature'. The IP High Court further decided that although the claimed invention involved a few additional operations to be carried out manually, this does not alter the above judgment, since the main operations characterising the claimed invention are carried out on the computer, and the claimed invention as a whole can be interpreted as utilising a law of nature.

Thus, this court decision provides a basis for the first step of the procedure for judging subject matter eligibility of software-related inventions (Step (a) of Figure 3).

4.3 Industrial applicability

Judgment of industrial applicability for software-related inventions is carried out in the same manner as that for other inventions, ie, in accordance with the procedure outlined in section 3 "Industrial applicability" above.

5. Chemical, pharmaceutical and biological arts

5.1 Subject matter eligibility

Judgment of subject matter eligibility for inventions in the chemical, pharmaceutical, and biological fields involves several issues, especially in relation to utilisation of a law of nature. We will briefly discuss three issues here: reproducibility of inventions; inventions relating to naturally occurring products; and inventions characterised by information.

(a) Reproducibility of inventions

In order for a claimed invention to utilise a law of nature, the claimed invention is required to be reproducible by a person skilled in the art. However, the reproducibility of an invention in the chemical, pharmaceutical, and biological fields need not be particularly high. For inventions relating to some biological products, eg, a new breed of plant, the reproducibility of the invention can be deemed to be sufficient as long as a person skilled in the art can reproduce it with some level of certainty.[11] As explained above, the characteristic of the technology is to be considered in determining whether a claimed invention as a whole utilises a law of nature (Examination Guidelines Part III, Chapter 1, Section 2.1.4).

---

11 See the Supreme Court decision on 29 February 2000, Case No. 1998 (Gyo-Tsu) 19, *Method of Breeding New Breed of Peach*, which ruled that even if the reproducibility of an invention relating to a method of breeding a new variety of plant is low, the invention can be considered a statutory 'invention' utilising a law of nature, provided that a person skilled in the art can reproduce it with some level of certainty.

(b) ***Inventions relating to naturally occurring products***

There has been an opinion that naturally occurring products in, eg, the human body, such as genes and proteins, should not be granted patents since they are merely naturally occurring and therefore do not utilise any law of nature. However, under the Japanese patent system, a naturally occurring gene or protein can be patented once it has been isolated and/or purified for the first time by artificial means, on the grounds that such an isolated gene or protein is no longer a naturally occurring product and therefore falls under the category of a statutory 'invention' which utilises a law of nature (see Part III, Chapter 1, Section 2.1.2 of the Examination Guidelines).

(c) ***Inventions characterised by information***

Even in the chemical, pharmaceutical, and biological fields, there has been an increase in recent years in the number of inventions characterised by data, such as computer models of proteins defined by atomic coordinates, data arrays of such atomic coordinates, and pharmacophores (representations of the characteristics of a molecule in terms of the spatial arrangement of chemical elements in the molecule). Such data as such is not patentable, since data is merely a presentation of information and usually does not correspond to a statutory 'invention' utilising a law of nature. However, a molecule such as a protein identified by such data can be deemed to utilise a law of nature and therefore be industrially applicable.

5.2 Industrial applicability

(a) ***Methods of surgery, therapy, or diagnosis of humans ('medical treatments')***

Judgment as to whether an invention in the pharmaceutical or biological field relies on whether the invention corresponds to a method of surgery, therapy, or diagnosis of humans ('medical treatment'). The 'medical treatment' in this context means an activity which is practised by medical doctors (including those who are directed by medical doctors) and falls under any of the following three categories (see Part III, Chapter 1, Section 3.1.3 of the Examination Guidelines):

(i) methods of surgery of humans; and
(ii) methods of therapy of humans; and
(iii) methods of diagnosis of humans.

For example, the methods of (a) and (b) below fall under 'medical treatments' and therefore lack industrial applicability:

(a) methods for contraception or delivery; and
(b) methods for processing samples that have been extracted from the human body (eg, a method of dialysing blood) or analysing the samples

during the process on the presumption that the samples are to be returned to the same body for therapy (except for the methods described in Part III, Chapter 1, Section 3.2.1(4)b) of the Examination Guidelines.

Even if the claimed invention relates to a method of surgery, therapy or diagnosis to be practised on animals in general, the method is deemed to be a 'medical treatment' which is to be practised on humans, unless humans are explicitly excluded from the subject on which the claimed method is practised.

Figure 4 summarises the flow of judgment of industrial applicability for pharmaceutical and biological inventions under Japanese examination practice.

Figure 4. Flowchart for judging industrial applicability for pharmaceutical and biological inventions

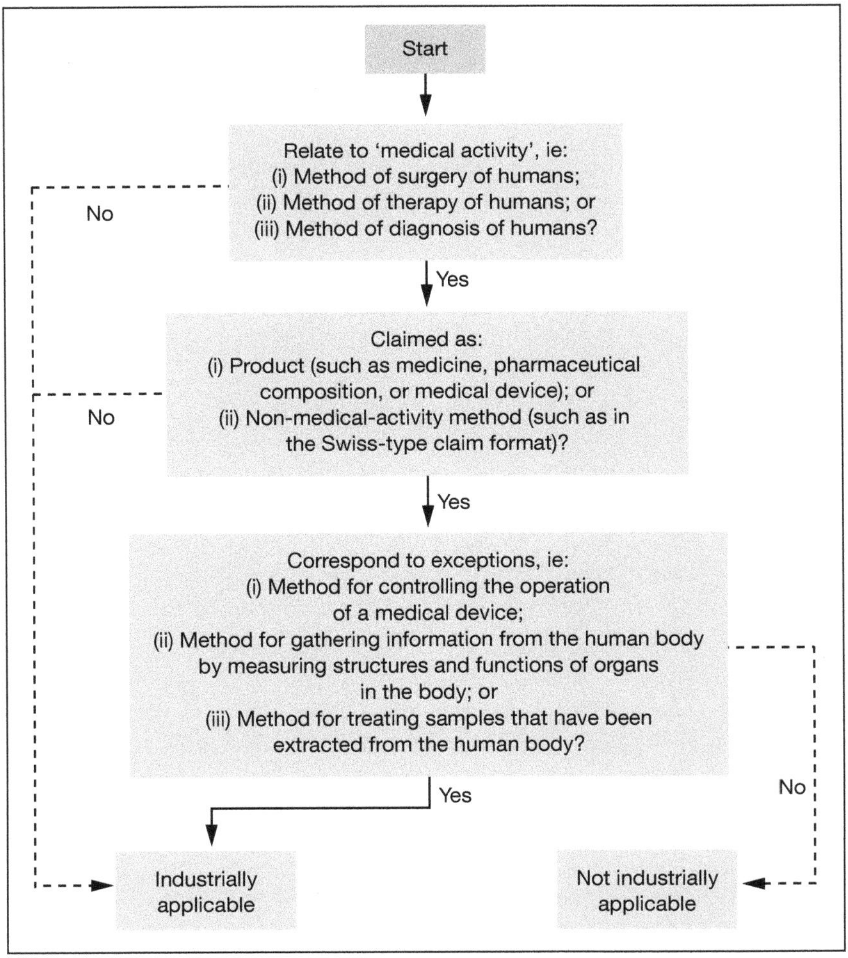

(b) ***Categories of inventions falling under 'medical treatments'***

Inventions falling under any of the categories mentioned below are deemed to be 'medical treatment' and therefore lack industrial applicability (see Part III, Chapter 1, Section 3.1.1 of the Examination Guidelines).

Methods of surgery on humans: inventions falling under any of categories (i) to (iii) below are deemed to be methods of surgery on humans and therefore lack industrial applicability (see Part III, Chapter 1, Section 3.1.1(1) of the Examination Guidelines):

(i) methods for surgical treatment (such as incision, excision, centesis, injection, and implant);

(ii) methods of using (eg, inserting, moving, maintaining, operating and extracting) a medical device (eg, a catheter or an endoscope) inside the human body (excluding inside the mouth, inside the external nostril, and inside the external ear canal); and

(iii) preparatory treatment for surgery (eg, anaesthetic treatment for surgery and method of disinfecting skin before injection).

Cosmetic methods including surgical operations are also deemed methods of surgery on humans even if their purpose is not therapeutic or diagnostic.

Methods of therapy of humans: inventions falling under any of categories (i) to (vi) below are deemed to be methods of therapy of humans and therefore lack industrial applicability (see Part III, Chapter 1, Section 3.1.1(2) of the Examination Guidelines):

(i) methods of administering medicine or giving physical treatment to a patient to cure or restrain a disease;

(ii) methods of implanting substitute organs such as artificial internal organs or artificial limbs;

(iii) methods of preventing a disease (eg, methods of preventing tooth decay or influenza);[12]

(iv) preparatory treatment for therapy (eg, method for arranging electrodes for electrotherapy);

(v) supplemental methods for improving treatment effects (eg, rehabilitation methods); and

(vi) methods for nursing associated with treatment (eg, methods to prevent bedsores).

Methods of diagnosis of humans: inventions relating to methods of

---

12 Methods of treatment for the maintenance of physical health (eg, methods of massage or shiatsu therapy) are also deemed to be methods of preventing a disease.

evaluating either (i) or (ii) below of the human body for medical purposes are deemed to be methods of diagnosis of humans and therefore lack industrial applicability (see Part III, Chapter 1, Section 3.1.1(3) of the Examination Guidelines):

(i) physical conditions of the human body (eg, conditions of diseases and physical health or mental conditions); and

(ii) prescription or treatment/surgery plans based on the conditions of (i) above (eg, methods of judging whether the patient has had a stroke by observing an image obtained by an MRI scan).

(c) Judgment of 'medical treatments' based on claim form

Even if the claimed invention substantially corresponds to a 'medical treatment', if the invention is recited in the claims as an invention of a 'product', such as a pharmaceutical composition or a medical device, the invention is not deemed to correspond to a 'medical treatment', but to have industrial applicability (see Part III, Chapter 1, Section 3.2.1(1) of the Examination Guidelines).

In addition, although it is not explicitly stated in the Examination Guidelines and Handbook, even if the claimed invention is described as a 'method', so long as the claimed method does not correspond to a 'medical treatment' based on the claim form (eg, Swiss-type claim), the invention is not deemed to have industrial applicability.

Table 1 indicates typical claim formats and their possible outcomes as to whether the claimed invention is deemed a 'medical treatment', taking as an example an invention characterised by using a known compound A for the treatment of disease X (hereinafter the model invention).

Table 1. Typical claim formats and possible outcomes

Claim format	Example	Possible outcome
(i) Treatment method	"A method of treating Disease X comprising administering to a subject in need thereof Compound A ..."	Medical treatment – not industrially applicable
(ii) Pharmaceutical composition	"A pharmaceutical composition for use in the treatment of Disease X comprising Compound A ..."	Not medical treatment – industrially applicable

continued on next page

Claim format	Example	Possible outcome
(iii) Swiss-type	"Use of Compound A in the manufacture of a medicament for use in the treatment of Disease X ..."	Not medical treatment – industrially applicable
(iv) EPC2000	"Compound A for use in the treatment of Disease X ..."	Not medical treatment – industrially applicable, but lacks novelty

Treatment method: if the model invention is recited in this claim format, the claimed invention will be deemed a 'medical treatment' and rejected as lacking industrial applicability. Therefore, this claim format should not be used.

Pharmaceutical composition: if the model invention is recited in this claim format, the claimed invention will not be deemed a 'medical treatment', but deemed to have industrial applicability.

Note that this claim format has another advantage: the use feature of the invention recited in the preamble, ie, "for use in the treatment of Disease X", will be considered in the examination of other patentability requirements such as novelty and inventive step. Therefore, this claim form is recommendable.

Swiss-type: similar to "Pharmaceutical composition" above. Specifically, if the model invention is recited in this claim format, the claimed invention will not be deemed a 'medical treatment', but deemed to have industrial applicability.

Note that this claim format also has another advantage: the use feature of the invention, ie, "for use in the treatment of Disease X", will be considered in the examination of other patentability requirements such as novelty and inventive step. Therefore, this claim form is also recommendable.

EPC2000-type: if the model invention is recited in this claim form, the claimed invention will not be deemed a 'medical treatment', but deemed to have industrial applicability.

Note, however, that this claim format should not be used, since the use feature recited in a EPC2000 claim is disregarded in the examination of other patentability requirements such as novelty and inventive step (see Part III, Chapter 2, Section 4.3 of the Examination Guidelines: "Expression Specifying the Product by its Use Application (Limitation of Use)").[13]

(d) ***Categories of inventions not falling under 'medical treatments'***

Inventions falling under any of the categories mentioned below are deemed not to correspond to a 'medical treatment', and therefore to satisfy the industrial applicability requirement (see Part III, Chapter 1, Section 3.2.1(3) of the Examination Guidelines).

Method for controlling the operation of a medical device: a method for controlling the operation of a medical device is not considered to be a 'method of surgery, therapy, or diagnosis of humans' as long as the function of the medical device itself is represented as a method (Examination Guidelines Part III, Chapter 1, Section 3.2.1(3)).

The "method for controlling the operation of the medical device" herein may include not only a method for controlling the internal operation of the medical device but also a functional or systematic operation provided to the medical device itself, such as the moving, opening, and/or closing of an incising means in accordance with an operating signal, the emission and/or receiving of a radioactive ray, an electromagnetic wave, a sound wave, or the like.

However, a method including either of the following steps (i) or (ii) is not considered to be a "method for controlling the operation of a medical device".

(i) an action of a medical doctor (for example, a step where a medical doctor operates a device in order to provide medical treatment in accordance with a symptom); and

(ii) a step with an influence on the human body by a device (for example, the incision or excision of a specific site of a patient's body by a device or the irradiation of radiation, electromagnetic wave or sound wave by a device).

If at least one of the steps constituting a claimed method corresponds to either conditions (i) or (ii) above, then the claimed method as a whole is deemed to be a "method for controlling the operation of a medical device" and therefore not industry applicable.

Method for gathering various kinds of information from the human body by measuring structures and functions of organs in the human body: the methods indicated in category (i) or (ii) below, which are intended to collect

---

13 This is a very confusing point. The difference in the possible outcomes between (ii) the 'pharmaceutical composition' claim and (iv) the "EPC2000-type" claim results from the difference in the JPO's interpretations of these claim forms. Specifically, since the former claim form is drawn to a composition of multiple (eg, two, three, four, ... or even countless) components, a limitation to the usage of the claimed composition can affect the selections and/or the ratios of the components thereof. Accordingly, the Examiner considers the use limitation upon examination. On the other hand, since the later claim form is drawn to a single compound, a limitation to the usage of the claimed compound cannot affect the structure or properties of the claimed compound. Accordingly, the Examiner disregards the use limitation as meaningless upon examination. See Part III, Chapter 2, Section 4.3 of the Examination Guidelines.

various types of data about the human body by measuring structures or functions of organs in the human body, are not considered to be 'methods of diagnosis of humans' (see Part III, Chapter 1, Section 3.2.1(3) of the Examination Guidelines):

(i) methods of extracting samples and data from the human body, or methods of analysing, eg, comparing such samples and data with standards, by utilising samples and data extracted from the human body (see Examples 1 to 5 in Table 2); and

(ii) methods of preparatory treatment for measuring structures or functions of various organs of the human body (see Example 6 in Table 2).

Table 2. Examples of methods for gathering various kinds of information from the human body by measuring structures and functions of organs

Category (i)	
Example 1	A method for an influenza test by extracting oral mucous membranes with a cotton bud
Example 2	A method for capturing the image of a lung by X-ray irradiation to the chest
Example 3	A method for measuring the body temperature by inserting an electronic ear thermometer into the external ear canal
Example 4	A method for judging the sugar level in urine by dipping a test strip in a collected urine sample, and comparing the colour of the test strip with colours on a colour chart
Example 5	A method of examining the susceptibility of the examinee to hypertension by determining the type of base on the nth line of the base sequence of the X gene of the examinee and comparing the base with a standard in which when the base type is A the susceptibility is low, and when the type is G the susceptibility is high
Category (ii)	
Example 6	A method of preventing the uneven smear of jelly for ultrasonography that is spread on the body

However, the Examination Handbook indicates two exceptions here. In exception 1, if the claimed invention falls under category (i) or (ii) above but relates to a method of evaluating either (i) or (ii) below of the human body for medical purposes, then the claimed invention is deemed to be a method of diagnosis of humans and therefore lacking industrial applicability (see Part III, Chapter 1, Section 3.1.1(3) of the Examination Guidelines; also see Section 5.2.b.iii above).

(i) physical conditions of the human body (eg, conditions of diseases and physical health or mental conditions); and
(ii) prescription or treatment/surgery plans based on the conditions of (i) above (eg, methods of judging whether the patient has had a stroke by observing an image obtained by an MRI scan).

In exception 2, if the claimed invention falls under category (i) or (ii) above but includes a step corresponding to a method of surgery or therapy of humans, then the claimed invention is deemed to be a 'method of surgery or therapy of humans'.

Method for treating samples that have been extracted from the human body: methods for treating a sample extracted from the human body (eg, blood, urine, skin, hair, cells, or tissue) or gathering data by analysing such a sample are not deemed to be 'medical treatments' and to have industrial applicability, provided that either condition (i) or (ii) below is satisfied (see Part III, Chapter 1, Section 3.2.1(4) of the Examination Guidelines).

(i) The sample extracted from the human body is not to be returned to the same human body.
(ii) The sample extracted from the human body is to be returned to the same human body in a method of:
    (1) manufacturing a medicinal product (eg, blood preparation, vaccine, genetically modified preparation and cell medicine) by utilising raw material collected from the human body;
    (2) manufacturing a medical material (eg, an artificial substitute or alternative for a part of the human body, such as an artificial bone, a cultured skin sheet, etc) by utilising raw material collected from the human body;
    (3) manufacturing an intermediate product for a medicinal product or a medical material (eg, methods for differentiation and induction of the cells, methods for separation and purification of the cells) by utilising raw material collected from the human body; or
    (4) analysing a medicinal product or a medical material, or an intermediate product thereof, which is manufactured by utilising raw material collected from the human body.

South Korea

Hankil D Kang
Kijoong Kang
Kil-chae Park
Bae, Kim & Lee LLC

1. Introduction

The patent system in South Korea is authorised by Article 22, Paragraph 2 of the Constitution of the Republic of Korea, which states that "the rights of authors, inventors, scientists, engineers and artists shall be protected by the Acts"[1] and governed by the Patent Act (the 'Patent Act'). Article 1 of the Patent Act explains that its purpose is to "promote the development of technologies and to contribute to industrial development by protecting and supporting inventions and promoting the use of inventions."[2] Furthermore, Article 29, Paragraph 1 of the Patent Act requires that, to be eligible for patenting, an invention needs to be one "having industrial applicability."[3] The statutory requirement under Article 29 of the Patent Act, and thus whether something can be patent eligible, can be broken down into two elements: an invention and its industrial applicability.

1.1 Invention

The Patent Act defines the term 'invention' as a "highly advanced creation of a technical idea utilising the laws of nature".[4] According to the Patent Court, the requirement for "highly advanced creation" is a relative concept that refers to the invention not being obvious to the person of ordinary skill in the art. The purpose of the highly advanced creation requirement is to differentiate between a patent-eligible invention – which is of comparatively higher level of technology – and a 'device' eligible for a utility model, which is a separate intellectual property right on its own.[5] As such, in practice, the 'highly advanced creation' part of the definition of the term 'invention' does not need to be considered to be an inherent feature or a requirement of the invention.[6] A patent-eligible invention is required to 'utilise' the laws of nature, which refer to certain unchangeable and unavoidable laws that govern the natural

1 The Constitution, Article 22, Paragraph 2.
2 The Patent Act, Article 1.
3 The Patent Act, Article 29, Paragraph 1.
4 The Patent Act, Article 2, Paragraph 1.
5 Patent Court 2001Heo4937, rendered on 21 February 2002.
6 Patent Court 2001Heo4937, rendered on 21 February 2002.

phenomena of the world, eg, law of gravity, thermodynamics, energy conservation, etc.[7] Laws contrived or discovered through the intellectual activities of human beings, on the other hand, are not considered a part of the laws of nature.[8] The Korean Intellectual Property Office (KIPO) explains that to utilise the laws of nature means to "apply the law of cause and effect in the context of natural science."[9] To provide guidance in determining whether a thing qualifies as an 'invention' under the Patent Act, the KIPO provides a helpful explanation and examples in its Patent Examination Guidelines, as amended on 14 December 2020.[10]

To be patent eligible, the invention needs to be a creation, and the term 'creation' does not mean a 'discovery' which denotes mere identification of an already existing substance or principle in nature, therefore discovery of naturally occurring substances (eg, minerals) or natural phenomena does not qualify as an invention.[11] However, if things in nature are isolated artificially from their surroundings, and not merely discovered, the methods of such isolation and the isolated natural substance or microorganisms are considered to be patent-eligible inventions.[12] Similarly, a new use of a known material in accordance with its inherent but newly found property is also distinguishable from a 'mere discovery of unknown property of a known material' if such new use is closely related with non-obvious inventive activities, and such new use shall be considered a patent-eligible use invention.[13]

Those claimed inventions that are contrary to the laws of nature or do not utilise the laws of nature, are not patent-eligible inventions. In its decision 98Hu744, the Supreme Court ruled that an alleged invention utilising perpetual motion was not patent eligible because perpetual motion is against the law of conservation of energy.[14] Additionally, if the claimed invention uses artificial regulations, such as rules contrived for playing games, products of human mental activities, such as a method for doing business, a teaching method, principles of a financial insurance scheme, tax codes, or any laws other than the laws of nature, including economic laws, mathematical formulae, laws of logic, or geometrical constructions, such invention shall not be patent eligible.[15] However, where the claimed invention does not claim the logical principle or mathematical principle or the method of using such principles, but claims a

7 KIPO, *Understanding the Patent Act of the Republic of Korea*, p41, available at www.kipo.go.kr/upload/en/download/UNDERSTANDING%20THE%20PATENT%20ACT%20OF%20THE%20REPUBLIC%20OF%20KOREA_201308.pdf.

8 *Ibid.*

9 *Ibid*, p42.

10 Available at www.kipo.go.kr/upload/en/download/Patent_Examination_Guidelines_2021.pdf.

11 Supreme Court 2002Hu1935, rendered on 24 October 2003.

12 Patent Examination Guidelines, p240.

13 *Ibid.*

14 Supreme Court 98Hu744, rendered on 4 September 1998.

15 Supreme Court 2007Hu265, rendered on 24 December 2008, and 2007Hu494, rendered on 11 December 2008.

technical device or method that uses the data resulting from a mathematical calculation to enhance performance of a certain technical means or controls such means to generate useful, specific, and practical results, if the technical device or the method is considered to be a reasonable means to achieve a specific purpose and is universal, repeatable, and objective, then such invention will be deemed to be a patent-eligible invention.[16] In determining whether a claimed invention utilises the law of nature or not, the claim as a whole needs to be considered, and even if a part of the claimed invention utilises the law of nature, if the claim as a whole does not utilise the law of nature, then the invention is not a patent-eligible invention, and conversely, even if a part of the claimed invention utilises a law other than the law of nature, eg, mathematical formula, if the claim as a whole is deemed to utilise the law of nature, then the invention will be deemed patent eligible.[17]

Additionally, a personal skill is not considered a patent-eligible invention as it lacks objectivity that can be transferred to a third party. For example, a method of playing musical instruments or a pitching method of a split-fingered fastball characterised by a specific grip using finger placements or throwing motion would not be eligible.[18] Simply presenting information where the content of the information contains the inventive feature is not deemed a patent-eligible invention. For example, a CD containing specific music or data captured using a digital camera would fall into such category. However, if the method of presenting the information has novel technical features, such presentation of information, the means containing the information, and the method of presenting the information can all be considered patent-eligible inventions. For example, a plastic card on which information is recorded using embossed letters, numbers, and signs is a novel means of presenting the information, and is patent eligible.[19] Further, an aesthetic creation may contain a technical aspect and a visual aspect, and thus may be evaluated based on subjective criteria, and the mere aesthetic effect (for example, paintings and sculptures) is not considered a patent-eligible invention, but if the aesthetic effect is obtained through the technical composition or other technical means, such means to obtain aesthetic effect may be patent eligible.[20] If the claimed invention formally provides a means to achieve the goal of the invention, but one cannot achieve objectively similar results to those the inventor achieved using the provided means – that is, the results cannot be executed repeatedly – then the stated invention is not an invention at all and thus not patent eligible.

16 Patent Examination Guidelines, pp240–241.
17 Patent Court 2006Heo1742, rendered 14 December 2008.
18 Patent Examination Guidelines, p242.
19 *Ibid.*
20 The closest Korean equivalent of a design patent is a 'registered design' which is protected by a separate statute, the Design Protection Act, and is not a subject of this chapter. See also Patent Examination Guidelines, p243.

The law, however, does not require a 100% success rate in repeatedly achieving the goal of the invention for it to be deemed an invention, and even at less than 100% if it is certain that the desired effect is achievable, then it is deemed repeatable and therefore patent eligible.[21]

Likewise, a patent-eligible invention needs to be complete, and a complete invention is a specifically and objectively comprised invention that a person of ordinary skill in the art can repeatedly practice and achieve the desired goal of the invention; the determination of an invention's completeness shall be made by considering the goal, composition, and effect of the invention as stated in the specification of the patent application and in accordance with the state of the art at the time of the filing.[22] If there is no specific means provided in order to solve the problem that is the object of the invention or it is determined that it is clearly impossible to solve the problem with the provided means, then the stated invention is not an invention for the purposes of the Patent Act, and thus not patent eligible.[23] However, the completeness of an invention, which goes to the question of whether the stated invention qualifies as an invention, is distinguishable from the lack of written description issue, which goes to the question of adequate disclosure in the application. The written description issue may be of a patent-eligible invention that is missing or lacking the required description in the application, which can be cured by an amendment during the prosecution after filing the application, whereas the incomplete invention is not a complete invention as of the filing date and thus not patent eligible to begin with.[24]

1.2 Industrial applicability

The purpose of granting a patent is to contribute to industrial development through technological progress. Accordingly, to be patent eligible, the invention must have industrial applicability, meaning an invention which cannot be used industrially or can only be used in areas other than industry is not patent eligible.[25] The term 'industry' under Article 29, Paragraph 1 of the Patent Act is generally interpreted as including not only primary or secondary industries such as agriculture, farming, forestry, fishery, mining and manufacturing, but also tertiary industries such as commerce, finance, transportation and service industries.[26] In essence, industrial applicability is interpreted very broadly and only inventions (a) that are related to medical practices that deal with human bodies, (b) that are purely for personal use, academic or experimental purposes, or (c) that theoretically work but clearly

---

21 *Ibid.*
22 *Ibid*, pp243–44, Supreme Court 93Hu1810, rendered on 27 December 1994.
23 *Ibid*, p244.
24 *Ibid.*
25 *Understanding the Patent Act of the Republic of Korea*, p46.
26 *Ibid.*

cannot be implemented or practised in reality are deemed to have no industrial application and not patent eligible.[27]

1.3 Patent-ineligible invention for public policy reason

Even if the invention meets the requirement of Article 29, Paragraph 1 of the Patent Act, ie, it is an invention having industrial applicability, the invention may not be patent eligible for public policy reasons under Article 32, which states, "no invention that violates public order or sound morals or is likely to harm public health is patentable."[28] As explained by the KIPO, 'public order' refers to the general interest of society or country, while 'sound morals' refer to the common and moral notion generally accepted by society.[29] The Patent Examination Guideline cites the following examples:

- an invention relating to sexual aides that explicitly depict human sexual parts such that it is obscene or lewd, or the practice of the invention necessarily requires lewd acts to be performed in public; or
- an invention that requires use of the human body so that practising the invention would necessarily injure the body or inhumanely restricts one's freedom of movement or harms one's human dignity.[30]

However, if the invention violates public order or sound morals due to improper use of the invention contrary to the original purpose of the invention, then such invention is not eligible. For example, a bingo-related invention, the original purpose of which is for entertainment, but is used as a gambling device, would not be eligible.

The prohibition of patentability based on the invention 'likely to harm public health' is applied sparingly because the purpose of the Patent Act is to encourage inventions and use thereof so that there will be technological improvement. Therefore, if the product safety or quality are presently deficient, such invention should nevertheless be encouraged as such invention may later stimulate or encourage inventions that will become the basis of or the incentive for such technological progress; on the other hand, securing the product's safety or quality should be separate issues to be regulated by other statutes.[31] An example cited by KIPO is an invention, the practice of which necessarily harms the public health; any invention will be reasonably suspected of harming the public health if the invention contains certain prohibited material or includes a material widely known to be hazardous and it can be clearly predicted that practising the invention will necessarily harm the public health, and the means

27 *Ibid*, pp46–47, Patent Examination Guidelines, pp246, 256; See also Patent Court 2003Heo6104, rendered 15 July 2004, regarding medical practices having no industrial applicability.
28 The Patent Act, Article 32.
29 Patent Examination Guidelines, p371.
30 *Ibid*, pp371–72; Patent Court 2014Heo4555, rendered 4 December 2014.
31 *Ibid*, pp372–73.

to remedy the harm to the public health from practising such invention is not generally known, despite the harmful side effect from practising the invention outweighing the benefit of it.[32]

2. Electrical and computer arts

The patent-eligibility issues in the electrical and computer arts generally arise in regard to whether the invention is utilising the laws of nature, particularly in the field of computer software and business method patents. A computer software or program is a series of commands and instructions to be performed by the computer; therefore, the computer program itself cannot be a patent-eligible invention as it does not utilise the laws of nature.[33]

However, in the case of an invention where the information processing by or with a computer program is specifically executed using hardware, the data processing device operating in association with the computer program (device), the operating method (method), computer readable medium storing the computer program or data (medium) and the computer program stored in the medium (program; applicable to applications filed on or after 1 July 2014) are all considered to be a creation or technical idea utilising the laws of nature, therefore a patent-eligible invention.[34]

In determining whether a software invention is a patent-eligible invention, it must first be determined whether the invention utilises the laws of nature: if the invention is utilising known examples that are not utilising laws of nature, including laws other than the laws of nature, artificial rules, human mental activities or simply providing information, then the invention is not a patent-eligible invention.

However, if the invention is specifically (a) performing control of a device or processes required for such control of a device, or (b) processing information based on the subject's technical characteristics (for example, including physical, electrical, chemical, biological characteristics of the subject to be processed), such invention is utilising the laws of nature and thus qualifies as a patent-eligible invention.[35]

If the invention does not fall into examples of those utilising or not utilising the laws of nature as stated above, then it should be examined whether the invention involves processing of information by software specifically being practised using the hardware.[36] More specifically, to be a patent-eligible software

32 *Ibid*, p374.
33 *Ibid*, p243.
34 *Ibid*.
35 KIPO, Examination Guidelines by Technology (December 2020), Older Technology Section, pp74, 75, available at www.kipo.go.kr/kpo/fileDown?path=/upload/ip_info/&fn1=simsaguide2020_12.pdf&fn2=%B1%E2%BC%FA%BA%D0%BE%DF%BA%B0_%BD%C9%BB%E7%BD%C7%B9%AB%B0%A1%C0%CC%B5%E5.pdf.
36 *Ibid*; see also, Supreme Court 2001Hu3149, 2007Hu494; Patent Court 2005Heo11094, 2006Heo1742.

invention for utilising the laws of nature, the software may not merely be read by the computer, but rather, it requires the software to be read by the computer to establish an information processing device or method that performs specific information processing by certain mutual cooperation between the software and the hardware for achieving a particular purpose that is different from the normal or typical usage of the computer or the internet; further, the claimed invention in the application may not be a mere expression of ideas but needs to state specifically and clearly all of the required elements to achieve the purpose of the invention in order to be deemed patent eligible.[37]

In addition, business method patents in South Korea are generally defined as 'patented inventions that realise business methods through utilising information technologies' and treated in a similar way to computer programs in that they require the processing of information by software on the computer to be specifically realised using the hardware.[38] Because the subject of a patent eligibility determination is based on what is claimed in the patent application, even if the specification contains references to computer hardware, if the claims do not specifically state how the information processing by software is utilising the hardware, the invention is not patent eligible.[39] As for inventions related to artificial intelligence, the claim must recite specific means or a specific method using the software and hardware in collaboration to realise the unique information operations or processing in accordance with the purpose of the invention and such effect needs to be consistently repeated without an intervention of human mental activities.[40]

3. Biological and pharmaceutical arts

3.1 Medical practice

As briefly mentioned under industrially inapplicable inventions, medical practices, such as methods of surgery, therapy, or diagnosis involving human bodies are deemed as industrially inapplicable inventions and not patent eligible.[41] Even if the invention is not a medical practice by a medical doctor, in view of the purpose, composition, and effect of the invention, if the invention is directed to a method of treatment or preventing human disease or promoting or maintaining health conditions, the invention shall be deemed industrially inapplicable and not patent eligible.[42]

In the case of an invention having both therapeutic and non-therapeutic effects (eg, cosmetic effect) simultaneously, if the two effects cannot be

37 Patent Court 2006Heo8910, rendered on 27 June 2007.
38 Supreme Court 2007Hu265, rendered on 24 December 2008.
39 KIPO, Examination Guidelines by Technology (December 2020), Older Technology Section, p87.
40 *Ibid*, p87.
41 Patent Examination Guidelines, pp246–247.
42 *Ibid*, p247.

Figure 1. Process flow for determining patent eligibility of a software or computer related invention

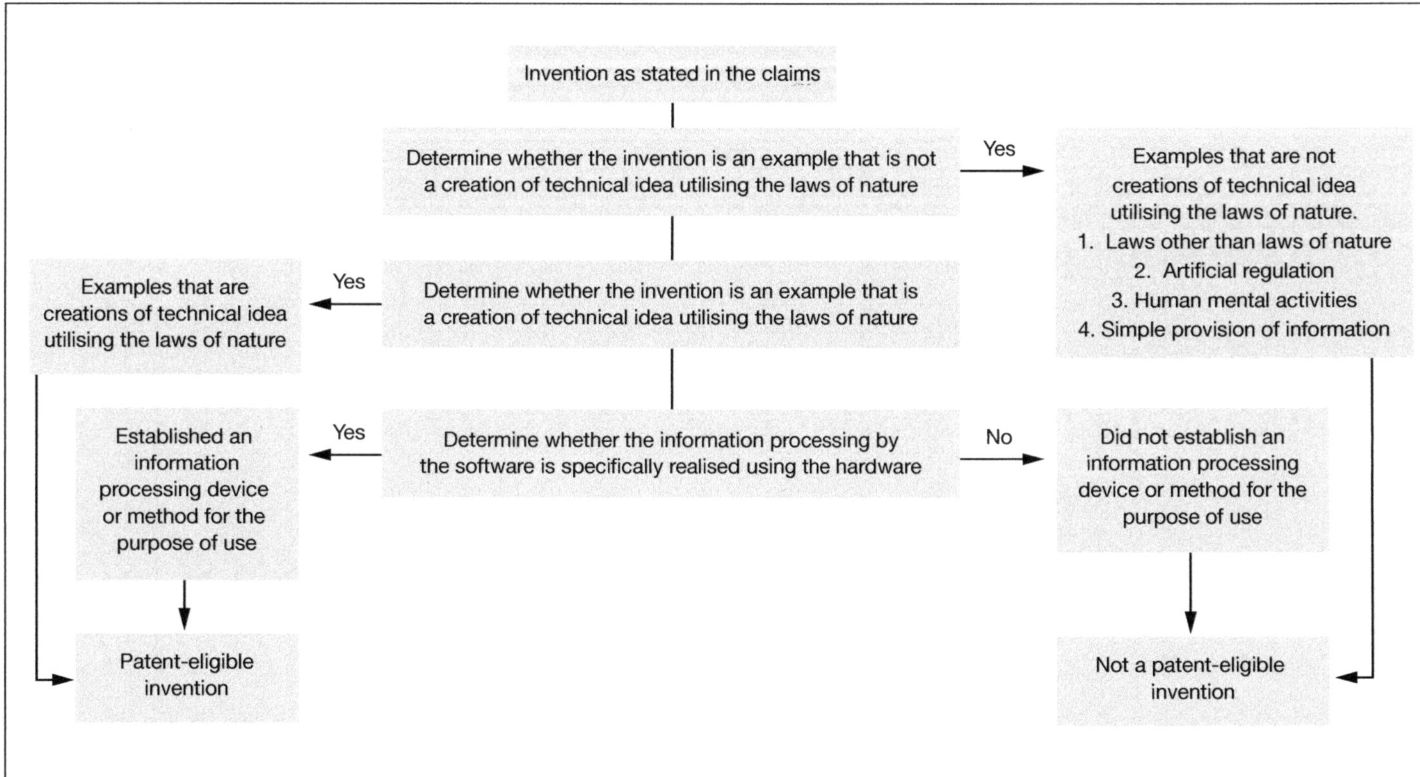

Reproduced with kind permission of the Korean Intellectual Property Office from the Examination Guidelines by Technology (December 2020), p13.

distinguished and separated, then the invention will be deemed as a method of treatment and industrially inapplicable; however, if the claim is solely directed to the non-therapeutic effect of the invention, even if the therapeutic effect is achieved in practising the non-therapeutic invention as a side effect, then the invention is deemed to be industrially applicable and thus patent eligible.[43] The medical devices used for medical practice, including surgery, treatment or diagnosis, as well as method of such use to gather data, methods of processing samples extracted or excreted from human bodies, methods of diagnosis without clinical judgement, methods of surgery, therapy, or diagnosis involving animals, and methods limited to non-therapeutic use are all considered industrially applicable although they are related to medical practice.[44]

3.2 Biotechnological inventions

For biotechnological inventions, including genes, DNA fragments, antisense nucleotides, vectors, recombinant vectors, transgenic organisms, cells, proteins, recombinant proteins, monoclonal antibodies, microorganisms, plants and animals, if the effects or utilities of the use of such inventions are not stated or otherwise cannot be inferred, the industrial applicability is not recognised, and as such they are not patent-eligible inventions.[45] For naturally existing matter such as genes, simply verifying the existence of such matter does not render it an invention, but one must prove the utility of the subject matter to show that new technical contents have been added to the prior art for the invention to be patent eligible.[46] The KIPO's recently published Examination Guidelines by Technology provides a new section for that of biotechnological inventions that reorganises previous categories of biotechnical inventions, including genetic engineering, microorganisms, animals and plants, etc into three simple categories:[47]

- nucleic acids, including genes, nucleic acid fragments, and vectors;
- proteins, including peptides and monoclonal antibodies; and
- cells, including microorganisms and transgenic organisms.

For nucleic acids, a gene sequence is a simple presentation of information; therefore, it is not considered an invention. Further, if a gene is presumed to be that of a specific protein based on a homology search using a public database, there is in principle no industrial applicability to the invention unless the gene is concretely established to encode that protein.[48] Likewise, an invention simply listing the sequence of a nucleic acid fragment is deemed to lack industrial

43 *Ibid.*
44 *Ibid*, pp251–255.
45 Examination Guidelines by Technology, Biotechnology Section, p15.
46 Patent Court 2007Heo5116, rendered 20 December 2019.
47 Examination Guidelines by Technology, Biotechnology section in general.
48 Examination Guidelines by Technology, Biotechnology section, p16.

applicability. By contrast, if the fragment's utility is specifically proven, such as regulating the activity of a specific protein or use in diagnosing a specific disease, then such invention is deemed to be industrially applicable and patent eligible.[49]

For proteins, similar to genes, the sequence of amino acids or atomic coordinates of the three dimensional structure of a protein is considered a simple presentation of information, and thus lacking industrial applicability.[50] Furthermore, if only the amino acid sequence is provided and no other characteristics of the protein, such as physical, chemical, or biological characteristics, are verified, then in general such an invention is considered to lack industrial applicability and is considered ineligible for patenting.[51]

For cells, the utility of an invention based on a new microorganism must be stated in the specification of the patent. Otherwise, the invention is a simple discovery of naturally existing matter and is not considered to be industrially applicable.[52] For an invention involving transgenic organisms, the genes introduced for transformation must yield a meaningful difference in the organism after transformation compared to the organism before transformation, and the utility resulting from such difference must be clearly stated in the specification or easily inferred.[53]

3.3 Pharmaceutical inventions

Similar to the Biotechnological Inventions above, the KIPO's recently published Examination Guidelines by Technology also provides a new section for that of pharmaceutical inventions defined as an invention that recites a medicinal use in the claims, and even if the medicinal use is not explicitly recited, if the medicinal use is disclosed in the description of the invention and such disclosure may affect the claim scope as a medicine through an amendment at a later point, then the invention should be treated as a pharmaceutical invention.[54] As defined, medicine means an article used for the purpose of diagnosis, cure, alleviation, treatment, or prevention of disease of animals, including humans, but excludes the following:

- apparatus, machine, or other devices;
- cosmetics; and
- (health) foods.

Further, 'use of the medicine' is use of the medicinal efficacy of the substance (or combination of substances) based on the discovery of the specific medical effect thereof. It is expressed as applying the medicinal substance:

---

49 *Ibid.*
50 *Ibid*, p17.
51 *Ibid*, p18.
52 *Ibid*, p18.
53 *Ibid.*
54 Examination Guidelines by Technology, Pharmaceutical Section, p3.

- to a specific disease; or
- to a specific disease which has limited administration method and dosage (administration cycle, administration time, administration area, administration path, administration amount, etc) or target patient group.[55]

The KIPO further breaks down pharmaceutical inventions into the following four broad categories:

(1) compound pharmaceutical invention, ie, medicines using synthetic compounds or compounds from small molecules refined from natural substance as the active ingredients;
(2) natural substance pharmaceutical invention, ie, medicines using results from processing, converting or extracting animals, plants, or microorganisms, etc, which exist in nature as the active ingredients;
(3) bio pharmaceutical invention, ie, medicines made from substances derived from an organism, including gene recombinant medicines such as vaccines, plasma derivatives, cell therapeutics and gene therapy; and
(4) medicinal formulation invention, ie, manufacturing drugs into suitable form for administration, such as formulation through physical manipulation or improvement in pharmaceutical property.[56]

As stated above, medical practices, such as methods of surgery, therapy, or diagnosis involving human bodies are deemed industrially inapplicable inventions and not patent eligible, as well as the preliminary treatments thereto (eg, administering anaesthesia) and any treatment related to contraception or childbirth.[57] Additionally, under Article 32, stated above, any medicine or a method of manufacturing the same using as the base material a part of a human body that was collected using a method harming a person or violating a person's human dignity by confining the person, etc, shall not be patent eligible.[58] However, any medicine or a method of manufacturing the same that uses human body parts as the base material but is not in danger of violating human dignity, eg, human blood or placenta, shall be a patent-eligible invention.[59]

4. Chemical arts

There is no specific issue regarding chemical arts that is worth noting in terms of the patent-eligible subject matter in addition to the basic requirements

55 *Ibid*, p2.
56 *Ibid*, p4.
57 *Ibid*, p22.
58 *Ibid*.
59 *Ibid*.

mentioned above. As long as the invention at issue is a "highly advanced creation of a technical idea utilising the laws of nature" that has industrial applicability and is not otherwise prohibited for public policy reasons under Article 32, the invention shall be patent eligible.

5. Statistics

According to the latest data on patent applications at the KIPO, in 2020 there were a total of 226,759 patent applications filed at the KIPO, and 134,766 patents were registered, which represent a 3.6% and 7.2% increase over the 2019 figures in the respective categories.[60]

Figure 2. Number of applications over the past five years[61]

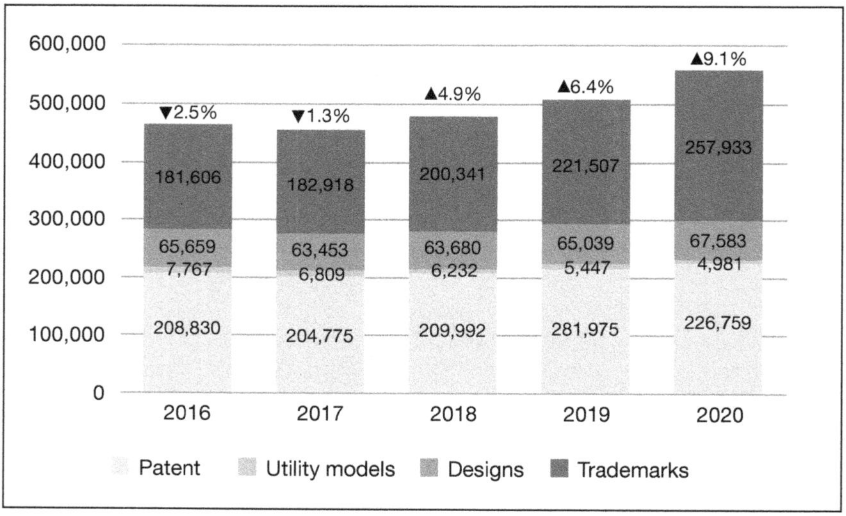

Reproduced with kind permission of the Korean Intellectual Property Office from KIPO, Intellectual Property Statistics FOCUS, Issue No 2017.

60 The KIPO, *Intellectual Property Statistics FOCUS*, Issue No 2017 (first half of 2021), p1, available at www.kipo.go.kr/kpo/download?f=/upload/kipo/ip_info/stat/20210312135233107019_1.pdf&fn=%C1%F6%BD%C4%C0%E7%BB%EA+%C5%EB%B0%E8+FOCUS+17%C8%A3%282021-%BB%F3%29.pdf.

61 *Ibid*, p2.

Figure 3. Number of registrations over the past five years[62]

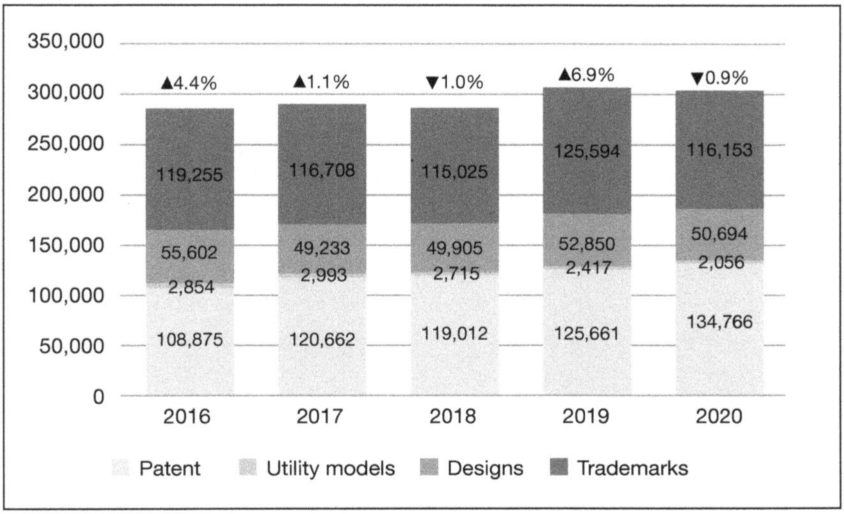

Reproduced with kind permission of the Korean Intellectual Property Office from KIPO, Intellectual Property Statistics FOCUS, Issue No 2017.

Of particular note, patent applications in the areas of medical technology (16.8%), pharmaceuticals (10.6%), biotechnologies (10.9%), and e-commerce (16.8%) each saw a larger than 10% increase in the respective number of applications, primarily attributable to the effect of the COVID-19 pandemic.[63] Among domestic patent applicants, Samsung Electronics topped the list with the number of applications at 7,446, followed by LG Electronics (5,345), LG Chemical (4,423), Hyundai Motors (3,000) and Samsung Display (2,957). The top five foreign patent applicants were Japan's Tokyo Electron Ltd, aka TEL (623), Taiwan's TSMC (603), Japan's Semiconductor Energy Laboratory Co, Ltd, aka SEL (527), China's Oppo (509) and China's Huawei (505).[64]

6. Hot topics: how emerging technology is going to be handled

The KIPO's Examination Guidelines by Technology published in January 2021, provides its examination guidelines not only for the aforementioned biotechnology and pharmaceutical inventions, but also for inventions related to two other emerging technologies; artificial intelligence (AI) and IoT (Internet of Things) services.

---

62 *Ibid.*
63 *Ibid*, p16.
64 *Ibid*, p5.

6.1 AI inventions

In the Examination Guidelines by Technology AI Invention section, the KIPO explains that AI-related inventions are applicable to inventions that require AI technology based on machine learning.[65] AI Inventions are further broken down into AI inventions related to learning models and those related to applications, where the AI inventions related to learning models focus on creating learned models based on raw data and learning models, such as a method of accelerating calculations, a method of data normalisation, and a method of creating learning models, etc, whereas the AI inventions related to applications focus on applying learned models or learned data to perform a specific task in various technological areas, such as AI self-driving robots, an AI medical device, or a business model using AI.[66]

In examining AI related inventions, for the purposes of patent-eligible subject matter AI inventions are treated in a similar way to computer software patents. In other words, AI related inventions are those based on data processing through software by using computer hardware, therefore the patentability requirements are the same as that of a computer software invention.[67] In view of the foregoing, patent registration of the AI related inventions is largely dictated by procedural issues such as enablement and written description as well as novelty and inventiveness of the inventions rather than patentability issue.

6.2 IoT inventions

The KIPO's Examination Guidelines by Technology IoT Invention section describes IoT invention as application technology developed to create value by applying information of things that were collected or analysed by devices such as sensors to various industrial fields.[68] IoT service related inventions are basically composed of a combination of IoT devices (hardware, such as sensor, device, servers, etc) and service method (software), therefore IoT service related inventions are known as a combination invention, which is an invention comprising novel solutions by gathering technical features disclosed in the prior art as a whole in order to solve a technical problem.[69] With IoT service related inventions, the patentability questions hinge upon whether there is an inventive step found in the combination invention – that is, whether the combination of the known prior art elements is such that a person skilled in the art can easily combine the references at the time of filing, similar to an obviousness inquiry in the US.[70]

---

65 Examination Guidelines by Technology, AI Invention Section, p1.
66 *Ibid*, p36.
67 *Ibid*, p11.
68 Examination Guidelines by Technology, IoT Invention Section, p1.
69 *Ibid*, p5, Patent Examination Guidelines, pp329–330.
70 *Ibid*, p330.

Taiwan

Roger Chang
Ivy Chin
Joyce Liou
Lee and Li Attorneys-at-Law

1. Background and executive summary

According to Article 21 of the Taiwan Patent Act, an 'invention' refers to the creation of technical ideas utilising the laws of nature. Details on verifying the eligibility of inventions are described in the Patent Examination Guidelines ('the Guidelines') provided by the Taiwan Intellectual Property Office (TIPO), similar to the Manual of Patent Examining Procedure (MPEP) in the US. Specific guidelines are given by technical field for inventions relating to computer software, pharmaceuticals, biology and Chinese herbal medicine. Generally speaking, patent eligibility is not a major issue before either the TIPO or the Taiwan Courts.

2. Electrical and computer arts

2.1 Discussion of case law

The number of cases in this area is limited because relatively little attention is paid to this issue. In Case 101-*Tai-Shang-Zi*-1673 decided by the Supreme Court in October 2012, the Supreme Court ruled on this issue for the first time. In this case, the claim cited a business method that could connect brands and advertising channels. Investigation showed that the claims failed to require computer technology to perform the business method. The Supreme Court accordingly ruled the claim to be invalid due to a lack of utilisation of the laws of nature. The ruling did not impose a high threshold on the eligibility issue.

2.2 How are eligibility issues handled by the Patent Office?

According to the Guidelines, a computer software-related invention is deemed to show eligible subject matter if its technical features have technical character, ie, a characterisation requiring, upon execution of the computer program, a technical effect other than normal physical phenomena. The normal physical phenomena may be, for example, current flow or a change in voltage level of the computer.

Due to the nature of computer software inventions, the steps or conditions cited in the claims can appear abstract. The Guidelines request that examiners review the specification and the drawings of an invention and then interpret each technical feature listed in the claim of the invention based on the disclosure of the specification and the drawings and general knowledge in the field underlying the invention on the filing date. Even though the specification, drawings, and general knowledge as of the filing date should be considered, the eligibility of computer software-related inventions should be determined based solely on the wording of the claims. In other words, the specification, drawings, and general knowledge in the field are merely used to illustrate or provide context to the claim and are not to be construed as limiting the claim.

It is emphasised in the Guidelines that a claimed invention shall not be considered ineligible merely due to its preamble. For example, an invention with a preamble such as a program module, a neural network, a data structure, or a packet may be eligible subject matter if the claim as a whole has technical character. The examiner shall determine whether the claimed invention has technical character based on the claim, considered as a whole, in view of the specification, drawings, and general knowledge in the field as of the filing date.

Examples of ineligible subject matter listed in the Guidelines include the following.

(a) Program code

Program code, either source code or object code, relates to an artificial arrangement without utilising the laws of nature, and thus does not conform to the definition of an invention. Although program code is ineligible subject matter for a patentable invention, it can be protected under copyright.

(b) Business methods with solely artificial rules

Business methods with solely artificial rules, such as social rules, empirical rules and economic rules, are not eligible subject matter. On the other hand, a business method implemented by a computer program may be eligible subject matter if it contains technical features beyond the artificial rules.

***(c) Presentation of information* per se**

The presentation of information *per se*, such as data, signals and packets, is not the creation of technical ideas, and thus does not conform to the definition of an invention. Only when data, signals, or packets, upon being read into a computer by use of machines, are functionally or structurally interrelated to the processing performed by the computer are they not categorised as the mere presentation of information *per se* but rather as involving a technical character.

(d) Simple usage of the computer

Simply using the computer to implement a method or an algorithm fails to meet the requirements for a computer software-related invention, and is not eligible subject matter. If the claimed computer software or hardware that implements a method or an algorithm completes tasks originally intended for human beings while yielding merely traditional benefits of computer software or hardware, such as increased speed and accuracy, the claimed computer software or hardware fails to meet the requirements for a computer software-related invention.

Conversely, if upon execution of the computer program or operation of the hardware, a technical effect produced is other than traditional benefits of computer software or hardware, such as enhanced data security or improved system stability, the claimed computer software or hardware meets the requirements for a computer software-related invention.

In 2020, the TIPO released a draft amended chapter of the Patent Examination Guidelines on computer software-related inventions ('the amended chapter'), and later held a public hearing in March 2021. Since the amended chapter is not yet finalised, the preceding paragraphs are based on the current Guidelines.

The amended chapter defines eligible computer software-related inventions using the stipulation in the Patent Act, ie, "'invention' meaning the creation of technical ideas utilising the laws of nature". The concept of 'technical character' mentioned here is removed from the definition of eligible computer software-related inventions. Furthermore, the amended chapter states that a computer software-related invention involving "controlling of machines or one that performs the controlling" or "one that performs data processing according to technical data of an object" is eligible subject matter. Meanwhile, simple usage of a computer is no longer explicitly categorised as ineligible subject matter. Accordingly, it may be easier for a computer software-related invention to be determined as eligible subject matter if the amended chapter is enforced.

3. Biological and pharmaceutical arts

3.1 Discussion of case law

There are no reported cases in this area.

3.2 How are eligibility issues handled by the Patent Office?

Article 24 of the Patent Act stipulates that an invention patent shall not be granted in respect of any of the following:

- animals, plants, and essential biological processes for the production of animals or plants, except for processes for producing microorganisms;
- diagnostic, therapeutic and surgical methods for the treatment of humans or animals; or
- inventions contrary to public order or morality.

Regarding Item 1 of Article 24, the Guidelines, Volume II, Chapter 14 on Biology-Related Inventions (the 'Biology Guidelines') state that it covers all kinds of animals and plants including transgenic animals or plants. However, processes for producing animals or plants utilising non-biological or microbiological processes (such as genetic engineering processes) are eligible subject matter. Furthermore, microorganisms are eligible subject matter.

Regarding Item 2 of Article 24, the Biology Guidelines and the Guidelines, Volume II, Chapter 13 on Pharmaceuticals-Related Inventions (the 'Pharmaceuticals Guidelines') provide certain criteria for determining whether an invention relates to unpatentable diagnostic, therapeutic, or surgical methods.

(a) Diagnostic methods

A diagnostic method is deemed unpatentable if the method is conducted on humans or animals, relates to diagnosis of a disease, or is implemented for the purpose of obtaining the results of diagnosis of a disease directly. That is, *in vitro/ex vivo* diagnostic methods, such as measuring the concentration of a protein in a sample obtained from a subject to determine whether the subject has a disease, are not considered unpatentable diagnostic methods.

The following examples are provided in the Guidelines to illustrate patentable diagnostic methods.

***In vitro/ex vivo* diagnostic methods:** a method for determining whether a subject has a kidney disease comprising the steps of:

(i) obtaining a urine sample from the subject;
(ii) measuring the concentration of protein X in the urine sample *in vitro*;
(iii) comparing the concentration obtained in step (ii) with the concentration of protein X in normal urine; and
(iv) if the concentration of protein X in the urine sample from the subject is lower than that in normal urine, determining that the subject is likely to have a kidney disease.

The Guidelines explain that although the method comprises steps of obtaining results for diagnosing a disease, since the testing is conducted *in vitro* on a sample rather than on humans or animals, the method is not considered a diagnostic method for the treatment of humans or animals.

Methods irrelevant to the diagnosis of diseases: methods such as measuring the height or body weight or detecting the quality of skin of a subject are irrelevant to the diagnosis of a disease, so they are not considered unpatentable diagnostic methods even though they are conducted on humans or animals.

Methods that cannot directly obtain the results for diagnosing disease: a cardiac imaging method comprising the steps of:

(i) positioning a subject having a cardiac blood flow path in a magnetic resonance imaging (MRI) system,
(ii) delivering polarised 129Xe to the subject;
(iii) dissolving at least a portion of the polarised 129Xe into the subject's cardiac blood flow path;
(iv) exciting dissolved polarised 129Xe in a target region along the blood flow path with at least one large angle RF excitation pulse; and
(v) generating a MR image associated with the excited dissolved polarised 129Xe.

The Guidelines explain that although the specification discloses that the data obtained from the method can be used for diagnosis, since the method only involves imaging and lacks the steps for evaluating symptoms and determining the cause or disease status based on the image, the method does not include all the steps from obtaining data and diagnosing a disease based thereon. Thus, the method is not considered an unpatentable diagnostic method.

(b) Therapeutic methods

A method is deemed a therapeutic method, and thus ineligible for patent protection, if the purpose of the method is to treat a disease or eliminate the cause of a disease that improves or recovers the health of a human or animal. As long as the method comprises a step that has a therapeutic effect, the method is considered a therapeutic method no matter whether the method contains non-therapeutic steps. If a method (such as a method for reducing body weight) has both a therapeutic effect (treating obesity) and a non-therapeutic effect (improving body shape), the method is still considered a therapeutic method.

Specifically, the Biology Guidelines indicate that the methods for gene therapy conducted on humans or animals are unpatentable therapeutic methods. On the other hand, the *in vitro* methods of gene editing, *in vitro* methods for modifying cells for cell therapy, and genes, vectors, or recombinant vectors for gene therapy may be patent eligible.

According to the Guidelines, medical use inventions (such as therapeutic methods) can be pursued in Swiss-type use claims. Under TIPO practice, specifying the technical features of therapeutic methods, such as dosing regimens, routes of administration and patient populations in a Swiss-type use claim will be taken into consideration when determining the scope or patentability of the claimed invention.

(c) Surgical methods

A method is deemed a patent-ineligible surgical method if it is conducted on humans or animals and involves invasive procedures or treatments, such as dissection, resection, suture, puncture, injection, blood sampling and the like, regardless of whether the method is for a therapeutic or non-therapeutic purpose. For example, in the diagnostic method described above, if polarised 129Xe in step (ii) is delivered to the subject by injection or a similar invasive procedure, the method as a whole involves an ineligible surgical method.

Regarding Item 3 of Article 24, the Biology Guidelines state that human cloning, the method of cloning humans, methods for modifying the genetic characteristics of human germlines and the products obtained therefrom, chimeras made from human or animal germ cells or totipotent stem cells and the method of preparing the same are all inventions contrary to public order or morality and cannot be patented. However, the human embryonic pluripotent stem cells derived from totipotent stem cells that are unable to grow into a human will not be considered to be contrary to public order or morality, and thus may be eligible for patenting.

4. Chemical arts

4.1 Discussion of case law

There are no reported cases in this area.

4.2 How are eligibility issues handled by the Patent Office?

There are no eligibility issues in the chemical arts other than for therapeutic methods involving pharmaceuticals as discussed previously. Chemical compounds, as long as they are novel, inventive, and have industrial applicability, can be eligible subject matter irrespective of whether they are products of nature.

5. Statistics

According to the latest official data released by the Intellectual Property Court, the highest patent invalidity rate in patent infringement suits was 69.12% in 2010, and the lowest was 33.33% in Q1 of 2021 (available at https://ipc.judicial.gov.tw/tw/lp-1391-091.html). Patent invalidation rate before the TIPO (patent cancellation cases, similar to the US PTAB) was 27% in 2020 (available at https://topic.tipo.gov.tw/patents-tw/cp-780-889175-b1475-101.html).

There are no statistics with respect to invalidation rates for ineligibility. One would be entitled to assert ineligibility to attack patent validity (Articles 21 and 71 of the Taiwanese Patent Act) by filing a patent cancellation action before the patent office or asserting it as a defence before the infringement trial. However, ineligibility has rarely been asserted before the court or the TIPO.

United Kingdom

Victoria Barker
Harrison Chang
Luigi Distefano
Nicholas Fox
Finnegan Europe LLP

1. Statutory basis

Patentable subject matter in the United Kingdom is governed by Section 1 of the Patents Act 1977, Subsections 1–4 of which read as follows:[1]

> *(1) A patent may be granted only for an invention in respect of which the following conditions are satisfied, that is to say—*
> *(a) the invention is new;*
> *(b) it involves an inventive step;*
> *(c) it is capable of industrial application;*
> *(d) the grant of a patent for it is not excluded by subsections (2) and (3) or section 4A below;*
> *and references in this Act to a patentable invention shall be construed accordingly.*
>
> *(2) It is hereby declared that the following (among other things) are not inventions for the purposes of this Act, that is to say, anything which consists of—*
> *(a) a discovery, scientific theory or mathematical method;*
> *(b) a literary, dramatic, musical or artistic work or any other aesthetic creation whatsoever;*
> *(c) a scheme, rule or method for performing a mental act, playing a game or doing business, or a program for a computer;*
> *(d) the presentation of information;*
> *but the foregoing provision shall prevent anything from being treated as an invention for the purposes of this Act only to the extent that a patent or application for a patent relates to that thing as such.*
>
> *(3) A patent shall not be granted for an invention the commercial exploitation of which would be contrary to public policy or morality.*
>
> *(4) For the purposes of subsection (3) above exploitation shall not be regarded as contrary to public policy or morality only because it is prohibited by any law in force in the United Kingdom or any part of it.*

---

1 Subsection 5, the final subsection of Section 1 provides the Secretary of State with the power to amend or supplement the list of 'non-inventions' appearing in Subsection (2) by order for the purposes of conformity with developments in science and technology. No such orders have been made.

Section 4A then further explains:

4A (1) A patent shall not be granted for the invention of:

(a) a method of treatment of the human or animal body by surgery or therapy, or

(b) a method of diagnosis practised on the human or animal body.

(2) Subsection (1) above does not apply to an invention consisting of a substance or composition for use in any such method.

(3) In the case of an invention consisting of a substance or composition for use in any such method, the fact that the substance or composition forms part of the state of the art shall not prevent the invention from being taken to be new if the use of the substance or composition in any such method does not form part of the state of the art.

(4) In the case of an invention consisting of a substance or composition for a specific use in any such method, the fact that the substance or composition forms part of the state of the art shall not prevent the invention from being taken to be new if that specific use does not form part of the state of the art.

2. Relationship between UK and EPO law

The wording of Sections 1 and 4A of the Patents Act deliberately mirrors the wording of Articles 52 and 53 of the European Patent Convention (EPC) to which the UK is a party and Section 130(7) of the Patents Act declares that, along with other key sections of the Act, Section 1(1) to (4) and Section 4A are: "framed to have, as nearly as practicable, the same effects in the United Kingdom as the corresponding provisions of the European Patent Convention".

As UK law is, in principle, harmonised with the EPC, the hurdles an application needs to overcome in the United Kingdom are very similar to those in the European Patent Office (EPO). However, differences between the two have arisen, particularly in relation to computer-implemented inventions.

The United Kingdom is a common law jurisdiction where the doctrine of precedent applies. This means that the earlier decisions of higher courts are binding authorities and must subsequently be followed. The Court of Appeal is bound by its earlier decisions unless a previous decision is inconsistent with a subsequent decision of the Supreme Court or was reached without reference to a relevant statute or other authority.[2]

EPO decisions are not decisions of an English court. Hence, they are only persuasive and do not constitute binding authority. The effect of this is that only those EPO decisions which have been expressly endorsed by a UK court decision are binding on the UK courts and the UKIPO.[3] This selective

2 *Young v Bristol Aeroplane Co Ltd* [1944] KB 718.

3 This remains the case even following *Actavis UK Limited v Merck and Co Inc* [2008] EWCA Civ 444 where the Court of Appeal acknowledged that UK law must now be construed in a European context and that the Court of Appeal could depart from its previous decisions where it was satisfied that the EPO Boards of Appeal had formed a settled view on a point of law which differs from earlier UK decisions.

application of EPO decisions by the UK courts has resulted in the United Kingdom's approach to patentability diverging from the approach of the EPO. In the United Kingdom, computer-implemented inventions lacking technical character are rejected as relating to unpatentable subject matter whereas equivalent inventions in the EPO are considered to lack inventive step.

It is difficult however to identify circumstances where these differences have any significant practical consequences. As the Court of Appeal in *Symbian's Application*, stated: "as a matter of broad principle, it seems to us that the approaches in [...] the great majority of cases in this jurisdiction and in the EPO, are, on a fair analysis, capable of reconciliation."[4] Later UK judgments have supported and reiterated this. For example, Kitchin LJ observed in *HTC v Apple*: "... in terms of result [...] it seems to me that whichever route is followed, one ought to end up at the same destination."[5] And more recently, Birss J commented in *Lenovo's Application*: "although in methodological terms the approach in the UK and the approach in the EPO may look different, in practice they reach the same result, at least usually."[6]

In summary, the UK and EPO approaches tend to be two different ways to arrive at the same destination. Ultimately, an applicant may not care whether his or her application is rejected on the grounds of unpatentable subject matter or lack of inventive step; either way, the applicant does not get a patent.

3. Computer-implemented inventions

3.1 UK courts' approach to software inventions

In the 1980s and 1990s the relationship between computer-implemented inventions and the excluded subject matter provisions was considered by the English Court of Appeal on three occasions: in *Merrill Lynch's Application*,[7] *Gale's Application*[8] and *Fujitsu's Application*.[9]

In *Merrill Lynch*, the Court of Appeal endorsed the then current approach of the EPO established in T208/84 *Vicom/computer-related invention*. This approach required, as a matter of patentable subject matter, the presence of a 'technical effect'.

Previously, the EPO Board of Appeal in *Vicom* had stated that:

> 12. *The Board is of the opinion that a claim directed to a technical process which process is carried out under the control of a program (be this implemented in hardware or in software), cannot be regarded as relating to a computer programme as such within the meaning of Article 54(3) EPC as it is the*

---

4 *Symbian's Application* [2009] RPC 1, [1].
5 *HTC Europe Co Ltd v Apple Inc* [2013] EWCA Civ 451, [41].
6 *Lenovo (Singapore) PTE Ltd v Comptroller General of Patents* [2020] EWHC 1706 (Pat), [9].
7 [1989] RPC 561.
8 [1991] RPC 305 discussed in section 3.2(e) below.
9 [1997] RPC 608.

application of the programme for determining the sequence of steps in the process for which in effect protection is sought. Consequently, such a claim is allowable under Article 52(2) EPC and (3) EPC.

The board continued:

16. *In arriving at this conclusion the Board has additionally considered that making a distinction between embodiments of the same invention carried out in hardware or in software is inappropriate as it can be fairly said that the choice between these two possibilities is not of an essential nature but is based on technical and economic considerations which bear no relationship to the inventive concept as such. Generally speaking, an invention which would be patentable in accordance with conventional patentability criteria should not be excluded from protection by the mere fact that for its implementation modern technical means in the form of a computer program are used. Decisive is what technical contribution the invention as defined in the claim when considered as a whole makes to the known art. Finally it would seem illogical to grant protection for a technical process itself controlled by a suitably programmed computer but not the computer itself when set up to execute the control.*

Fox LJ crystalised the requirement that for a software invention to be patentable it must give rise to a 'technical effect' into English law when in *Merrill Lynch* he stated:

... it seems to me to be clear ... that it cannot be permissible to patent an item excluded by section 1(2) under the guise of an item which contains that item – that is to say in the case of a computer programme, the patenting of a conventional computer containing that programme. Something further is necessary. The nature of that addition is, I think to be found in the Vicom case where it is stated: "Decisive is what technical contribution the invention makes to the known art". There must, I think, be some technical advance over the prior art in the form of a new result (e.g., a substantial increase in processing speed as in Vicom).[10]

Subsequent UK cases have then reiterated the requirement for patentable inventions to have a 'technical effect'.

For example, the Court of Appeal in Fujitsu stated:[11]

... it is and always has been a principle of patent law that mere discoveries or ideas are not patentable, but those ideas and discoveries which have a technical aspect or make a technical contribution are. Thus the concept of what is needed to make an excluded thing patentable is a technical contribution is not surprising. That was the basis of the decision in the Vicom. It has been accepted by this Court and by the EPO and has been applied since 1987. It is a concept at the heart of patent law.

The Court of Appeal revisited the question of the patentability of computer software in 2006 in the conjoined appeals *Aerotel Limited v Telco Holdings Limited*

10 *Merrill Lynch*, at p569, lines 2–10.
11 *Fujitsu*, at p614, lines 40–46.

and Macrossan's Patent Application.[12] By that time, the EPO had modified the test in *Vicom* through the T931/95 *PBS partnership*, T258/03 *Hitachi* and T641/00 *COMVIK* decisions, as a result of which the requirement that an invention provide a technical solution to a technical problem no longer formed part of the assessment of patentable subject matter before the EPO.

However, due to the doctrine of precedent, the UK Court of Appeal considered itself bound by its own earlier decisions, and hence the Court declined to follow the EPO's lead. Instead, it restated a test for patentable subject matter which retains the requirement for a 'technical effect' to be present.

This test[13] (often referred to as the *Aerotel* test) is as follows:

- properly construe the claim;
- identify the actual or alleged contribution;
- ask whether it (the identified actual or alleged contribution) falls solely within the excluded subject matter; and
- check whether the contribution is actually technical in nature.

The Court of Appeal explained[14] each of these steps as follows:

No one would quarrel with first step, construction. You have to decide what the monopoly is before going on the question of whether it is excluded. Any test must involve this first step.

The second step – identify the contribution – is set to be more problematical. How do you assess the contribution? Mr Birss submits the test is workable – it is an exercise in judgement, probably involving the problem said to be solved, how the invention works, what its advantages are. What has the inventor really added that perhaps best sums up the exercise. The formulation involved looking at substance not form – which is surely what the legislator intended.

Mr Birss added the words "or alleged contribution" in his formulation of the second step. That will do at the application stage – where the office must generally accept what the inventor says is his contribution. It cannot actually be conclusive, however. If an inventor claims a computer when programmed with his new programme, it will not assist him if he alleges wrongly that he has invented the computer itself, even if he specifies all the detailed elements of a computer in his claim. In the end the test must be what contribution has actually been made, not what the inventor says he has made.

The third step – is the contribution solely of excluded matter? – is merely an expression of the "as such" qualification of Article 52(3). During the course of argument Mr Birss accepted a reformulation of the third step – ask whether the contribution thus identified consists of excluded matter as such? We think either formulation will do – they mean the same thing.

12 [2006] EWCA Civ 1371
13 *Aerotel*, [40].
14 *Ibid*, [42]–[46].

The fourth step – check whether the contribution is 'technical' – may not be necessary because the third step should have covered that. It is a necessary check, however, if one is to follow Merrill Lynch as we must.

In 2009, in *Symbian's Application*, the Court of Appeal had an opportunity to realign UK law with that of the EPO. By that date, the Court of Appeal had held in *Actavis UK Limited v Merck and Co Inc*[15] that the Court could depart from its previous decisions where it was satisfied that the EPO Boards of Appeal had formed a settled view on a point of law which differs from earlier UK decisions. The Court, however, declined to do so. Instead, the Court reiterated its position that software inventions would continue to be allowable in the UK based on the existence of a 'technical contribution'.[16]

Subsequently, in *AT&T Knowledge Ventures and CVON Innovations Limited Applications*[17] the English High Court provided further guidance on the correct approach to determining technical contribution under the *Aerotel* test. Noting that it was impossible to define the meaning of 'technical' in the context of the *Aerotel* test, the Court set out a number of signposts for identifying a relevant technical effect:[18]

(i) whether the claimed technical effect has a technical effect on a process which is carried out outside the computer;

(ii) whether the claimed technical effect operates at the level of the architecture of the computer, that is to say whether the effect is produced irrespective of the data being processed or the applications being run;

(iii) whether the claimed technical effect results in the computer being made to operate in the new way;

(iv) whether there is an increase in the speed or reliability of the computer; and

(v) whether the perceived problem is overcome by the claimed invention as opposed to merely being circumvented.

Lewison LJ reviewed these signposts in the Court of Appeal decision in *HTC Europe Co Ltd v Apple*,[19] approving a less restrictive interpretation of the above fourth signpost by Mann J in *Gemstar-TV Guide International Inc v Virgin Media Ltd*,[20] ie, that a program makes a computer a better computer in the sense of running more efficiently and effectively as a computer and not only when there is an increase in the speed or reliability of the computer.

In *Lantana's Application*,[21] after stating that there is no comprehensive test for determining technical contribution, Kitchin LJ repeated and commented

---

15 [2008] EWCA Civ 444.

16 Such a decision was taken prior to the ruling of the Enlarged Board of Appeal in G3/08 which upheld the current EPO practice and arguably gives this area the status of 'settled law' which would have permitted the Court of Appeal to bring UK law into line with the practice of the EPO.

17 [2009] EWHC 343 (Pat).

18 *AT&T*, [40].

19 [2013] EWCA Civ 451.

20 [2009] EWHC 3068 (Ch).

21 [2014] EWCA Civ 1463.

favourably on Lewison LJ's summary in *HTC Europe Co Ltd v Apple* and set out the following summary of the UK courts' approach.

- *First, it is not possible to define a clear rule to determine whether or not a program is excluded, and each case must be determined on its own facts. …*
- *Second, the fact that improvements are made to the software programmed into the computer rather than hardware forming part of the computer does not make a difference. … the analysis must be carried out as a matter of substance not form.*
- *Third, the exclusions operate cumulatively. So, for example, the invention in Gale related to a new way of calculating a square root of a number with the aid of a computer and Mr Gale sought to claim it as a ROM in which his program was stored. This was not permissible. The incorporation of the program in a ROM did not alter its nature: it was still a computer program (excluded matter) incorporating a mathematical method (also excluded matter). …*
- *Fourth, it follows that it is helpful to ask: what does the invention contribute to the art as a matter of practical reality over and above the fact that it relates to a program for a computer? If the only contribution lies in excluded matter then it is not patentable.*
- *Fifth, and conversely, it is also helpful to consider whether the invention may be regarded as solving a problem which is essentially technical, and that is so whether that problem lies inside or outside the computer. An invention which solves a technical problem within the computer will have a relevant technical effect in that it will make the computer, as a computer, an improved device, for example by increasing its speed. An invention which solves a technical problem outside the computer will also have a relevant technical effect, for example by controlling an improved technical process. In either case it will not be excluded by Art 52 as relating to a computer program as such.*[22]

In 2020, the High Court applied this law in *Lenovo's Application*[23] in relation to a patent application concerning a contactless payment card, and more particularly an invention relating to the avoidance of 'card clash' (ie, the selection of which card to use for a payment when multiple cards are presented to a contactless payment device at the same time as may occur when multiple cards are present in the same wallet).

In *Lenovo*, after reviewing the law, Birss J as he then was, focused on two of the signposts mentioned in *AT&T* – whether the claimed technical effect impacts a process which is carried out outside a computer and whether a technical problem is overcome by the claimed invention as opposed to merely

22 *HTC v Apple*, [45]–[49].
23 *Lenovo (Singapore) PTE Ltd v Comptroller General of Patents* [2020] EWHC 1706 (Pat).

being circumvented.[24] The judge observed that the claimed invention involved a different physical interaction to what had occurred in the prior art. Unlike the prior art, the invention avoided a requirement of a user to press a button to allocate a payment to a payment card when card clash occurred. The judge considered this was a sufficient difference to overcome the invention being considered a computer program or a method of doing business as such.

3.2 Individual exceptions to patentability

In addition to establishing the basic framework for assessing the patentability of computer-implemented inventions, the UK courts have also commented on the individual exceptions appearing in Section 1 of the Act, each of which is discussed below.

(a) Methods for doing business

There is little case law in the United Kingdom on the patentability of business methods. What limited jurisprudence exists suggests that it is very difficult to persuade the courts that a patent application should be granted where a claimed invention is a computer-implemented business method.

The leading case is *Merrill Lynch's Application*,[25] where the Court of Appeal rejected an application directed to a computerised trading system which accommodated real-time order flow. The Court considered that the only possible technical advance arising from the invention was the production of a novel trading system – that is, a data-processing system for implementing a specific business. The Court went on to reject the application reasoning that although a data-processing system operating to produce a novel technical result would normally be patentable, this would not be the case when the end result was a method of doing business and hence itself a prohibited item under Section 1(2) of the Patents Act 1977.

The High Court took a similar approach in *Oneida Indian Nation's Application*,[26] which related to a computer system for online gambling. In that case, the Court accepted that the claimed system gave rise to a number of technical advantages in that the number of processing steps per bet were reduced, the number of data transmission steps were reduced, and the system dispensed with the need to make an account check for every bet, and hence the system was more secure and robust. However, the Court still rejected the application because the Court found all these advantages were the direct result of implementing a new business method.

---

24 Notably Birss J referred to the other signposts – technical effects at the level of computer architecture causing a computer to operate in a new way and improving the speed or efficiency of a computer as being relevant for "the better computer cases", in other words the more technical computer cases.

25 Note 7, *supra*.

26 [2007] EWHC 954 (Pat).

In contrast, the judge, in *Lenovo's Application*[27] did not consider the invention to constitute a business method "as such". In *Lenovo's Application*, the judge expressly asked the question "what more is the Lenovo invention than a method of doing business?"[28] Answering that question, the judge analysed the alleged invention in terms of the physical differences between the invention and the prior art concluding that the differences between the two were not merely a computer program or a method of doing business, but rather technical in character because they solved a specific problem of how to deal with card clash in an automatic way which did not require any user input as had been required in the past.

(b) Mental acts

The mental acts exclusion is construed narrowly in the United Kingdom. As confirmed by the High Court in *Halliburton's Application*,[29] the exclusion only applies to acts carried out mentally.

Previously in *Fujitsu's Application*,[30] the Court of Appeal proposed taking a broad view of the exclusion, which would exclude from patentability any methods which were capable of being performed mentally, regardless of whether the methods were in fact performed in that way. The Court of Appeal however doubted this view in *Aerotel*[31] and it was finally rejected by the Court in the *Halliburton* case. As a result, the mental acts exclusion is of very limited relevance to the patentability of computer programs as this exclusion can easily be avoided by specifying that a method is undertaken by a computer rather than by a human being.

(c) Presentation of information

The application of the *Aerotel* test to presentation of information was considered in *Gemstar TV Guide International v Virgin Media*[32] in a case concerning electronic program guides. There, the Court confirmed that the UK courts, like the EPO, will distinguish between content and delivery of information and any technical aspects of that delivery. In *Gemstar*, the Court accepted that the actual contribution of the claimed invention was a better, more intuitive electronic program guide. This meant that the invention had an independent effect which went beyond the mere presentation of information.

The Court in *HTC v Apple*[33] followed the same approach. This case involved four patents including Apple's 'slide to unlock' patent. Although the Court

27 Note 23 *supra*.
28 *Lenovo*, [35].
29 [2011] EWHC 2508 (Pat).
30 *Fujitsu*, at p619 line 10 to p621 line 30.
31 *Aerotel*, at p98.
32 Note 20 *supra*.
33 [2012] EWHC 1789 (Pat).

ultimately found the claimed invention obvious in the light of the prior art, the Court was happy to accept that the provision of a novel and intuitive user interface for activating a mobile phone was clearly suitable subject matter for a patent.

(d) Aesthetic creations

The exclusion of 'literary, dramatic, musical or artistic work or any other aesthetic creation whatsoever' from patentability has generated very little case law in the United Kingdom.

The UKIPO's view is that if an article is distinguished from the prior art solely by its design, ornamentation or colour then it will be excluded from patentability. However, a distinction with a practical effect can save the article from exclusion.[34]

Practically the only case law considering the exclusion is *ITS Rubber Ltd's Application*,[35] which was decided under the pre-1977 law and concerned a claim to a squash ball characterised by its blue colour. In that case, the application was allowed because presented evidence demonstrated that the difference in colour resulted in surprisingly enhanced visibility during play.

The paucity of case law on this provision demonstrates the relative lack of importance of this provision.

Finally, it should be noted that the UKIPO considers that in contrast to an aesthetic creation, the means for obtaining a purely aesthetic effect can be patentable when characterised by non-excluded features, such as the structure of an article or the steps in a manufacturing process.[36]

(e) Mathematical methods

Purely abstract mathematical methods are not patentable under UK law. However, mathematical methods having practical application are not necessarily excluded and may be patentable.

This follows from the Court of Appeal decision in *Gale's Application*[37] where the Court stated that:

> *In the present case Mr Gale claims to have discovered an algorithm. Clearly that, as such is not patentable. It is an intellectual discovery which, for good measure, falls squarely within one of the items, mathematical method, listed in s.1(2). But the nature of this discovery is such that it has a practical application, in that it enables instruction to be written for conventional computers in a way which will, so it is claimed, expedite one of the calculations frequently made with the aid of a computer. In my view the application of Mr Gale's mathematical formulae for the*

34 UKIPO Manual of Patent Practice, paragraph 1.30.
35 [1979] RPC 318.
36 UKIPO Manual of Patent Practice, paragraph 1.30.2.
37 Note 8 *supra*.

purpose of writing computer instruction is sufficient to dispose of the contention that he is claiming a mathematical method as such.

Following *Gale's Application*, the UKIPO will only reject patent applications relating to mathematical modelling or the implementations of algorithms if no benefit arising from the algorithm can be identified or the algorithm is entirely unconnected with real world phenomena.[38]

Thus, for example, in *Halliburton Energy Services Inc's Applications*[39] both a method of designing a drill bit using computer simulation and a method of simulating drilling a directional wellbore were found not excluded despite each involving mathematics. In that case, the judge summarised the UK approach to such matters as follows:

Although obviously some mathematics is involved, the contribution is not solely a mathematical method (on top of being a computer program) because the data on which the mathematics is performed has been specified in the claim in such a way as to represent something concrete (a drill bit design etc).[40]

The UKIPO however considers that many computer-implemented inventions, particularly inventions involving computer simulation and artificial intelligence, may well be objected to on the grounds that they relate in some way to a mathematical method.[41]

This is still a developing area of law and jurisprudence is limited on the matter.

(f) Scheme, rule or method for playing a game

Where an invention relates solely to the rules of a game, a patent application for the invention will be rejected as relating to unpatentable subject matter. For example, in *IGT's Application*,[42] the claimed invention related to a gaming apparatus where success in a main game led to a chance to play a bonus game. The High Court therefore found that the invention related solely to the rules of the game being played, and hence rejected the application as being unpatentable for relating to excluded subject matter as such.

4. Life sciences and chemical inventions

For the life sciences and chemical fields, prospective applicants will be pleased to hear that there are no real surprises when considering subject matter eligibility at the UK courts. Indeed, questions of subject matter eligibility are not

38 Compare *Schlumberger Holdings* BL O/016/09 – provision of quality control indicators based on processing sonic well logging data – allowed; *Western Gecco* BL O/135/07 – determining one or more parameters relating to physical properties of the earth's interior from seismic data – allowed. But note also *Institut du Français Petrol & Elf* BL O/201/03 – case rejected due to lack of any link to physical benefit or measurement.

39 [2011] EWHC 2508 (Pat).

40 *Haliburton*, [72].

41 UKIPO Manual of Patent Practice, paragraph 1.29.5.

42 [2007] EWHC 1341.

raised very often during UK Court proceedings. One reason for this is that most UK patents in the life sciences and chemical fields start life as European patent applications.[43] As is noted in the chapter on patentability under the European Patent Convention, in general patentable subject matter issues primarily arise during the grant process and rarely arise in post-grant litigation.

4.1 Ethical exclusions

The Patents Act 1977 prohibits the patenting of inventions that are contrary to public policy or morality.[44] The main difference between the wording of the Patents Act compared with the EPC is the Act's reference to 'public policy', rather than to '*ordre public*' as used in the EPC. The UK Patents Act 1977 also explicitly specifies that this exclusion does not prohibit any inventions simply because they are illegal in the United Kingdom.[45] However, as discussed earlier, Section 1 of the Patents Act is one of the sections of the Patents Act which is expressly stated to be "framed to have, as nearly as practicable, the same effects in the United Kingdom as the corresponding provisions of the European Patent Convention".[46] Hence, this difference in wording is not intended to have any practical effect.

Some more concrete guidance on subject matter excluded from patentability is provided by paragraphs 3(a)–3(e) of Schedule A2 to the Patents Act 1977, which was added to UK law as a result of the EU Biotech Directive.[47]

This states that the following are not patentable inventions:

(a) the human body, at the various stages of its formation and development, and the simple discovery of one of its elements, including the sequence or partial sequence of a gene;

(b) processes for cloning human beings;

(c) processes for modifying the germ line genetic identity of human beings;

(d) uses of human embryos for industrial or commercial purposes;

(e) processes for modifying the genetic identity of animals which are likely to cause them suffering without any substantial medical benefit to man or animal, and also animals resulting from such processes.

UK-specific case law is limited in this area. The UK courts have, however, held 'embryo', as referred to in Schedule A2, to include not only a live human embryo produced by the fertilisation of a female egg, but also embryos produced without such fertilisation, such as those created by cell nuclear replacement.[48]

---

43 Over 90% of patents in force in the UK are European patents (UK) granted by the European Patent Office. However, the proportion of chemical and life science patents originating from the EPO is even higher than that given the commercial imperatives for protecting such innovations across multiple jurisdictions.

44 Patents Act 1977, Section (1)(3).

45 Patents Act 1977, Section (1)(4).

46 Patents Act 1977, Section 130(7).

47 European Directive 98/44/EC.

48 *R (Quintavalle) v Sec of State for Health* [2003] UKHL 137.

4.2 Plant and animal varieties

Paragraphs 3(f), 4 and 11 of Schedule A2 to the Patents Act 1977 set out the rules for the patentability of plant and animal varieties in the United Kingdom.

These provisions provide that:

- *any variety of animal or plant or any essentially biological process for the production of animals or plants, not being a micro-biological or other technical process or the product of such a process, is not a patentable invention;*
- *Inventions which concern plants or animals may be patentable if the technical feasibility of the invention is not confined to a particular plant or animal variety;*
- *"essentially biological process" means a process for the production of animals and plants which consists entirely of natural phenomena such as crossing and selection;*
- *"microbiological process" means any process involving or performed upon or resulting in microbiological material; and*
- *"plant variety" means a plant grouping within a single botanical taxon of the lowest known rank, which grouping can be:*
    - *defined by the expression of the characteristics that results from a given genotype or combination of genotypes;*
    - *distinguished from any other plant grouping by the expression of at least one of the said characteristics; and*
    - *considered as a unit with regard to its suitability for being propagated unchanged.*

These provisions were also introduced into UK law to implement the EU Biotech Directive and similar rules[49] exist governing the patentability of plants and animals under the European Patent Convention. Consequently, there is very little divergence in the approach adopted in the UK from that of the EPO.

In addition, a specialist protection scheme for protecting plant varieties is available under the Plant Varieties Act 1997. The only point of note here is that after Brexit (ie, from 31 January 2020), the UK is no longer part of the EU, and therefore protection in the UK through the Community Plant Variety Office is no longer possible.

4.3 Medical, surgical and diagnostic methods

Similarly, as with the EPO, methods practised on the human or animal body are not patentable in the United Kingdom,[50] and there is little divergence from the EPO in this area.

One notable exception is, however, the differing outcomes in the so-called 'homeopathy' applications filed at both the EPO and at the UKIPO.

---

49 Rules 26(4)(6) and 28(2) EPC.
50 Patents Act 1977, Section 4A(1).

Homeopathy is a holistic treatment based on the use of highly diluted substances, which practitioners claim can cause the body to heal itself. A 2010 House of Commons Science and Technology Committee[51] report on homeopathy said that the principles on which homeopathy is based are "scientifically implausible".

In 2015, the UKIPO Hearing Officer[52] considered the patentability of eleven applications relating to ultra-dilute-homeopathic-antibody solutions. The dilution was so great that each dose would be unlikely to contain a single antibody molecule, a fact admitted in the applications. The Hearing Officer rejected the applications on the grounds that ultra-low doses of antibodies having any effect beyond the placebo effect was not considered plausible. Consequently, the inventions lacked industrial application[53] and sufficiency. A finding of a lack of sufficiency was also confirmed by the EPO Board of Appeal in the corresponding EP proceedings.[54]

The applicant subsequently appealed the decision of the UKIPO Hearing Officer in the UK courts. On appeal it was held that the Hearing Officer had unfairly rejected the data in the applications which included a double-blind placebo-controlled study in 146 children. Consequently, the applications did have a plausible, albeit mysterious, technical effect and thus were also industrially applicable.[55] The cases were remitted to the UKIPO and subsequently granted.

4.4 Natural products

Mere discoveries are not patentable in the United Kingdom.[56] However, in line with the approach adopted by the EPO, the practical application of a discovery can be patentable.

In *Genentech Inc's Patent*,[57] the Court of Appeal held that the discovery of an amino acid sequence for the substance tPA led to a valid claim when incorporated into a conventional manufacturing process for the manufacture of tPA. Similarly, in *Kirin-Amgen v Hoechst Marion Roussel*,[58] the House of Lords held that a DNA sequence of a gene was not an invention on its own. However, if it were necessary to isolate and extract a DNA sequence, then a process developed for this purpose and the material when obtained by this process could both be patentable.

In line with the EU Biotech Directive, patents to gene sequences may be allowed, but must include data.[59]

---

51 https://publications.parliament.uk/pa/cm200910/cmselect/cmsctech/45/4502.htm.

52 BL O/508/15.

53 Inventions must be capable of industrial application in order to be patentable (see Patents Act 1977, Section 1(1)(c)). Section 4(1) further states that an invention is capable of industrial application if it "can be made or used in any kind of industry". The same requirements exist in the EPC.

54 T 1273/09.

55 *Oleg Iliich Epshtein v the Comptroller General of Patents, Designs and Trade Marks* [2016] EWHC 1511 (Ch).

56 Patents Act 1977, Section 1(2)(c).

57 [1989] RPC 147.

58 [2005] RPC 9.

59 Patents Act 1977, Schedule A2, paragraphs 5 and 6.

In the UKIPO Examination Guidelines for Patent Applications relating to Biotechnological Inventions, special mention is made of claims to 3D-structures of proteins, stating that these are not patentable "not the least because such structures are merely representations of the atomic coordinates of a peptide in space, do not have any technical character, and do not solve any technical problem".[60] The 3D structure of a protein is therefore excluded from patentability as a mere discovery, although the Examination Guidelines leave open the possibility of this changing in the future, noting that each application should be considered on its own merits.

5. Impact of Brexit

European Directive 98/44/EC (the Biotech Directive) concerns subject matter eligibility for biotechnological inventions. As an EU member state at the time the Directive was implemented, UK law was amended to incorporate the Biotech Directive.[61]

Following the UK's departure from the European Union on 31 January 2020, the UK courts are no longer bound by decisions of the Court of Justice of the European Union (CJEU) or future European directives. This might result in future divergence of UK and EU law, as the UK courts and CJEU may decide upon points of law independently after Brexit. However, this seems unlikely when considering the specific area of patent subject matter eligibility as this is not a sufficiently contentious issue at the present time in either the UK or the EU.

Consequently, the impact of Brexit on how the UK courts approach questions of patentable subject matter for biotechnological inventions is likely to be small, and divergence between the UK courts and the CJEU is only likely to be seen when considering future technologies that have not yet been envisaged.

6. Statistics

Since 2000, the UKIPO has issued 608 Hearing Officer decisions relating to patentable subject matter; such decisions constitute just over 30% of the total number of all decisions issued by Hearing Officers between 2000 and 2020. As the UKIPO considers very few patent applications in the chemical and life science fields, almost all of these decisions concern the patentability of computer-implemented inventions.[62]

In 89% of cases, the Hearing Officer upheld the view of the examiner handling an application that the case in question related to unpatentable

60 Guidelines at [116].

61 See discussed in section 4.1 on "Ethical Exclusions" and section 4.2 on "Plant and Animal Varieties" above.

62 A small number, around 2% to 3%, concern applications by private inventors where issues of patentability arise due to applications not being compliant with physical laws or other fundamental reasons.

subject matter with only 11% of cases causing the Hearing Officer to overturn an examiner's preliminary opinion on the matter.

As Figure 1 indicates, the numbers of Hearing Officer decisions each year varied from a high of 77 in 2007 to a low of three in 2000.

Due to the relatively low numbers of cases each year and particularly due to the low numbers of successful hearings, the allowance rate varies significantly year-to-year, as shown in Figure 2. In 2014 and 2018, 27% of cases resulted in Hearing Officers overturning the preliminary views of a patent examiner that an invention related to unpatentable subject matter. In contrast, no hearings overturned a patent examiner's finding on patentable subject matter between 2000 and 2003, or in 2013 or 2016.

Figure 1. UKIPO patent hearings on patentable subject matter

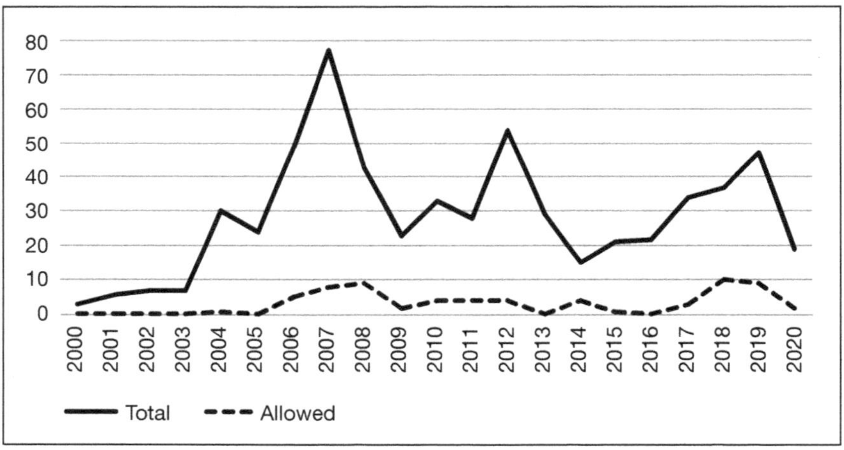

Figure 2. UKIPO allowance rate at Patent Office hearings

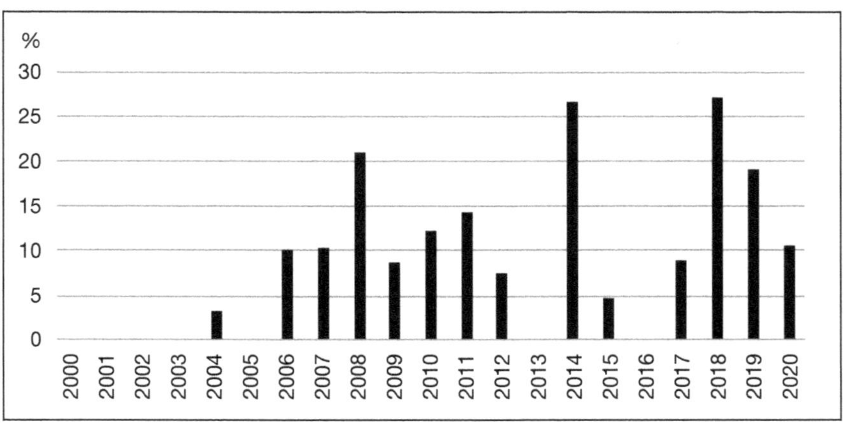

Table 1. Total number of hearings

	Total number of hearings	**Allowed**	**Refused**	**Percentage allowed**
2000	3	0	3	0%
2001	6	0	6	0%
2002	7	0	7	0%
2003	7	0	7	0%
2004	30	1	29	3%
2005	24	0	24	0%
2006	49	5	44	10%
2007	77	8	69	10%
2008	43	9	34	21%
2009	23	2	21	9%
2010	33	4	29	12%
2011	28	4	24	14%
2012	54	4	50	7%
2013	29	0	29	0%
2014	15	4	11	27%
2015	21	1	20	5%
2016	22	0	22	0%
2017	34	3	31	9%
2018	37	10	27	27%
2019	47	9	38	19%
2020	19	2	17	11%
TOTAL	**608**	**66**	**542**	**11%**

The figures in Table 1 should, however, be put in perspective. The UKIPO examines around 12,000 patent applications a year,[63] roughly half of which proceed to grant. The 30 or so applications a year, which are rejected on the grounds of lack of patentable subject matter following a Hearing Officer decision, therefore represent a very small percentage of the applications rejected by the UKIPO.

7. Practical considerations

It is overwhelmingly computer-implemented inventions which are assessed at hearings before the UKIPO. As a result, lessons which can be derived from the case law primarily relate to the drafting and prosecution of computer-implemented inventions and may have limited relevance beyond that field.

7.1 Absence of any technical benefits will result in an application being rejected

The case law as it has developed has had a consistent focus on the technical differences between a claimed invention and the prior art. Where that difference exclusively relates to excluded subject matter, an application will be refused.

Cases which were doomed to fail are well exemplified by the inventions in *Shopolotto's Application*[64] and *Macrossan's Application* which was considered in the *Aerotel* appeal itself.[65]

The concept at the heart of *Shopolotto's Application* was the idea of replacing the markings on a computer-implemented casino slot machine with representations of brands. This was the sole feature which could be said to distinguish the claimed invention from the prior art. The presentation of images of brands on a computer-implemented slot machine was seen to fall solely within the sphere of methods of doing business, and no suggestion was put forward to counter this.

Macrossan's Application considered in the *Aerotel* appeal related to a computer-based system for creating documents for incorporating businesses. According to the system, a user was presented with questions relating to certain types of business entity and, in response to the user's input, incorporation documents were generated. Again, there was no suggestion that the system amounted to anything more than the automation of existing business processes. Automation of an otherwise non-technical process, without more, does not constitute a technical benefit.

---

63 Intellectual Property Office, "Facts and Figures, Patent, trade mark, design and hearing data" (UKIPO, 2019).
64 [2005] EWHC 2416 (Pat).
65 Note 12, *supra*.

7.2 The UKIPO will take an applicant's own presentation of an invention as non-technical at face value

Although it may be the case that some applications are destined for failure because they simply do not relate to any kind of technical advance, the mere existence of some technical advantage is not sufficient. Presentation of such advantages in a patent application matters. *Gale's Application* and *Oneida Indian Nation's Application* illustrate this point.

As discussed above, *Gale's Application* concerned a novel method of calculating square roots.[66] Mr Gale's method has been widely adopted and is almost the exclusive method for calculating square roots used by computers and pocket calculators. The reason for this is the method involves fewer division steps than previous methods. Division is relatively time consuming and difficult to computerise compared with other mathematical operations, such as addition, subtraction, or multiplication. Hence, Mr Gale's approach could be implemented using fewer computer resources than previously conventional methods.

Although, in hindsight, Mr Gale's invention had a clear potential for an arguable technical benefit, the Court of Appeal ruled otherwise, and the application failed. This was in large part due to how the application was written. Mr Gale was a private applicant who did not engage a professional patent attorney and the application almost exclusively comprised a mathematical proof that Mr Gale's new approach was suitable for calculating square roots. As the application presented the claimed invention as a novel mathematical method and nothing more, the Court of Appeal ruled that the application solely concerned excluded subject matter.

Oneida Indian Nation's Application[67] related to a computer system for online gambling, which the Court accepted reduced the amount of processing for dealing with individual bets. At face value, it would be expected that the demonstration of reduced processing and increased system robustness forms a good basis for arguing the disclosed system was patentable.

However, after listing the technical advantages which were said to flow from the invention,[68] the judge commented:

> *It is fair to say... the way that Oneida describe their invention in the application is not the way in which they describe it in this appeal. The advantages relied on in this appeal are nowhere pointed out in the application. There is not said to be any problem with permitting any number of processing or data transmission steps, or allowing an account check on every transaction, or of a lack of security or robustness. Moreover in the application as filed the advantages are described purely*

---

66 More accurately approximations of square roots.
67 [2007] EWHC 954 (Pat).
68 *Ibid*, [24].

in terms of the advantages for gaming ..., including advantages as to how the new method may avoid restrictions imposed by local gaming laws.[69]

The judge concluded:[70]

The advantages relied on by Oneida seem to me to fall within the rider in Merrill Lynch. They are advantages of the new method of doing business and so fall wholly within the exclusion. Although they can be described as "technical", they do not count as such: they are not a relevant technical effect. They are merely the consequence of putting the new business method into effect.

These decisions illustrate the limits of what can be done to overcome a finding of non-patentable subject matter after the application has been filed. In both cases, neither *Gale's Application* nor *Oneida Indian Nation's Application* presented the claimed invention in terms of a technical advance or a technical solution to a technical problem. Given that, there were limits on the extent to which later argument could persuade the Court that the claimed inventions amounted to anything more than the applicants had originally claimed.

7.3 Identification and description of technical benefits in an application increases likelihood of the patent-eligibility finding

Given the above, the importance of identifying and describing technical benefits arising from a claimed invention in an application cannot be over-emphasised.

In most cases, it is possible to identify, in advance of drafting, applications where issues relating to patentable subject matter may arise by analysing the differences between the claimed invention and known prior art. If, as in *Shopolotto* or *Macrossan's applications*, there is nothing which the application could be said to add outside of the fields of excluded subject matter, then there is very little which can be done to pre-empt patent office objections. If, however, there are any arguable technical differences, such as there were with *Gale's* and *Oneida Indian Nation's applications*, then challenges to patent eligibility can be alleviated or avoided by presenting the invention in terms of addressing a specific technical problem. In Mr Gale's case, the outcome might have been different if the application had explained computational burdens imposed by large numbers of division steps and how these would be reduced using the claimed invention. Similarly, the decision in *Oneida Indian Nation's Application* might have been different if the application had identified the benefits relied upon by the advocate at court as part of the application itself, rather than presenting the invention purely in terms of advantages of complying with local gaming laws.

---

69 *Ibid*, [25].
70 *Ibid*, [28].

7.4 The importance of an assessment and presentation of the invention relative to the prior art

Oneida Indian Nation's Application and the successful appeal in *Lenovo's Application* indicate the benefits of being able to present an invention in terms of an advance over the prior art.

In *Oneida Indian Nation's Application*, the application was based on a PCT application, and a prior art search had been conducted in the international phase. This meant that it was possible at the prosecution stage to compare the claimed invention with the prior art and identify potential technical benefits which arose from the differences between the two. Although the application failed for other reasons, a technical assessment relative to the prior art was sufficient to persuade the Court that some technical advance existed.

Similarly, Lenovo overcame patent office objections by presenting their invention as a development in relation to specific items of prior art. Because the Lenovo system differed physically from the prior art, presenting the Lenovo system as a further technical development based on such physical differences produced a persuasive argument that the Lenovo system is more than merely a simple implementation of a business method.

These two cases illustrate the importance of assessing and presenting an invention in terms of an advance over the prior art, not only at the drafting stage but also during the prosecution stage, even when such advances change between the two stages due to the patent office citing new prior art.

7.5 Advice for avoiding and addressing subject matter objections in the UKIPO

The approach for avoiding or overcoming unpatentable subject matter objections at the UKIPO can be summarised as follows.

- An invention should be assessed at the initial drafting stage to try to identify whether it is likely to run into unpatentable subject matter issues. If the only differences between a claimed invention and the prior art lie in excluded fields, eg, relate solely to business advantages as in *Shopolotto* and *Macrossan*, then an unpatentable subject matter objection is likely to be fatal to the application's chances of being granted. In such circumstances, it may be preferable to avoid filing the application at all, given the low chances of success, and consider relying on other forms of intellectual property protection.
- Conversely, if any arguments exist that the differences between a claimed invention and the prior art give rise to any technical advantages then the application should be drafted to highlight those potential advantages and how they arise. Had this been done in *Gale's Application* or *Oneida Indian Nation's Application*, the outcomes of those cases might have been different.
- To highlight any technical advantages in an application, attorneys

should identify the actual contribution the claimed invention makes (see *Aerotel* test) and consider whether this actual contribution is or involves a technical solution to any technical problems (or problems that are essentially technical).

- As well as at the drafting stage, during prosecution, attorneys should be creative in trying to identify suitable 'technical advantages'. If any differences can be ascertained between an invention and prior art, they should be assessed to see if they can be presented as giving rise to some form of 'technical character'. The 'improved visibility' argument for a different coloured squash ball presented in *ITS Rubber Ltd's Application* is a good example of creative advocacy supporting a conclusion that an apparently non-technical feature (in that case the colour of a squash ball) could be linked with an arguable technical advantage (improved visibility).
- Potential technical advantages may only become apparent in the light of a comparison with the prior art, as was the case in *Oneida Indian Nation's Application* and *Lenovo's Application*. The UKIPO is under no obligation to search applications which an examiner considers relate to unpatentable subject matter. In such cases an applicant's identification of prior art and technical advantages of the invention over that prior art may assist with advancement of an application. In particularly challenging cases, where potential unpatentable subject matter issues are identifiable at the drafting stage, conducting pre-filing searches to identify prior art can facilitate drafting an application in a way which presents the invention as a technical advance over the prior art.
- If the UKIPO raises an unpatentable subject matter objection during prosecution it is rarely advantageous to present arguments that the objection is incorrect as a matter of law. A more effective approach is to focus on persuading a patent examiner that the application describes something inventive which gives rise to some kind of technical advantage.
- As noted above, a patent application will preferably be drafted so that it contains an indication of the technical problem being addressed. However, that is not essential. Rather the more important issue is to ensure that the application as filed does not itself identify advantages which relate solely to unpatentable subject matter, such as identifying the application as merely relating to a mathematical algorithm (see *Gale's Application* discussed above) or solely addressing a business problem (see *Oneida Indian Nation's Application* discussed above). Being completely silent about the nature of advantages is preferable to identifying advantages as being solely non-technical in nature.
- Naturally, the UKIPO will be influenced in its assessment of an invention

by the terminology used by an applicant. Although it is not necessary to try to conceal the business context of an invention, use of business terminology in a patent application (eg, customers, prices, sales, etc) should be minimised. Instead, an application should focus on the technical structures and processes which are performed by a computer implementing a computer implemented invention.

- When there is a question about a potential unpatentable subject matter in a computer-implemented invention, the UKIPO Examiners will look to the *AT&T* signposts as indicators for a 'technical' invention. Thus, when drafting an application, embodiments should be presented with features which lead to technical advantages that fall under these *AT&T* signposts wherever possible.
- Not all of the *AT&T* signposts to the existence of a 'technical' invention are equal. As noted in *Lenovo's Application*, technical effects which arise at the level of computer architecture and cause a computer to operate in a new way or improve the speed or efficiency of the computer are more likely to be accepted by the UKIPO and the courts as establishing that an invention relates to patentable subject matter. Arguments based on technical effects arising from processes outside a computer or on an alleged new way of processing tend to be less persuasive. So, when drafting an application, features and their technical advantages relating to the more persuasive signposts should be presented whenever possible.
- If an application is of importance, applicants should consider filing the application both in the UKIPO and with the EPO. Although the approaches between the two offices are similar, they are not identical and an application may be successful in one forum and not in the other.
- Similarly in borderline cases, it can be worthwhile appealing decisions of a Hearing Officer to the UK Courts. As noted above, Hearing Officers generally uphold the objections raised during prosecution. However, the courts seem to be more open to allowing applications to proceed if there is an arguable case that a claimed invention has technical character as was the case both with *Symbian's Application* and *Lenovo's Application*.

The authors would like to thank their colleagues Yelena Morozova and Maeve O'Flynn for their assistance in drafting this chapter.

United States

Paul W Browning
Christopher C Johns
Sara A Leiman
Finnegan LLP

1. Background and executive summary

United States courts and the US Patent and Trademark Office (USPTO) allow for the patenting of a broad range of subject matter, with few limitations. The US Constitution provides the origins of US patent law, granting Congress broad power to legislate to "promote the Progress of Science and useful Arts, by securing for limited Times to Authors and Inventors the exclusive Right to their respective Writings and Discoveries".[1] Congress has exercised that power in the US Patent Act, which provides:

> *[w]hoever invents or discovers any new and useful process, machine, manufacture, or composition of matter, or any new and useful improvement thereof, may obtain a patent therefor, subject to the conditions and requirements of this title.*[2]

The US Supreme Court has recognised that this expansive language in the Patent Act indicates Congressional intent to allow for a wide scope of patentable subject matter.[3] This intent is further revealed in the Committee Reports accompanying the 1952 Patent Act, which codified the current language of 35 USC §101. These Reports state that the intent of the Act was to permit the patenting of "anything under the sun that is made by man".[4] Thus, while other countries may forbid patenting of business methods or methods of medical treatment, the US patent system does not, and instead allows for the patenting of a wide range of subject matter.

But this broad scope of patent-eligible subject matter has limits. US courts have held that not all subject matter is eligible for patenting under 35 USC §101, and, in particular, "laws of nature, natural phenomena, and abstract ideas" may not be patented under US law.[5] The Supreme Court has explained that these exceptions to patent eligibility constitute the "basic tools of scientific and technological work" and that permitting the monopolisation of these tools by granting patent rights may impede innovation rather than promote it.[6] Thus,

---

1 Article I, §8, clause 8.
2 35 USC §101.
3 *See Diamond v Chakrabarty*, 447 US 303, 308 (1980).
4 S Rep No 1979, 82d Cong, 2d Sess, 5 (1952); H R Rep No 1923, 82d Cong, 2d Sess, 6 (1952).
5 *Diamond v Diehr*, 450 US 175, 185 (1981).
6 *Alice Corp Pty v CLS Bank Int'l*, 573 US 208, 216 (2014).

courts have additionally rejected, as patent ineligible, attempts to patent inventions that either apply these three categories of forbidden subject matter in an unduly broad manner, or in a manner the courts deem to have no inventive contribution beyond the identification of a natural law, phenomenon or abstract idea. The prohibition against patenting laws of nature, natural phenomena, or abstract ideas cannot be circumvented, for example, by limiting their use to a particular technological environment or by adding insignificant post-solution activity.[7] At the same time, courts have also recognised that:

too broad an interpretation of this exclusionary principle could eviscerate patent law ... [because] all inventions at some level embody, use, reflect, rest upon or apply laws of nature, natural phenomena, or abstract ideas.[8]

The challenge for practitioners, agencies and the courts has been identifying the precise boundaries of the murky line between patent-eligible and patent-ineligible subject matter. The US Supreme Court, through its decisions in *Mayo v Prometheus Labs, Inc* and *Alice Corp Pty v CLS Bank Int'l,* has provided a two-step test (the *Mayo/Alice* test) for resolving this question. In the first step of the test, the claims at issue are examined to determine whether they are directed to any of the 'judicial exceptions' to patent eligibility, namely, laws of nature, natural phenomena, or abstract ideas.[9] If not, then the patent claims are patent eligible. If the claims are directed to a judicial exception, however, the examination proceeds to the second step of the test. In the second step, the elements of each claim are considered, "both individually and 'as an ordered combination' to determine whether the additional elements 'transform the nature of the claim' into a patent-eligible application".[10] The Supreme Court has

described step two of this analysis as a search for an 'inventive concept'—i.e., an element or combination of elements that is 'sufficient to ensure that the patent in practice amounts to significantly more than a patent upon the [ineligible concept] itself.'[11]

The Court of Appeals for the Federal Circuit ('Federal Circuit')[12] has determined that this second step of the *Mayo/Alice* test is satisfied if, aside from the judicial exception, the limitations of the claim at issue "involve more than performance of 'well-understood, routine [and] conventional activities previously known to the industry'".[13]

The USPTO has described the *Mayo/Alice* test with the framework below, which further elaborates on the Supreme Court's two-step analysis. The USPTO

---

7 *Mayo v Prometheus Labs, Inc,* 566 US 66, 73 (2012).

8 *Mayo,* 566 US at 71.

9 *Alice,* 573 US at 217.

10 *Alice,* 573 US at 217–218 (citing *Mayo,* 566 US at 79, 78).

11 *Ibid* (citing *Mayo,* 566 US at 77).

12 The Federal Circuit is the only court of appeals that reviews decisions in patent cases. It reviews decisions by district courts and the USPTO.

13 *Content Extraction and Transmission LLC v Wells Fargo Bank, Nat'l Ass'n,* 776 F 3d 1343, 1347–1348 (Fed Cir 2014) (quoting *Alice,* 573 US at 225).

adds a preliminary first step[14] that determines if the claims are directed to one of the traditional classes of patentable subject matter enumerated in 35 USC §101:

- *Step 1* – is the claim to a process, machine, manufacture, or composition of matter?
- *Step 2A* (*Mayo/Alice* Step One) – is the claim directed to a judicial exception, eg, a law of nature, natural phenomenon (product of nature), or an abstract idea?
- *Step 2B* (*Mayo/Alice* Step Two) – does the claim recite additional elements that amount to significantly more than the judicial exception?

The USPTO has also created a flowchart to illustrate this analysis:

Figure 1. Subject matter eligibility test for products and processes

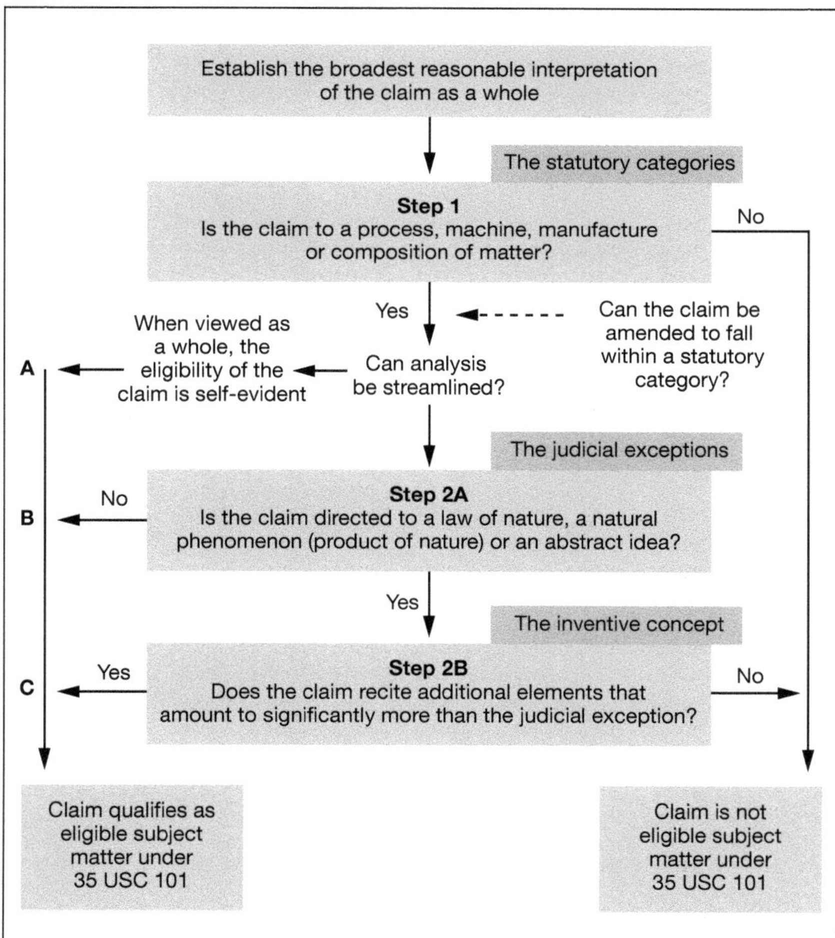

The USPTO further converts step one of the *Mayo/Alice* test (the USPTO's Step 2A) into a two-prong enquiry:

- Prong One of Step 2A – does the claim recite a judicial exception?
- Prong Two of Step 2A – if the claim recites a judicial exception, does it integrate that exception into a practical application?

The USPTO has provided the following flowchart to illustrate these prongs:

Figure 2: The USPTO's two-prong enquiry

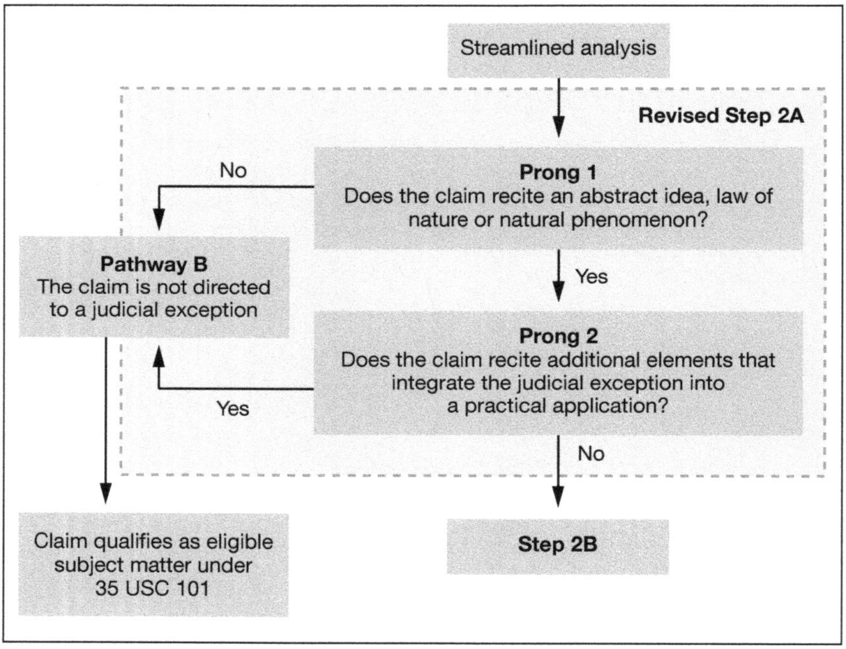

Thus, if USPTO finds the answer to the question in Step 1 is 'yes' and either the answer to the question in Step 2A is 'no' (ie, the claim does not recite a judicial exception or the claim integrates the judicial exception into a practical application) or the answer to the question in Step 2B is 'yes', then the claim is patent eligible. Otherwise, it is not.[15] Notably, following the Federal Circuit's

14 In an effort to reduce the burden on patent examiners, the USPTO further directs examiners to consider at the outset of their analysis whether the claim is suitable for a 'streamlined analysis' for patent eligibility, where eligibility is self-evident and no further analysis is necessary. See Manual of Patent Examination Procedure (MPEP) §2106.06 ("A streamlined eligibility analysis can be used for a claim that may or may not recite a judicial exception but, when viewed as a whole, clearly does not seek to tie up any judicial exception such that others cannot practice it. Such claims do not need to proceed through the full analysis herein as their eligibility will be self-evident.").

15 See MPEP §2106 (Revision 10.2019).

decision in *Berkheimer v HP, Inc,*[16] the USPTO announced that patent examiners would be required to cite to specific support if they determine, in Step 2B, that a claim is ineligible for patenting because the additional claim limitations (beyond the judicial exception) involve only "well-understood, routine and conventional activities".[17]

The *Mayo/Alice* two-step analysis (or the USPTO's variation on that analysis) may be simple to recite, but courts and the USPTO have found it challenging to apply. According to Judge Plager of the Federal Circuit, the state of the law following the Supreme Court's *Mayo* and *Alice* decisions "renders it near impossible to know with any certainty whether the invention is or is not patent eligible".[18] Judge Plager's frustrations have been echoed by several other Federal Circuit judges in multiple decisions in the wake of the Supreme Court's *Mayo* and *Alice* decisions, including in several contentious decisions denying petitions for rehearing *en banc.*[19] Notably, in both *Athena Diagnostics* and *American Axle,* the Court was split over whether to rehear the case, resulting in a denial of a petition for rehearing *en banc* in each of these cases. The vehement dissenting opinions in each of these decisions, joined by nearly half of the sitting judges, demonstrate the magnitude of the disagreement, in some circumstances, over how to resolve questions of patent eligibility.

The USPTO has also struggled to apply the *Mayo/Alice* two-step analysis in assessing patent eligibility during patent examination. A publication by the USPTO's Office of the Chief Economist reported that uncertainty in patent examination increased by 26% in the 18 months following the Supreme Court's Alice decision.[20] The USPTO responded to this uncertainty by issuing a series of guidance documents. The Office of the Chief Economist concluded that this guidance by the USPTO resulted in a marked reduction in uncertainty in patent examination.[21] The USPTO has continued to issue updates to its subject matter eligibility guidance and provides a range of useful information and examples on its website.[22] Much of the USPTO's guidance is derived from examples drawn from the case law, which may be the most practical way to determine the patent eligibility of any given patent claim.

The following sections examine the current state of the law in the US for patent subject matter eligibility in the electrical and computer arts, the

---

16 890 F 3d 1369 (2018).

17 See "Change in Examination Procedure Pertaining to Subject Matter Eligibility, Recent Subject Matter Eligibility Decision (*Berkheimer v HP, Inc.*)" (USPTO, 19 April 2018).

18 *Interval Licensing LLC v AOL, Inc,* 896 F 3d 1335, 1348 (2018) (Judge Plager, concurring-in part and dissenting-in-part).

19 See *Berkheimer v HP, Inc,* 890 F 3d 1369 (2018); *Athena Diagnostics, Inc v Mayo Collaborative Servs, LLC,* 927 F 3d 1333 (Fed Cir 2019); and *American Axle & Manufacturing, Inc v Neapco Holdings LLC,* 966 F 3d 1347 (Fed Cir 2020).

20 See Adjusting to Alice USPTO patent examination outcomes after *Alice Corp v CLS Bank International,* IP DATA HIGHLIGHTS No 3 at 4 (USPTO, April 2020).

21 *Ibid,* at 5–7.

22 See www.uspto.gov/patent/laws-and-regulations/examination-policy/subject-matter-eligibility.

biological and pharmaceutical arts, and the chemical and mechanical arts. Examination of the body of case law and USPTO guidance relating to each of these categories of subject matter provides guidance for obtaining patent-eligible claims under current US law.

2. Electrical and computer arts

2.1 Case law discussion

Much of case law relating to software and electronics comes from a few seminal Supreme Court cases, as well as a handful of recent Federal Circuit cases.

The Supreme Court's June 2014 decision in *Alice v CLS Bank* helped establish the *Mayo/Alice* two-step test for patent eligibility, as discussed above. *Alice* is also the most important case for software and electronics patents.[23] The four patents reviewed in *Alice* related to methods of mitigating settlement risk in a financial exchange. The Court found that the claims were ineligible for patenting because they failed to claim significantly more than the abstract idea of intermediated settlement.[24] The representative method claim was as follows:

> *A method of exchanging obligations as between parties, each party holding a credit record and a debit record with an exchange institution, the credit records and debit records for exchange of predetermined obligations, the method comprising the steps of:*
>
> *(a) creating a shadow credit record and a shadow debit record for each stakeholder party to be held independently by a supervisory institution from the exchange institutions;*
>
> *(b) obtaining from each exchange institution a start-of-day balance for each shadow credit record and shadow debit record;*
>
> *(c) for every transaction resulting in an exchange obligation, the supervisory institution adjusting each respective party's shadow credit record or shadow debit record, allowing only these transactions that do not result in the value of the shadow debit record being less than the value of the shadow credit record at any time, each said adjustment taking place in chronological order; and*
>
> *(d) at the end-of-day, the supervisory institution instructing on[e] of the exchange institutions to exchange credits or debits to the credit record and debit record of the respective parties in accordance with the adjustments of the said permitted transactions, the credits and debits being irrevocable, time invariant obligations placed on the exchange institutions.*[25]

---

23 *Alice Corp Pty v CLS Bank Int'l*, 573 US 208 (2014).
24 *Ibid*, at 225–227.
25 *Ibid*, at 213 n 2. While the claim does not literally recite a 'computer', the parties to the case agreed that one was implied. *Ibid*, at 214.

(a) Mayo/Alice *step one – abstract ideas*

Under the first step of the *Mayo/Alice* framework, the Court explained that the concern behind the eligibility question was one of 'pre-emption' – the concern that monopolising the 'basic tools of scientific and technological work' could impede innovation.[26] The Court found that the claims were 'directed to' the abstract idea of 'intermediated settlement' of banking transactions.[27] The Justices justified this decision in part by pointing to century-old evidence to demonstrate that the concept underlying the invention was a "fundamental economic practice long prevalent in our system of commerce".[28] However, the Court decided not to "delimit the precise contours of the 'abstract ideas' category"[29] including what makes a claim 'directed to' an abstract idea rather than, for instance, involving, building upon, or merely relating to such an idea.

(b) Mayo/Alice *step two – 'significantly more'*

Under step two of the *Mayo/Alice* framework, the *Alice* Court found that the method claims at issue required only a 'generic computer implementation'.[30] The Court looked to a few historical cases to determine whether the claims recited an 'inventive concept' that was sufficient to transform the abstract idea into a patent-eligible invention. Looking to their analysis in *Mayo*, the Court noted that a valid claim reciting an abstract idea needed 'additional features' to ensure that it was more than a "drafting effort designed to monopolise the [idea itself]".[31] Indeed, the ineligible claims in *Mayo* were found to recite nothing more than a judicial exception with an instruction to apply the exception.[32]

The Court distinguished between claimed inventions that transformed an abstract idea into something 'significantly more' by improving upon an existing technological process, and those that merely implemented an abstract idea on a generic computer.[33] For example, the eligible claim in *Diamond v Diehr* related to a computer-implemented process for curing rubber.[34] While the claim used a known equation, the Supreme Court found it eligible because the equation was used in conjunction with specific hardware that constantly measured the temperature of the rubber mould and fed temperatures to the computer for use with the equation.[35] In contrast, the Supreme Court found that patents to algorithms that converted binary-coded decimal numbers to pure binary

26 *Ibid,* at 216 (quoting *Mayo Collaborative Servs v Prometheus Labs, Inc,* 566 US 66, 71 (2012)).
27 *Alice,* 573 US at 219.
28 *Ibid,* at 219–220.
29 *Ibid,* at 221.
30 *Ibid,* at 219.
31 *Mayo,* 566 US at 77.
32 *Ibid,* at 79.
33 *Alice,* 573 US at 222.
34 *Diamond v Diehr,* 450 US 175 (1980).
35 *Ibid,* at 187.

numbers (*Benson*)[36] and updated 'alarm limits' for operating conditions (*Flook*)[37] failed to do more than claim abstract ideas in the form of algorithms.[38]

2.2 Federal Circuit cases since *Mayo/Alice*

The Supreme Court's rather open-ended mandate in *Alice* left the Federal Circuit to continue the task of developing the law. This has led to some confusion in the software and electronics space, particularly when the claims include financial or business concepts. Two cases decided shortly after *Alice* (*Ultramercial III*[39] and *DDR Holdings*)[40] illustrate this difficulty.

The *Ultramercial III* case had spent several years bouncing between the Federal Circuit and the Supreme Court over subject matter eligibility issues, with the Federal Circuit's final decision issuing after the Supreme Court's decision in *Alice*. The patent in question included an eleven-step method for distributing copyrighted media over the internet to consumers in exchange for viewing an advertisement.[41] Claim 1 recited:

A method for distribution of products over the Internet via a facilitator, said method comprising the steps of:

- *a first step of receiving, from a content provider,* ***media products that are covered by intellectual property rights protection and are available for purchase****, wherein each said media product being comprised of at least one of text data, music data, and video data;*
- *a second step of* ***selecting a sponsor message*** *to be associated with the media product, said sponsor message being selected from a plurality of sponsor messages, said second step including accessing an activity log to verify that the total number of times which the sponsor message has been previously presented is less than the number of transaction cycles contracted by the sponsor of the sponsor message;*
- *a third step of providing the media product for sale at an Internet website;*
- *a fourth step of restricting general public access to said media product;*
- *a fifth step of offering to a consumer access to the media product without charge to the consumer on the precondition that the consumer views the sponsor message;*
- *a sixth step of receiving from the consumer a request to view the sponsor message, wherein the consumer submits said request in response to being offered access to the media product;*
- *a seventh step of, in response to receiving the request from the consumer,* ***facilitating the display of a sponsor message to the consumer****;*
- *an eighth step of, if the sponsor message is not an interactive message,* ***allowing***

---

36 *Gottschalk v Benson*, 409 US 63 (1972).
37 *Parker v Flook*, 437 US 584 (1978).
38 *Alice*, 573 US at 222–224.
39 *Ultramercial, Inc v Hulu, LLC and Wildtangent, Inc*, 772 F 3d 709 (Fed Cir 2014).
40 *DDR Holdings, LLC v Hotels.com, LP*, 773 F 3d 1245 (Fed Cir 2014).
41 *Ultramercial*, 772 F 3d at 714–715.

said consumer access to said media product *after said step of facilitating the display of said sponsor message;*

- *a ninth step of, if the sponsor message is an interactive message, presenting at least one query to the consumer and* ***allowing*** *said consumer access to said media product* ***after receiving a response to said at least one query;***
- *a tenth step of* ***recording the transaction event to the activity log****, said tenth step including updating the total number of times the sponsor message has been presented; and*
- *an eleventh step of* ***receiving payment from the sponsor of the sponsor message displayed****.[42]

This multi-step process, on its face, appears to recite a specific technical method. It requires a content provider to make available a media product via an internet website, conditioned on the viewing of a sponsor's message (ie, an advertisement), recording the viewing of the sponsor's message in an interactive log, and providing the viewer with the media product. But under step one of the *Mayo/Alice* test, the Federal Circuit found the claims to be directed to the "abstract idea of showing an advertisement before delivering free content", an idea with "no particular concrete or tangible form".[43] And under step two, the Federal Circuit found that the claims did not transform the abstract idea into eligible subject matter because they simply instructed implementation with "routine, conventional activity".[44] The Court found that the majority of the steps related to the basic advertising concept and that the remainder of the steps – updating an activity log, receiving a request to view the advertisement, and restricting public access – were "conventional", "specified at a high level of generality" and did not supply the required "inventive concept".[45]

Three weeks after *Ultramercial III*, the Federal Circuit decided *DDR Holdings*. The claims related to a system for creating a composite web page using content of one web page with the look and feel of another web page.[46] Representative claim 19 recited:

19. A system useful in an outsource provider serving web pages offering commercial opportunities, the system comprising:

(a) a computer store containing data, for each of a plurality of first web pages, defining a plurality of visually perceptible elements, which visually perceptible elements correspond to the plurality of first web pages;

(i) wherein each of the first web pages belongs to one of a plurality of web page owners;

(ii) wherein each of the first web pages displays at least one ***active link***

42 *Ibid,* at 712 (emphases added).
43 *Ibid,* at 715.
44 *Ibid.*
45 *Ibid,* at 716.
46 *DDR Holdings, LLC v Hotels.com, LP*, 773 F 3d at 1248–1249.

associated with a commerce object *associated with a buying opportunity of a selected one of a plurality of merchants; and*

(iii) wherein the selected merchant, the outsource provider, and the owner of the first web page displaying the associated link are each third parties with respect to one other;

(b) a computer server at the outsource provider, which computer server is coupled to the computer store and programmed to:

(i) receive from the web browser of a computer user a signal indicating activation of one of the links displayed by one of the first web pages;

(ii) ***automatically identify as the source page*** *the one of the first web pages on which the link has been activated;*

(iii) in response to identification of the source page, ***automatically retrieve the stored data corresponding to the source page****; and*

(iv) using the data retrieved, ***automatically generate and transmit to the web browser a second web page*** *that displays:*

(A) information associated with the commerce object associated with the link that has been activated, and

(B) ***the plurality of visually perceptible elements visually corresponding to the source page.***[47]

Like in *Ultramercial III*, the claims at issue in *DDR Holdings* included economic concepts: web pages offering 'commercial opportunities', commerce objects associated with a 'buying opportunity of a selected one of a plurality of merchants', generating web pages that include information associated with a selected commerce object, and having a merchant, outsource provider, and owner of the first web page be 'third parties with respect to one other'. But, unlike *Ultramercial III*, the Federal Circuit in *DDR Holdings* struggled to identify a specific abstract idea in the claim. Potential ideas the Court considered included "making two web pages look the same", "syndicated commerce on the computer using the internet", "making two e-commerce web pages look alike by using licensed trademarks, logos, color schemes and layouts" and the "entrepreneurial goal" of increasing sales by making "two web pages have the same 'look and feel'".[48] In the end, no matter the idea(s), the Court found that under step one of the *Mayo/Alice* test, that the claims did not merely recite a business practice from the pre-internet world combined with a requirement to "perform it on the internet". Instead, the Court found that the claims recited a claimed solution "necessarily rooted in computer technology in order to overcome a problem specifically arising in the realm of computer networks".[49] Further, the Court held the claims patent eligible under step two of the

47 773 F 3d at 1249–1250 (emphases added).

48 *Ibid*, at 1257.

49 *Ibid*.

Mayo/Alice test because they specified "how interactions with the internet are manipulated to yield a desired result" and because they overrode the "routine and conventional sequence of events" normally triggered when clicking on a hyperlink to an internet page.[50] Thus, the Court found that the claims in *DDR Holdings* were "necessarily rooted in computer technology in order to overcome a problem specifically arising in the realm of computer networks" and therefore patent eligible.[51]

While it may be difficult to see much of a difference between the claims in *DDR Holdings* and *Ultramercial III*, the Federal Circuit reasoned that Ultramercial's claims relied on a generic use of the internet in a routine and conventional manner. So even though there was a high degree of specificity in the eleven steps in those claims, that was less important than how the non-abstract elements were implemented and whether that implementation was typical. The claims in *Ultramercial III* broadly and generically claimed normal, expected uses of the internet to perform its method: "providing the media product for sale at an internet website", "receiving from the consumer a request to view the sponsor message" and "facilitating the display of a sponsor message to the consumer". In contrast, the claims in *DDR Holdings* used a network that did not operate in its normal, expected manner. Instead of sending users to a requested website, it generated and sent a hybrid web page having a 'commerce object' from one party with the look and feel of a different party's web page.

Indeed, subsequent Federal Circuit cases have distinguished between claims that "focus on a specific means or method that improves [a] relevant technology" (which are not abstract and thus eligible) and claims that are "directed to a result or effect" that simply invoke "generic processes and machinery" (which are abstract and thus ineligible).[52] These cases suggest that the more standard operating properties of computer technology recited in a claim, the less likely it is the claim will be eligible.

One common factor among many patent-ineligible claims in the electrical and computer arts is an attempt to claim straightforward collection, processing and analysing of data – a traditional dominion of computer technology. Transforming that standard process in some way can be a crucial step toward eligibility. This trend is reflected by the cases summarised in Tables 1–3.

---

50 *DDR Holdings*, 773 F 3d at 1258.
51 *Ibid*, at 1257.
52 *McRO, Inc v Bandai Namco Games America Inc*, 837 F 3d 1299, 1314 (Fed Cir 2016).

Table 1. Select case law focused on transforming standard data processing

Ineligible	**Eligible**
Fairwarning[53] **Claims:** method of analysing access information against rules to determine if data had been improperly accessed. **Rationale:** The claims[54] did nothing more than implement an old practice – inspecting audit log data using rules – using a computer. They failed to add enough 'more' to transform the claims into an eligible process.[55] Any technological improvement related only to the mere use of a computer to speed up applying rules to data.[56]	*McRO*[57] **Claims:** a system for animating a CGI human to simulate speech, using unconventional 'rules' that related subsequences of phonemes, timings and morph weight sets. **Rationale:** The typical way of animating speech was to manually determine 'morph weight' sets based on phoneme timings, determine what the animated face should look like at different times, and then 'draw' the face appropriately.[58] The court found the claims not directed to an abstract idea under step one, in part because it did not merely automate conventional activity but performed a fundamentally different process.[59]
Electric Power Group[60] **Claims:** monitoring an electric power grid by collecting data from multiple sources, analysing it and displaying the results. **Rationale:** The claims did not contain any inventive technology for any of the component parts of the process and were abstract under step one.[61] Nor did the claims provide anything more than the use of generic technology to perform standard processes under step two.[62]	*Amdocs*[63] **Claims:** system for collection and filtering of network usage accounting data. **Rationale:** While the claims were relatively short – receiving an accounting record from a first source, correlating it with information from a second source and using the accounting information to 'enhance' the accounting record – the patent explained that enhancing the network accounting record using a distributed arrangement of components was a 'critical advancement' over the prior art.[64] This was enough for an 'unconventional technological solution' and the claims were eligible under step two of *Mayo/Alice*.[65]

53 *Fairwarning IP, LLC v Iatric Systems, Inc*, 839 F 3d 1089 (Fed Cir 2016).
54 *Ibid*, at 1092.
55 *Ibid*, at 1094–1095.
56 *Ibid*, at 1095.

Some cases in this area focus on the specificity of the claimed invention. These cases indicate that particular arrangements – whether 'unconventional' steps or a specific 'arrangement' of components – can be helpful in passing the *Mayo/Alice* eligibility test.

Table 2. Select case law focused on specific, unconventional arrangements of common components

Ineligible	Eligible
Intellectual Ventures v Symantec[66] **Claims:** email filtering methods to prevent computer virus transmission. One set of claims related to applying business rules to redirect/redistribute email. **Rationale:** The Federal Circuit analogised the claims to a corporate mailroom that receives mail, applies business rules to the mail, and takes actions based on those rules, and found it abstract under step one of *Mayo/Alice*. Under step two, the Federal Circuit noted that the specification listed only 'conventional' computer systems implementing the abstract idea in a 'routine and conventional' manner.[67]	*BASCOM*[68] **Claims:** an internet content filtering system located on a remote ISP server. The claims recited only "generic computer, network, and internet components".[69] **Rationale:** While abstract under step one of *Mayo/Alice*, the Federal Circuit found the claims eligible under step two because of the specific arrangement of parts. The filtering tool was located on an ISP server, remote from the end-users, but had specific filtering features for each user. This specific arrangement gave "both the benefits of a filter on a local computer and the benefits of a filter on the ISP server".[70]

continued on next page

57 *McRO, Inc v Bandai Namco Games America Inc*, 837 F 3d 1299 (Fed Cir 2016).
58 *Ibid*, at 1306.
59 *Ibid*, at 1314–1315.
60 *Electric Power Group, LLC v Alstom SA*, 830 F 3d 1350 (Fed Cir 2016).
61 *Ibid*, at 1354.
62 *Ibid*, at 1355–1356.
63 *Amdocs (Israel) Limited v Openet Telecom Inc*, 841 F 3d 1288 (Fed Cir 2016).
64 *Ibid*, at 1300. 'Groundbreaking, innovative, or even brilliant' innovations may not have enough for eligibility. *SAP Am, Inc v InvestPic, LLC*, 898 F 3d 1161, 1163 (Fed Cir 2018) (quoting *Ass'n for Molecular Pathology v Myriad Genetics, Inc*, 569 US 576, 591 (2013)).
65 *Amdocs*, 841 F 3d at 1306.
66 *Intellectual Ventures I LLC v Symantec Corp*, 838 F 3d 1307 (Fed Cir 2016).
67 *Ibid*, at 1318.
68 *BASCOM Glob Internet Svcs, Inc v AT&T Mobility LLC*, 827 F 3d 1341 (Fed Cir 2016).
69 *Ibid*, at 1349.
70 *Ibid*, at 1350.

Ineligible	Eligible
Automated Tracking Solutions v Coca-Cola[71] **Claims:** method and apparatus for using RFID for tracking items. **Rationale:** The patentee argued that the claims required a 'particular configuration'. But the claims required only standard RFID equipment. The claims were abstract under step one of *Alice* as they simply collected data from well-known sensors, analysed it, and broadly determined results.[72] Under step two, the court found the remaining aspects of the claims to be conventional. The specification admitted that a scanner, a transponder, and a computer, as "recited in the representative claims" was a "conventional" and "simple RFID system".[73]	*Thales Visionix*[74] **Claims:** an inertial motion-tracking system. Traditional tracking systems measured inertial changes with respect to the earth; the claimed system measured changes with respect to a moving reference frame. **Rationale:** While the orientation was determined using mathematical formulas, the court found that the claims sought "to protect only the application of physics to the unconventional configuration of sensors".[75]

Another important lesson from the case law is that a claim's length and complexity are not the sole deciding factors for patent eligibility. Highlighting an inventive concept is markedly more important.

71 *Automated Tracking Solutions, LLC v The Coca-Cola Company*, 723 Fed Appx. 989 (Fed Cir 2018) (non-precedential).
72 *Ibid*, at 993.
73 *Ibid*, at 995.
74 *Thales Visionix Inc v United States*, 850 F 3d 1343 (Fed Cir 2017).
75 *Ibid*, at 1349.

Table 3. Select case law focused on a specific improvement as an inventive concept

Ineligible	Eligible
Interval Licensing[76] **Claims:** nine separate elements in an independent claim for attention manager software making use of 'unused capacity' of a display device.[77] The invention obtained data, enabled a user to request data, scheduled instructions for providing 'temporal constraints' on the display of the information, and retrieved and displayed the information. **Rationale:** The Federal Circuit saw the claims as directed to the abstract idea of 'providing information to a person' without interrupting them under step one.[78] Under step two, the claims were too 'high level' and 'conventional' to be found eligible.[79]	*Core Wireless*[80] **Claims:** a computing device that displayed a menu with 'one or more applications' and 'an application summary that can be reached directly from the menu' that enables access to a limited set of data "while the one or more applications are in an un-launched state".[81] **Rationale:** eligible at step one as they were not directed to an abstract idea but to a "specific improvement over prior systems, resulting in an improved user interface for electronic devices".[82]

continued on next page

76 *Interval Licensing LLC v AOL, Inc,* 896 F 3d 1335 (Fed Cir 2018).
77 *Ibid,* at 1339–1340 (listing representative claim 18).
78 *Ibid,* at 1344.
79 *Ibid,* at 1346–1348.
80 *Core Wireless Licensing SARL v LG Electronics, Inc,* 880 F 3d 1356 (Fed Cir 2018).
81 *Ibid,* at 1359 (listing representative claim 1).
82 *Ibid,* at 1363.

Ineligible	Eligible
Ameranth[83] **Claims:** system for generating a second menu based on selections in first menu. For example, selecting a salad in a first menu could generate a second menu that enables selection of a dressing.[84] **Rationale:** Under step one, the Federal Circuit reasoned that the claims were directed to generating menus with features.[85] And under step two, the claims and patent failed to provide more than typical, commonly known implementations of this idea, and that any of the detailed aspects were mere "post-solution activity".[86]	*Enfish*[87] **Claims:** a 'self-referential' structure for a database, one which improves upon the standard 'relational' model of databases by including all entity types (normally stored in multiple tables) in a single table.[88] **Rationale:** The Federal Circuit found the claims not abstract at step one, reasoning that they were directed to a "specific improvement to the way computers operate".[89] (Interestingly, after this decision, the Federal Circuit found some of the claims unpatentable over prior art.)[90]

These cases were, of course, decided on fact-specific grounds. Analogising a particular technological advancement to the exact set of facts of a previously decided case can be challenging. The teaching point from all of these cases is that a patent application for computer inventions should focus on what differentiates the claims from the standard set of procedures, arrangements and components that go along with what the courts understand makes up a computer – the known processors, storage and memory that cooperate to ingest data, understand it and produce output. The best source for such information – both in front of district courts and the USPTO – has and will continue to be the patent specification. As mentioned in the opening to this chapter, the question of whether claim elements are well-understood, routine and conventional is a question of fact, one which requires more than a simple legal analysis.[91]

83 *Apple, Inc v Ameranth, Inc,* 842 F 3d 1229 (Fed Cir 2016).
84 *Ibid,* at 1235.
85 *Ibid,* at 1240–1241.
86 *Ibid,* at 1241–1245.
87 *Enfish, LLC v Microsoft Corp,* 822 F 3d 1327 (Fed Cir 2016).
88 *Ibid,* at 1330–1333.
89 *Ibid,* at 1336–1338.
90 *Microsoft Corp v Enfish, LLC,* 662 F App'x 981 (Fed Cir 2016).
91 *Berkheimer,* 881 F 3d at 1368–1369.

2.3 How eligibility issues are handled by the USPTO

Recent guidance from the USPTO has expanded upon both steps of the *Mayo/Alice* test. The USPTO's earliest guidance[92] on steps one and two was stark: determine if the claim is directed to a judicial exception (eg, an abstract idea),[93] and if so, determine whether it recites additional elements that amount to significantly more than the judicial exception.[94] As noted in the opening to this chapter, recent guidance from the USPTO, including Guidance from January 2019[95] and an update from October 2019,[96] clarified this test, dividing the USPTO's Step 2A (*Mayo/Alice* step one) into two parts – known as Prong One and Prong Two. Under this new two-prong enquiry, a claim would be eligible at revised Step 2A unless it recites a judicial exception (Prong One) and does not integrate that application into a 'practical application' of the exception (Prong Two).[97]

The USPTO has delineated three categories of abstract ideas (the types of judicial exceptions most frequently found in computer- and electronics-related claims). In recognition of the fact that many patent examiners do not have formal legal training, the USPTO's groupings attempt to shift the focus away from individual decisions in the case law and toward a more uniform approach based on a coarsely filtered version of case law:

- **Mathematical concepts:** mathematical relationships; mathematical formulas or equations; mathematical calculations. Claims do not 'recite' such a concept if it is only based on or recites a mathematical concept.
- **Certain methods of organising human activity:** fundamental economic principles or practices; commercial or legal interactions; or managing personal behaviour or relationships or interactions between people.
- **Mental processes:** concepts performed in the human mind.[98]

Under Prong One of Step 2A, the 2019 USPTO Guidance instructs patent examiners to consider whether claims that are potentially directed to an abstract idea recite limitations that fall within one of these groupings. Examiners are directed to a) identify the specific limitation(s) that allegedly recite an abstract idea, then b) determine whether the limitation(s) falls within the groupings listed above.[99] If not, the claim is not directed to an abstract idea

92 2014 Interim Guidance on Patent Subject Matter Eligibility, 79 Fed Reg 74618 (16 December 2014).
93 The USPTO refers to this as 'Step 2A'.
94 The USPTO refers to this as 'Step 2B'. Note that the USPTO recognises a 'streamlined' analysis when the eligibility of the claim is 'self-evident'. In practice, the units examining computer- and electronics-related inventions tend to skip this analysis.
95 2019 Revised Patent Subject Matter Eligibility Guidance, 84 Fed Reg 50 (7 January 2019).
96 October 2019 Update: Subject Matter Eligibility, www.uspto.gov/sites/default/files/documents/peg_oct_2019_update.pdf (17 October 2019).
97 84 Fed Reg at 54.
98 *Ibid.*
99 *Ibid.*

and the analysis is over (assuming the claim is not directed to a natural phenomenon or law of nature).[100] If the claim limitation(s) reciting the abstract idea does fall within one of the groupings, the analysis moves to Prong Two.

In Prong Two of Step 2A, the 2019 USPTO Guidance instructs examiners to consider whether the claims 'integrate' the abstract idea into a 'practical application', by determining whether there are additional elements in the claims that make the claim more than a drafting effort designed to monopolise the abstract idea.[101] This is not a consideration of whether the additional elements are 'well-understood, routine, or conventional' activity but is rather a first-level review of whether the claims do something beyond recite or merely implement the abstract idea. In fact, the 2019 Guidance explicitly cautions examiners to not inject analysis of 'well-understood, routine, or conventional' activity (a Step 2B consideration) at Prong Two of Step 2A.[102] The 2019 Guidance includes a sample set of considerations that an additional claim element may represent an integration of the abstract idea into a practical application, including whether the element reflects an improvement to computer functionality or a technical field. The guidance includes many other examples; each of them generally relates to finding something in the claim ensuring that the abstract idea itself is not being claimed.

If a claim fails to integrate the abstract idea into a practical application in Prong Two of Step 2A, the examiner evaluates the claim under Step 2B to determine whether the claim provides an 'inventive concept' (the 'significantly more' part of the *Mayo/Alice* test (*Mayo/Alice* step two)).[103] Notably, the considerations are mostly the same as those listed above for Prong Two of Step 2A: is there some element in the claims that provides more than the mere abstract concept?

2.4 Hot topics: how emerging technology will be handled

One question for consideration is how patent claims to artificial intelligence (AI) will be handled as AI permeates more and more areas of technology. At the moment, some public stakeholders believe that such inventions should be examined consistent with other computer-related inventions and believe there are no separate considerations for AI inventions.[104]

---

100 If the examiner determines that a claim limitation which does not fall within one of these groupings should still be treated as reciting an abstract idea, the Technology Center Director (a high-level supervisor) must approve treating the claim limitation as abstract in writing. In the authors' experience, this almost never happens.

101 *Ibid*, at 54–55.

102 *Ibid*, at 55 ("Examiners should note, however, that revised Step 2A specifically excludes consideration of whether the additional elements represent well-understood, routine, conventional activity. Instead, analysis of well-understood, routine, conventional activity is done in Step 2B.").

103 *Ibid*, at 55–56.

104 USPTO, "Public Views on Artificial Intelligence and Intellectual Property Policy", October 2020 (available at www.uspto.gov/sites/default/files/documents/USPTO_AI-Report_2020-10-07.pdf).

One case[105] pending in front of the Eastern District of Virginia is a good example of the difficult decisions to come. The USPTO rejected applications based on subject matter generated by an AI engine called DABUS (the "Device for the Autonomous Bootstrapping of Unified Sentience"). Here, the core issue was not that the claimed subject matter was itself ineligible for patent protection, but rather that the sole inventor, an AI, failed to meet the statutory requirement that an inventor be a natural person. Though the district court has not yet decided this case, it also appears likely that the human creator of DABUS would not be a suitable inventor in the AI's stead, as he did not conceive DABUS's inventions.

3. Life sciences

Like the electrical and computer arts, the life sciences have generated many significant patent-eligibility disputes in the US. Patent claims to inventions in the life sciences were at issue in some of the most important Supreme Court and Federal Circuit decisions on subject matter eligibility. Notable life sciences cases include the *Mayo* decision, which helped formulate the *Mayo/Alice* two-step test, and the *Myriad* decision, which severely limited the patent eligibility of claims to DNA and other genetic material.[106]

Life sciences patent-eligibility decisions can be divided into two broad categories: those relating to natural compositions and those relating to medical methods. We discuss both of these categories, and their respective sub-categories, below, and describe how these types of patent claims have been addressed by the courts and the USPTO.

3.1 Natural compositions: biomolecules and organisms – case law discussion

Following the Supreme Court's decision in *Myriad*, a naturally occurring nucleic acid sequence, even if isolated or synthetically produced, is not eligible for patent protection.[107] While *Myriad* is sometimes also cited as holding that complementary DNA (cDNA) "is patent eligible because it is not naturally occurring", the opinion more precisely concludes that cDNA is patent eligible so long as the cDNA is not naturally occurring.[108] Consistent with the Supreme Court's holding in *Myriad*, the Federal Circuit has since held that claims to DNA primers that match native sequences are not patent eligible.[109]

Similarly, other natural biomolecules, such as proteins and metabolites, are ineligible for patent protection in the US. However, like cDNA, these other biomolecules may constitute patent-eligible subject matter if they are engineered and differ in character from native biomolecules.

---

105 *Thaler v Iancu*, Case No 1:20-cv-00903 (E D Va, filed 6 August 2020).
106 *Association for Molecular Pathology v Myriad Genetics, Inc*, 569 US 576 (2013).
107 *Ibid.*
108 *Ibid*, at 576, 595.
109 See *In re BRCA1- & BRCA2-Based Hereditary Cancer Test Patent Litig*, 774 F 3d 755 (Fed Cir 2014); *Roche Molecular Systems, Inc v Cepheid*, 905 F 3d 1363 (Fed Cir 2018).

That said, engineering of a native molecule is not always needed for patent eligibility. A combination or formulation of natural products may be patent eligible if, as a result of that combination or formulation, the natural products have a markedly different characteristic compared to their native forms. For example, in *Nat Alternatives Int'l, Inc v Creative Compounds, LLC*, the Federal Circuit declined to hold that claims to a dietary supplement or sports drink comprising naturally occurring molecules (eg, glycine and beta-alanine) were patent ineligible.[110] Instead, the Court credited a construction of the claims that the dietary supplement or sports drink necessarily contained a non-natural, non-conventional amount of the natural product(s), and that the supplement or drink was effective to enhance athletic performance.[111] In other words, the Federal Circuit interpreted the claims to encompass amounts and effects of a natural product that were markedly different from its native form. It thus remanded to the lower court to evaluate the facts further, to better inform a decision on patent eligibility.[112] By contrast, courts have found that a combination of natural components that does not result in a new or different property does not constitute patentable subject matter.[113]

Like naturally occurring products, naturally occurring organisms are not patentable under 35 USC §101.[114] However, like engineered proteins and other biomolecules, engineered organisms may satisfy the patent-eligibility requirement.[115] The Supreme Court in *Chakrabarty* clarified that the claimed genetically modified bacterium, which was able to break down crude oil components, had "markedly different characteristics from any found in nature and one having the potential for significant utility".[116] Applying this analysis, the Federal Circuit held that Dolly the cloned sheep was not eligible for patent protection, as she was genetically identical to her donor parent.[117] While Roslin argued that Dolly had different mitochondrial DNA than her donor parent, the Court found this difference did not make Dolly patent eligible, noting that Roslin had not claimed this aspect of Dolly, and further noting that Roslin's patent application did not identify how having different mitochondrial DNA could change the characteristics of cloned animals.[118] Importantly, while engineered non-human animals are potentially patentable, humans, however, cannot be patented under any circumstances.[119]

---

110 918 F 3d 1338 (Fed Cir 2019).
111 See *Ibid,* at 1343.
112 See *Ibid,* at 1348.
113 See, eg, *Funk Bros Seed Co v Kalo Inoculant Co,* 333 US 127 (1948).
114 *Funk Bros,* 333 US at 130–131 (holding a mixture of naturally occurring bacterial strains ineligible for patent protection).
115 *See Diamond v Chakrabarty,* 447 US 303 (1980) (holding a genetically engineered bacterium eligible for patent protection).
116 *Ibid,* at 310.
117 *In re Roslin Inst (Edinburgh),* 750 F 3d 1333, 1337 (Fed Cir 2014).
118 *Ibid,* at 1338.
119 The Leahy-Smith America Invents Act (AIA), Pub L 112–129, sec 33(a), 125 Stat 284 (16 September 2011) (prohibiting patent claims to or encompassing human organisms).

Meanwhile, 'newly discovered plants' can be patentable subject matter under 35 USC §101.[120] Plants also have two other avenues for protection, aside from utility patents. First, the Plant Patent Act provides eligibility criteria for protection by a 'plant patent'.

> *Whoever invents or discovers and asexually reproduces any distinct and new variety of plant, including cultivated sports, mutants, hybrids, and newly found seedlings, other than a tuber propagated plant or a plant found in an uncultivated state, may obtain a patent therefor, subject to the conditions and requirements of this title.*[121]

Thus, plants are eligible for 'plant patent' protection if an inventor has created the plant through breeding or other agricultural and horticultural means.[122]

Secondly, the Plant Variety Protection Act (PVPA) provides (non-patent) exclusivity for "[t]he breeder of any sexually reproduced or tuber propagated plant variety" so long as the breeder has reproduced the plant variety.[123]

3.2 How eligibility issues are handled by the USPTO

In 2016 and 2019, the USPTO published guidance on natural product claims, including Examples 30 and 44 summarised in Table 4.[124] These examples from the USPTO Guidance are consistent with US case law.

Table 4. USPTO Guidance – Examples 30 and 44

Example 30	
Background: Sap of the Texas mint plant naturally contains 10% texiol. Compound N reduces texiol's bitterness.	
Claim	**USPTO Analysis**
A dietary sweetener comprising: a) 1–5% texiol, and b) at least 90% water.	Ineligible, because adding water to texiol does not change the native properties of the natural products. Also, adding water to a sweetener is routine (for instance, making a simple syrup in baking).
A dietary sweetener comprising: a) 1–5% texiol, b) at least 90% water; and c) 1–2% compound N.	Eligible (under Step 2A), because N reduces texiol's bitterness, thus yielding a markedly different property than the natural product in its native form.

continued on next page

120 *J E M Ag Supply, Inc v Pioneer Hi-Bred Int'l, Inc*, 534 US 124 (2001).
121 35 USC §161.
122 *In re Beineke*, 690 F 3d 1344, 1352 (Fed Cir 2012).
123 7 USC §2402(a).
124 www.uspto.gov/sites/default/files/documents/101_examples_1to36.pdf; www.uspto.gov/sites/default/files/documents/peg_oct_2019_app1.pdf.

Example 44	
Background: Denveric acid is a natural protein with short-acting glycemic control properties. Longer-acting glycemic control is desired to reduce diabetic patients' need for insulin while they sleep. Combining denveric acid and protamine (which do not naturally occur together) enhances their glycemic control properties.	
Claim	**USPTO Analysis**
A dosage unit comprising denveric acid in a container.	Ineligible, because the claim broadly encompasses a natural product in a generic container. Placing a natural product in a container does not change the properties of the natural product and is a routine activity.
The dosage unit of claim 1, wherein the denveric acid is an intermediate-acting denveric acid.	Eligible, because an intermediate-acting denveric acid is functionally different, and presumed structurally different, from its native, short-acting counterpart.
The dosage unit of claim 1, further comprising protamine that is mixed with the denveric acid in the container in an amount of 0.75 mg to 1.5 mg protamine per every mg of denveric acid.	Eligible, because, even though longer-acting glycemic control is not explicitly recited, a skilled person would understand that the claim is directed to a combination of denveric acid and protamine that provides longer-acting glycemic control compared to either natural product acting alone.

3.3 Medical methods – case law discussion

(a) Mayo, *of the* Mayo/Alice *test, and its impact on medical methods patents*

Mayo provides the most authoritative guidance for the various types of medical methods discussed below. In *Mayo,* decided in 2012, the Supreme Court considered Prometheus's claims directed to their discovery that a metabolite could predict whether a drug dose would be too low to be effective, or too high to be safe.[125] This discovery allowed physicians to personalise a dosing regimen according to a patient's needs. A representative claim at issue is reproduced below.

> 1. *A method of optimizing therapeutic efficacy for treatment of an immune-mediated gastrointestinal disorder, comprising:*
>   - (a) *administering a drug providing 6–thioguanine to a subject having said immune-mediated gastrointestinal disorder; and*
>   - (b) *determining the level of 6–thioguanine in said subject having said immune-mediated gastrointestinal disorder,*

125 *Mayo,* 566 US at 74–75.

wherein the level of 6–thioguanine less than about 230 pmol per $8x10^8$ red blood cells indicates a need to increase the amount of said drug subsequently administered to said subject and
wherein the level of 6–thioguanine greater than about 400 pmol per $8x10^8$ red blood cells indicates a need to decrease the amount of said drug subsequently administered to said subject.[126]

The Supreme Court interpreted the 'administering' step as telling doctors to treat a pre-existing patient population (having an autoimmune disease) with a thiopurine drug already used to treat such patients; the 'determining' step as telling doctors to determine the level of relevant metabolites using techniques known in the art; and the 'wherein' clauses as telling doctors about a natural correlation and, at most, suggesting the doctors apply that correlation in the future.[127] But the claims did not require doctors to apply that correlation, ie, by reciting an affirmative step of administering the improved dosing regimen once it was identified. As a result of this omission, the Supreme Court found that "the steps [of the claims] are not sufficient to transform unpatentable natural correlations into patentable applications of those regularities" and held Prometheus's claims to be patent ineligible.[128]

(b) Methods of diagnosis

Following the Supreme Court's decision in *Mayo*, US courts have consistently held that diagnostic methods are not eligible for patent protection when those methods use only routine and conventional techniques (even where the overall method is non-obvious or even revolutionary). Routine and conventional diagnostic techniques include standard immunoassays such as ELISA and standard sequencing technologies such as PCR. Other routine and conventional techniques may be apparent from statements in the specification or prosecution history of a patent or descriptions in prior art references, or may be identified by experts during litigation.[129]

In *Athena Diagnostics, Inc v Mayo Collaborative Servs, LLC*, Mayo challenged Athena's claims to a method of diagnosing Myasthenia gravis (MG) by detecting muscle specific tyrosine kinase (MuSK) autoantibodies in a patient's bodily fluid.[130] The claimed method recites incubating the bodily fluid with radiolabelled MuSK and detecting the label.[131] The Federal Circuit agreed with Mayo's argument that Athena's claimed steps "apart from the natural law are

126 *Ibid.*
127 *Ibid*, at 78–79.
128 *Ibid*, at 80.
129 As evidenced by the analysis and holding in *Mayo*, US courts (and the USPTO) view prognostic methods, methods of predicting treatment efficacy, and other such inventions that rely on a natural correlation and mental step as patent ineligible, so long as those methods are implemented using only routine and conventional activities.
130 915 F 3d 743 (Fed Cir 2019).
131 *Ibid*, at 747.

concededly standard immunoassay techniques" and therefore found the claims were patent ineligible.[132] Athena petitioned for *en banc* review of this decision. Though the full panel denied *en banc* review, it did so with a 7–5 split and eight contentious opinions (four concurrences and four dissents).[133] The judges took different views of how the *Athena* decision should have been rendered, with a narrow majority feeling bound by the precedent set in *Mayo* and the other judges believing Athena's claims were patent eligible even when applying *Mayo*.[134] Oddly, the panel appeared to be unanimous on one thing: that Athena's claims – and diagnostic claims like it – should be patent-eligible subject matter.[135] Many Federal Circuit judges worried for the future of the diagnostics industry without patent protection, and about courts applying 35 USC §101 in an overexpansive fashion to invalidate innovations deserving patent protection.[136] In her prescient dissent, Judge Moore stressed the importance of diagnostics in combating pandemics.[137]

Athena next petitioned the Supreme Court for *certiorari*. The Solicitor General of the US Department of Justice implored the Supreme Court to hear this appeal, asking the Court to revisit *Mayo* and the patent eligibility of diagnostic tests. But on 13 January 2020, the Supreme Court denied Athena's petition.[138] Though it is possible another diagnostic case will make it to the Supreme Court in the coming years, it appears the diagnostic industry's best hope at patent eligibility is legislative reform. Two senators proposed such reform in 2019; however, that bill has not progressed as of the publication of this book.

(c) Methods of detection

US courts give detection claims and diagnostic claims the same unfavourable treatment. They consistently hold that claims to detection methods using routine and conventional techniques are patent ineligible.

For example, in *Ariosa Diagnostics, Inc v Sequenom, Inc*, the Federal Circuit held that Sequenom's claims began with a natural phenomenon (cell-free fetal DNA in a maternal blood sample) and ended with a natural phenomenon (a portion of that cell-free fetal DNA that was paternally inherited), and thus were "directed to matter that is naturally occurring".[139] The Court then considered step two of the *Mayo/Alice* test, whether the claims contained additional features that amount to an 'inventive concept' beyond a judicial exception.[140] The Court

132 *Ibid*, at 750.
133 See generally *Athena Diagnostics, Inc v Mayo Collaborative Servs, LLC*, 927 F 3d 1333 (Fed Cir 2019).
134 See *Ibid*.
135 See *Ibid*.
136 See *Ibid*.
137 *Ibid, at* 1356–1357 (J Moore's dissent).
138 *Athena Diagnostics, Inc v Mayo Collaborative Servs, LLC*, 140 S Ct 855 (2020).
139 788 F 3d 1371, 1376 (Fed Cir 2015).
140 *Ibid*, at 1376.

explained that "[f]or process claims that encompass a natural phenomenon, the process steps are the additional features that must be new and useful", thus continuing the blurring of 35 USC §101 with prior art-based restrictions on patentability.[141] Because the Federal Circuit found that Sequenom's claims merely observed a natural phenomenon using routine steps, it held the claims patent ineligible.[142]

The Federal Circuit's decision in *Ariosa* published just under a year before the USPTO released their guidance, suggesting an opposing approach to detection method claims. Example 29 of the 2016 USPTO Guidance suggested that detection method claims using routine steps are not directed to a judicial exception and are eligible for patent protection.[143] In the wake of this confusion, the USPTO granted *Cleveland Clinic* a patent with claims modelled after claim 1 of the USPTO's Example 29. True Health Diagnostics challenged the patent eligibility of *Cleveland Clinic*'s claims. Thus, in 2019, the Federal Circuit once again had an opportunity to weigh in on the subject matter eligibility of detection method claims. When it did, the Court explicitly chose its analogous decision in *Ariosa* over the 'expertise' of the USPTO, declined to follow claim 1 of Example 29 from the 2016 USPTO Guidance, and held *Cleveland Clinic*'s claims to be patent ineligible.[144]

A comparison of the claims in *Ariosa*, the 2016 USPTO Guidance, and *Cleveland Clinic* appear in Table 5.[145]

141 *Ibid*, at 1377.
142 *Ibid*, at 1380.
143 See section 3.4b for further details on the USPTO approach to detection method claims.
144 *Cleveland Clinic Foundation v True Health Diagnostics LLC*, 760 Fed Appx 1013, 1020–1021 (Fed Cir 2019) (non-precedential).
145 *Ariosa*, 788 F 3d at 1373–1374; www.uspto.gov/sites/default/files/documents/101_examples_1to36.pdf; *Cleveland Clinic*, 760 Fed Appx at 1017.

Table 5. Comparison of claims in *Ariosa*, the 2016 USPTO Guidance and *Cleveland Clinic*

***Ariosa* (Fed Cir 2015)**	**2016 USPTO Guidance**	***Cleveland Clinic* (Fed Cir 2019)**
1. A method for detecting a paternally inherited nucleic acid of fetal origin performed on a maternal serum or plasma sample from a pregnant female, which method comprises amplifying a paternally inherited nucleic acid from the serum or plasma sample and detecting the presence of a paternally inherited nucleic acid of fetal origin in the sample.	1. A method of detecting JUL-1 in a patient, said method comprising: a. obtaining a plasma sample from a human patient; b. detecting whether JUL-1 is present in the plasma sample by contacting the plasma sample with an anti-JUL-1 antibody and detecting binding between JUL-1 and the antibody.	1. A method of detecting elevated MPO mass in a patient sample comprising: a. obtaining a plasma sample from a human patient having atherosclerotic cardiovascular disease (CVD); and b. detecting elevated MPO mass in said plasma sample, as compared to a control MPO mass level from the general population or apparently healthy subjects, by contacting said plasma sample with anti-MPO antibodies and detecting binding between MPO in said plasma sample and said anti-MPO antibodies.
Held ineligible (precedential)	Advised eligible (guidance; not binding)	Held ineligible (non-precedential)

Though non-precedential, the Federal Circuit decision in *Cleveland Clinic* confirms the Court's view of method of detection claims as presented in the precedential *Ariosa* decision. Further, *Cleveland Clinic* shows there is some risk in relying on USPTO guidance. While the USPTO often adjusts its guidance to align with case law (see section 3.2(c)), it has not revised its published analysis of claim 1, Example 29. Thus, it is important to be aware of discrepancies between US case law and USPTO practice and, where those discrepancies remain, defer to case law.

(d) *Methods of preparation*

In *Illumina, Inc v Ariosa Diagnostics, Inc*, the Federal Circuit considered claims to "methods of preparing a fraction of cell-free DNA that is enriched in fetal DNA".[146] The Federal Circuit emphasised the claimed methods' use of 'human-engineered' size parameters based on the inventors' observation that fetal DNA is often (but not always) shorter than maternal DNA.[147] Because some sizes of fetal and maternal DNA overlap, the Court held the inventors' chosen size parameters were not "dictated by any natural phenomenon" but instead only informed by a natural phenomenon.[148] Further, the Court found that "[t]he claims include physical process steps that change the composition of the mixture, resulting in a DNA fraction that is different from the naturally occurring fraction in the mother's blood".[149] Thus, the Court held Illumina's claims patent eligible.

The Court also contrasted the patent-eligible claims in *Illumina* against the patent-ineligible claims in *Ariosa*, which are shown in Table 6.[150]

Table 6. Comparison of claims in *Ariosa* and *Illumina*

***Ariosa* (Fed Cir 2015)**	***Illumina* (Fed Cir 2020)**
1. A method for detecting a paternally inherited nucleic acid of fetal origin performed on a maternal serum or plasma sample from a pregnant female, which method comprises amplifying a paternally inherited nucleic acid from the serum or plasma sample and detecting the presence of a paternally inherited nucleic acid of fetal origin in the sample.	1. A method for preparing a deoxyribonucleic acid (DNA) fraction from a pregnant human female useful for analysing a genetic locus involved in a fetal chromosomal aberration, comprising: (a) extracting DNA from a substantially cell-free sample of blood plasma or blood serum of a pregnant human female to obtain extracellular circulatory fetal and maternal DNA fragments; (b) producing a fraction of the DNA extracted in (a) by: (i) size discrimination of extracellular circulatory DNA fragments, and (ii) selectively removing the DNA fragments greater than approximately 500 base pairs, wherein the DNA fraction after (b) comprises a plurality of genetic loci of the extracellular circulatory fetal and maternal DNA; and (c) analysing a genetic locus in the fraction of DNA produced in (b).
Ineligible method of detection	Eligible method of preparation

146 967 F 3d 1319, 1322 (Fed Cir 2020).
147 *Ibid*, at 1326.
148 *Ibid*.
149 *Ibid*.
150 *Ariosa*, 788 F 3d at 1373–1374; *Illumina*, 967 F 3d 1323.

The Federal Circuit stated that "like the invalid diagnostic claims at issue in *Mayo, Athena* and *Cleveland Clinic*", the claims at issue in *Ariosa* "were directed to detecting a natural phenomenon *after* a sample has been prepared or extracted".[151] But in *Illumina*, the Court explained, the claims at issue did not recite the natural correlation between a DNA molecule's length and its source, but rather "exploit that natural size distribution during the sample preparation steps to remove some maternal DNA from the mother's blood".[152] The distinction the Court drew between the facts of *Ariosa* and *Illumina* illustrate that what a patentee omits from a claim may be just as important to the eligibility analysis as what a patentee recites.

(e) *Methods of treatment*

In stark contrast to many other jurisdictions discussed in this book, the US not only permits patenting methods of administering medical treatment to a human or animal body, but its courts have often held that reciting this subject matter can be the reason a claim meets patent-eligibility requirements. In its 2018 *Vanda* decision, the Federal Circuit clarified that claims reciting an active step that transforms the natural state of the human body may be patent eligible at step one of the *Mayo/Alice* test.[153] In other words, a claim directed to a specific therapeutic application of a natural law is deemed to be more than an attempt to claim the natural law. The Federal Circuit held that claims, like *Vanda*'s, that recite "a specific method of treatment for specific patients using a specific compound at specific doses to achieve a specific outcome" are not directed to a judicial exception.[154] Thus, a court need not address whether the natural law is applied in a routine or conventional way. Instead, this type of scrutiny is left to assessing non-obviousness of the claim under 35 USC §103.

In recent years, the claims at issue in *Vanda* have become a standard-bearer for subject matter eligibility. And, since *Vanda*, the Federal Circuit has stressed and clarified its emphasis on the eligibility requirements of "a specific method of treatment for specific patients using a specific compound at specific doses to achieve a specific outcome".[155] For example, in *Nat Alternatives*, the treatment claims at issue did not explicitly recite a 'specific dose'. Still, the Federal Circuit found that the claims satisfied this element because they recited administering an 'effective' dose, and the specification provided guidance on effective dosing.[156] The Court was also unconcerned that the claims did not address a

---

151 *Illumina*, 967 F 3d at 1327 (emphasis added).

152 *Ibid*; accord *Rapid Litigation Management Ltd v CellzDirect, Inc*, 827 F 3d 1042 (Fed Cir 2016) (holding claims to a "method of producing a desired preparation of multi-cryopreserved hepatocytes" patent eligible).

153 *Vanda Pharms v West-Ward Pharms*, 887 F 3d 1117 (Fed Cir 2018) (distinguishing patent-eligible claims requiring a drug administration step from patent-ineligible claims, from *Mayo*, that do not require a drug administration step).

154 *Ibid*, at 1136.

155 *Ibid*.

156 *Nat Alternatives*, 918 F 3d at 1346.

specific patient population.[157] Meanwhile, in *Endo Pharm Inc v Teva Pharm USA, Inc*, the Federal Circuit held that the claims' instruction to administer 'a lower dosage' was specific enough to make Endo's claims "legally indistinguishable from the representative claim in *Vanda*".[158] Table 7 shows representative method of treatment claims from *Vanda, Nat. Alternatives* and *Endo.*[159]

Table 7. Representative method of treatment claims from *Vanda, Nat Alternatives* and *Endo*

Case	Representative method of treatment claim
Vanda	1. A method for treating a patient with iloperidone, wherein the patient is suffering from schizophrenia, the method comprising the steps of: determining whether the patient is a CYP2D6 poor metabolizer by: obtaining or having obtained a biological sample from the patient; and performing or having performed a genotyping assay on the biological sample to determine if the patient has a CYP2D6 poor metabolizer genotype; and if the patient has a CYP2D6 poor metabolizer genotype, then internally administering iloperidone to the patient in an amount of 12 mg/day or less, and if the patient does not have a CYP2D6 poor metabolizer genotype, then internally administering iloperidone to the patient in an amount that is greater than 12 mg/day, up to 24 mg/day, wherein a risk of QTc prolongation for a patient having a CYP2D6 poor metabolizer genotype is lower following the internal administration of 12 mg/day or less than it would be if the iloperidone were administered in an amount greater than 12 mg/day, up to 24 mg/day.

continued on next page

157 *Ibid*, at 1345.
158 919 F 3d 1347, 1353 (Fed Cir 2019).
159 *Vanda*, 887 F 3d at 1121; *Nat Alternatives*, 918 F 3d at 1343–1344; *Endo*, 919 F 3d at 1350–1351.

Case	Representative method of treatment claim
Nat Alternatives	1. A method of increasing anaerobic working capacity in a human subject, the method comprising: a) providing to the human subject an amount of an amino acid to blood or blood plasma effective to increase beta-alanylhistidine dipeptide synthesis in the tissue, wherein said amino acid is at least one of: i) beta-alanine that is not part of a dipeptide, polypeptide or oligopeptide; ii) an ester of beta-alanine that is not part of a dipeptide, polypeptide or oligopeptide; or iii) an amide of beta-alanine that is not part of a dipeptide, polypeptide or oligopeptide; and b) exposing the tissue to the blood or blood plasma, whereby the concentration of beta-alanylhistidine is increased in the tissue, wherein the amino acid is provided through a dietary supplement.
Endo	1. A method of treating pain in a renally impaired patient, comprising the steps of: a. providing a solid oral controlled release dosage form, comprising: (i) about 5 mg to about 80 mg of oxymorphone or a pharmaceutically acceptable salt thereof as the sole active ingredient; and (ii) a controlled release matrix; b. measuring a creatinine clearance rate of the patient and determining it to be (a) less than about 30 mL/min, (b) about 30 mL/min to about 50 mL/min, (c) about 51 mL/min to about 80 mL/min, or (d) above about 80 mL/min; and c. orally administering to said patient, in dependence on which creatinine clearance rate is found, a lower dosage of the dosage form to provide pain relief; wherein after said administration to the patient, the average AUC of oxymorphone over a 12-hour period is less than about 21 ng·hr/mL.

Also, since *Vanda*, the Federal Circuit has identified limitations to the patent eligibility of method of treatment claims.[160] In the non-precedential decision INO, the Court considered claims reciting a method of identifying a first patient who is a candidate for nitric oxide treatment and a second patient who is not,

160 See, eg, *INO Therapeutics LLC v Praxair Distribution Inc*, 782 Fed Appx 1001 (Fed Cir 2019).

due to left ventricular dysfunction, and administering the standard of care nitric oxide treatment to the first patient but not the second.[161] The Federal Circuit held that:

> *The patent claim* ***does no more than add an instruction to withhold*** *iNO treatment from the identified patients; it does not recite giving any affirmative treatment for the iNO-excluded group, and so it* ***covers a method in which, for the iNO-excluded patients, the body's natural processes are simply allowed to take place****. Consequently, the claim here is directed to the natural phenomenon. The claim, apart from the natural phenomenon itself, involves* ***only well-understood, routine, and conventional steps****.*[162]

Thus, the Court held INO's claims patent ineligible. While non-precedential, considering this holding in view of *Vanda* and *Mayo*, patent applicants are advised to consider reciting only the patient populations in their claims that the claims also recite treating, or to at least refrain from an explicit instruction not to treat.

3.4 How eligibility issues are handled by the USPTO

The most notable guidance from the USPTO in the life sciences applies to inventions in the fields of medical diagnostics, detection assays and treatments.

(a) Methods of diagnosis

Just as US courts apply *Mayo* to invalidate diagnostic claims as patent ineligible, the USPTO consistently declines to grant such claims. This trend is reflected in Example 29 of the 2016 USPTO Subject Matter Eligibility Guidance. Claim 2 of this Example recites a method of diagnosing the hypothetical disease julitis by detecting the protein JUL-1 in a patient's plasma sample.

> 2. *A method of diagnosing julitis in a patient, said method comprising:*
>   a. *obtaining a plasma sample from a human patient;*
>   b. *detecting whether JUL-1 is present in the plasma sample by contacting the plasma sample with an anti-JUL-1 antibody and detecting binding between JUL-1 and the antibody; and*
>   c. *diagnosing the patient with julitis when the presence of JUL-1 in the plasma sample is detected.*[163]

According to the 2016 Guidance, the claimed method employs the routine technology of antibody detection to observe a natural correlation (between a disease marker and a disease) to determine the health status of a patient (a mental step). The USPTO notes that the discovery underlying the invention represents an important clinical advance, facilitating the differential diagnosis of julitis from rosacea so that doctors can prescribe more effective medication

---

161 *Ibid*, at 1003.
162 *Ibid*, at 1005 (emphases added).
163 www.uspto.gov/sites/default/files/documents/101_examples_1to36.pdf.

to properly diagnosed patients. However, because the method merely applies a natural correlation using conventional activity, it is not eligible for patent protection.[164]

(b) *Methods of detection*

While US courts and patent examiners adopt the same approach to diagnostic method claims, they take conflicting positions on claims to methods of detection that do not include a diagnostic step. The USPTO approach aligns closely with the approach taken by jurisdictions such as Europe and China. This is perhaps best illustrated by Example 29, claim 1, of the 2016 USPTO Subject Matter Eligibility Guidance briefly referenced in section 3.3(c). This claim, reproduced at Table 8, recites a method of detecting a disease marker by contacting a patient sample with an antibody that specifically binds that marker, and detecting that binding.[165]

Table 8. Example 29, claims 1 and 2, of the 2016 USPTO Subject Matter Eligibility Guidance

Example 29	
Eligible*	**Ineligible**
1. A method of detecting JUL-1 in a patient, said method comprising: a. obtaining a plasma sample from a human patient; b. detecting whether JUL-1 is present in the plasma sample by contacting the plasma sample with an anti-JUL-1 antibody and detecting binding between JUL-1 and the antibody.	2. A method of diagnosing julitis in a patient, said method comprising: a. obtaining a plasma sample from a human patient; b. detecting whether JUL-1 is present in the plasma sample by contacting the plasma sample with an anti-JUL-1 antibody and detecting binding between JUL-1 and the antibody; and c. diagnosing the patient with julitis when the presence of JUL-1 in the plasma sample is detected.

* *As discussed above, a US court would find this claim ineligible.*

As shown in Table 8, detection claim 1 and diagnosis claim 2 share two core steps: observing and detecting. They differ in their preambles and the absence (claim 1) or presence (claim 2) of diagnostic step c. The USPTO finds that, while claim 1 recites natural phenomena (a plasma sample and the disease marker JUL-1), the claim as a whole is directed to a process of detecting a natural

164 *Ibid.*
165 *Ibid.*

phenomenon (the presence of a disease marker), which is not a judicial exception *per se*. Thus, under Step 2A of the *Mayo/Alice* test (corresponding to step one as applied by courts), the USPTO finds claim 1 to be patent eligible.[166] Meanwhile, the USPTO finds that claim 2, having step c, is directed to identifying a natural correlation and a mental step of making a diagnosis based on that correlation, and thus is patent ineligible.[167] Further, under Step 2B (corresponding to step two as applied by courts), the USPTO considers the observing and detecting limitations of claim 2. While, again, these steps are not themselves judicial exceptions, they are routine and conventional and not enough to transform the diagnostic method into something more than a natural law and mental step.

(c) Methods of treatment

In response to recent case law, largely *Vanda*, the USPTO adapted its guidance on method of treatment claims. Example 29 of the 2016 Guidance previously advised that claim 6, reciting a method of diagnosing and treating julitis, was eligible for patent protection because treatment step d added the inventive concept of ensuring patients are accurately treated based on their differential diagnosis.[168] After *Vanda*, the USPTO clarified that claim 6 of Example 29 is eligible for patent protection because it is not directed to a judicial exception at all.[169]

Table 9. Example 29, claims 2 and 6, of the 2016 USPTO Subject Matter Eligibility Guidance

Example 29	
Ineligible	**Eligible**
2. A method of diagnosing julitis in a patient, said method comprising: a. obtaining a plasma sample from a human patient; b. detecting whether JUL-1 is present in the plasma sample by contacting the plasma sample with an anti-JUL-1 antibody and detecting binding between JUL-1 and the antibody; and c. diagnosing the patient with julitis when the presence of JUL-1 in the plasma sample is detected.	6. A method of diagnosing and treating julitis in a patient, said method comprising: a. obtaining a plasma sample from a human patient; b. detecting whether JUL-1 is present in the plasma sample; c. diagnosing the patient with julitis when the presence of JUL-1 in the plasma sample is detected; and d. administering an effective amount of anti-tumour necrosis factor (TNF) antibodies to the diagnosed patient.

166 *Ibid.*
167 *Ibid.*
168 www.uspto.gov/sites/default/files/documents/101_examples_1to36.pdf.
169 www.uspto.gov/sites/default/files/documents/memo-vanda-20180607.PDF.

In 2019, the USPTO published further guidance advising that patent-eligible method of treatment claims must have some (but not much) specificity. Example 43 of the 2019 Guidance (Table 10) features claims reciting a method of treating a patient with a generic therapy (claim 1), a broad genus of therapies (claim 2), or a standard of care treatment (claim 3).[170]

Table 10. Example 43, claims 1–3, of the 2019 USPTO Subject Matter Eligibility Guidance

Example 43	
Ineligible	**Eligible**
1. A treatment method comprising: (a) calculating a ratio of C11 to C13 levels measured in a blood sample from a patient diagnosed with Nephritic Autoimmune Syndrome Type 3 (NAS-3) to identify the patient as having a non-responder phenotype; (b) administering a treatment to the patient having a non-responder phenotype.	2. The method of claim 1, wherein the treatment is a non-steroidal agent capable of treating NAS-3. 3. The method of claim 1, wherein the treatment is rapamycin.

The USPTO advises that claim 1 is too general to be patent eligible, while claims 2 and 3 are directed to sufficiently specific applications of a natural law to be patent eligible.[171]

It is not yet clear whether US courts will agree with this portion of the USPTO Guidance or find it too permissive. Thus, practitioners should proceed with caution when following this guidance.

4. Chemical and mechanical arts

Chemical compounds, mechanical devices and processes involving the same have traditionally been deemed patentable and claims to this subject matter are less likely to be challenged as not eligible for patenting. Nevertheless, when such claims are drafted too broadly and incorporate a judicial exception, such as an algorithm or a natural law, these claims have been found ineligible for patenting by the US courts and USPTO. Moreover, claims to chemical compounds or processes that relate to products found in nature such as known compounds, organisms, or genetic material, have also been found ineligible for patenting. These general principles are set forth in a series of Supreme Court

170 www.uspto.gov/sites/default/files/documents/peg_oct_2019_app1.pdf.
171 *Ibid.*

cases, which have been applied, with some difficulty and disagreement, by the lower courts and the USPTO.

4.1 Case law discussion

The *Flook* and *Diehr* Supreme Court cases, discussed above in section 2 relating to the electrical arts, are also instructive as to the dividing line between patent-eligible and patent-ineligible claims for inventions directed to chemical or mechanical processes.[172]

The claims at issue in *Flook* recited a three-step method for updating alarm limits:

> *an initial step which merely measures the present value of the process variable (e.g., the temperature); an intermediate step which uses an algorithm 1 to calculate an updated alarm-limit value; and a final step in which the actual alarm limit is adjusted to the updated value.*[173]

Methods for updating alarm limits existed in the art, and the only difference between the claimed method and previous conventional methods was the use of the specific algorithm.[174] The Supreme Court held these claims patent-ineligible, determining that 'conventional or obvious' post-solution activity cannot "transform an unpatentable principle into a patentable process".[175]

The Court reached a different outcome in *Diamond v Diehr*.[176] The Court reaffirmed the principle in *Flook* that "insignificant post-solution activity will not transform an unpatentable principle into a patentable process".[177] But the Court determined that in this case the claims were not directed to an unpatentable principle. The Court explained that the claimed process for moulding and curing rubber involved "transformation of an article, in this case raw, uncured synthetic rubber, into a different state or thing" and that "[i]ndustrial processes such as this are the types which have historically been eligible to receive the protection of our patent laws".[178] The Court acknowledged that the claimed invention relied on a mathematical equation, but determined that it did not seek to pre-empt all uses of that equation. The Court observed that the claims were directed to the use of the equation in conjunction with a number of specific steps, namely:

> *installing rubber in a press, closing the mold, constantly determining the temperature of the mold, constantly recalculating the appropriate cure time through the use of the formula and a digital computer, and automatically opening the press at the proper time.*[179]

---

172 *Parker v Flook,* 437 US 584 (1978); *Diamond v Diehr,* 450 US 175, 185 (1981).
173 *Ibid,* at 585.
174 *Ibid.*
175 *Ibid.*
176 450 US 175 (1981).
177 *Ibid,* at 191–192.
178 *Ibid,* at 184.
179 *Ibid,* at 187.

Accordingly, the Court concluded that the claims were directed to "a process for moulding rubber products and [were] not … an attempt to patent a mathematical formula".[180]

The key differences between *Flook* and *Diehr* are summarised in Table 11:

Table 11. Key differences between *Flook* and *Diehr*

***Flook* – patent ineligible**	***Diehr* – patent eligible**
Involved updating of alarm limits – did not transform any specific article into a different state Claim terms were broad and covered a broad range of potential uses Claims were found to be directed to a judicial exception (algorithm) and additional post-solution limitations were conventional or obvious	Involved transformation of an article into a different state (raw rubber to cured rubber) Claims involved multiple specific steps directed to a specific use – moulding and curing rubber Claims were found to be directed to a process of moulding and curing rubber that incorporated the use of a judicial exception (a natural law)

The Court relied on the analysis in *Flook* and *Diehr*, among other cases, in developing the *Mayo/Alice* two-step approach for determining patent eligibility. For example, in determining that the claims at issue in *Mayo* were directed to patent-ineligible subject matter – in that case a natural law – the Court observed that "the steps in the claimed processes (apart from the natural laws themselves) involve well-understood, routine, conventional activity previously engaged in by researchers in the field".[181] Similarly, in *Alice*, the Court determined that the claims were directed to an abstract idea and that "all of these [additional] computer functions [required by the claims] [we]re 'well-understood, routine, conventional activit[ies]' previously known to the industry" that did not render the claims patent eligible.[182] The Court further reaffirmed in *Mayo* and *Alice* the principle in *Flook* that a claim directed to a patent-ineligible abstract idea, natural phenomenon, or natural law cannot be transformed into a patent-eligible claim simply by limiting it to a specific technical environment.[183]

The dividing line between patent-eligible subject matter in *Diehr* and patent-ineligible subject matter in *Flook* is not precisely defined, but in these two cases, as well as subsequent decisions, the Supreme Court has provided some guiding principles, set out in Table 12.

180 *Ibid*, at 191.
181 *Mayo*, 566 US at 73.
182 *Alice*, 573 US at 225 (citing *Mayo*, 566 US at 73).
183 *Mayo*, 566 US at 67; *Alice*, 573 US at 222.

Table 12. Guiding principles from *Flook, Diehr* and subsequent Supreme Court decisions

Lessons from *Flook, Diehr* and subsequent Supreme Court decisions:
1. Overly broad claims that run the risk of preempting all uses of the abstract idea, natural phenomenon, or natural law are likely not patent eligible.
2. A claim directed to an abstract idea, natural phenomenon, or natural law cannot be rendered patent-eligible by restricting it to a specific technical environment.
3. If, after excluding the limitations of the patent claim directed to the abstract idea, natural phenomenon, or natural law, the remainder of the claim is directed to routine, conventional activity, the claim is likely not patent eligible.
4. If a claim is directed to a specific machine or transforms an article into a different state then it is more likely to be patent eligible.
5. Claims with sufficient specificity and non-conventional details, in addition to the limitations directed to the abstract idea, natural phenomenon, or natural law, such that they appear like claims to devices or processes traditionally protected by patent law, are likely patent eligible.

Recently, the Federal Circuit applied these principles when considered the patent eligibility of claims directed to automotive machinery in *American Axle & Manufacturing, Inc v Neapco Holdings LLC*[184] and heart-monitoring devices in *Cardionet LLC v Infobionic, Inc.*[185] In *American Axle*, the Court found certain claims, including claim 22, patent ineligible as directed to a natural law. Claim 22 read as follows:

> *22. A method for manufacturing a shaft assembly of a driveline system, the driveline system further including a first driveline component and a second driveline component, the shaft assembly being adapted to transmit torque between the first driveline component and the second driveline component, the method comprising:*
> *providing a hollow shaft member;*
> *tuning a mass and a stiffness of at least one liner, and*
> *inserting the at least one liner into the shaft member;*
> *wherein the at least one liner is a tuned resistive absorber for attenuating shell mode vibrations and wherein the at least one liner is a tuned reactive absorber for attenuating bending mode vibrations.*[186]

184 967 F 3d 1285 (Fed Cir 2020).
185 955 F 3d 1358 (Fed Cir 2020).
186 *American Axle*, 967 F 3d at 1290.

The Court focused on the claim language "tuning a mass and stiffness of at least one liner" and determined that this was simply an application of Hooke's law, an equation "that describes the relationship between an object's mass, its stiffness, and the frequency at which the object vibrates".[187] The Court thus found this claim ineligible for patenting. Notably, the Court took a different approach with claim 1, which more broadly recited "tuning at least one liner to attenuate at least two types of vibration transmitted through the shaft member" and thus did not explicitly limit the tuning actions to adjustments of mass and stiffness, which implicated Hooke's law. The Court remanded the case to the district court to further assess the eligibility of claim 1.[188]

In *Cardionet*, the Court considered patent claims directed to a device for detecting and reporting the presence of atrial fibrillation or atrial flutter. For example, claim 1 read as follows:

1. A device, comprising:
a beat detector to identify a beat-to-beat timing of cardiac activity;
a ventricular beat detector to identify ventricular beats in the cardiac activity;
variability determination logic to determine a variability in the beat-to-beat timing of a collection of beats;
relevance determination logic to identify a relevance of the variability in the beat-to-beat timing to at least one of atrial fibrillation and atrial flutter; and
an event generator to generate an event when the variability in the beat-to-beat timing is identified as relevant to the at least one of atrial fibrillation and atrial flutter in light of the variability in the beat-to-beat timing caused by ventricular beats identified by the ventricular beat detector.

The district court had determined that the claims were "directed to the abstract idea that atrial fibrillation and atrial flutter 'can be distinguished by focusing on the variability of the irregular heartbeat'" and found the claims ineligible for patenting. The Federal Circuit reversed this decision, concluding that these claims described a "specific means or method that improves cardiac monitoring technology" and therefore were not improperly directed to a judicial exception and were eligible for patenting.[189]

The *American Axle* and *Cardionet* cases are difficult to reconcile in that the claims in each case were directed to a specific practical application of a natural relationship. The claims held ineligible in *American Axle*, however, included claim language that specifically implicated a well-known natural law, and this appears to have driven the outcome in that case.

Another line of Supreme Court case law illuminates how the courts have determined the patent eligibility of patent claims directed to natural products,

187 *Ibid*, at 1291.
188 *Ibid*, at 1301.
189 *Cardionet*, 955 F 3d at 1368.

including naturally occurring chemical compositions. As noted in section 3.1 above, *Funk Brothers*[190] determined that claims directed to specific mixed cultures of naturally occurring bacteria were not eligible for patenting because the "qualities [of the claimed mixtures] are the work of nature ... [and] patents cannot issue for the discovery of the phenomena of nature".[191] The Court later determined in *Chakrabarty*[192] that claims to genetically engineered bacteria were eligible for patenting because the claims were not directed to "a hitherto unknown natural phenomenon, but to a non-naturally occurring or composition of matter – a product of human ingenuity having a distinctive name, character [and] use".[193] The Court further commented that the engineered bacteria had "markedly different characteristics from any found in nature".[194] The Federal Circuit has applied these holdings in its eligibility decisions relating to natural products and chemical compositions, holding that "discoveries that possess 'markedly different characteristics from any found in nature' ... are eligible for patent protection".[195]

4.2 How eligibility issues are handled by the USPTO

The USPTO recites, in the Manual of Patent Examining Procedure (MPEP), examples of types of claims to mechanical and chemical inventions that may be eligible for patenting, despite the incorporation of a judicial exception:

> *Improvements to any other technology or technical field, e.g., a modification of conventional rubber-molding processes to utilise a thermocouple inside the mold to constantly monitor the temperature and thus reduce under- and over-curing problems common in the art, as discussed in Diamond v Diehr, 450 U.S. 175, 191-92, 209 USPQ 1, 10 (1981)*[196]*...*
>
> *Applying the judicial exception with, or by use of, a particular machine, e.g., a Fourdrinier machine (which is understood in the art to have a specific structure comprising a headbox, a paper-making wire, and a series of rolls) that is arranged in a particular way to optimise the speed of the machine while maintaining quality of the formed paper web, as discussed in Eibel Process Co. v Minn. & Ont. Paper Co., 261 U.S. 45, 64-65 (1923)*[197]*...*
>
> *Effecting a transformation or reduction of a particular article to a different state or thing, e.g., a process that transforms raw, uncured synthetic rubber into precision-molded synthetic rubber products, as discussed in Diehr, 450 U.S. at 184, 209 USPQ at 21.*[198]

---

190 333 US 127 (1948).
191 *Ibid,* at 130.
192 447 US 303 (1980).
193 *Ibid,* at 309.
194 *Ibid,* at 310.
195 *In re Roslin*, 750 F 3d at 1336 (quoting *Chakrabarty*, 447 US at 310, 206).
196 MPEP §2106.05(a).
197 MPEP §2106.05(b).
198 MPEP §2106.05(c).

For claims directed to natural products, chemicals or organisms, the claims are analysed in Prong One of Step 2A of the USPTO's modified *Mayo/Alice* analysis to determine whether they are directed to a natural phenomenon or product of nature. In doing so, the USPTO follows the Supreme Court's guidance in *Chakrabarty* and considers whether the claim is directed to subject matter that has "markedly different characteristics from any found in nature".[199] The MPEP explains that the "markedly different characteristics" can relate to:

- biological or pharmacological functions or activities;
- chemical and physical properties;
- phenotype, including functional and structural characteristics; and
- structure and form, whether chemical, genetic or physical.[200]

Claimed subject matter that does not exhibit such "markedly different characteristics" is deemed to recite a natural phenomenon or product of nature and is subject to further analysis for patent eligibility.

The USPTO has further published on its website many case studies exemplifying what types of claims may be eligible for patenting, including case studies of mechanical and chemical inventions. In one example, the USPTO examines the eligibility of a patent claim directed to an internal combustion engine that provides for exhaust gas recirculation. The claim specifies an air intake manifold, an exhaust manifold, a combustion chamber, a drive shaft, a throttle position sensor and a control system "comprising a processor and memory, to receive the engine throttle position from the throttle position sensor, calculate a position of the exhaust gas recirculation valve based upon the rate of change of the engine throttle position". The USPTO explains that the eligibility of this claim is "immediately evident" because, while it recites the abstract idea of calculating the "position of the exhaust gas recirculation valve based upon the rate of change of the engine throttle position", it does not "seek to tie up this mathematical relationship so that others cannot practice it". The USPTO further notes that the numerous structural limitations detailing the specific structure of the engine amounts to "significantly more" than the judicial exception.[201]

The USPTO provides additional examples directed to chemical compositions and other inventions derived from natural materials. For example, the USPTO considers a patent claim directed to gunpowder. Because the claim is directed to a nature-based product, ie, a combination of three naturally occurring substances (potassium nitrate, charcoal and sulphur), the claim is analysed to determine whether the combination has markedly different characteristics from any naturally occurring counterpart(s) in their natural state. As the USPTO explains:

---

199 *Diamond,* 447 US at 310.
200 MPEP §2106.04(c).
201 See Example 26 at www.uspto.gov/sites/default/files/documents/101_examples_1to36.pdf.

In this case, there is no naturally occurring counterpart to the claimed combination (the components do not occur together in nature), so the combination is compared to the individual components as they occur in nature. None of the three claimed substances are explosive in nature. When the substances are finely-ground and intimately mixed in the claimed ratio, however, the claimed combination is explosive upon ignition. This explosive property of the claimed combination is markedly different from the non-explosive properties of the substances by themselves in nature.

The USPTO concludes that the claim to gunpowder does not recite a natural product or phenomenon and is eligible for patenting at Prong One of Step 2A of the analysis.[202]

The USPTO also describes eligibility considerations for claims directed to the hypothetical natural product 'amazonic acid'.[203]

Table 13. Eligibility considerations for claims directed to the hypothetical natural product 'amazonic acid'

	Ineligible for patenting	Eligible for patenting
Claimed subject matter	'Purified amazonic acid' isolated from the leaves of the Amazonian cherry tree	5-methyl amazonic acid – a chemically modified form of amazonic acid
Explanation	Because amazonic acid is naturally occurring, and purifying it does not alter its properties, the claims are not eligible for patenting	The chemically modified form of amazonic acid does not exist in nature and the addition of the 5-methyl group creates a different chemical structure such that the claimed modified acid has 'markedly different characteristics' than naturally occurring amazonic acid

The USPTO has continued to update its guidance in the MPEP and published examples, which may be located on the USPTO's website, as new decisions issue and practitioners seeking the most recent guidance from the USPTO should consult this section.

5. Conclusion

Patent-eligibility requirements in the US are often complex and seldom consistent. However, there are a few notable rules of thumb. In particular,

202 See Example 9 at www.uspto.gov/sites/default/files/documents/101_examples_1to36.pdf.
203 See Example 11 at www.uspto.gov/sites/default/files/documents/101_examples_1to36.pdf.

greater claim specificity and highlighting an inventive element can help persuade a patent examiner or a court that a claim is directed to a concrete and patent-eligible application of a judicial exception, and not to the judicial exception itself. It is interesting that these elements – specificity and inventiveness – appear to be more appropriately considered when analysing the separate patentability requirements of enablement, definiteness and non-obviousness. In fact, after prompting by Congress, the USPTO plans to implement a (voluntary) pilot programme in which examiners may delay raising a rejection under 35 USC §101 until they find all other patentability requirements have been met.[204] One goal of this approach is to reduce the number of rejections made under 35 USC §101 that would be more effectively handled under another statutory provision. Further, this approach may reduce the perceived overuse of 35 USC §101 rejections and focus eligibility rejections on the claims that truly merit them. This, in turn, may help avoid creating further confusion in US case law pertaining to subject matter eligibility.

Recent case law shows that the appropriate bounds of 35 USC §101 need clarification. In *Yu v Apple*, a split panel of the Federal Circuit found claims for a digital camera with multiple sensors and multiple lenses ineligible under 35 USC §101.[205] Unlike earlier cases such as *Ultramercial III*,[206] which found methods to be improperly directed to abstract ideas, the claims in Yu were directed to a physical object – namely, a camera: "image sensor[s]", "lenses", an "analog-to-digital converting circuitry" outputting digital images and a "processor" producing a resulting digital image by enhancing one digital image with another.[207] Yet, two of the judges in *Yu* found the claims directed to the abstract idea of "taking two pictures ... and using one picture to enhance the other in some way".[208] The majority found that the claims had only a well-understood, routine and conventional arrangement of generic parts.[209] One judge dissented, decrying the court's enlargement of 35 USC §101 beyond a "general statement of the type of subject matter" eligible for patenting to encompass statutorily distinct requirements for patentability, such as novelty and non-obviousness.[210] At the time of writing, the patent owner in *Yu* had requested a rehearing in front of the entire Federal Circuit.

The authors wish to thank Leonard Stewart for his comments and feedback.

204 Andrew Hirshfeld, Response to Senators Tillis and Cotton on Sequenced Examination: https://aboutblaw.com/W0F.

205 *Yanbin Yu v Apple, Inc.*, 1 F 4th 1040 (Fed Cir 2021).

206 *Supra* n 41.

207 *Yu v Apple*, 1 F 4th at 1042.

208 *Ibid*, at 1043.

209 *Ibid*, at 1045.

210 *Ibid*, at 1047.

About the authors

Victoria Barker
Associate, Finnegan Europe LLP
victoria.barker@finnegan.com

Victoria Barker, PhD is a chartered UK and European patent attorney with experience in all areas of patent portfolio management from drafting and filing applications to prosecution strategy, and beyond to EPO opposition and appeal procedures. Victoria's experience spans a broad range of chemical and life sciences technologies and key jurisdictions including China, Japan and Korea.

Thomas Becher
Partner, Hoffmann Eitle Dusseldorf
TBecher@hoffmanneitle.com

Thomas Becher studied general mechanical engineering at the Technical University (RWTH) in Aachen. In 1995/96 he completed his final thesis at the Massachusetts Institute of Technology (MIT) and the Fraunhofer-Institute for Production Technology (IPT) on 3D printing. Thomas joined Hoffmann Eitle's mechanical practice group in 1996. He qualified as a German patent attorney in 2000, as a European patent attorney in 2001, and as a Higher Courts litigator for England and Wales in 2016. Thomas was the founding partner of the firm's Dusseldorf office in 2012, which he continues to manage.

Thomas specialises in *inter partes* cases on utility and design patents, ie, in cancellation and opposition procedures before the German office and courts, in opposition and appeal procedures before the EPO, and in German infringement and nullity actions.

Thomas handles a diverse portfolio of cases in the mechanical arts, with some overlap into optics and other physics. He puts a special emphasis on medical devices, particularly implants. His clients are predominantly headquartered in the US, which he regularly visits.

Graeme Boocock
Partner, Borden Ladner Gervais LLP
gboocock@blg.com

Graeme Boocock, PhD is a partner and patent agent with Borden Ladner Gervais LLP. Graeme takes particular interest in the unique challenges facing antibody, diagnostic and personalised medicine inventions. Graeme's doctoral research, undertaken at the Hospital for Sick Children in Toronto, culminated in discovery of the gene that is mutated in Shwachman-Diamond syndrome, a rare inherited disorder featuring bone marrow failure, leukemia risk and pancreatic exocrine insufficiency. He then worked for three years as post-doctoral researcher in the department of Protein and Nucleic Acid Chemistry (PNAC) at the Medical Research Council's Laboratory of Molecular Biology (LMB) in Cambridge (UK), where his research focused on protein engineering. Graeme counsels clients on patenting strategies and assists with managing international portfolios. Graeme also assists with Canadian Plant Breeders' Rights (PBR) applications and is keen amateur breeder of Passiflora.

Paul W Browning
Partner, Finnegan LLP
paul.browning@finnegan.com

Paul Browning, PhD is a first chair litigator focusing on patent litigation and appeals, primarily in the chemical and pharmaceutical areas, including Hatch-Waxman litigation. He has tried cases before judges in various US district courts and has handled arbitrations and mediations. In addition to his litigation practice, Paul advises clients on a variety of patent matters, including strategic development of their patent portfolios and coordination of prosecution and US and foreign litigation strategy and related proceedings before the Patent Trial and Appeal Board (PTAB).

Anne Buchet
Managing partner, Laurent & Charras
anne.buchet@laurentcharras.com

Anne Buchet is a French and European patent attorney. She has a degree in Biochemical Engineering from the National Institute of Applied Sciences (INSA) in Lyon, a PhD in Microbiology (University of Paris 7 – Institut Pasteur) and the CEIPI Intellectual Property Diploma from the University of Strasbourg. She began her career in 1998 as an Examiner at the European Patent Office in Munich, then joined Laurent & Charras in 2003 and has been a managing partner since 2013.

Anne's practice includes IP strategy and counselling, patent drafting and prosecution, post-grant procedures such as oppositions and appeals, as well as infringement and freedom to operate analysis.

Her practice mainly relates to cosmetics, pharmacy and biotechnologies.

Harrison Chang
Associate, Finnegan Europe LLP
harrison.chang@finnegan.com

Harrison (Hoon Seok) Chang, PhD is a European and UK patent attorney. Harrison assists clients based on his experience as an in-house attorney of an award-winning IP team at a multinational corporation, where he managed patent prosecution before various patent offices such as the EPO, the UKIPO, the USPTO, CNIPA, RUPTO, KIPO and others. Harrison works across a wide range of electronics- and software-related technologies including telecommunications, image processing, video compression, computer security, processors, memory devices, mobile phones, unmanned aerial systems and unmanned underwater vehicles. He has particular experience in Standard Essential Patents (SEP) and patent pools. Harrison is bilingual in Korean and English, having moved to the UK as a teenager. As well as his degrees in mathematical physics from Imperial College London and computer science from the University of Cambridge, Harrison holds a MSc in microsystems & nanotechnology and a doctorate in enhanced pyroelectric effect from Cranfield University.

Roger Chang
Partner, Lee and Li Attorneys-at-Law
rogerchang@leeandli.com

Roger Chang has extensive experience in intellectual property infringement litigation, licensing, strategy planning and antitrust and competition regulation advice.

Roger is active in trademark, copyright, and

patent litigation for various industries. In 2019, represented by Roger, AVIS was awarded US$3 million by the Intellectual Property Court in a trademark infringement case. In 2019, Entegris was awarded US$32 million in a patent infringement case. In 2017, Philips was awarded US$35 million in a patent infringement suit. In 2013, Philips was awarded US$10 million in a patent case. In 2011, ESI, a NASDAQ-listed company based in Oregon, was awarded US$24 million in a patent infringement suit. In 2010, in another case represented by Roger, Philips was awarded US$68 million for patent infringement damages. In 2009, the Intellectual Property Court awarded Philips US$75 million as royalty of patent licensing. In 2007, in a landmark case that he participated in, the Taipei District Court awarded Celanese US$68 million as damages for patent infringement.

Known for his in-depth understanding of complex matters involving intellectual property and ability to provide innovative and constructive solutions, Roger is regularly invited to speak at seminars and workshops and to publish articles on intellectual property and antitrust laws. Roger has also assisted Taiwanese government agencies in amendments to intellectual property and competition-related laws and regulations.

Himanshu Chawla
Partner, K&S Partners
himanshu@knspartners.com

Himanshu Chawla is a partner in the computer and electronics department of K&S Partners. Himanshu is an engineering graduate with a degree in electronics and instrumentation. Himanshu has been associated with K&S Partners for more than 13 years and during his employment he has completed his law degree and obtained patent agent certification.

Himanshu handles patent drafting, patent prosecution and patent oppositions in the fields of electronics, electrical, instrumentation, mechanical, telecommunication, computer science, AI, robotics and blockchain. Himanshu also handles issues relating to patentability, freedom to operate, due diligence, invalidity searches and patent infringement.

Ivy Chin
Counsellor, Lee and Li Attorneys-at-Law
ivychin@leeandli.com

Ivy Chin has been involved in the patent field for more than 15 years. Her current practice consists primarily of preparing and prosecuting patent applications in a wide variety of electronic engineering, communication system, memory device, semiconductor and computer software.

Ivy has extensive experience counselling clients, and helps them build valuable, high-quality patent portfolios in an efficient manner. She has drafted and maintained standard essential patents for 5G New Radio standards for many years.

She has handled patent-related disputes and licensing cases, which involve memory devices, hand-held devices, semiconductor equipment or financial technology, for multinational companies.

Luigi Distefano
Associate, Finnegan Europe LLP
luigi.distefano@finnegan.com

Luigi Distefano is a chartered UK and European patent attorney whose practice focuses on patent prosecution, global portfolio development strategies, drafting, IP strategy counselling, and oppositions and appeals before the European Patent Office (EPO). Luigi predominantly handles subject matter in the fields of electronic and mechanical engineering and has extensive experience in dealing with the nuances of prosecuting computer implemented inventions in Europe, and speaks regularly on this topic.

Nicholas Fox
Partner, Finnegan Europe LLP
nicholas.fox@finnegan.com

Nicholas Fox is a partner at Finnegan Europe LLP specialising in intellectual property law with a focus on electronics, telecoms and software. In addition to being qualified as a solicitor, he is also qualified as a European and chartered British patent attorney and is qualified and admitted as an Attorney-at-Law in the State of New York.

Nicholas has degrees in mathematics, computer science and law and has technical experience in the areas of electronics and software having acted on behalf of a wide variety of multinational firms dealing with subject matter ranging from image processing and voice recognition through to telecoms and e-commerce.

Nicholas is the author of the practitioner's work, *A Guide to the EPC 2000* and the consulting editor and author of the UK intellectual property, European patents and European enforcement chapters of the book *Intellectual Property in Electronics and Software* published by Globe Law and Business.

Uri Fruchtman
Intellectual property lawyer
uri.fruchtman@icloud.com

Uri Fruchtman is a seasoned intellectual property lawyer. He has been practising IP law for over a decade and specialises in particular in drafting complex motions and briefs.

Uri has a very strong theoretical knowledge of patent laws with a unique expertise in matters relating to patent term extensions and data exclusivity. He successfully briefed and argued cases at the Patent Office, District Courts and the Supreme Court and developed winning arguments. In addition to his patent practice, Uri is also involved in numerous trademark cases involving look-alikes and protection for non-traditional trademarks.

Uri is a graduate of Tel Aviv University and was associate editor of the *Tel Aviv University Law Review*. He has also been a teaching assistant in Jurisprudence and Intellectual Property and Contract Law. Uri has published several chapters and articles on IP law including the Israeli chapter of *Patent Transactions in the Life Sciences* (Globe Law and Business, 2014).

Steve Gledhill
Partner, FB Rice
sgledhill@fbrice.com.au

Steve Gledhill leads the Sydney biotechnology practice at Australian IP boutique firm FB Rice. Steve provides an extensive range of intellectual property services for clients, ranging from contentious matters including patent oppositions and litigation support in Australia and internationally to advising on due diligence, infringement and freedom to operate matters and devising patent prosecution strategies from drafting through to global patent portfolio management. Of particular note is Steve's involvement in contentious proceedings before the Australian Patent Office, the Federal Court of Australia and the European Patent Office, in which he has achieved notable successes. Steve has also qualified as a European and UK patent attorney, which assists his practice advising on multijurisdictional disputes. Since obtaining his first-class degree in Biological Sciences at Oxford University, Steve has served clients across the life sciences sector and has particular experience in patent matters relating to vaccines, antibodies, diagnostics, gene therapy and bioinformatics.

Natasha Gulati
Associate, Borden Ladner Gervais LLP
ngulati@blg.com

Natasha Gulati is a lawyer and associate with Borden Ladner Gervais LLP practising intellectual property law. Natasha provides patent, copyright, trademark and other IP portfolio strategy advice to innovators and entrepreneurs. She also maintains a litigation practice and has successfully represented clients in patent and copyright disputes before the Federal Court. Natasha holds a BSc (Hons), JD and MBA from the University of Ottawa, a Certificate in Intellectual Property Licensing from Osgoode Hall Law School, and a Lean Six Sigma Yellow Belt for Services.

Chong He
Partner, Advance China IP Law Office
hc@aciplaw.com

Chong He joined Advance China IP Law Office (ACIP) in 2005 and has been a partner for more than 10 years, managing the international patent department. Before starting his IP career, Chong worked in a foreign high-tech company as an engineer, which gives him a good understanding of the working process of foreign companies. Chong has been recently elected as CEO to supervise overall management of the firm, while he continues to lead the international patent team at ACIP, focusing on providing high-quality and customised IP services.

With rich experience in patent prosecution and counselling to corporates in terms of international patent drafting, infringement analysis, freedom to operate investigation, invalidation and patent strategy, Chong has helped clients to successfully obtain patent rights and win patent re-examinations and invalidation, especially in the fields of engineering and electronics. Chong is also a member of the ACIP enforcement team for international clients. He has participated in many enforcement cases and successfully combats counterfeiting that involves patents and trademarks.

He was a recommended individual for patent prosecution in IAM Patent 1000 2019–2021.

Ephraim Heiliczer
Partner, Pearl Cohen
eheiliczer@pearlcohen.com

Ephraim Heiliczer is a partner in the Intellectual Property and Regulatory Compliance Group at Pearl Cohen's Tel Aviv office. Ephraim has a strong background in medical science and has been involved in numerous life science and medical device oppositions and infringement actions as well as in patent prosecution and patent term extensions.

Ephraim also utilises his scientific background in regulatory matters involving the Israeli Ministry of Health and Israeli Standards Institute. In addition to regulatory work, Ephraim has broad experience in compliance. Ephraim has authored book chapters on pharmaceutical and intellectual property compliance.

He has also been active in litigation, litigating cases involving drug release profiles and pharmacokinetics, metabolism, anti-HIV agents, CNS drugs and medical devices. In addition, he has been involved in precedent-setting PTE litigation. Ephraim is a graduate of Hebrew University (LLB, MSc) and Columbia Law School (LLM), and is presently a JSD candidate at Columbia Law School.

Christopher C Johns
Associate, Finnegan LLP
christopher.johns@finnegan.com

Christopher C Johns is an associate in the Washington DC office of Finnegan LLP.

Christopher works with domestic and international clients on strategic portfolio counselling, including portfolio management, drafting strategies, and *ex parte* appeals. He has nearly 15 years of experience in the patent field and speaks and writes regularly on topics such as patent eligibility and prosecution practice. He has worked on appeals to the Federal Circuit, litigation at the International Trade Commission (ITC), district court litigation, and Patent Trial and Appeal Board (PTAB) trials.

Before joining Finnegan, Christopher served as a USPTO patent examiner for nearly five years, where he examined applications related to business methods and software. He also has experience as a network technician at a major research university.

Hankil D Kang
Foreign attorney, Bae, Kim & Lee LLC
hankil.kang@bkl.co.kr

Hankil D Kang is a foreign attorney (admitted in the state of New York and Washington DC) at Bae, Kim & Lee LLC. His main practice areas include IP-related international disputes and IP-related transactions. Prior to joining BKL, he handled patent suits and licensing matters at major US law firms and a global electronics company. Since joining the IP Team of BKL in 2016, he has handled various disputes involving patents, trade secrets, copyrights, trademarks and other intellectual property rights, as well as advising on licensing agreements and other contracts involving intellectual property issues.

Kijoong Kang
Partner, Bae, Kim & Lee LLC
kijoong.kang@bkl.co.kr

Kijoong Kang is a partner at Bae, Kim & Lee LLC (BKL) and current head of BKL's IP Group. Before joining BKL, Kijoong served as a judge specialising in intellectual property matters, including patents, designs, trademarks and copyrights, as well as being the managing partner of an IP law firm, an executive vice president and the head of the IP litigation team of a global electronics manufacturer.

Kijoong began his career as a judge in 1989, and he earned his LLM from New York University Law School in 1999 focusing on intellectual property laws. Upon returning to Korea, he served as a judge at the Patent Court, then as a research judge in the IP division of the Supreme Court of Korea. After retiring from the bench in 2006, Kijoong served as the managing partner of AIP Patent & Law Firm. He then joined Samsung Electronics Co Ltd (Samsung) as an executive vice president and the head of the IP litigation team at the IP Center of Samsung. As the head of the IP litigation team at Samsung, Kijoong led a team of in-house attorneys, including many US attorneys, and oversaw various global litigations involving IP matters, including the case against Apple that involved multiple countries (including the US, Germany, the UK, France, the Netherlands, Spain, Australia, Japan and Korea) and encompassed various IP issues, including the design patent case which he managed from the district court level to the Supreme Court.

Kijoong has extensively managed foreign law firms with IP speciality and experienced dozens of global IP litigation cases at the forefront, building upon his Korean IP litigation experience with those at the various foreign legal venues.

Madeleine Kelly
Partner, FB Rice
mkelly@fbrice.com.au

Madeleine Kelly is a partner at FB Rice, a leading Australian IP firm. Her expertise lies in software and electronics, with a particular focus on fintech and e-health sectors. She specialises in providing strategic advice, navigating complicated patent landscapes and managing global patent portfolios to support her clients in meeting their business objectives. Prior registrations as an Irish and European patent attorney in combination with her Australian and New Zealand patent attorney qualifications equip her to take a wide and informed perspective when approaching IP strategy. Madeleine has been recognised in the IAM Global Leaders list for 2021 and the IAM Patent Prosecution Recommended list for 2020.

Gaëtan Lassere
Attorney, Laurent & Charras
gaetan.lassere@laurentcharras.com

Gaëtan Lassere graduated from ESIREM (engineer in electronics and IT), and has a PhD in electronics and signal processing, and the CEIPI intellectual property diploma from the University of Strasbourg. He is an industrial property attorney and a European patent representative.

Prior to working in intellectual property, Gaëtan worked on the neural network domain and the radio frequency identification (RFID) domain.

Gaëtan's practice includes IP strategy and counselling, patent drafting and prosecution, post-grant procedures such as oppositions and appeals, as well as infringement and freedom to operate analysis.

His practice mainly relates to electronics, signal processing and informatics.

Sara A Leiman
Associate, Finnegan LLP
sara.leiman@finnegan.com

Sara Leiman, PhD is an associate in Finnegan LLP's Boston office. Sara works with domestic and international clients across the life sciences on global patent prosecution, strategic counselling, due diligence, and validity and infringement opinions. She writes and speaks regularly on topics in intellectual property, particularly patent-eligibility requirements, case law, and patent office guidance in the US. Before joining Finnegan, Sara completed her graduate studies in biochemistry, with a research focus in microbiology.

Joyce Liou
Counsellor, Lee and Li Attorneys-at-Law
joyceliou@leeandli.com

Joyce Liou graduated from the National Taiwan University, and obtained double Bachelor's degrees in zoology and veterinary medicine. After two years of practice and two years of doctoral study in veterinary medicine, Joyce focused her study in data analysis and obtained her Master's degree in bioinformatics at the University of Manchester. During her career as a bioinformatics analyst in a biotech company, Joyce noticed the importance of patents, and decided to join Lee and Li as a patent engineer in the Chemical Group of the Patent and Technology Department, and passed the Taiwan patent bar exam in 2008 and the China patent bar exam in 2011. Joyce has extensive experience in patent prosecution, patent search, patent term extension, patent invalidation actions, administrates remedy procedures and patent infringement suits, especially in the pharmaceutical and biotech fields, and won the first patent linkage litigation in Taiwan in 2020.

Ping Luo
Patent attorney, Advance China IP Law Office
luoping@aciplaw.com

Ping Luo specialises in patent prosecution as well as litigation in the field of computer science, software, telecommunication, electronics etc. He has been practising in patent law since 2011.

Before joining Advance China IP, he actively worked with US or EU attorneys to counsel local clients and, as a litigator, participated in several major patent matters such as *Qualcomm v Meizu, Samsung v Huawei, Ericsson v Yulong, Philips v Desay* and *Whirlpool v Jiaxipera*, etc. He also helps with patent licensing from time to time. Ping has a comprehensive understanding of patent law.

Tsuyoshi Miura
Partner, Seiwa Patent & Law
tmiura@seiwapat.co.jp

Tsuyoshi Miura is a partner in Seiwa Patent & Law. His practice focuses on patent prosecution, post-grant procedure and litigation cases in various fields including electronics, artificial intelligence, information and communication technology and mechanical engineering, both in Japan and abroad.

Tsuyoshi obtained a Bachelor's degree in applied communication engineering from Osaka University in 1994. He worked for Fujitsu Limited as a software engineer developing image processing systems, image transmitting systems and security systems, etc, for 14 years. Tsuyoshi worked as a patent specialist for three years, and has been working as a Japanese patent attorney for eight years.

Tsuyoshi is a member of JPAA.

Beverley Moore
Partner, Borden Ladner Gervais LLP
bmoore@blg.com

Beverley Moore is a partner and lawyer with Borden Ladner Gervais LLP and practises in all areas of intellectual property litigation, with a focus on complex patent litigation and actions under the Patented Medicines (Notice of Compliance) Regulations. She also advises clients on patent portfolio management, including how to navigate IP regulatory issues such as listing patents on the Patent Register, and reporting patents to the Patented Medicines Prices Review Board, Certificates of Supplementary Protection, and the Register of Innovative Drugs as it relates to data protection. In addition, Beverley advises on patentability, validity and freedom-to-operate issues, and aids in the prosecution of patent applications in Canada. Beverley has advocated before the Federal Courts and Federal Court of Appeal, as well as the Patented Medicine Prices Review Board. Beverley is national leader of BLG's Intellectual Property Litigation Group and serves on the firm's thought leadership committee. She also mentors several of the firm's students and associates.

Yelena Morozova
Associate, Finnegan Europe LLP
yelena.morozova@finnegan.com

Yelena Morozova's professional career spans across three countries, with more than 15 years of legal experience across two continents. Yelena's unique background enables her to understand cultural nuances and helps her to advise a broad range of clients across the world. Qualified as a patent attorney in the US and Europe, Yelena focuses her practice on patent procurement and portfolio development in all fields of engineering on both sides of the Atlantic.

Jason Mueller-Neuhaus
Partner, Borden Ladner Gervais LLP
jmuellerneuhaus@blg.com

Jason Mueller-Neuhaus is a partner and patent agent with Borden Ladner Gervais LLP, and assists inventors and businesses in protecting and profiting from their technological innovations in all physics-related fields. This includes mechanical devices, electronics, industrial processes, communications and computing solutions. He has substantial knowledge and experience in computer information processing systems. Jason provides strategic advice to help clients navigate the intellectual property landscape, including invention patentability, patent infringement and validity, and freedom-to-operate. He drafts and prosecutes patent applications to grant, for Canada, the US and worldwide, and manages patent portfolios for innovators and enterprises. Jason has appeared before the Canadian Patent Appeal Board and the Trademarks Opposition Board and has represented clients before the Federal Court of Canada and the US Patent Trial and Appeal Board.

Durgesh Mukharya
Partner, K&S Partners
durgesh@knspartners.com

Durgesh Mukharya is a partner with the Life Science practice at K&S Partners. He has a background in biotechnology and is a qualified patent agent and attorney. His core practice is built on years of patent drafting and prosecution in different domains within the Life Sciences for domestic and international clients.

Over the last 13 years, he has developed considerable expertise in advising clients on IP strategy and worldwide portfolio management, in sync with their business models. This involves deep conversations around markets of interest, feasibility of IP generated revenue, licensing issues and advice on critical IP issues including contentious matters related to patentability, freedom to operate, due diligence and the technology landscape. Durgesh regularly appears before the Indian Patent Office, the Intellectual Property Appellate Board and various courts in connection with prosecution and litigation of patent applications and related matters. Most recently, Durgesh was recognised as an IP Star 2021 by the MIP.

On a personal front, Durgesh is a fitness enthusiast and enjoys music, sports and meditation.

Markus Georg Müller
Partner, Hoffmann Eitle Munich
MMueller@hoffmanneitle.com

Dr Markus Georg Müller studied Physics at the University of Heidelberg, University of Massachusetts and Massachusetts Institute of Technology. He obtained a Master of Science degree in 1997 with a thesis on the optical characterisation of quantum dot structures and completed his Diploma degree in 1999 and PhD thesis in 2002 in the field of biomedical optics. Before joining Hoffmann Eitle's Electrical Engineering Group in 2002, he worked for six months as a temporary analyst with Siemens Management Consulting. After training periods at the Federal Patent Court and Civil Court in Munich he qualified as a European and German patent attorney and is now a partner at Hoffmann Eitle.

Markus specialises in opposition and appeal proceedings before the EPO and German nullity and infringement proceedings. He is regularly involved in international litigation projects.

Markus's practice covers technical areas including optoelectronics, photonics, medical physics and imaging, telecommunications, automotive and lighting electronics.

Masaru Nakajima
Partner, Seiwa Patent & Law
mnakajima@seiwapat.co.jp

Masaru Nakajima is a partner in Seiwa Patent & Law. His practice focuses on patent prosecution, post-grant procedure, and litigation cases in various fields including pharmaceuticals, biotechnology and organic chemistry, both in Japan and abroad.

He obtained a Master's degree in applied

zoology from the Graduate School of the University of Tokyo in 1995, passed the patent bar exam in Japan in 2005, and has been working as a Japanese patent attorney for 15 years. He also studied US patent law and practice as a trainee in Foley and Lardner LLP in 2014 and passed the patent bar exam for the US.

He is a member of JPAA and AIPPI (senior director of the Japan group since 2018).

Maeve O'Flynn
Partner, Finnegan Europe LLP
maeve.oflynn@finnegan.com

Maeve O'Flynn is a European and chartered UK patent attorney with more than a decade of in-house experience, having worked at some of the world's largest multinational corporations in the oil and chemical industries. She has worked for a range of clients, from startups to multinationals, covering diverse technologies such as cosmetics, sustainable chemistry and catalysis.

Kil-chae Park
Patent attorney, Bae, Kim & Lee LLC
kilchae.park@bkl.co.kr

Kil-chae Park entered the public office by public competition in 1995 at deputy-director level, and served at the Ministry of Trade and Industry, the Korean Intellectual Property Office (as an examiner of the Organic Chemistry Examination Division, Agriculture, Forestry and Fisheries Examination Division, and the Biotechnology Examination Division, and as a director of the Fine Chemistry Examination Division, Environment and Energy Examination Division and the Housing Technology Examination Division), the IP Tribunal (advisory officer, litigation representative for KIPO, re-examiner), the Supreme Court (patent adviser) and the Ministry of Foreign Affairs and Trade (diplomat), etc. Kil-chae is an expert who has handled more than 400 patent trials and litigation cases, and currently specialises in litigation in the fields of chemical engineering, chemicals, and pharmaceuticals, and conducts research, analysis and consultations regarding IP.

Vincent Pons
Partner, Laurent & Charras
vincent.pons@laurentcharras.com

Vincent Pons is a French and European patent attorney partner. He holds a PhD in chemistry from the University of Washington and the CEIPI Intellectual Property Diploma and the CEIPI Diploma in Patent Litigation in Europe from the University of Strasbourg. Prior to working in Intellectual Property, Vincent worked on chemical hydrogen storage at Los Alamos National Laboratory in close collaboration with the University of Pennsylvania.

Vincent's practice includes IP strategy and counselling, patent drafting and prosecution, post-grant procedures such as oppositions and appeals, as well as infringement and freedom-to-operate analysis. His practice mainly relates to chemistry, materials and energy matters.

Andreas Stefferl
Partner, Hoffmann Eitle Munich
AStefferl@hoffmanneitle.com

Dr Andreas Stefferl studied Biology at the University of Vienna and the University of Manchester and completed his diploma thesis in the field of neurobiology in 1995. Andreas joined Hoffmann Eitle's Biotechnology Group in 2003 and is qualified as a European and German patent attorney. He is now a senior partner at Hoffmann Eitle.

Andreas specialises in expert opinions, examination procedures, opposition procedures and appeal procedures before the EPO. Besides the EPO work, he is involved in pan-European litigation projects and handles German infringement and nullity actions before the German courts.

Andreas's cases are exclusively in the field of biotechnological inventions, with a diverse portfolio ranging, eg, from various enzyme-related cases to stem cell technology, numerous antibody cases and fermentation procedures for fine chemicals.

In addition to his case work, Andreas frequently presents at conferences, eg, the annual Comparative Patent Practice Conference (CPPC) and the Japan Intellectual Property Association (JIPA) in Tokyo. He contributes articles to various journals including *Patents & Licensing* and *Going Public* magazine. The majority of Andreas's clients are based in Japan, where he travels on a regular basis to advise his clients in face-to-face meetings.

Cheng Wang
Patent attorney, Advance China IP Law Office
wangc@aciplaw.com

Cheng Wang has practised in the field of intellectual property since 2010. She maintains an active patent prosecution practice, preparing and prosecuting Chinese and foreign patent applications on behalf of domestic and foreign clients. She has extensive experience in patent applications in China, the US, and Europe. In addition to patent prosecution, Cheng has experience in patent reexamination and patent infringement analysis in electronics, computer science, mechanical and semiconductor industries.

Wenwen Wang
Partner, Advance China IP Law Office
wangww@aciplaw.com

Wenwen Wang received her PhD in biological sciences from the University of California, Irvine, and is a registered patent attorney and attorney-at-law of China. Wenwen joined Advance China IP Law Office in 2013 and later became a partner. She has been providing IP services to various domestic and foreign companies, universities and research institutes in patent drafting, prosecution, analysis, and consulting of patentability and infringement, etc, in the fields of biotech, pharmaceuticals, chemistry, materials and medical devices. She also has IP experience in products and manufacturing processes of cosmetics, food industry, biofuel, nanofilm, etc.

Wenwen actively participates in international communications and conferences. She serves as a committee member of the IP in China Committee of AIPLA, the Asian Practice Committee of IPO and the Bio-Pharma Professional Committee of the Guangdong Division of the All-China Patent Attorney Association (ACPAA). She has also participated in a number of IP investigation and research projects funded by CNIPA and WIPO.

Wenwen was recommended in the individual rankings for patent prosecution of China-Mainland in IAM Patent 1000 2020–2021.

Hui Yuan
Patent attorney, client relationship manager of Asia-Pacific Area, Advance China IP Law Office
yuanhui@aciplaw.com

Hui Yuan has been working in the IP field for 12 years and is well versed in Chinese patent law. She qualified as a Chinese patent attorney in 2015 and has handled filing and prosecuting matters for more than a hundred Chinese patent applications in the technical fields of materials, chemistry and biology. She is specialised in providing legal advice for domestic and foreign clients, and also excels at searching for, collecting and analysing data.